Consumer
Research

For John A. Howard—
Teacher, Mentor, Colleague, Friend—
An Inspiration in Every Way

Consumer Research

Introspective Essays on
the Study of Consumption

Morris B. Holbrook

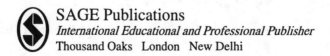

SAGE Publications
International Educational and Professional Publisher
Thousand Oaks   London   New Delhi

For information address:

SAGE Publications, Inc.
2455 Teller Road
Thousand Oaks, California 91320

SAGE Publications Ltd.
6 Bonhill Street
London EC2A 4PU
United Kingdom

SAGE Publications India Pvt. Ltd.
M-32 Market
Greater Kailash I
New Delhi 110 048 India

Printed in the United States of America

Library of Congress Cataloging-in-Publication Data

Holbrook, Morris B.
    Consumer research : Introspective essays on the study of
consumption / Morris B. Holbrook.
        p.   cm.
    Includes bibliographical references and index.
    ISBN 0-8039-7296-2 (hc. : acid-free paper). — ISBN 0-8039-7297-0
(pbk. : acid-free paper)
    1. Consumers—Research.   2. Consumer behavior.   I. Title.
HF5415.3.H637   1995
658.8'34—dc20   95-7712

This book is printed on acid-free paper.

95 96 97 98 99 10 9 8 7 6 5 4 3 2 1

Production Editor: Tricia K. Bennett   Typesetter: Christina M. Hill

Man need not be surprised that animals have animal instincts that are so much like his own. . . . Man may learn from the animals, for they are his parents.
—*Paracelsus (1492-1541)*

CONTENTS

PREFACE

In recent years, consumer research has emerged as an academic specialty of growing concern to marketing scholars and of increased importance on today's college and university campuses. Courses on consumer behavior, taught in virtually every program of business or management, draw heavily on work by consumer researchers. Over half of the students who receive their doctoral degrees in marketing specialize in consumer studies. Marketing MBAs traditionally take at least one course in consumer behavior, as do many college undergraduates concentrating in business. Furthermore, other academic disciplines—psychology, sociology, cultural anthropology, social history, communication, economics, home economics, textiles/clothing, and even law—draw major portions of their content from the area of consumption-related phenomena. These cross-disciplinary connections received formal recognition 20 years ago in the formation of the Association for Consumer Research and the *Journal of Consumer Research*—now widely regarded as the major professional organization and leading academic journal in the field.

Many books have given comprehensive coverage to the topic of consumer *behavior*. Yet, despite its wide and growing recognition as an emergent area of study, no book appears to exist on the subject of consumer *research*. To the best of my knowledge, no one has completed a full-length treatment of the history, nature, and types of consumer research or of the varied and often hotly debated issues that surround this field of inquiry. Hence, a gap that badly needs filling exists in the marketing literature.

In this book, I aim to close that gap by providing an account of some recent historical developments in consumer research and by showing how the evolution of this discipline has affected one researcher in particular—namely, me. Hence, the book offers a personal and subjective glance at how various changes in the field have come about and how they have shaped my own studies of consumption. This account borrows from introspective essays originally written to elucidate various aspects of the relevant issues but now revised and collected to sketch a sustained picture of how consumer research has grown and blossomed during the past 25 years.

By virtue of my habitual use of animal metaphors, this collection resembles a menagerie—that is, a gathering of creatures intended for exhibition. I hope the reader will find that this menagerie of introspective chapters sheds light on various facets of consumer research not accessible from the more scattered writings of those who have treated aspects of the topic with greater gravity, heavier sobriety, or higher seriousness.

In closing these prefatory remarks, I wish to express my sincere gratitude to the innumerable people who helped me create this book. Thanks, first, to the many coauthors whose names appear throughout: Rajeev Batra, Russ Belk, Steve Bell, Steve Bertges, Lauren Block, Bob Chestnut, Kim Corfman, Ellen Day, Glenn Dixon, Gavan Fitzsimons, Meryl Gardner, Rashi Glazer, Mark Grayson, Eric Greenleaf, Bill Havlena, Beth Hirschman, Donna Hoffman, Doug Holloway, John Howard, Joel Huber, Don Lehmann, Bill Moore, Terry Oliva, T. J. Olney, John O'Shaughnessy, Scott Roberts, Mike Ryan, Robert Schindler, John Sherry, Barbara Stern, Melanie Wallendorf, Rebecca Williams, Russ Winer, and Bob Zirlin. Among these, special thanks to Ellen Day, Beth Hirschman, John Howard, and John O'Shaughnessy, who gave me countless ideas that show up here. Thanks to Anne Smith of HarperCollins, who initially encouraged the project during its early stages. Thanks to Judith Leet, also of HarperCollins, who made detailed editorial suggestions. Thanks to Ron Hill for his gracious support as a liaison with Sage. Thanks to Marquita Flemming, Dale Grenfell, Linda Poderski, and Tricia Bennett of Sage for their enthusiasm and expert editorial advice. Profound thanks to my beloved family for filling the center of my life as a consumer. And boundless thanks to John Howard—my teacher, mentor, colleague, and friend—to whom I dedicate this book with deep appreciation and great affection.

A BRIEF HISTORY
OF MORRIS THE CAT
Still Crazy After All These Years

And we talked about some old times;
And we drank ourselves some beers—
Still crazy after all these years;
Still crazy after all these years.
 —Paul Simon (1975),
 "Still Crazy After All These Years"[1]

As its title implies, this book presents a series of introspective essays on consumer research. A brief glance at the table of contents suggests that I draw frequently on the idea of a *menagerie* or metaphors connected with various members of the animal kingdom: a cat (Morris), a bird (Charlie Parker), an elephant (Horton), a gorilla (Koko), bears (not to mention Baltimore and baseball), the wolf (not to mention Peter), skylarks (the power of song), dogs (vs. cats and fish), and the turtle (another way to view Morris).

Merriam-Webster's Collegiate Dictionary defines *menagerie* as "a place where animals are kept . . . a collection . . . for exhibition" (1993, p. 725). This definition strikes me as an apt description for my use of animal metaphors in this book. I use these metaphors to reflect various different but complementary viewpoints on consumers, consumer research, and consumer research-

1

ers. Like a menagerie, this book collects these animal metaphors in order to exhibit them for purposes of illustrating my perspective on consumer research.

In this spirit, let me begin with a few words of comparison between a consumer researcher and a cat.

❑ *The Cat*

If you come back from the supermarket with a box of groceries, unload the box into your refrigerator, and then put the empty box on the floor, the first thing your cat will do—if he or she is anything like my cat—is climb inside. Sometimes, if the box is particularly comfortable, it can even be rather difficult to persuade the cat to come out. This, after all, is how cats earned their well-deserved reputation for curiosity. And independence.

By contrast, if you buy an expensive bed for your cat at a fancy pet store, spend a lot of money on soft cushions and cozy pillows, put this well-intentioned gift in a place of honor near the warmest radiator you can find, pick up your cat tenderly, and gently place him or her inside, the first thing your cat will do is climb out. After which, your cat probably will scowl at you, stalk into the next room, and curl up in your favorite armchair. Cats, it seems, have minds of their own. They like to take up positions where *they* want to be.

Similarly, researchers in general and consumer researchers in particular spend much effort trying to build their identities, to assert their individualities, to establish their reputations, to find their niches, and to distinguish themselves from the crowd. Furthermore, like a cat, if you put a consumer researcher into a conceptual closet, he or she will immediately try to escape. In other words, consumer researchers tend to resist attempts to stick them into pigeonholes, categories, or single cells of a typology. For a consumer researcher, as for most academicians, being typecast, classified, or labeled is about as odious as sitting in a box of cat litter.

So it was with mixed emotions that I greeted Beth Hirschman's article on styles of consumer research (Hirschman, 1985b). In that piece, Beth drew on a framework suggested by Mitroff and Kilmann (1978) to classify me (Morris) as a conceptual humanist—that is, as a consumer researcher who writes in a style high on intuition and feeling. On the one hand, I admired Beth's paper as a typically creative and insightful series of comparisons. And,

Figure 1.1. Left-Brained Self-Portrait
SOURCE: From Holbrook and Zirlin (1985), p. 17. Reprinted with permission.

I must admit, I found it most gratifying—indeed, ego-inflating—to see my own two self-portraits reproduced for posterity in the *Journal of Consumer Research* (Holbrook & Zirlin, 1985, pp. 17, 18), as shown in Figures 1.1 and 1.2. On the other hand, I also felt a strong impulse to shout, "Wait a minute! That's not the only sort of work I do. I'm not exclusively a conceptual humanist. Hey, I can be just as data-driven and nonhumane—just as counterintuitive and unfeeling—as the next person."

On balance, a decade later, I now see that Beth used the Mitroff-Kilmann taxonomy to signal some important differences among styles of doing consumer research. I have to agree that my approach to my own work does differ from that of my distinguished colleagues who occupy the other cells in Beth's taxonomic jail. I would add, however, that my own work also differs from that of virtually any other consumer researcher whom one might care to name. At least, I fervently hope it does. Indeed, that difference motivates my writing of this book.

Figure 1.2. Right-Brained Self-Portrait
SOURCE: From Holbrook and Zirlin (1985), p. 18. Reprinted with permission.

❏ *Still Crazy*

For me, these reflections reached the point of epistemological crisis amid a moment of existential angst during the summer of 1991 when I was invited to attend the annual Marketing Camp hosted by the Graduate School of Business at Stanford University and to present a paper on past trends, recent developments, and future directions in approaches to consumer research—with an emphasis on how my own evolving perspective has fit into the changing field as a whole.

I gladly accepted this invitation and responded by creating a narrative account intended to convey some sense of the evolution in our field as seen—rather idiosyncratically or even egocentrically—through my own eyes as a consumer researcher. This story charts the progress of what I believe was

1. Scientific Marketing Research Is Neopositivistic Managerially Relevant Studies of Decisions to Buy Goods and Services.

2. Scientific -------- Research Is Neopositivistic Managerially Relevant Studies of Decisions to Buy Goods and Services.

3. Scientific -------- Research Is Neopositivistic Managerially Relevant Studies of Decisions to buy ----- --- --------.

4. Scientific -------- Research Is Neopositivistic Managerially Relevant Studies of Decisions -- --- ----- --- --------.

5. Scientific -------- Research Is Neopositivistic Managerially Relevant Studies -- ---------- -- --- ----- --- --------.

6. Scientific -------- Research Is Neopositivistic ------------ -------- Studies -- ---------- -- --- ----- --- --------.

7. Scientific -------- Research Is ------------- ------------ -------- Studies -- ---------- -- --- ----- --- --------.

8. ---------- --------- Research Is ------------- ------------ -------- Studies -- ---------- -- --- ----- --- --------.

9. ---------- --------- Research -- ------------- ------------ -------- -------- -- ---------- -- --- ----- --- --------.

10. Humanistic Consumer Research in Marketing Includes Interpretive Intrinsically Motivated Studies of Experiences in the Consumption of Artwork and Entertainment.

11. Scientific and Humanistic Marketing and Consumer Research Includes Neopositivistic and Interpretive Managerially Relevant and Intrinsically Motivated Studies of Decisions to Buy Goods and Services and of Experiences in the Consumption of Artwork and Entertainment.

Figure 1.3. A Brief History of Consumer Research: From the 1960s to the 1990s

the party line, received view, or conventional wisdom circa 1965 (when I first entered the field as a student). This prevailing doctrine may be expressed:

SCIENTIFIC MARKETING RESEARCH IS NEOPOSITIVISTIC MANAGERIALLY RELEVANT STUDIES OF DECISIONS TO BUY GOODS AND SERVICES.

During the ensuing years, each part of this doctrine has been questioned and has fallen by the wayside. These changes, in rough chronological order, appear in Figure 1.3, one by one, as key parts of the conventional wisdom are successively crossed out. Ultimately, as the progression through the various stages shows, very little of the traditional view remains. It is replaced by a perspective more pluralistic, more all-embracing, and more inviting in its scope.

❏ Consumer Research: A Historical Perspective

In this first chapter, I present a brief personal narrative of these changes in the field as I see them and as they have affected me. Furthermore, I use this historical perspective as a key to explaining the structure that underlies this book. In other words, Chapter 1 recounts the historical developments that led to the viewpoints expressed in Chapters 2 through 11. Each stage in Figure 1.3 corresponds to a chapter.

Quite obviously, others who work in different areas of marketing or consumer research would tell very different tales. For some, what seemed true in 1965 remains just as true today. (Such people showed signs of extreme discomfort when I made my presentation at Stanford.) For others, one or two of the developments shown in Figure 1.3 are acceptable, but the rest are anathema. (These people tended to latch on to one of the key points and to forget or repress the rest.) For still others, Figure 1.3 may stop short of the revolutionary departures they seek. (These tend to be Marxists, opponents of the capitalist system, or other critics of the consumer culture.) The best I can offer is a subjective account of how changes in the field have shaped the intellectual life of a few consumer researchers in general and mine in particular. Hence, like the rest of this book, Chapter 1 is about introspection.

Scientific Marketing Research Is Neopositivistic Managerially Relevant Studies of Decisions to Buy Goods and Services

Once upon a time—say, in the mid-1960s—most marketing academics believed in the conventional wisdom expressed by the self-confident claim that "scientific marketing research is neopositivistic managerially relevant studies of decisions to buy goods and services." This modernistic faith in progress had arisen, however, only after serious struggles that had set the stage for the received view circa 1965.

Specifically, a far-reaching study sponsored by the Ford Foundation in the early 1960s had cast doubt on the academic credentials of business education (Howard, 1963a; Myers, Massy, & Greyser, 1980; Porter & McKibbin,

1988). As centers for professional training, business schools were called into question on the grounds of both their methodological refinement (rigor) and their usefulness to managerial practice (relevance). In the wake of this disturbing study, business school faculty members were left with a troubled feeling of intellectual inferiority. Hence, business teachers perceived the need to become more academically respectable, more scientific, more rigorous, and more helpful to managers.

Quite naturally, this reevaluation of business education led to attempts to shake the "trade school" image, to alterations in the curriculum, and to revised standards for hiring and promoting. Increasingly, a professor could not hope to earn tenure without a PhD and a long list of research publications in refereed journals. Not surprisingly, the standards for excellence in such research borrowed heavily from the "received view" in the philosophy of science (that branch of inquiry dealing with the nature and proper construction of scientific knowledge). The new credo therefore adopted was the "positivistic" approach, or what (in deference to Hunt, 1991) I refer to as the "neopositivistic" perspective.

Essentially, the neopositivistic approach assumes that the researcher begins with *hypotheses* derived by *deduction* from a theory and, therefore, is sometimes also called the "hypothetico-deductive" method. The key terms or constructs in these hypotheses are defined by a set of procedures or operations that permit their measurement. These operational definitions then guide the collection of data to test the hypotheses under consideration. Such empirical tests may or may not refute the hypotheses. If refuted or falsified, the theory requires revision to generate new hypotheses for subsequent testing. If not refuted, the hypotheses and underlying theory are viewed as corroborated. Thus, although theories can never be proven to be true, they can at least fail to be refuted; that is, they can be corroborated as not false. In this way, scientific knowledge evolves toward truth (e.g., see Popper 1959/ 1968, 1976).

For Morris the Cat, who began his graduate studies in business during the fall of 1965, this neopositivistic approach was the foundation of his MBA and PhD training. That training amounted to a thorough grounding in the conventional wisdom and continues to characterize the MBA or PhD programs in marketing at most schools in this country, where the traditional neopositivistic view is still taught with great dedication, where the fundamentals of experimental design and survey methods are still honored, and where students are still coached on the merits of meticulous model building and rigorous hypothesis testing.

Despite this lingering allegiance to the traditional perspective, many researchers have moved steadily in the direction of modified, extended, or even liberated views of their work as scientists or scholars. Chapter 1, therefore, traces how that conventional wisdom has been revised since the 1960s and, from a personal point of view, shows what some of those revisions have meant to Morris the Cat.

*Scientific ~~marketing~~ Research Is Neopositivistic Managerially
Relevant Studies of Decisions to Buy Goods and Services*

Probably the first great change in the established credo involved replacing the single-minded emphasis on marketing with an emerging *awareness of the customer* and the recognition that buyer behavior represented a viable subdiscipline. The central impetus in this direction stemmed from Peter Drucker's (1954) profoundly dedicated emphasis on customer value in his *Practice of Management*. Ted Levitt adopted and adapted Drucker's principles to celebrate the virtues of *customer orientation* in his famous piece "Marketing Myopia" (1960). According to Drucker and Levitt, satisfying customer needs and wants is the key to business success: The Customer Is King or Queen. Clearly, from this customer-oriented perspective, the importance of studying buyer behavior follows as ineluctably as summer follows spring.

However exciting this discovery might have seemed to the legions of marketing scholars who embraced the teachings of Drucker and Levitt, it was not news to the so-called motivation researchers—such as Ernest Dichter (1960), Sid Levy (1959), and Pierre Martineau (1957)—who for years had drawn heavily on clinical and psychoanalytic approaches to study consumer motivations but whose work, because of its nonconformity to the neopositivistic credo, had failed to receive the attention it doubtless deserved. Thus, motivation research was criticized both on scientific grounds and on the basis of social welfare. For example, Kassarjian (1974) faulted motivation research for its tendency to use clinical and qualitative, rather than experimental and quantitative, methods. Meanwhile, Packard (1957) heaped opprobrium on what he considered the manipulative techniques of those who design advertising and other marketing communications to appeal to the unconscious desires of consumers via what he called "hidden persuasion." Hence, by branding motivation research as both unscientific and immoral, these critics discouraged its acceptance in academic circles on both methodological and ethical grounds. (Unfortunately, the critics did not pause to consider the apparent self-contradiction inherent in claiming that motivation research was both ineffective and damaging to society.)

For these reasons, the growth of consumer-oriented studies had to await the appearance of a strong and charismatic intellectual leader who could make peace with the forces of neopositivism. Such a figure emerged in 1963 when John Howard (initially at the University of Pittsburgh and later at Columbia University) took the conventional wisdom in marketing theory strongly in the direction of applying the neopositivistic viewpoint to the study of buyer behavior.

Howard's innovations appeared originally in a revision of his textbook on marketing management (Howard, 1963b). This initial formulation of a theory of buyer behavior was followed rapidly and, in some cases, almost simultaneously by elaborations from Howard and Sheth (1969); Engel, Kollat, and Blackwell (1968); Franco Nicosia (1966); and others. These early attempts at model building all featured the boxes-and-arrows style of representation that Howard (1963b) had borrowed from Herbert Simon and that now served as the backbone for a new paradigm—that is, a new set of concepts, methods, and aims for the study of buyer behavior.

Among other insights, this new paradigm suggested the need for a multidisciplinary approach to the study of customers: organizational buyers and consumers. Howard and other buyer-behavior researchers began to borrow heavily from the social sciences (defined broadly to include psychology, sociology, anthropology, communication theory, public opinion research, statistics, economics, home economics, management science, and so on). By the end of the 1960s, such borrowings from other disciplines were commonplace. They were officially recognized in 1975 with the founding of the *Journal of Consumer Research*—defined as *An Interdisciplinary Quarterly* and sponsored by a number of associations in the fields just mentioned. Similarly, from its beginnings in the early 1970s, the Association for Consumer Research attempted to draw its membership from a wide variety of disciplines (although the concentration of members from academic departments of marketing remains extremely high to the present day).

During this critical period, Morris the Cat was lucky enough to study for several years with John Howard himself, whose excellence as a scholar is surpassed only by his dedication as a teacher and warmth as a friend (hence the dedication of this book). As a mentor, Howard provided an inspirational grounding in the importance of buyer behavior and the need to study consumers' purchasing decisions from a variety of disciplinary viewpoints. In this embrace of multiple disciplines, Howard ranged far beyond most other buyer-behavior theorists and welcomed the opportunity to borrow from such fields of study as psycholinguistics and semiotics—sources of knowledge that have proven quite important to the subsequent work of Morris the Cat. Later chapters draw heavily on these expanded horizons encouraged by John Howard. In particular, Chapter 2 uses Howard's work to illustrate the role of theory development in our field and compares Howard's ability to innovate with that of the great artistic genius Charlie Parker, the pioneering jazz saxophonist often referred to as "Bird."

Scientific Research Is Neopositivistic Managerially
Relevant Studies of Decisions to Buy goods and services

The next "casualty" in the received view concerned its time-honored preoccupation with traditional "goods and services" (e.g., coffee, cigarettes, toothpaste, refrigerators, automobiles, restaurants, life insurance). Here, in the late 1960s and early 1970s, Philip Kotler and Sid Levy (both from the Kellogg School at Northwestern University) attacked the conventional wisdom by opening researchers' eyes to the possibility that marketing and therefore buyer behavior involve a whole constellation of products not encompassed by the familiar definition of goods and services. Thus, in broadening the concept of marketing, Kotler and Levy (1969; Kotler, 1972) suggested that a "product" can be literally anything of value that enters into an exchange. Products therefore include not only goods (e.g., beer) and services (e.g., credit cards) but also various people (e.g., politicians), places (e.g., cities), and things (e.g., works of art) not previously conceptualized as part of the marketing-exchange process. Furthermore, products can include ideas (e.g., social causes) and events (e.g., music festivals). Ultimately, the producers of a symphony concert may engage in marketing activities as fully as does a manufacturer of diet cola.

This enlarged view of marketing was a revelation to Morris the Cat, who by this time had begun his career as a marketing academic, struggling unsuccessfully to interest himself in research on such traditional products as automobiles or even whole fleets of cars. After basing his dissertation on an experimental study of consumer responses to automobile advertising (Holbrook, 1975), Morris had dutifully embarked on a large empirical project concerned with decision making among members of the National Association of Fleet Administrators—NAFA (Holbrook & Ryan, 1982).

Unfortunately, the term *fleet administrator* refers not to customers who make especially quick decisions, but rather to those who plan the acquisition of automotive vehicles for corporations that need large "fleets" of cars for their sales or service people. Try as he might, Morris could not manage to find this topic exciting.

As an escape from such mundane preoccupations, Kotler and Levy opened possibilities for studying hitherto neglected kinds of products such as those found in commercial communication in general and in entertainment, the arts, advertising, and the media in particular. Indeed, Kotler and Levy's expansive view tended to legitimate a sphere of interests that, by temperament, Morris the Cat found virtually irresistible—including music, visual art, movies, and television.

One day in about the fourth year of a four-times-a-week adventure in Freudian psychoanalysis, as Morris lay on the couch and droned on about how much he disliked his dreary routine of research on the automotive industry and how much he enjoyed a little project he had started for a local jazz-oriented radio station, his analyst suddenly asked him—with the mock innocence that only a true Freudian could manage—whether he had ever considered doing more research on music. This little question caused a fundamental change in the life of Morris the Cat.

Thus inspired, Morris began a series of studies on such topics as preferences among popular singers, liking for jazz artists, radio listening, record buying, aesthetic appreciation, artistic perceptions, visual artworks, musical performance styles, and the development of tastes over time. For example, one series of studies dealt with the visual representation of consumers' tastes for jazz musicians by building preference spaces in which artists located close together tend to be liked by the same people (Holbrook, 1982; Holbrook & Dixon, 1985; Holbrook & Holloway, 1984; Holbrook & Huber, 1979b).

A chronicle of these research adventures—all related to the study of communication—appears in Chapter 3, which deals with some issues that arise in "hatching" a program of consumer research and which develops a metaphor based on a favorite character—Horton from the Dr. Seuss book—to illustrate the importance of patience, persistence, and perseverance ("An Elephant's Faithful, One Hundred Percent").

This area of research on communication, which I call "consumer aesthetics," studies the consumer's appreciative responses to artworks, to entertainment, to advertising, to the media, or to other products that provide aesthetic experiences ranging in intensity from the simplest hedonic pleasure to the most profound ecstatic rapture (Holbrook, 1980). Although many consumer researchers have begun to subject these phenomena to increasingly sophisticated neopositivistic methods of empirical study, they remain endlessly complicated and elusive (Holbrook, 1987e, 1987g). As some of the most compelling human experiences, they deserve the most dedicated investigation from a variety of methodological perspectives (Holbrook & Zirlin, 1985). Furthermore, these observations point the way to a broader focus on the experiential nature of consumption behavior.

Scientific Research Is Neopositivistic
Managerially Relevant Studies of Decisions ~~to buy~~

As originally argued by Jacoby (1975, 1978) and Sheth (1979), consumer behavior includes all activities involved in acquiring, using, and disposing of products (Holbrook, 1987h). Yet traditionally, the vast majority of empirical consumer research has focused on acquisition in general and on purchasing decisions in particular, rather than on studying the nature of consumption experiences themselves (let alone disposition activities). In short, we as marketing researchers have tended to direct our scientific scrutiny at buying, rather than at *consuming*; at brand selection, rather than at *product usage*; or at choosing, rather than at *using* (Holbrook & Hirschman, 1982). Given the desire of most marketing researchers to produce results of relevance to marketing managers, this state of affairs is hardly surprising. After all, marketing managers care about market share. Market share implies sales of the brand. Sales hinge on decisions to buy.

The first attempts, just described, to study consumer behavior in the arts and entertainment were still characterized by the typical focus on attitude toward the brand, intentions to purchase, or buying decisions. By the early 1980s, however, some consumer researchers had suggested that purchasing decisions tend to rest on what happens during consumption activities—that choosing depends on using, that customers' choices depend on their experiences, that buying depends on consuming. As in so many other cases of apparent "breakthroughs," nothing was all that new in this shift of attention from the purchase to the experience. Indeed, as noted in Chapters 4 and 5, it was "radical" only in the sense that it entailed a return to the "roots" of marketing thought.

Years earlier, Wroe Alderson (1957) had emphasized the rather fundamental proposition that buying decisions depend on consumption experiences. Rediscovering this bedrock premise, a few consumer researchers by the early 1980s began to insist on the importance of usage experiences as the basis for "hedonic" consumption (Hirschman & Holbrook, 1982)—that is, the role of "fantasies, feelings, and fun" in the lives of consumers (Holbrook & Hirschman, 1982).

Working closely with Beth Hirschman, Morris the Cat welcomed this shift of emphasis from buying choices to consumption experiences. In particular, he looked for ways to study consumption experiences independent of their effects on buying decisions or purchasing behavior. This focus appears strongly in Chapter 4, where I ask the fundamental question, "What is consumer research?" and formulate an answer based on the centrality of the consumption experience. From this experiential perspective, many types of consumption deserve rigorous study. These include play (e.g., many sports and games), leisure activities (e.g., various hobbies and social events), and self-improvement programs (e.g., dieting and working out). Thus, Nintendo, Emily Post, and Cory Everson all have something to say to consumer researchers. Furthermore, this concern for experiences in general leads inevitably toward a focus on emotions in particular.

Scientific Research Is Neopositivistic
Managerially Relevant Studies ~~of decisions~~

The new emphasis on consumption experiences raised the possibility of a shift away from the prevailing focus on purchase decisions and brand choices (the traditional view) toward a greater concern for the role of emotions, feelings, moods, and other affective aspects of consumption (a new experiential perspective). Although many consumer researchers continued to deal almost exclusively with information processing and buying decisions, the maturing work on consumption experiences during the late 1980s led others to look at the sorts of emotions experienced while consuming products or attending to advertisements. Thus, a number of consumer researchers began to investigate the emotional aspects of advertising and the feelings derived from consumption. Increasingly, the contrast between cognitive and emotional factors—the respective roles of thoughts and feelings—became a theme of great urgency in consumer research.

Quite early in the game, Morris the Cat pounced on this emerging area of research as a theme near to his heart. Almost as if the topic had been rubbed with catnip, he devoted much of his curiosity and energy to exploring the mediating role of emotions along the chain of effects from receiving information through product usage. In other words, he addressed questions concerned with how information produces emotions that, in turn, encourage favorable attitudes toward an advertisement or brand. Rewards for Morris have included the chances to pursue the theme of consumer emotions with people like Rajeev Batra, Bob Chestnut, Meryl Gardner, Eric Greenleaf, Bill Havlena, Terry Oliva, T. J. Olney, John O'Shaughnessy, Dick Westwood, and others cited in the references.

At the moment, for the record, the greatest gap in studies of consumer emotions seems to be that we as researchers have tended to focus on the affective aspects of advertising (e.g., the Fears, Cheers, and Tears Conference sponsored by the Marketing Science Institute and held at Duke University in 1991) while tending to neglect the equally important feelings associated with consumption experiences themselves (as studied in Havlena's dissertation on "the varieties of consumption experience") (Havlena & Holbrook, 1986). For this reason, in collaboration with Meryl Gardner, Morris has begun to follow his own advice by devoting increased attention to the emotional aspects of the consumption experience (Holbrook & Gardner, 1993). This interest in emotions appears strongly in Chapter 5 and calls for an approach to research that treats the human consumer more like a living creature (Koko the gorilla) and less like an inanimate machine (the mechanical computer).

Scientific Research Is Neopositivistic ~~managerially relevant~~ *Studies*

By the time some of us as researchers had turned to an emphasis on the emotional aspects of consumption experiences, our style of doing consumer research had moved fairly far away from the traditional preoccupation with making discoveries useful to marketing managers. Indeed, for some time, an increasingly vocal group of management-oriented thinkers had complained about the lack of practical relevance characteristic of much academic work devoted to marketing studies in general and to consumer research in particular. For example, this viewpoint has tended to prevail among people active at the Marketing Science Institute (MSI), where it gave birth to attacks on irrelevant research such as those summarized initially by Myers et al. (1980)

and later repeated by Webster (1988). Similar concerns have been voiced by several consumer researchers (Jacoby, 1985a, 1985b).

With a few lonely compatriot spirits—Jim Bettman, Beth Hirschman, Hal Kassarjian, Sid Levy, Melanie Wallendorf, Peter Wright—on this particular issue, Morris the Cat found himself fairly far to the left (or is it the right?). Specifically, he advocates consumer research pursued for its own sake *as an end in itself*—an advocacy that surfaces strongly in Chapter 6. Obviously, this perspective argues against the privileged position of consulting or other strictly practical concerns. Moreover, it supports essentially useless, impractical, a-relevant research pursued for its intrinsic value. Here, *a-relevant* implies that the issue of managerial relevance is itself not relevant. For these reasons, the perspective in question strikes many as at least controversial and maybe even heretical.

In Chapter 6, I distinguish between marketing research and consumer research on the basis of their guiding purposes. In my view, *marketing research* (as opposed to research *in* marketing, which may aspire to a much broader scope of inquiry) is—and, in some sense, should be—conducted for the sake of providing knowledge useful to practitioners. In other words, marketing research is properly utilitarian, instrumental, or banausic in nature.

The word *banausic* is, for me, a relatively recent semantic acquisition—a term that I propose as a worthwhile addition to the marketing vocabulary and one that I have analyzed elsewhere at some length (Holbrook, 1987f). It came to me through the influence of a calendar that attempts to teach its owner a new word every day by defining some unfamiliar lexical specimen and employing it in a sentence that illustrates its proper usage. My wife and I installed such a calendar on our breakfast table a few years ago in an effort to help our then-teenage son, Chris, prepare for his SATs. On the first 9 days of its presence at our morning meal, it impressed us with case after case of abstruse and pedantic vocabulary. Finally, on January 10, it yielded what I now regard as a truly useful semantic discovery—namely, the word *banausic*.

According to our daily calendar, *banausic* is an adjective that means "governed by or suggestive of utilitarian purposes," "practical," "commercial," or "materialistic." I can think of no term that so admirably captures the essence of marketing research (narrowly conceived) or that so convincingly encapsulates the concerns of those who inveigh against the irrelevancy of some research on consumer behavior. Indeed, when confronted with the task of correctly using *banausic* in a sentence, our calendar produced the following illustration: "I now regret the *banausic* impulse that led me to take a degree in business rather than in literature." Thus, the calendar suggests, darkly, that something might be wrong with the banausics of business and that this ominous source of regrets might be avoided by turning to more intrinsically motivated endeavors.

By contrast with the banausic side of marketing research, in my view, *consumer research* is and should be conducted for the sake of studying consumer behavior where that type of knowledge serves as an end in itself. In this sense, consumer research ought to be *ludic* (playful) and *autotelic* (self-justifying) in nature (to pick two more million-dollar words that deserve careful attention). This contrast between the banausic and the ludic or autotelic parallels the familiar distinction between extrinsic and intrinsic motivation. There is good reason to believe that *many activities thrive best when they are pursued for their own sake*. I believe that, like sports, art, and sex, academic research is such an activity and that it tends to prosper best when it is fun, pursued as an end in itself, and given freely rather than bartered for the sake of its potential relevance to managerial problems. Further expressions of this viewpoint, aided by analogies with "The Three Bears," appear in Chapter 6, which asks the question, "Whither consumer research?"

Scientific Research Is ~~neopositivistic~~ *Studies*

At about the same time that this controversy concerning managerial irrelevance or a-relevance began to heat up, changes had also begun in the adherence of some consumer researchers to the received view in the philosophy of science. Thus, questioning of the old neopositivistic premises had emerged. Specifically, fundamental problems were raised in a watershed issue of the *Journal of Marketing*, which featured provocative pieces by Peter and Olson (1983), Deshpande (1983), and Anderson (1983).

This and other work cast doubt on the neopositivistic underpinnings of science for marketing in general and for consumer research in particular. Essentially, the new critiques borrowed from such thinkers as Kuhn (1970a, 1970b, 1977), Feyerabend (1975, 1982), Polanyi (1958), and others to propose the need for revising consumer researchers' devotion to the hypothetico-deductive method.

At first, this general line of thought marched under the banner of "postpositivism." However, this term has been cogently attacked by Shelby Hunt, who has also inveighed against the incorrect application of the term *positiv-*

ism itself (Hunt, 1991; a major reason for my substituting *neopositivism* in the present discussion). In his review of the current state of the art, Sherry (1991) kept *post* but dropped *positivism* and changed the term to *postmodernism*. However—with the exception of a few architects, art historians, and devotees of the avant garde in popular culture—very few people seem really to understand what *postmodernism* means. Its variety of definitions is staggering. Hence, like a few others such as Hirschman (1989) or Hudson and Ozanne (1988), I have tended to prefer the term *interpretivism* or the phrase "interpretive approaches to knowledge."

Even a confirmed neopositivist tends to acknowledge the interpretive contributions to be found in the area of theory development (the "context of discovery") as distinguished from the area of hypothesis testing (the "context of justification") (Reichenbach, 1938). In the neopositivistic view, hypothesis testing proceeds by rigid rules of operationalization and statistical inference. Yet, even for someone devoted to this hypothetico-deductive approach, theory development legitimately draws on virtually any source capable of suggesting potentially fruitful concepts, whether philosophical treatises, historical accounts, works of art, stories, metaphors, intuitions, or even mystical encounters with the Great Unknown. In short, although neopositivists impose tight standards on hypothesis testing, they loosen up considerably in accepting various routes to theory building.

Partly for this reason, I have turned increasingly to the task of conceptual development and hypothesis formulation—aspects of exploration that are relatively sheltered from the iron paw of the ruthless neopositivist. Thus, I have often focused on clarifying theory and on integrating concepts apart from the context of empirical testing. This approach helps protect fragile ideas from rejection before they are sufficiently well structured to bear the burden of confrontation with data.

When studying consumer behavior in general and consumption experiences in particular, however, I have also increasingly accepted the contribution made by interpretive approaches in their own right. In this connection, I have grown convinced that some of the biggest, most profound questions that confront consumer research—What constitutes happiness? What role does consumption play in people's lives? What determines greatness in art?—cannot necessarily be resolved via neopositivistic studies of the type generally conducted by mainstream consumer researchers. Rather, I believe that progress on such questions often requires the application of a more interpretive approach to consumer research.

Interpretive methods view consumer behavior as a text composed of many subtexts that require explication according to a more semiotic or hermeneutic inquiry. This view of consumption as text appears in a monograph by Hirschman and Holbrook (1992) and aligns closely with the semiological-hermeneutic viewpoint adopted by, among others, Paul Ricoeur (1976, 1981). The hermeneutic approach—as explained, for example, by Gadamer (1975)—views an interpreter as moving between a holistic view of the meaning in a text and a scrutiny of its individual parts or elements in a way that establishes a self-correcting cycle that eventually converges on a valid interpretation via the celebrated *hermeneutic circle*.

Morris the Cat has devoted increased effort to the interpretive, hermeneutic, or semiological side of consumer research—including work on the meaning of films, plays, novels, epic poems, music, television programs, and so on—as examined via close readings of their symbolic consumption. Furthermore, this focus has included a push toward the greater use of what I call "subjective personal introspection"—that is, observations on the nature of consumption drawn from one's own direct experience of the human condition.

In a sense, as a consumer, one can meaningfully conduct participant observation on one's own life. In general, participant observation involves the attempt to gain a fuller understanding of some phenomenon by becoming part of it. Analogously, introspective studies in consumer research entail a form of participant observation in the world of everyday consumption experiences. Hence, an emphasis on the importance of introspection as a window on consumption informs this book throughout. This perspective receives special emphasis in Chapter 7, which argues for the role of subjective personal introspection in consumer research and which bases its advocacy of the introspective essay on a tradition that began with Montaigne, reached its pinnacle with Walter Pater, and led to my own self-reflections entitled "I Am an Animal."

~~scientific~~ *Research Is Studies*

As suggested in Chapter 7, interpretivists can defend themselves against the neopositivistic charge of not being scientific. Yet, more fundamentally, it appears that perhaps the conventional devotion to science must itself fall. In this spirit—as argued in Chapter 8, "The Role of Lyricism in Consumer Research"—another way of replying to the neopositivists is to admit that interpretive work is basically humanistic and scholarly, rather than scientific in their sense, and then to agree with their implicit admission that, as a path toward generating knowledge, sound scholarship is often more useful than misplaced scientism (Holbrook, Bell, & Grayson, 1989). Here, one wonders whether consumer researchers perhaps have expended too much energy on trying to be scientists and not enough effort on trying to become scholars.

Years ago, one lone prophet—Herbert Rotfeld—spoke about the need for greater scholarship in marketing and consumer research (Rotfeld, 1985). Thus far, few have heeded this call; rather, consumer researchers tend to use the term *scientific* as synonymous with *rigorous, respectable, worthwhile,* or even *good.* But increasingly, one wonders whether being scientific should constitute consumer researchers' ultimate goal. First, one sadly recognizes that the scientists themselves (even leaders in their respective fields) sometimes have engaged in *questionable practices,* as in the cases of Linus Pauling with vitamin C, Stanley Pons and Martin Fleischmann with cold fusion, or David Baltimore and Thereza Imanishi-Kari with immunology. Second, one senses that *some truths lie buried at a level of human experience too deep for science to penetrate.* Hence, in pursuit of such buried truths about the human condition, some of us attach growing interest to applications of the humanities in marketing and consumer research.

Lately, I have been persuaded that this second defense is potentially even more important than the first. Thus, I have pursued the interpretive focus in the direction of the humanities. This more humanistic research orientation has opened the door to a variety of insights from semiology, hermeneutics, literary criticism, cultural studies, critical theory, interpretive perspectives, phenomenology, existentialism, philosophy of art, aesthetics, axiology, ethics, law, and so on. Among other benefits, this approach countenances the role of subjective personal introspection as an appropriate avenue of consumer research and accepts the desirability of self-revelatory expressiveness in writing by consumer researchers. This lyrical impetus toward a more passionate authorial voice in consumer research emerges in Chapter 8, "The Role of Lyricism" and draws on a metaphor that recalls the song "Skylark."

Research is studies

Finally, with all of these changes occurring apace, it would seem highly presumptuous to make any pronouncements at all on the subject of what research really is. Rather, like other branches of the social sciences, the fields of marketing in general and consumer research in particular seem to be headed for a period of pluralism in which many approaches exist side by side. Such pluralism entails a willingness to embrace perspectives drawn from a number of disciplines and from a variety of methodological orientations. This new ecumenicalism recognizes that competing points of view may shed light on the same issue. It signals the acceptance of diversity that Rich Lutz celebrated in his presidential address to the Association for Consumer Research (Lutz, 1989).

As for Morris the Cat, the new pluralism spells an end to the project of making pronouncements about what constitutes good, worthwhile, or valuable research. Increasingly, Morris believes that honest endeavor in the pursuit of knowledge can take innumerable forms and that it is futile to box oneself in by limiting the directions of one's inquiries. In the last analysis, as argued in Chapter 9, "good" research is whatever the researcher finds fascinating, fruitful, and fulfilling.

Chapter 9, "Dogmatism and Catastrophe in the Development of Marketing Thought," reflects some tensions anticipated in Chapter 6 within the context of studies on consumption that have larger implications for the study of marketing as a whole. Specifically, as his career in research has lengthened, Morris has tended increasingly to extend the view expressed in Chapter 6 past the boundaries of consumer research and into his perspective on research *in* marketing itself (Hirschman, 1986b; Levy, 1976). Ultimately, Morris and some other sympathetic souls managed to smuggle this orientation into a position paper prepared by the Task Force on the Development of Marketing Thought sponsored by the American Marketing Association (AMA Task Force, 1988). After the brain trust at the MSI attacked this position paper as "self-serving" (Webster, 1988), I found myself defending what I called the "feline," as opposed to the "canine," side of the research enterprise (with comments later added on the subject of "fishiness"). This defense appears in Chapter 9 on *dog*matism and *cat*astrophe, couched in the most forceful comparisons based on members of the animal kingdom that I am able to muster.

To anticipate, the essence of my argument in Chapter 9 is that, like cats but unlike dogs, scholars in marketing should do the research that they value, unencumbered by distorting intrusions on academic freedom. On the basis of this logic, for example, Morris the Cat might suggest that, for his own purposes, one promising revisionist expression of a liberated unconventional wisdom might take the form of the next heading borrowed from Figure 1.3.

Humanistic Consumer Research in Marketing Includes
Interpretive Intrinsically Motivated Studies of Experiences in
the Consumption of Artwork and Entertainment.

This revised slogan in the section heading simply reverses all of the language incorporated into the piece of conventional wisdom with which I began and thereby represents one possible position among many. If every term in the original doctrine is replaced by one of the alternative concepts for which I have been arguing, something like this alternative statement results. This new slogan represents one possible view among many others that deserve attention. For example, from the perspective of this book, it opens the way to an expanded focus on the usefulness of insights into consumption experiences to be gained from subjective personal introspection.

In connection with the role of subjective personal introspection, in the chapters that follow I assume that all consumer researchers enjoy a privileged role as participant observers in the consumption experiences of their own everyday lives. I believe that careful and systematic analyses of impressionistic, private self-observations concerning one's own consumption behavior can shed considerable light on the phenomena in question. This conviction has led me to explore phenomenological, autobiographical, and even psychoanalytic accounts of my own consumption activities. This book presents some of these self-analyses in the form of self-reflective essays that read, I hope, less like scientific research papers and more like humanistic scholarship—though, doubtless, this goal remains more an aspiration than an achievement.

I wish I could say that everyone has greeted these self-explorations with warm enthusiasm. Many chapters of this book, however, evince tensions with those who would hold fast to all or part of the narrower view with which I began. Thus, my attempts at self-reflective analysis have proven quite distressing to some critics, who have accused me of egocentric eccentricity.

In part, this book provides a defense of subjective personal introspection against such criticisms. Toward this end, my main arguments on behalf of subjective personal introspection appear in Chapter 7. In conclusion, however, I offer one extended example concerning my personal consumption experiences. Specifically, I have chosen the illustration that remains nearest and dearest to my heart because it was the first. Thus, Chapter 10 presents a revised and expanded version of my introspective essay "I'm Hip: An Autobiographical Account of Some Musical Consumption Experiences."

At the time I wrote the original version in 1985, it took all of my chutzpah to compose a paper that so conspicuously broke virtually every rule and convention then in existence within the discipline (Holbrook, 1986e). During the intervening years, however, several people have told me that "I'm Hip" gave them a new sense of the possibilities inherent in studies of consumer behavior. Hence, I offer this introspective essay as a mere indication or glimmer of the enormous potential for self-analysis that remains largely unexplored in the field of consumer research.

Scientific and Humanistic Marketing and Consumer Research
Includes Neopositivistic and Interpretive Managerially Relevant and
Intrinsically Motivated Studies of Decisions to Buy Goods and Services
and of Experiences in the Consumption of Artwork and Entertainment.

Still, from a personal perspective, I must conclude this brief history by suggesting several important qualifications.

First, Morris the Cat espouses the advantages of subjective personal introspection only as a partial guide for himself and not as a formula that he wishes to thrust on others (who inevitably will pursue whatever approaches they find most congenial). Again and again, the history of consumer research has shown that those who subscribe to a new paradigm tend to be all too anxious to impose that paradigm on the work of others. Thus, those enamored of experimental studies on cognition tend to want to see cognitive experiments. Those fond of the neopositivistic approach look for what they regard as methodological rigor. Those who subscribe to naturalistic inquiry insist on the virtues of ethnography. Morris has no wish to add his own name to the list of critics who have ignored the lessons of pluralism.

Second, even for his own case, Morris emphasizes that the operative force of the word *includes* means that Statement 10 applies only to some research and not to all the different types of studies that he would like to do. Some of my own research remains resolutely empirical, quantitative, and neopositivistic. For certain kinds of problems that lend themselves to empirical investigation within traditional paradigms, I would not have it any other way.

Third, Morris warns those early in their careers—college students, MBAs, PhD candidates, and even young assistant professors—that the viewpoint advocated in the last subsection and developed at greater length in the remaining chapters can be quite dangerous as an employment strategy for those just starting out as marketing academics. It is often prudent to establish oneself via conventional approaches before engaging in more esoteric endeavors.

Fourth, like the proverbial cat, Morris believes passionately in the sanctity of free inquiry. Here, he recognizes the need to avoid imposing restrictions on others, the goal of remaining tolerant of different approaches, the importance of embracing a diversity of ideas, the wisdom of encouraging all researchers to remain true to themselves, and the ultimate irreducible value of academic freedom. Fundamentally, there is only one major reason to engage in the life of a university professor—namely, that it ensures a degree of intellectual independence not to be found elsewhere. Anyone who questions that freedom of inquiry threatens the blessed right to educational liberty that those in academia cherish and share.

So, ultimately, all of this suggests a new ecumenical statement:

SCIENTIFIC AND HUMANISTIC
MARKETING AND CONSUMER
RESEARCH INCLUDES
NEOPOSITIVISTIC AND INTERPRETIVE
MANAGERIALLY RELEVANT AND
INTRINSICALLY MOTIVATED STUDIES OF
DECISIONS TO BUY GOODS AND SERVICES
AND OF EXPERIENCES IN THE CONSUMPTION
OF ARTWORK AND ENTERTAINMENT.

❏ Epilogue

Taken together, the introspective essays previewed in this introductory chapter advocate the presence of a subjective authorial voice, a voice concerned with personal revelations and devoted to the pursuit of self-reflective analysis. Thus, they build toward an acceptance of phenomenological, private, self-analytic insights. They deal with the impressionistic, inward, self-conscious world of the author.

Briefly, in this book I attempt to convey a point of view—a way of looking at the world of consumer research, a perspective on consumption experiences, a manner in which to regard the lives of human consumers. I propose no methodological cookbook, but rather illustrate a general approach that I refer to as "subjective personal introspection." These introspective essays reveal various feelings and confessions that stem from deep convictions concerning the possibilities for new directions in the research stream. And throughout, they express heavily value-laden hopes for a personal vision that I attempt to summarize in Chapter 11—the Epilogue—wherein I add one more animal metaphor to the menagerie that has appeared throughout the book (cat, bird, elephant, gorilla, bears, skylark, dogs, fish) by referring to myself as The Turtle. I hope the reader will not find it imaginatively confusing to learn that, catlike though I may be, a turtle is also what I am.

Above all, I have tried to write these introspective essays in a way that departs dramatically from the normal conventions of social science in general and of consumer research in particular. Usually, social scientists seek academic respectability by striving to present their material in a style that one might describe as "the bland, the impersonal, the remote, and the colorless militantly on parade." By contrast, I plead for an infusion of imaginative sensibilities into our approach to the social sciences. I plead for an approach that borrows from the liberal arts to the extent that it encourages us as consumer researchers to make our words mean something by virtue of their resonance in human lives. I plead for a view of consumer research that has scope and space for the insights gained from subjective personal introspection.

> But I would not be convicted
> By a jury of my peers—
> Still crazy;
> Still crazy;
> Still crazy after all these years.
>   —Paul Simon (1975)[1]

❏ Note

1. Copyright © 1974 Paul Simon. Used by permission of the Publisher, Paul Simon Music.

THEORY DEVELOPMENT IS A JAZZ SOLO

Bird Lives!

> Come reminisce with me
> and think about the Bird.
> Remember everything he did
> and all the things you heard.
> —*Eddie Jefferson (1968),*
> *lyrics to Charlie Parker's "Now's the Time"*

> Everybody knows,
> The more you hesitate, the more you lose.
> If you be still and fail to move,
> You're gonna dig yourself a well-intentioned rut
> And think you've found a groove.
> Waitin' for your time to come,
> You might not ever move.
> —*Jon Hendricks (1959),*
> *lyrics to Charlie Parker's "Now's the Time"* [1]

❏ Introduction

Progenitors

If God is Progenitor of the Universe; if Necessity is the Mother of Invention; and if George Washington is the Father of His Country; then who is the Father, Mother, or Progenitor of Consumer Research?

25

Many people could plausibly make some sort of claim to that honorific title. For example, as early as the 1940s, the so-called motivation researchers, such as Dichter (1947, 1949), Martineau (1957), and Gardner and Levy (1955), began the practice of clinical interviews to plumb the depths of consumer motivations (Levy, 1959; McMurry, 1944; Newman, 1955). Meanwhile, economists such as Robinson (1954) and Chamberlin (1956) had built models of imperfect or monopolistic competition that recognized differences in consumer needs and wants as manifested by the role of product differentiation (Abbott, 1955). Also, those interested in consumer welfare and devoted to such projects as the launching of *Consumer Reports* had long studied the nature of consumption (Morris, 1941). Even earlier, some wise retailer from the preliterate days of marketing knowledge had declared that "the customer is always right."

Within marketing theory, these early explorations still awaited a more coherent formal recognition when Peter Drucker (1954) announced his famous dictum in *The Practice of Management*: "There is only one valid definition of business purpose: *to create a customer*" (p. 37). This early statement of the doctrine later known as "customer orientation" won wide recognition when Ted Levitt (1960) published his influential piece "Marketing Myopia." According to Levitt (1960, 1962), marketing myopia occurs when a firm subscribes to the "better mousetrap" fallacy represented by Ralph Waldo Emerson's immortal phrase, "If a man can make . . . a better mousetrap . . . the world will make a beaten path to his door" (as quoted in Bartlett, 1992, p. 430). Here, problematically, this Emersonian aphorism embodies the essence of "product orientation" by ignoring the fact that people *may not want* a better mousetrap—in which case, the business will fail. Far better, Levitt argued, the firm must recognize that survival (let alone success) requires getting (and keeping) customers by finding ways to please them: "The primary business of every business is to stay in business. And to do that you have to get and keep customers" (Levitt, 1962, p. 1). From this, still in the words of Levitt, it follows that "a business is . . . defined by the want the customer satisfies when he buys a product or a service. To satisfy the customer is the mission and purpose of every business" (Drucker, 1954, p. 79). In short, the gist communicated by these famous statements of customer orientation can be expressed in two simple, never-to-be-forgotten steps:

1. Find out what the customers want.
2. Give it to them.

With the growing acceptance of this customer orientation, serious work on the study of consumption inevitably appeared. In October 1964, consumer studies gained broader attention when a group of prominent marketing scholars—including Ray Bauer (Harvard), Paul Green (Wharton), Al Kuehn (Carnegie), Sid Levy (Northwestern), Bill Massy (Stanford), Charles Ramond (Columbia), Gary Steiner (Chicago), and Bill Wells (Rutgers)—gathered at Stanford for a symposium on consumer behavior. The papers presented later appeared as *On Knowing the Consumer*, a set of essays edited by Joe Newman (1966). Collectively, this work represented a broad range of methodological and theoretical perspectives, each focusing on some aspect of consumer behavior. Despite the heroic summary chapter provided by Newman, however, an integrated viewpoint capable of inspiring and coordinating the efforts of followers and disciples was still missing. The formulation of such a viewpoint awaited the arrival of a visionary leader—someone to create an overall framework for organizing the efforts of other consumer researchers. Such a leader emerged during the mid-1960s in the person of John A. Howard. To answer the question with which I began, by any reasonable standards John Howard is the Father of Consumer Research.

Theory Development

John Howard deserves recognition for his seminal role in the development of buyer-behavior theory or the theory of consumer behavior. This role first surfaced in 1963 when he published a chapter on what turned out to be the first formal model of consumer behavior in a revision of his textbook *Marketing Management* (Howard, 1963b). As explained in a videotaped interview conducted for the American Marketing Association's Oral History Project and entitled *John A. Howard: A Life in Learning* (Holbrook, 1989b), while teaching at the University of Pittsburgh, Howard drew on the work of the future Nobel laureate in economics Herbert Simon at the nearby Carnegie Institute of Technology (now Carnegie-Mellon). Simon had introduced models of human behavior based on computer-oriented logical flowcharts. Howard subsequently adapted these boxes-and-arrows diagrams to the task of describing consumer behavior. He then dedicated the next 30 years to the job of developing and refining these boxes-and-arrows models. In his hands, to accommodate a variety of complex behavioral phenomena, the models first grew more complicated. Later, they became simpler. The rest, as they say, is history.

In this chapter, I explore the nature of Howard's theory building in particular and that of theory development in general. I suggest that theory development in consumer research is a creative enterprise comparable to any artistic endeavor and that the factors encouraging greatness in theory development therefore deserve comparison with those that lead toward greatness in art. Toward this end, I compare theory development by a pioneering consumer researcher (John Howard) with the creative masterpieces of a great artistic genius (Charlie Parker, otherwise known as "Bird").

Disclaimers

As the reader will have sensed, I have moved in the direction of making some big claims. Hence, to hedge carefully, I begin with some important *disclaimers* concerning the role of theory development in consumer research generally and my own humble position within that grand project in particular.

First, unlike some of my more iconoclastic colleagues, I still do believe in empiricism and still do subscribe to the importance of testing theory against data. Elsewhere in this book (particularly Chapter 7), I refer to the problems of specifying what marketing researchers mean by "data" and the dangers of defining that concept so narrowly as to force researchers into a neopositivistic dead end. In this chapter, I focus on questions of hypothesis generation and theory construction, speaking primarily about the development of theory, rather than about its empirical validation. (A resolute neopositivist might say that this chapter dwells on the so-called context of discovery, rather than on the context of justification, though as described in Chapter 7 this distinction may itself prove somewhat problematic.)

Second, I do not claim to have developed any theory myself. At most, I might have generated a few hypotheses in my time and formulated a few concepts here and there, but certainly nothing so grand as a theory. Indeed, I claim no knowledge of how to create anything, whether it be theory or something more mundane. Rather, I see the creative process as an almost mystical endeavor involving elusive components of magic and luck.

Third, I recall a lecture I once gave to some marketing doctoral students on how to write a paper. On the way back to my office, I stopped at my mailbox and found two rejection letters from journal editors. Here and elsewhere, a principle of irony often seems to govern our daily lives. This principle suggests that the moment one becomes cocky, feels self-satisfied, relaxes into complacency, or (face it) wallows in happiness, something bad is bound to happen. When you get up in the morning, if your spouse happens to mention that it certainly looks like a gorgeous day, you can count on rain (if not a hurricane). If the Knicks are winning by 16 points going into the last 2 minutes and the announcer foolishly comments that it feels great finally to win one in Boston, you can bet that the Celtics will sink six 3-point shots in a row. On similar logic, any claim to understand creativity probably would result in my never creating anything again for as long as I lived. In other words, I sincerely believe that, in this area, the assertion of mastery practically guarantees subsequent failure.

Fourth, it follows that my approach here differs dramatically from that of those who believe that creativity lends itself to explanation and even to organization—in short, that creativity can be taught. In this vein, for example, Mike Ray has created a series of stimulating books written with various coauthors to describe his perspective as a teacher of the course on creativity in management at Stanford's Graduate School of Business (Catford & Ray, 1991; Goleman, Kaufman, & Ray, 1992; Ray & Myers, 1986). Although I admire and even envy the optimism with which Ray and his colleagues preach the gospel of creative endeavor, I believe that my own chances of announcing how-to principles for guiding creativity are about as remote as my hope of successfully prescribing procedures for drawing blood from a turnip. Hence, my purpose is not to offer *prescriptions* for what strikes me as the essentially magical process of successful theory development, but rather to suggest some *descriptions* of what I regard as creative genius in the development of theory and of how this genius parallels greatness in art.

Claimer

After all of these *disclaimers*, I need some "claimer" to justify the existence of this chapter. Toward that end, I propose to focus on aesthetics as it applies to the development of marketing theory in general and of consumer-behavior theory in particular. Specifically, I argue that successful theory development parallels the process of artistic creativity so that, in this sense, scientific and aesthetic concerns begin to merge.

One test of greatness in the arts is that great aesthetic value tends to endure. If one defines durability as the length of time over which a product yields its characteristic value-conferring services, one must recognize artwork such as Michelangelo's *David*, Shakespeare's *Hamlet*, or Bach's *Mass in B-Minor* as the ultimate consumer durables. Lesser consumer durables—automobiles, say, or refrigerators—might produce valued consumption experiences for 10 to 20 years. But people still appreciate the works of Michelangelo, Shakespeare, and Bach hundreds of years after their original creation. Even more dramatically, when one admires Homer's epic poems, classical Greek sculpture, or the Egyptian pyramids, one appreciates works that have stood the test of time for thousands of years.

Similarly, one measure of greatness in theory development is how long the theory lasts. Like great art, great theory endures for generations. Like a great artistic masterpiece, a great theoretical contribution is cited, referenced, copied, borrowed, reformulated, revised, expanded, refined, and extended.

Here, I want to compare an instance of greatness in artistic creativity (the musical genius of Charlie Parker) with a similar instance in the development of consumer-behavior theory (the pioneering contributions of John Howard). From these examples, I abstract a general descriptive view of the creative process in both art and science, suggesting how parallel considerations apply to the case of jazz improvisation and the activities of consumer-behavior theorists. Furthermore, this perspective may indicate ways of facilitating the creative process in both art and theory development.

I wrote an earlier version of the comments to follow (Holbrook, 1984) prior to the appearance of two films—the first, a movie on the life of Charlie "Bird" Parker produced and directed by Clint Eastwood; the second, a videotape on John Howard called "A Life in Learning" mentioned earlier (Holbrook, 1989b). My viewing of the first and participation in the second provided some confirmation for the intersubjective validity of my chosen examples. Equally important to me is the chance to pay tribute to one of my great musical inspirations and to honor a teacher—my mentor, colleague, and friend—whose quest for knowledge has placed him at the forefront of scholarship in the field of consumer research.

❑ Greatness in Artistic Creativity

To exemplify greatness in artistic creativity, I have selected the work of Charlie Parker—the legendary jazz saxophonist, sometimes called "Bird"—who died in 1955 from a host of drug- and alcohol-related problems at the tragically young age of 35 (though the coroner's report described his physical appearance as that of someone in his 60s). Commentators speculate that Parker's original nickname "Yardbird" stemmed (in the African American vernacular of the day) from his fondness for eating chicken but that this epithet later shrank to just plain "Bird" out of respect for his ability to soar on flights of improvisatory imagination. On innumerable occasions, Bird carried his alto sax into a recording studio or concert hall and *improvised*—that is, invented spontaneously on the spot—masterpieces of musical innovativeness that still are listened to, admired, studied, loved, and copied 40 to 50 years later. More important, Bird's spontaneous creations have inspired subsequent generations of jazz musicians to borrow from and extend his melodic and harmonic vision.

One illustration of how others have extended Parker's musical ideas involves a tune called "Now's the Time," which he first recorded for Savoy in 1945. Its simple melody on the conventional 12-bar blues pattern later became a popular hit when some rhythm 'n' blues musicians retitled it "The Hucklebuck." In his own version, Bird played a three-chorus solo that listeners still greet with admiring wonder half a century after he first conjured it up out of thin air (Parker, 1945/1988). (Other recorded performances of the same tune on the same day establish that Parker did not even come close to repeating himself from one version to the next.)

In the late 1950s, Hal McKusick (1957) recorded an arrangement by Ernie Wilkins of Bird's solo on "Now's the Time" orchestrated for a full sax section. A few years later, Lambert, Hendricks, and Ross (1959) performed the piece with lyrics composed by Jon Hendricks to match Parker's solo note for note. A decade later, Eddie Jefferson (1968) added his own version to the discography, with completely new lyrics set to the same solo.

Of course, Parker continued to develop his own thoughts on the blues. In the early 1950s, he rerecorded "Now's the Time" for Verve (Parker, 1953/1988). Taken at a much faster tempo, his new solo extended his earlier ideas in a performance that itself has served as the basis for subsequent recapitulation and elaboration. Thus, in the late 1970s (32 years after the original recording of "Now's the Time"), Warne Marsh took Bird's second solo and arranged it for a group of Los Angeles jazz musicians called Supersax (1977).

In sum, after originating in a burst of creative spontaneity, the impromptu ideas reflected in a great jazz solo have been borrowed, modified, and extended over a period of 50 years. *That* constitutes greatness in music.

❏ *Greatness in Marketing*
   and Consumer-Behavior Theory

To exemplify greatness in developing marketing or consumer-behavior theory, I focus on the work of John Howard, partly because he has made such important contributions to the history of consumer research, partly because I am familiar with (and enormously indebted to) his writings, and partly because his contributions so clearly parallel the kind of creative evolution just examined in the case of Charlie Parker. I remember sitting in John's consumer-behavior class during the spring of 1966, shortly after he had arrived at Columbia University, where I then was studying for my MBA. We students in that class felt a powerful sense of excitement in watching the almost feverish unfolding of the creative adventure in which John and Jagdish Sheth produced their masterpiece *The Theory of Buyer Behavior* (Howard & Sheth, 1969). This book immediately established both as leaders in the field of consumer research and has remained influential to the present day. But the full story of John's role is not that simple; indeed, it requires a brief synopsis.

Just as Bird took the basic blues form and elaborated it, John adopted and adapted an old paradigm—cognitions → affect → behavior—whose use extends back to Plato. This framework initially appeared in his 1963 revision of *Marketing Management* (Howard, 1963b), wherein he traced the flow of effects from "information seeking" (cognitions) to "predispositions" (affect) to "purchase" (behavior). It thereby provided the original springboard for subsequent elaborations of the theory.

Just as musicians continue to take Charlie Parker's ideas and develop them, many consumer-behavior theorists (myself included) continue to play variations on essentially the same cognitions-affect-behavior or C-A-B theme that Howard introduced 30 years ago. Thus, as shown in Table 2.1, Howard and Sheth (1969) developed an enormously influential extension in their theory of buyer behavior by focusing on the linkages from brand comprehension (cognitions) to attitude (affect) to intention (behavior). Howard (1977) retained this C-A-B terminology—brand comprehension, attitude, intention—in his later reformulation, drawing on Farley and Ring's (1970) groundbreaking representation of the model as a system of simultaneous equations.

Others have provided empirically testable structural models on the same C-A-B theme. For example, numerous researchers (reviewed by Holbrook &

—— **TABLE 2.1** ——
Evolving Terminology in the Howard Model of Buyer Behavior

	Basic Concept		
	Cognitions	*Affect*	*Behavior*
Howard (1963b)	Information seeking	Predispositions	Purchase
Howard & Sheth (1969)	Brand comprehension	Attitude	Intention
Howard (1977)	Brand comprehension	Attitude	Intention
Howard (1983)	Information/ Identification	Attitude/ Confidence	Intention/ Purchase
Howard (1989)	Information/ Recognition	Attitude/ Confidence	Intention/ Purchase
Howard (1994)	Information/ Recognition	Attitude/ Confidence	Intention/ Purchase

Batra, 1987) have refined the model by incorporating the mediating effects of attitude-toward-the-ad (A_{Ad}). Here, it is assumed that one kind of cognition-shaping informational input (advertising) influences a particular type of affective response (liking for the ad) that, in turn, intervenes in explaining behavioral tendencies (intention to purchase a brand). In other words, embedded within the C-A-B scheme are variations on a subordinate theme:

$$C_{Ad} \rightarrow A_{Ad} \text{ and } A_{Brand} \rightarrow B_{Brand}$$

Much of my own work has drawn heavily on Howard's style of constructing boxes-and-arrows diagrams based on the C-A-B framework. Thus, when I teach a consumer-behavior course, I lean heavily on the model of individual consumer behavior shown in Figure 2.1. This model represents my own attempt to capture the key relationships of interest in schematic form. The reader perhaps will be relieved to learn that I do not plan to explicate the entire model in this chapter. Indeed, it takes me twenty-four 80-minute classes to cover the schema in anything like the degree of detail that it appears to deserve. Rather, my purpose here is simply to indicate the extent to which this and other elaborations of consumer-behavior theory often proceed by building on Howard's original C-A-B formulation. Thus, as before, we encounter the familiar three elements as the model's central core:

Cognition (thoughts) → Affect (emotions) → Behavior (activity)

In addition, as in Howard's work, the model contains a feedback loop in the lower right-hand corner, wherein satisfaction (value) affects the subsequent learning of brand loyalty via habit formation. Furthermore, search processes associated with involvement and arousal appear in the upper left of the diagram, whereas an elaboration of cognition (thoughts) appears in the more detailed specification of reception-perception-memory at the bottom. Thus, this particular version of the model extends Howard's earlier framework but retains his basic C-A-B design. (More dramatically, as described in Chapter 4, my work with Beth Hirschman—even while attempting to break away from the traditional focus on *buyer* behavior by emphasizing the role of the *consumption experience*—retains the familiar three terms *cognition, affect,* and *behavior* renamed as *fantasies, feelings,* and *fun.*)

Meanwhile, as indicated by Table 2.1, Howard has continued to tinker with his C-A-B model, reducing it to the streamlined version that appeared in the *Journal of Marketing* (Howard, 1983) and in the text *Consumer Behavior in Marketing Strategy* (Howard, 1989). Stripped to its essence to provide a more parsimonious representation—especially by comparison with the convoluted diagram shown in Figure 2.1—the new, more compact theory includes only a few major variables to represent cognitions via information/ identification (1983) or information/recognition (1989); affect via attitude/ confidence; and behavior via intention/purchase.

More recently, John worked tirelessly on a second edition of his consumer text (Howard, 1994). This revision retains the earlier focus on information/ recognition, attitude/confidence, and intention/purchase, but it provides a more elaborate treatment of the *stages* in buyer behavior—which Howard calls extensive, limited, and routinized problem solving (shown as "eps," "lps," and "rps" at the top of Figure 2.1)—and how these decision-oriented processes change over the course of the product life cycle (including the decline phase in which nostalgic problem solving or "nps" seems to play a

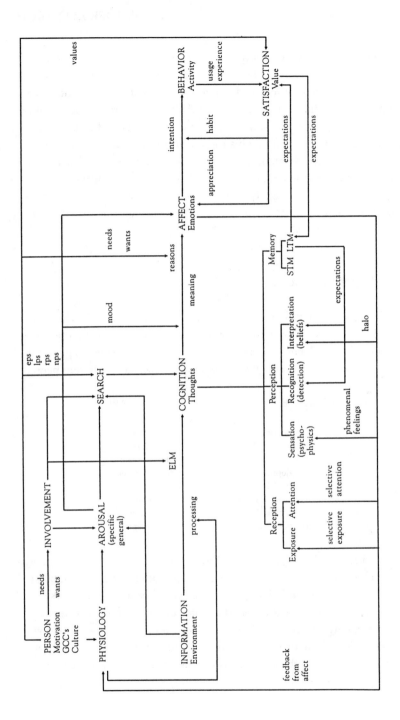

Figure 2.1. A Model of the Individual Consumer

35

major role). Briefly, as sales of a product category first increase and then decrease (the product life cycle), buyers move through a series of phases characterized by different levels of search for information, different aspects of comprehending the product or brand, and different degrees of deliberation in making purchasing choices. In working out these issues, Howard has pursued the task of further refining his theory with ceaseless dedication. With his typical curiosity, eclecticism, and multidisciplinary zeal, he has reached out for advice from scholars in diverse fields scattered worldwide. Needless to say, John's colleagues eagerly awaited the publication of his latest book, somewhat in the way that Charlie Parker's fans awaited the arrival of each new recording from Bird.

❏ The Creative Process

Do the parallels that I have suggested between the work of Charlie Parker and John Howard stem from common characteristics shared by these two extraordinarily gifted men? Obviously not. As the following personality profiles suggest, one would find it difficult to imagine two more different people:

CHARLIE PARKER	JOHN HOWARD
musical	verbal
reckless	careful
disorderly	orderly
emotional	intellectual
manic depressive	well-adjusted
overweight	thin
addicted to drugs	abstemious
self-centered	generous
irresponsible	considerate

Apparently, the shared greatness of Bird's music and John's theory lies not in any similarity between their two personalities, but rather in a resemblance between the processes underlying their creativity. I believe that, in essence, both processes involve a *dialectic* that also underlies the occurrence of profound aesthetic experience. In this dialectical process, a *thesis* gives way to an *antithesis*; ultimately, the thesis and antithesis combine to form a *synthesis*; subsequently, the synthesis serves as a *new thesis* on which to base further rounds of progress.

The Dialectic

In previous essays—drawing from the research on creativity (Koestler, 1964), perception (Platt, 1970), memory (Mandler, 1975), the philosophy of art (Arnheim, 1966), experimental aesthetics (Berlyne, 1960, 1971), and especially musicology (Meyer, 1956, 1967)—I have proposed a model of the dialectic that results in *profound aesthetic experience* (Holbrook, 1980; Holbrook & Zirlin, 1985). In this view of profound aesthetic experience, the relevant dialectic process is one of *structure-departure*-and-*reconciliation* or *configuration-deviation*-and-*integration*. First, the hypothesized process begins with an awareness of *configuration* involving the formation of probabilistic expectations (e.g., based on the observation of various stylistic norms or conventions). Second, such expectations are violated by the occurrence of some *deviation* that produces surprise (e.g., when an artwork contains elements of novelty or incongruity). Third, the resulting arousal motivates a reinterpretation of the surprising event and its cognitive *integration* into a newly perceived larger pattern that, in turn, becomes the structural framework for the next cycle of the aesthetic process (e.g., when clashing aspects in a work of art appear to fuse into an appealing overall pattern or gestalt). The corresponding reduction in arousal via the achievement of resolution or reconciliation is so satisfying as to create a deeply felt emotional response (Holbrook, 1980, p. 106).

In the present context, I would suggest that creativity in both music and theory development appears to involve a comparable dialectic process like that shown in Figure 2.2. In this conception, *structure* or "configuration" (the thesis) entails the patterns, contexts, motivations, categories, norms, and conventions that build probabilistic expectations (Meyer, 1956, pp. 30-32) corresponding to what Koestler (1964) calls a "matrix"—that is, "any ability, habit, or skill, any pattern of ordered behavior governed by a *code* of fixed rules" (p. 38). In other words, the artist or scholar operates within a preexisting framework of rules concerning how things are done, something like what Kuhn (1970b) called a "paradigm."

Departure or "deviation" (the antithesis) occurs when some inconsistency, conflict, incongruity, or other clash arises due to "the frustration of expectation" (Meyer, 1956, p. 43), "the confrontation of incompatible matrices" (Koestler, 1964, p. 304), or "oblique orientation" as a "means of obtaining directed tension" (Arnheim, 1966, p. 407). Berlyne (1960, 1971)

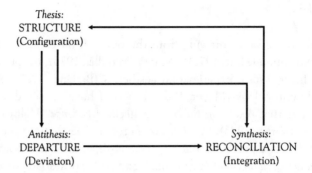

Figure 2.2. The Dialectic of Creativity in Music and Theory Development
SOURCE: From Holbrook (1984). Adapted with permission.

called these clashes "collative properties" because they involve the comparison of one element in an object with another. Here, when the "object" in question is a work of art or a theoretical formulation, the artist or scholar violates the governing norms or paradigmatic conventions by "breaking the rules" to engage in *deviant practices* or *divergent thinking.*

Finally, the creative moment of *reconciliation* or "integration" (the synthesis) arrives when the creator "discovers some new structure that incorporates the deviation and thereby resolves the tension arising from the violation of expectations" (Holbrook & Zirlin, 1985, p. 43). Thus, the artist or scholar finds a way to make the audacious departure fit into a new pattern that contains the deviation by resolving it into an emergent order; we as researchers call the breakthrough "creative" instead of merely "innovative" or "different" because it works. The new structure of reconciliation, integration, or synthesis, in turn, is fed back to serve as the basis for a further round of the dialectic creative process. In this sense, it endures.

Berlyne (1960, 1971) called this dynamic creative process of first arousing and then reducing tension "the arousal jag." In Koestler's (1964) terms, it corresponds to the eureka experience in which, suddenly, "the bisociative act connects previously unconnected matrices of experience" (p. 45); that is, two previously independent or even antagonistic realms of thought or feeling are fused into a new whole. Speaking specifically of music, Meyer (1956) summarizes the dialectic process most succinctly: "By raising our expectations, disappointing them, and finally satisfying them, the composer-performer molds an exciting and moving experience" (p. 239).

Jazz and Theory

This creative or dialectic process of structure-departure-and-reconciliation pertains both to the jazz solo and to the development of marketing and consumer-behavior theory. Indeed, metaphorically, I hope to show—as indicated by the title of this chapter—that theory development *is* a jazz solo.

Other recent work on creativity has played on its connection with jazz. Thus, Goleman et al. (1992) have drawn on analogies with jazz and include illustrative material from the great jazz composer and tenor saxophonist Benny Golson. Along similar lines, Max DePree has pursued the impact of aesthetics on business management in *Leadership Is an Art* (DePree, 1989) and has emphasized the relevant musical parallels in his book *Leadership Jazz* (DePree, 1992). Hence, I find some support for my contention that these parallels deserve probing in greater depth.

❏ The Jazz Solo

The Dialectic

In a jazz solo, *structure* (the thesis) consists of such organizational elements as the basic melody and the harmonic progression of a piece. The jazz musician begins with these structural elements and introduces *departures* (the antithesis) in the form of melodic variations and harmonic extensions or substitutions. The all-important *reconciliation* (the synthesis) occurs when these violations of organization and deviations from order are made to work via a reinterpretation of the piece within which they fit meaningfully. When jazz listeners experience such a resolution, they say that the performance "swings." It "cooks." The musician is "takin' care of business."

I believe that great jazz soloists do, consciously or unconsciously, construct their improvisations in something like the manner just described. For example, an analysis of a solo by Paul Desmond, one of the most masterful of jazz architects, reached the following conclusion:

> Desmond developed his use of the melodic sequence as the foundation of his improvisatory style. Typically, he would begin with a little figure in one key and then repeat it over the next chord change in a different key. He might repeat it once or twice more over subsequent stages in the harmonic progres-

sion until it had built up a kind of forward momentum that conditioned the listener's expectation of its continuance. Then, just as one thought he had committed himself to a further repetition of the fragment, he would begin it again only to depart suddenly in a totally unexpected direction. This violation of expectations would produce a tension that he would resolve almost immediately by transforming the departure itself into a new sequence, thus containing the listener's surprise by revealing the deviation as the basis for an emergent structure. (Holbrook & Zirlin, 1985, p. 45)

Lest anyone doubt that some so-called architectonic improvisers really do consciously construct their solos in this manner, consider the self-described approach employed by Jimmy Knepper, a noted trombonist:

I play sequences. . . . What I've tried to do . . . is play something and then imitate it. You might imitate it again or make a variation and then go off into something else. But it's not recommended for compositional purposes that you play a sequence more than three times. In fact, twice is enough. Three times is a little shaky and four times—forget it, it's just boring. . . . You see this [phrase], the next phrase is an imitation, the next phrase does [something different], and then the next one is a wrap-up of that. Then there's something else. . . . And the whole solo is like that. Anyway, that's the way I play. (Jimmy Knepper, quoted by Jeske, 1981, p. 67)

This process of artistic creativity can be facilitated by any factor that strengthens the achievement of structure, departure, or reconciliation. Here, unlike Ray, DePree, or others, I do not mean to *prescribe* ways of achieving creative success; rather, I wish merely to *describe* three important aspects of the artistic endeavor in jazz. In the following sections, I mention each briefly, with special emphasis on their relevance to the career of Charlie Parker. Throughout, my accounts of Parker's experiences draw on countless Bird-related books, articles, liner notes, and recordings in general and on the excellent biography by Ross Russell (1973) in particular.

Facilitating Structure: Woodshedding

Jazz musicians have coined a term for the facilitation of structure. They call it "woodshedding." Here, they refer to the arduous practice and strenuous preparation by which artists master their instruments and build a complete knowledge of the jazz repertoire. From countless hours of playing scales and studying the chord changes to standard tunes, jazz players build their "chops" and acquire the techniques needed to blow their horns. Ultimately, some jazz musicians sharpen these skills on their "axe" to the point where they can "cut" other players in a blowing session (thereby extending the language drawn from the woodshedding metaphor).

A famous story recounts the episode in which a young, inexperienced Charlie Parker sat in with some other musicians in Kansas City, many of them from the Count Basie Band. Apparently, Bird played so badly on that occasion that Basie's celebrated drummer Jo Jones used one of his ride cymbals like a Frisbee and threw it straight at Bird's head (Russell, 1973).

Narrowly escaping decapitation, Bird felt so humiliated that he withdrew to the wilderness and practiced morning, noon, and night until he had completely mastered every nuance of his horn. Blowing like a demon, he then returned to Kansas City and cut everybody in town. That's woodshedding.

Facilitating Departure: Playing

Notice that I speak of "playing" music. This linguistic habit carries significance because, as pointed out by Schiller, Freud, and many others, the essence of artistic creativity lies very close to the intrinsically motivated phenomenon called "play." Art, as opposed to craft, involves ludic or autotelic creative activity pursued for its own sake, apart from whatever practical results it might accomplish (Becker, 1978, 1982).

The term *ludic* (Huizinga, 1938) comes from the Latin *ludus* ("play, game, sport"), whereas *autotelic* (Csikszentmihalyi, 1975) means "self-motivated" or "self-justified." These terms reflect the general definition of play as essentially "useless activity" (Santayana, 1896, p. 18) that serves "no practical purpose" (Beardsley, 1981, p. 530) but rather is "intrinsically motivated" (Berlyne, 1969, p. 841) for its own sake as "the *free movement* which is itself end and means" (Schiller, 1795/1965, p. 134).

Many philosophers and psychologists have pointed out the close connection between ludic behavior and artistic creation. Schiller (1795/1965) emphasized the play impulse (*Spieltrieb*) as central to the process wherein artistic creation "breaks completely away from the fetters of exigency, and Beauty for her own sake becomes the object of its endeavor" (p. 136). This theme was continued in Bosanquet's (1915) description of the "joy of execution" (p. 199) and in Santayana's (1896) characterization of the "imaginative activities of man" (p. 18) as "whatever is done spontaneously and for its own sake" (p. 19).

Freud (1908/1959) extended this view of imaginative activity by regarding artistic creation as a surrogate form of wish fulfillment in which "the writer does the same as the child at play; he creates a world of phantasy which he takes very seriously" (p. 174). In Freud's conception, "imaginative creation, like day-dreaming, is a continuation of and substitute for the play of childhood" (p. 182).

At a more societal level, Huizinga (1938) regarded play as the very basis for cultural development and evolution, a point echoed and magnified by Stephenson's (1967) ludic theory of mass communication. On a similar theme, Becker (1978) points out that "artists create" according to standards wherein "a work's only utility will be as art: to be admired, appreciated, and experienced" (p. 869). In other words, unlike "banausic" craftsmanship, artistic activity is essentially "disinterested" (Ducasse, 1979; Hospers, 1967; Kant, 1790/1957). Thus, for Whyte (1961), "Creative activity . . . is the enemy of the utilitarian values of every existing mode of life" (p. 353). As in so many cases, Oscar Wilde (1891/1962) offered an appropriate aphorism (in his preface to *The Picture of Dorian Gray*): "We can forgive a man for making a useful thing as long as he does not admire it. The only excuse for making a useless thing is that one admires it intensely. . . . All art is quite useless" (p. 18).

Although this view of the artist as quintessentially playful has received relatively sketchy empirical support, it fits our subjective introspections concerning the mainsprings of artistic creation. In everyday usage, one speaks of playing a role on the stage or playing a musical instrument. From this perspective, much creative activity may itself be viewed as a form of consumption in which the artist consumes certain ludic experiences (Hirschman, 1983).

At times, these forms of autotelic or intrinsically motivated behavior may be extremely serious, even painful, in nature. For me, writing this chapter might be one illustration of the serious side of ludic experience. To pick a more lofty example, Michelangelo's celebrated adventures on the scaffold in the Sistine Chapel indicate the possible connection between play and pain— that is, *The Agony and the Ecstasy*. Similarly, Albert Innaurato has acknowledged that the ludic or autotelic aspects of writing plays, motivated by a love for the theater, may not always feel like fun in the conventional sense:

> I think you have to love the theater, beyond having a career. . . . Even when there was nobody interested in me and my work, I wrote plays. When no one

would read them, when I didn't have anyone to show them to, I wrote plays. I've written through the most terrible days. I don't want a badge for that, it's just my life. (quoted by Berkvist, 1980, p. C16)[2]

In short, as expressed in the poem "Adam's Curse" by William Butler Yeats (1904/1956), "we must labour to be beautiful": "It's certain there is no fine thing/Since Adam's fall but needs much labouring" (p. 78).

In happier instances, however, artists in general and jazz musicians in particular may engage conspicuously in the consumption of playful pleasure and ludic enjoyment. Consider, for example, the words of Johnny Griffin—a prominent jazz saxophonist—on this subject:

> I go on that bandstand to have fun. . . . Music is magic, man; it's just magic. . . . I've got this metal thing in my hands, but when I play it, it becomes part of my body. . . . All I want to do is blow, man. I want to blow my horn and have a nice public and a swingin' rhythm section and that's heaven for me. That's it, you understand. The rest is dross. (quoted by Stewart, 1979, p. 62)

This sense of intrinsically motivated play seems to spur jazz musicians to venture past the conventional bounds of the tunes they perform. A depressing fact is that, as an aid to musical deviance, many (maybe most) great jazz artists have used narcotics of one sort or another (heroin being a favorite during the 1940s and 1950s). The appallingly lengthy list includes Lester Young, Billie Holiday, Miles Davis, Red Rodney, Thelonious Monk, Stan Getz, Chet Baker, Art Pepper, Bill Evans, Ray Charles, and many more of my favorite heroes. Thus, although he constantly warned others against becoming junkies, Charlie Parker's notorious drug habits may have contributed to his own musical liberation.

But, equally likely, Bird's ability to deviate from the standard or the expected arose from his unfettered sense of humor and pursuit of fun. One finds enormous comedy and wit in Bird's playing. Indeed, paradoxically, Charlie Parker ultimately laughed himself to death.

Bird had grown seriously ill. Suffering from ulcers and cirrhosis of the liver, he went to recuperate at the home of his wealthy patron, the Baroness Pannonica De Koenigswarter, who occupied an apartment at the Stanhope Hotel on Fifth Avenue in New York City. After some bed rest, Bird recovered enough to sit up and watch television. Highly amused at a comedy juggling act, he began laughing so hard that he ruptured something deep inside. His laughter turned into a choking noise, and he died before anyone could do anything to save him (Russell, 1973). So, as an ironic tribute to his heroic sense of humor, Bird literally died laughing.

Facilitating Reconciliation: Swinging

When the musical dialectic of structure and departure—or configuration and deviation—comes together and works as an effectively integrated whole, the performance "swings." Unfortunately, no one can pinpoint where swinging comes from, specify what makes it work, or prescribe how to do it. Rather, swinging defies description. When a hapless lady once asked Fats Waller to define rhythm, the great jazz pianist replied, "Lady, if you got to ask you ain't got it" (as quoted in Bartlett, 1992, p. 703).

John Abercrombie, a contemporary jazz guitarist, comes as close as anyone I know to articulating the complex process by which a jazz musician reconciles elements of structure and departure into a well-integrated solo:

> In the improvising experience . . . there's a thought process going on. But it goes by so quickly that it's like the fastest decision-making I've ever done. . . . If I find myself playing a long, very even type of phrase, I'll suddenly realize that if I continue in this manner, it's going to get very boring. So I'll play a more broken phrase, or a phrase involving more triplets, anything to break up the monotony of what I've just played. What you play is the impetus for what comes next, and it all has to be with the general flow of your solo. (quoted by Schneckloth, 1979, p. 42)

The great singer-songwriter-pianist David Frishberg has captured the essence of this dialectic process in jazz via his words to the song "Zoot Walks In" (Frishberg, 1987; Holbrook, 1989c). This song celebrates the improvisatory genius of the brilliant tenor saxophonist Zoot Sims, who wrote the tune (with Gerry Mulligan) and for whom Frishberg often served as piano player in the rhythm section. In the opening phrase, Frishberg alludes briefly to the role of structure exerted by the pull of convention and imitation (the thesis):

> Jazz is a saxophone sound;
> Not every player's got his own sound.

He then quickly confirms the importance of departure (the antithesis) through deviation or uniqueness by assuring us that, when Zoot walks in, "You will know it's totally him you're hearing":

Got a tone all his own,
A happy kind of sadness,
With just a touch of tenor madness.

The point, of course, is that a great improvisor like Zoot Sims integrates structure (thesis) with departure (antithesis) to achieve a reconciliation (synthesis) that swings hard enough to delight an audience of jazz aficionados. In short:

When Zoot walks in,
All the tenormen in the joint start cheering.[3]

No one doubts that, like Zoot, Charlie Parker knew well how to swing. From the elements of structure and departure, Bird built an integrated style so personal and powerful that it transformed the history of jazz.

❏ Theory Development

The Dialectic

Like artistic creativity, theory development also involves a process of structure, departure, and reconciliation. *Structure* (the thesis) stems from a discipline's habits of thought, from its conventional wisdom, from its overarching paradigms, and from its standard practices. *Departure* (the antithesis) comes in the form of new insights, divergent thinking, the violation of hidden assumptions, and the breaking of explicit rules. Finally, both structure and departure achieve *reconciliation* (the synthesis) in some new combination, integration, pattern, or resolution that, in turn, serves as the emerging structure on which to base subsequent rounds of further elaboration in theory development.

For example, building on Howard's *Marketing: Executive and Buyer Behavior* (1963a) and on the aforementioned revision of *Marketing Management* (1963b), the integrative model proposed by Howard and Sheth (1969) in their *Theory of Buyer Behavior* provided a new synthesis of many previously divergent streams of thought. This contribution then became the structure for additional rounds of theoretical departure by Howard in subsequent years—*Consumer Behavior: Application of Theory* (1977), "Marketing Theory of the Firm" (1983), *Consumer Behavior in Marketing Strategy* (1989), and the second edition retitled *Buyer Behavior in Marketing Strategy* (1994). In short, the evolution of Howard's conceptualizations clearly illustrates the role of theory development in consumer research and vividly embodies the expansion of marketing scholarship to embrace the customer (Statement 2 in Figure 1.3 from Chapter 1).

How can we as researchers encourage this same kind of creative process in future theory development? Addressing this question, not prescriptively but descriptively, and using Howard's work as an example, I again consider ways of facilitating structure, departure, and reconciliation.

Facilitating Structure: The Prepared Mind

Marketing and consumer-behavior theorists customarily rely on several familiar approaches to facilitate their understanding of structure in a particular problem area. They immerse themselves in the issues. They visit the library. They peruse the literature. They talk with colleagues. They attend conferences. They introspect.

All of these activities help put one in touch with the conventional wisdom. In the sense discussed by Christine Moorman at an AMA Winter Conference on Marketing Theory (1984), they shape the "prepared mind."

In the videotape on his life's work, John Howard reveals that one of his primary ways of preparing himself has involved discussions with experts in consumer research and related disciplines (Holbrook, 1989b). In other words, unlike those researchers who tend to bury themselves in books and periodicals, John habitually does something straightforward but amazingly effective: He talks with people. This flair for meaningful conversation has put him in close touch with such influential thinkers as Herbert Simon, Bill McGuire, and Paul Lazarsfeld. Such communications have enabled him to share their ideas and have kept his thinking fresh for several decades.

Facilitating Departure: Play

To facilitate departures from the conventional wisdom, one might resort to various extreme measures such as taking drugs (not recommended) or sleeping a lot in hopes of having interesting dreams (not very efficient). We all hear these approaches touted implicitly by those who celebrate Coleridge and his "Kubla Khan" or Kekulé and his benzene rings (two of the more tiresome examples on everybody's favorite list of great creative break-throughs). But, ultimately, such methods may produce self-destruction or self-defeat, as in the sad case of Charlie Parker's ruinous narcotics addiction. Indeed, Beth Hirschman (1991) has spoken with great depth of feeling on the dangers of addiction or workaholism in the scholarly life as part of what she calls "the dark side of consumer research." Compared with the problems described by Hirschman and illustrated by Bird, most researchers would pre-fer a safer route to glory in theory development.

As in the case of jazz improvisation, the essence of finding new departures in theory development often lies in play. By "play," I refer to the mental habit of pursuing thoughts for their own sake, having fun with ideas, deriving joy from the activity of wrestling with puzzles, letting concepts take on a life of their own, investing one's intellectual products with so much energy that they practically jump up and dance around the room.

A similar emphasis on play emerges in Roger Von Oech's (1983) book on creativity, *A Whack on the Side of the Head*, and in the work by Mike Ray and his colleagues (Catford & Ray, 1991; Goleman et al., 1992; Ray & Myers, 1986), who urge us to stifle that noisily chattering "voice of judgment" that so often threatens to divert us from playful intent. The importance of deriv-ing fun from one's intellectual pursuits received glowing endorsement from Edward Tolman (1959) as he looked back over a distinguished career in psy-chology:

> I have liked to think about psychology in ways that have proved congenial to me. . . . The best that any individual scientist . . . can do seems to be to follow his own gleam and his own bent, however inadequate they may be. In fact, I suppose that actually this is what we all do. In the end, the only sure criterion is to have fun. And I have had fun. (p. 152)

More recently, the anthropologist Joseph Campbell articulated a slogan based on similar advice: "Follow your bliss" (Campbell, 1988). To paraphrase, the only sure criterion is to do the very thing that makes most of us feel guilty—namely, to pursue the most enjoyable parts of our work and, if possible, to find ways to make these even more rewarding while neglecting or at least downplaying the parts we find odious and tedious.

Although most of us cannot escape our share of dreary tasks and thank-less assignments, we must view these intrusions as temporary constraints and press toward maximizing the joy derived from the intellectual task that remains after satisfying our more mundane responsibilities.

Few academics receive enough pay to compensate them adequately for the hours spent on their daily chores. For many, only the intrinsic rewards gained in such academic activities as the development and testing of theory can justify the devotion of a lifetime to scholarly pursuits. For the lucky few, even independent wealth would not dim their desire to innovate conceptually.

Here, I recall the inspirational words of Muriel Costa-Greenspon, an opera singer who won $1.7 million in the lottery. When questioned by reporters, she admitted that her financial windfall was "really something." But she quickly added: "To tell the truth, nothing can compare to the thrill of going on stage and singing, of giving something special to an audience. That is pay that goes beyond any money, and it's my greatest joy" (quoted by Holbrook, 1984, p. 51).

To put it mildly, John Howard has displayed this same kind of unquenchable dedication in his role as a consumer-behavior theorist. For more than 20 years, his contagious enthusiasm permeated the halls of the Columbia Business School, where countless beneficiaries (myself included) absorbed the excitement for consumer research that Howard radiated. Since his retirement in the mid-1980s, during which time he could easily have rested on his impressive laurels, Howard has remained passionately committed to the discipline that he played such a major role in establishing. Specifically, since retiring from Columbia's faculty, he has written and then revised his latest book on consumer behavior (1989, 1994). I do not know whether I should call Howard's approach to consumer research "playful" or "fun"; he seems too serious for that. But I do know that it constitutes play in the highest sense of that term—the sense, suggested by Schiller (1795/1965), that connotes joy.

To capture Howard's perspective, it seems fitting to quote the conclusion of the videotape on his life's work (Holbrook, 1989b). As the interview reaches its end and the camera freezes on John's sensitive face in what may have been a rather emotional moment for him (as it certainly was for me), the following exchange occurs:

HOLBROOK: You've touched so many lives . . . so many students, so many colleagues, so many faculty, so many other researchers that have drawn on your support, your ideas, your wonderful creative mind, and your ability to inspire others to do work along the same lines. What has brought you the most satisfaction?

HOWARD: The greatest satisfaction that I have gotten is from interaction with people . . . talking together, putting ideas together, and ending up with a creative structure. It is very satisfying and almost a spiritual kind of satisfaction.

Facilitating Reconciliation: Matrix Thinking

Again, as in the case of artistic creativity, no one really knows how to foster the reconciliation that integrates structure and departure so as to promote hypothesis generation and theory construction. This reconciliation involves phenomena that Arthur Koestler calls "bisociation," that the Gestalt psychologists call "insight," and that many more familiarly call the "eureka experience" or the "light-bulb-in-the-head phenomenon." At the moment, I am calling it *theory development*.

I cannot say prescriptively how to make a reconciliation happen in general, but I can report descriptively that, for me, one helpful aid often relies on what I would call *matrix thinking*. Somewhat akin to Koestler's *bisociation*—the fusion of competing perspectives—this way of looking at problems clarifies conceptual issues by first forming key distinctions, dichotomies, or logical divisions and then cross-classifying or combining these contrasts to build typologies. These typologies take the form of $N \times M$ matrices, wherein N partitions based on one concept are arrayed against M partitions based on another to produce a cross-classification with $N \times M$ cells or categories.

Somebody (maybe it was Kenneth Boulding) once said that two kinds of people exist in the world: (a) those who divide everything into two groups and (b) those who don't. Beyond appreciating this reflexive joke, I have concluded that apparently I belong to the former group. At any rate, I find that sometimes, by thinking about the kinds of matrices based on cross-classified dichotomies just described in abstract terms, one can reach concrete new discoveries that might otherwise have escaped attention. Three examples follow.

The Fourth Monkey. We have all heard of the famous monkeys named Hear-No-Evil, See-No-Evil, and Speak-No-Evil. But suppose I classify these monkeys systematically by combining two dichotomies: their focus (inputs/outputs) and their response mode (verbal/visual). I thereby obtain the typology of morally concerned simians shown in Table 2.2. This matrix indicates that, all along, we have unjustly neglected an important fourth type of

───── **TABLE 2.2** ─────────────────────────────────
A Classification of Monkeys

	Response Mode	
Focus	*Verbal*	*Visual*
Inputs	Hear-No-Evil	See-No-Evil
Outputs	Speak-No-Evil	????????????

monkey—one concerned with avoiding nasty visual outputs. I picture this monkey wearing a trench coat with its collar turned up and a hat pulled down over his eyes. Not to be confused with the flasher who lurks around the playground after school, this fourth monkey carefully keeps his private parts covered. His name is Show-No-Evil.

Types and Degrees of Market Segmentation. Philip Kotler (1988) distinguishes among undifferentiated marketing, concentrated marketing, and differentiated marketing. The key underlying distinctions may be categorized by dichotomizing the *firm's view of the market* (homogeneous/segmented) and the *number of offerings* it produces (one or a few/many) to produce the typology shown in Table 2.3. This classification suggests that Kotler has neglected a fourth type of strategy, in which the firm produces many offerings for a market that it views as homogeneous. This strategy might be called *proliferational marketing.* Sober reflection on the number of questionably differentiated and fuzzily targeted brands of detergents from Procter & Gamble, coffees from General Foods, cereals from Kellogg's, or cars from General Motors suggests that proliferation indeed may represent a frequent occurrence in the marketplace.

Classification of Goods. Dating back to the 1920s, Melvin Copeland's famous classification of convenience, shopping, and specialty goods has received attention in virtually every marketing textbook written since then (e.g., Kotler, 1988). As shown in Table 2.4, however, this time-honored classification gains clarity if cast into a matrix derived from distinctions based on the *degree*

—— **TABLE 2.3** ————————————————————————
Types and Degrees of Market Segmentation

	Number of Offerings	
Firm's View of the Market	One or a Few Offerings	Many Offerings
Homogeneous market	Undifferentiated marketing	?????????
Segmented market	Concentrated marketing	Differentiated marketing

of physical shopping effort (low/high) and the *timing* of mental effort (during/prior to the shopping trip). *Convenience goods*—for example, fruits and vegetables—inspire relatively little shopping effort but do evoke comparisons made in the store itself, as when one inspects the tomato for bruises or thumps the cantaloupe. *Shopping goods*—for example, furniture and carpeting—also require comparisons between alternative offerings made during the shopping trip itself but inspire greater effort spent in going from store to store, looking for just the right fabric texture or the perfect shade of green. *Specialty goods*—for example, television sets and automobiles—involve a similarly substantial effort invested in shopping but also require a high degree of information seeking and deliberation prior to the actual purchase occasion via such activities as reading *Consumer Reports* to discover what brand has earned the "Best Buy" designation and then searching until one finds a store that carries this brand. In addition, Holbrook and Howard (1977) have suggested that this matrix potentially reveals a fourth type of goods—one not very important in Copeland's day but increasingly conspicuous in more recent marketing history—namely, goods on which consumers expend little physical shopping effort but for which they have formed some brand loyalty due to mental effort prior to the shopping trip. Examples are Bird's Eye frozen vegetables, Swanson TV dinners, Campbell's soups, and Sarah Lee cakes. This hitherto neglected fourth type of offering is called *preference goods*. Preference goods represent the vast majority of packaged and branded products found in today's grocery stores. Their "discovery" via the matrix just described has received some attention in the literature—for example, in the textbooks by Jerry Wind (1982) and Rick Bagozzi (1986). These citations provide partial validation for the power of matrix thinking.

—— **TABLE 2.4** ————————————————————————
A Classification of Goods

	Timing	
Degree	*Mental Effort During Shopping*	*Mental Effort Prior to Shopping*
Low physical shopping effort	Convenience goods	??????????
High physical shopping effort	Shopping goods	Specialty goods

Progress. This last example returns my focus to the work of John Howard and helps illustrate his characteristic mode of theory building. After Holbrook and Howard (1977) had introduced the concept of preference goods, I assumed that it bore little relation to my own primary interest in consumer research on commercial communication and moved on to other topics. Hence, chez Morris the Cat, the concept of preference goods lay dormant for many years, surfacing only in my lectures on marketing strategy concerned with channels of distribution in general and with retailing in particular. Meanwhile, in his ceaseless reconstruction of theory based on new insights, Howard found a way to incorporate the role of preference goods into his evolving model of consumer behavior (Howard, 1989, 1994). Briefly, in his typically eclectic manner, Howard has adapted the idea and integrated it into a revised view of retailing strategy in which types of stores are geared to types of goods sold. For example, Howard (1989) suggests: " 'Preference goods,' including convenience foods, are sold in [supermarkets or] *department stores.* There are several brands to compare, and stores are well located. However, the clerks know substantially less [than in specialty stores] about the products and the margin is lower—perhaps 39%" (p. 144). Thus does the progress of theory in consumer research depend on the constant infusion of new departures reconciled with the conventional wisdom.

❏ Conclusion

In this chapter, I have argued that theory development is for the philosophy of science what artistic creativity is for the study of aesthetics. I have

suggested that artistic creativity and theory development follow similar processes and that comparable logic applies to the facilitation of both.

I can envision two possible responses to these arguments. The first is, So
what? (Wells, 1993). As the painter Ben Shahn is supposed to have said,
"Aesthetics is for the artist like ornithology is for the birds." In other words,
the practicing artist (like Shahn) may regard the creative process as inexpli-
cable and may dismiss all attempts by psychologists and philosophers to explain it as a waste of time ("for the birds").

But speaking of birds, a second and more meaningful response is to remember the legend of Charlie "Bird" Parker and to preserve the ideal of
pursuing similar greatness in theory development. To the extent that this
chapter has a prescriptive, rather than a purely descriptive, point, this is it:
Birds fly. They soar aloft on beating wings toward the tops of mountain
peaks. Like them, those who develop theory in consumer research should
aspire to the pinnacle of greatness reached by such rare creative masters as
John Howard.

Still speaking of birds, the tale of Charlie Parker's death has grown to
resemble legends sometimes told about the death of Beethoven. When Bird
died, the Baroness Pannonica was holding his wrist and taking his pulse. At
the moment when his heart stopped and Charlie Parker passed away, she
heard a tremendous clap of thunder.

Within hours all around New York City, soon all across the country, and
before long all over the world, signs appeared on sidewalks, on the walls of
abandoned buildings, in subway stations, and in nightclub washrooms.
Scratched in chalk on the cement, printed in paint on the bricks, scrawled
in crayon on the tiles, and smeared in lipstick on cracked mirrors, these signs
all said the same thing. Unlike Charlie Parker—who never repeated himself—the graffiti reiterated just one simple phrase: BIRD LIVES!

❏ Notes

1. Reprinted by permission of Jon Hendricks.
2. Berkvist (1980), p. C16. Copyright © 1980 by The New York Times Company. Reprinted
by permission.
3. Reprinted by permission of Jeruvian Music and Elliot Music Co., Inc.

ON HATCHING
A PROGRAM OF
CONSUMER RESEARCH

An Elephant's Faithful, One Hundred Percent

Design and the environmental disciplines can be considered as one of the branches of mass communication. . . . From this moment on, our true environment is the universe of communication. . . . Environment is from the beginning a network of messages and signs, its laws being those of communication.

—Jean Baudrillard (1981), *For a Critique of the Political Economy of the Sign*, p. 200

❑ Introduction

Toward Consumer Aesthetics or the
Study of Commercial Communication

John Howard's work, described in the previous chapter, pushed the academic study of marketing strongly in the direction of dealing with the customer and, therefore, meeting the consumer face to face. Yet in many ways, Howard and his legion of disciples remained true to the conventional catechism described earlier (Statement 2 in Figure 1.3 from Chapter 1):

54

QUESTION: What Is Scientific Consumer Research?
ANSWER: Scientific Consumer Research Is Neopositivistic Managerially Relevant Studies of Decisions to Buy Goods and Services.

Thus, the famous empirical investigations by Howard and his colleagues applied his theory of buyer behavior to conventional frequently purchased consumer *nondurable goods* such as coffee (the Maxim study for General Foods) or other breakfast beverages (the Post Instant Breakfast study, also for General Foods) and to *durable goods* such as automobiles (the Vega study for General Motors) or electronics (the videodisc study for IBM). In these large-scale studies, investigators used advanced statistical methods to test structural models of the type illustrated earlier in Chapter 2 (Figure 2.1). But although the models and methods moved consumer research strongly forward, the data still reflected a preoccupation with traditional goods and services. Hence, it remained for Philip Kotler and Sid Levy to remind marketing scholars that consumption encompasses more than just the purchase of freeze-dried coffee, instant breakfast, compact cars, and electronic gadgets (Kotler, 1972; Kotler & Levy, 1969).

A Broadened View

When Philip Kotler and Sid Levy broadened the definition of marketing and enlarged the sphere of products suitable for study by consumer researchers (Kotler, 1972; Kotler & Levy, 1969), they moved in the direction represented by Statement 3 in Figure 1.3 from Chapter 1: Scientific Research Is Neopositivistic Managerially Relevant Studies of Decisions to Buy. They thereby opened a host of research possibilities as diverse as political campaigns (voting behavior), social causes (birth control), the arts (music or literature), and entertainment (movies or television). Other researchers have followed this somewhat centripetal expansion in many directions. My own particular response has involved a career-long focus on studies of *commercial communication*, which I would define broadly to include entertainment, the arts, advertising, and the media. In the late 1970s, I began referring to this general stream of research as "consumer aesthetics" (Holbrook, 1980). I thought then (and still do) that one can best position one's work by designating a trademark, logo, or slogan to set it apart and to capture people's attention. In this spirit, the term *consumer aesthetics* has proven useful. Nonetheless, this "trademark" is just a fancy name for studies of commercial communication. And my own scholarly career can be described as a series of variations on this basic theme.

The Researcher as Mythical Hero

When discussing theory development in their book on creativity, Catford and Ray (1991) describe the path of the everyday hero and emphasize "the power of myth to meet life's most important challenges." In particular, these authors stress the usefulness of finding "your own myth to live by" (p. 236). They suggest that such a "guiding myth" might be drawn from familiar tales like *Hansel and Gretel, Red Riding Hood, Peter Pan, Oedipus Rex, The Odyssey, Alice in Wonderland,* or *The Little Engine That Could* (p. 33). Such stories, they point out, can help people understand and shape their own lives by mythologizing aspects of their lived experiences and retelling them as personal narratives (pp. 238-239). In other words, people may gain clarity of purpose and sureness of direction by viewing their lives as myths of which they are the authors. Needless to say, each person needs to discover his or her own appropriate story to follow as a guide—a different narrative for each individual—perhaps borrowed, perhaps personally constructed, perhaps a combination of the two.

I must admit that sometimes, especially when I am lost in the throes of the writing and reviewing process, I tend to identify with Sisyphus, that unfortunate Greek hero condemned for eternity to push a heavy boulder up the side of a hill in Hades only to have it roll back down again. Without doubt, writing or revising a research paper for the 29th time constitutes a Sisyphean task—as anyone who has experienced such labors can readily attest.

But in more optimistic moments, I often recall my list of favorite animal metaphors and find more cheerful creatures with whom to identify. In this connection, I find plenty of use for cats (Chapter 1), birds (Chapter 2), gorillas (Chapter 5), bears (Chapter 6), other animals (Chapter 7), skylarks (Chapter 8), dogs or fishes (Chapter 9), and turtles (Chapter 11). In most of these animal analogies, I treat myself and my colleagues in a lighthearted way, in a tone that tries to avoid excessive solemnity.

When I turn to the theme of this chapter, however, I cannot help but grow at least a little serious. After all, Chapter 3 deals with the topic of my research program within the area of consumer research that focuses on commercial communication—in other words, my life's work. It addresses the question of how one launches, conducts, and sustains *programmatic research* on consumer behavior—that is, a coherent stream of closely related projects. In this regard, I find myself looking for an animal metaphor that provides more than just comic relief. I find myself looking for a guiding myth to live by, one that can truly inspire my own commitment to the study of consumption. For me, such a guiding myth appears in a cherished story by Dr. Seuss, one that describes the adventures of Horton the Elephant.

❑ Horton and the Essence of a Research Program

The Setting

Every year, the American Marketing Association sponsors a doctoral consortium that brings together the country's "best and brightest" PhD candidates in marketing to meet for 3 days and to listen to presentations by faculty members from the top schools. In August 1990, the University of Florida hosted this annual event. The chairmen of the 1990 Consortium—Rich Lutz and Alan Sawyer—invited me to say a few words about the nature of a marketing-research *program* in general and about my own approach to consumer research in particular. They asked me especially to explain the senses (if any) in which my own work might be viewed as *programmatic*—that is, the senses in which this work holds together in some sort of coherent body, as opposed to scattering all over the conceptual and methodological map (Holbrook, 1990b).

This assignment proved challenging and put me on the defensive. How, I asked myself, might I explicate and justify my own activities as a consumer researcher over the past 25 years? In short, how might I account for myself, my work, and my approach to the study of consumption?

As already mentioned, when faced with a hard problem or complex question like this, I tend to turn instinctively to animal metaphors. Hence, it should surprise no one that, in discussing the problematic nature of research programs in general and my own program in particular, I employ one more reference to animal imagery. This time, I wish to trace a theme that emphasizes the virtues of patience, persistence, and perseverance by invoking the example of a creature beloved by me since childhood, one that I regard as eminently worthy of the title Mythical Hero—specifically, the elephant named Horton.

Horton

When I was a little boy, my mother used to read me stories about Curious George the monkey, Babar the elephant, Elsie the cow, and Bambi the deer, not to mention tales with titles like *Peter Rabbit, Make Way for Ducklings, Morris the Big-Hearted Moose,* and *If I Ran the Zoo* (no wonder I have a "thing" about animal metaphors). But most often, on those cold, dark winter evenings in Milwaukee when the sun sets at about 3:30 p.m. and one desperately seeks some source of warmth and comfort, I used to ask for my all-time favorite literary masterpiece, the wonderful comic narrative poem by Dr. Seuss (1940) called *Horton Hatches the Egg.* Written by Theodor Seuss Geisel in 1940, just 3 years before I was born, this tale, more than any other I know, presents the case for patience rewarded, for persistence as the ultimate test of character, and for perseverance raised to its highest level of exaltation. Clearly, these themes bear directly on the subject of programmatic consumer research wherein the qualities of patience, persistence, and perseverance often prove decisive.

The Story

Because some readers may not recall this particular Dr. Seuss story, I briefly summarize the adventures of this magnificent elephant.

Horton is a large and handsome elephant with a very well developed sense of conscience. One day, an obnoxious and lazy bird named Mayzie asks Horton to sit on her red-and-white polka-dotted egg while she takes a short rest. Anticipating George Bush, Mayzie flatters Horton by reminding him that he is "gentle and kind." Reluctantly, he agrees to do her this favor and, after propping up the tree, "carefully, tenderly" creeps up the trunk to sit on the nest. (Please notice, Dear Reader, that long before the advent of women's liberation, Horton achieved a sensitivity to the feminist cause seldom equaled before or since. Score one for Dr. Seuss.)

But Horton soon learns that Mayzie birds should not be trusted. Mayzie has flown south to Florida for the winter and spends her time sunbathing on the beach, while Horton has begun to suffer intensely. Perched precariously on the delicate egg in Mayzie's tiny tree, the elephant undergoes a series of trials and tribulations. A terrible storm comes, with thunder, lightening, and pouring rain; but Horton patiently keeps his promise to sit on the nest. Winter arrives, bringing snow and sleet that cover Horton with icicles; but he persists in keeping his word and protecting the fragile egg. Horton's other animal friends tease him mercilessly, saying "how absurd" that he "thinks he's a bird"; but the brave elephant perseveres. Finally, three hunters sneak up behind Horton, put him in a large cage on a huge wagon, and drag him over the mountains and across the water to New York, where they sell him, his nest, and the tree on which he sits to a circus. This circus travels to Boston, Chicago, Washington—to Minnesota and North Dakota—with crowds of people flocking to see and laugh at the elephant up in the tree. (Notice the implication that folks from rural areas can be just as nasty and cruel as the residents of big cities. The work of Dr. Seuss is loaded with such interesting subtexts.)

But all the while, as the very embodiment of patience, persistence, and perseverance, Horton loyally honors his promise to protect the egg, constantly repeating a vow that gradually acquires the force of a sacred incantation:

> I meant what I said
> And I said what I meant. . . .
> An elephant's faithful
> One hundred per cent!

Ultimately, Horton's entourage reaches Florida, where Mayzie bird visits the circus and finds Horton still steadfastly sitting on the nest. Just then, the egg starts to hatch. At first, with all the work already done, Mayzie wants it back. But when the egg breaks open, it contains a marvelous anomaly, a kind of cross between a bird and an elephant—a baby elephant with wings.

In a tribute to Horton's faithfulness, the baby bears a miraculous resemblance to *him*. And the people are amazed:

> And out of the pieces of red and white shell,
> From the egg that he'd sat on so long and so well,
> *Horton the Elephant saw something whizz!*
> IT HAD EARS
> AND A TAIL
> AND A TRUNK JUST LIKE HIS!
> And the people came shouting, "*What's all this about. . .?*"
> They looked! And they stared with their eyes popping out!

Then they cheered and they *cheered* and they CHEERED more and more.
They'd never seen anything like it before!
"My goodness! My *gracious!*" they shouted. "MY WORD!
It's something brand new!
IT'S AN ELEPHANT-BIRD!! . . ."[1]

Thus, in this paean to patience, nature has been overcome by nurture. Persistence has earned its reward. The power of perseverance has creatively transformed the character of the offspring that Horton has hatched.

The Moral

Almost everyone will agree that this is a touching story. But one still might be tempted to ask, What has Horton got to do with programmatic consumer research? Here, I believe, the moral is as simple as the Dr. Seuss story is sweet.

Specifically, I suggest that, in undertaking studies of consumer behavior, researchers should emulate Horton the elephant. They should adopt some aspect of the marketplace or some view of consumption experiences as the focal point from which to perceive the world of business, marketing, and consumers that they study. Researchers should take a stance that ties their work directly to a perspective that they love and that they want to spend their entire lives investigating. They should then devote all of their energy, strength, and commitment to pursuing this vision with the full power of their utmost patience, persistence, and perseverance.

It will not be easy.

Like Horton the elephant, drenched by the torrential downpours, academic consumer researchers must patiently endure the agonies of designing, developing, and defending a PhD dissertation. Like Horton, battered by the bitter storms, they must persistently strive to meet the impossible standards of hiring and promotions committees. Like Horton, mocked by the cruel taunts of the other animals for tenaciously guarding his treasured egg, they must persevere in protecting their precious kernel of truth from the merciless review process. Like Horton, they may find themselves incarcerated in a van, dragged over the mountains and water to New York City, and paraded all across the country in a circuslike display (the AMA and ACR conferences) that eventually winds up in Florida (specifically, in Gainesville at the hottest peak of the summer season), where they are subjected to the mirthful scrutiny of curious spectators (PhD students gathered for the AMA Doctoral Consortium).

But also like Horton, they must constantly repeat to themselves the steadfast vow: "I meant what I said, and I said what I meant." Only then, like Horton, do they have any right to hope for eventual moments of breakthrough and discovery when they somehow miraculously transform the nature of the phenomena they study into something different from the expected—some new and exciting vision in which the hard-won object of their patience, persistence, and perseverance has magically taken flight.

Here, notice that the elephant metaphor has merged with the figure of the bird discussed in the previous chapter on the achievements of John Howard and Charlie Parker. Thus, as depicted in the dialectical view of the creative process in Chapter 2, Bird (*thesis*) and Elephant (*antithesis*) are reconciled by Seuss in the form of Elephant-Bird (*synthesis*). Along the lines suggested by Catford and Ray (1991), this memorable image evokes the celebratory greeting of a creative achievement:

> Then they cheered and they *cheered* and they CHEERED more and more.
> *They'd never seen anything like it before!*
> "My goodness! My *gracious!*" they shouted. "MY WORD!
> *It's something brand new!*
> IT'S AN ELEPHANT-BIRD!! . . ."[1]

❑ A Program of Consumer Research on Communication

The reader might wonder how I can dare to proclaim the virtues of patience, persistence, and perseverance in programmatic research when my own work, dealing with everything from automobiles to pop singers, appears to be characterized by such a conspicuous lack of continuity and coherence. To this criticism, I would reply, first, that I intend to speak less about what my own research *is* than about what it *should be*. Beyond that convenient copout, however, I would claim, second, that my work does conform to a common theme that tends to hold it together even where others might see it as diverging in too many directions or falling apart.

The Theme: Communication

Specifically, I believe that virtually all of the work I do bears directly on the theme of communication. When I entered Columbia's PhD program back in 1967, I applied for what was then the last of the Ford Fellowships for PhD students in business. The application asked me what focus I had chosen as my area of specialization and, having absolutely no idea about the correct answer to this question, I took a wild chance and just wrote down something that I cared about deeply—namely, the study of communication.

This was an old English major from Harvard talking. My 4 years as an unhappy undergraduate concentrating in English at that august institution had drained me of any desire to continue in the rigorous formal study of literature. Indeed, I had more or less been battered into submission by eight frustrating terms of fruitlessly trying to persuade my Harvard professors that I could read or write well enough to earn a living at either. Despite this disillusionment, however, I retained a deep interest in the arts and entertainment (music, literature, movies, television). And it had dawned on me that communication is the one major area that business and the arts share in common. Hence, communication struck me as a reasonable theme for my life's work—at least, for the relatively innocent purposes of a fellowship application.

To my surprise, I actually won that Ford Fellowship. Thereafter, recalling Horton, I felt an increasingly strong sense of moral obligation to pursue the theme I had identified as my chief area of interest. This sense pulled me in the direction of studying advertising effects—the quintessential topic of relevance to communication in marketing. So, ultimately, my dissertation dealt with an experiment on the consumer's attitudinal responses to factual, as opposed to evaluative, advertising content (Holbrook, 1975).

To summarize briefly, I defined *factual content* as "logical, objectively verifiable descriptions of tangible product features" and *evaluative content* as "emotional, subjective impressions of intangible aspects of the product" (Holbrook, 1978, p. 547). I manipulated this variable by designing advertising messages for a fictitious car called the "Vendome" that described this vehicle in terms of six key attributes: appearance, ease of handling, comfort, safety, service record, and economy. For example, the factual and evaluative descriptions of *economy* read as follows:

> *Factual*—It offers a purchase price starting at $2,879, 27 miles per gallon of regular gas, and a 6-year average life span.

Evaluative—It offers a surprisingly low initial purchase price, truly excellent gasoline mileage, and a lengthy life span.

These and the various other factual/evaluative descriptions were combined with filler material to create advertisements viewed by 104 subjects assigned to either the factual or the evaluative treatment. Among other tasks, these subjects rated the Vendome ad on such aspects of *attitude-toward-the-ad* as enjoyment, confidence, and credibility; rated the car itself on their *beliefs* concerning its likelihood of possessing the six attributes mentioned earlier; and evaluated their *affect* or overall liking for the Vendome. A path analysis produced the results shown in Figure 3.1. Specifically, factualness contributed positively to credibility, whereas evaluativeness encouraged confidence. Credibility supported more favorable beliefs. Beliefs, enjoyment, confidence, and credibility combined to determine affect. Thus, for this particular group of experimental subjects (MBA students) and this particular product category (automobiles), factualness (evaluativeness) contributed positively (negatively) to affect or attitude-toward-the-brand via its intervening effects on beliefs and on attitude-toward-the-ad (credibility and confidence).

This study for the dissertation and most of my research for the next few years were as narrow and neopositivistic as one might wish . . . or regret (depending on one's point of view). But, gradually, I expanded my horizons in two directions. First, some of my research became less narrow or *microscopic* and broader or more *macroscopic* in its conceptual orientation. Second, my approach sometimes grew less hypothetico-deductive or *neopositivistic* in its methodology and more *interpretive* or geared toward understanding the meaning of the various communications investigated. Yet, I would contend that, even while branching out in these ways, most of what I did remained true to the promise that I had made to myself and to the Ford Fellowship Committee. In this sense, when I told the committee that I wanted to study communication, I meant what I said, and I said what I meant.

The Matrix: A Classification of the
Programmatic Research on Communication

One can see that growing in the two directions just suggested opens plenty of room for developing a variety of interests around a central focus on communication. Indeed, these two axes of development provide another opportunity to illustrate the sort of matrix thinking recommended in

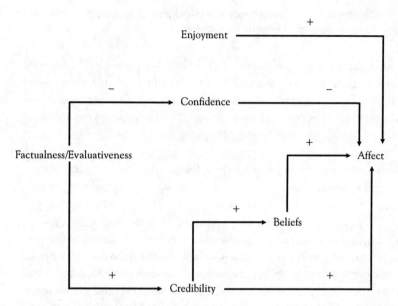

Figure 3.1. Path Analysis of How Factualness/Evaluativeness Determines Affect Toward the Vendome

Chapter 2 as a potential source of insights. In this case, the insights in question pertain to the nature of my program of consumer research on communication.

Specifically, if the two dimensions just mentioned are treated as simple dichotomies (microscopic/macroscopic, neopositivistic/interpretive), they prepare the way to at least four kinds of communication research, as identified by the two-by-two classification of possibilities shown in Table 3.1. My attempts to fill the four cells of this matrix probably account for my apparent diversity, divergence, or diffuseness.

Neopositivistic Microscopic
Consumer Research on Communication

First, the early research was resolutely neopositivistic in its approach and microscopic in its focus. For example, I did laboratory experiments on the attitudinal effects of advertising messages—as in the case of the Vendome

——— **TABLE 3.1** ———————————————————————
Classification of Possibilities for Consumer Research on
Communication

Conceptual Focus	Methodological Approach	
	Neopositivistic	Interpretive
Microscopic	Lab experiments on message effects	Studies of symbolic consumption
Macroscopic	Survey research on audience tastes	A view of consumption as text

Study just described—or I tested models of how artistic features influence evaluative judgments. Clearly, by focusing on ads, artworks, aesthetics, and entertainment, I managed always to deal with some form of commercial communication (for reviews and references to this work, see Holbrook, 1987e, 1987g).

Another illustration of this micro-neopositivistic approach appeared in some research I conducted with Stephen Bertges, an MBA student at Columbia as well as a conservatory-trained concert pianist (Holbrook, 1981; Holbrook & Bertges, 1981). In general, this study examined the effects of various stylistic practices in performing piano music on the perceptual and affective responses of listeners. In particular, Bertges recorded a piece by J. S. Bach—the "Allemande" from his *English Suite in G-Minor*—using all 16 possible combinations of the following four stylistic features:

Rhythm: Steady (no fluctuations in pulse)
       Rubato (slight fluctuations in pulse)
Tempo: Slow (about 69 beats per minute)
      Fast (about 88 beats per minute)
Dynamics: Flat (constant loudness)
       Varied (some crescendo and diminuendo)
Phrasing: Legato (all notes connected)
       Detached (16th notes connected, but 8th notes staccato)

Controversies have long existed concerning the "correct" performance style in playing Baroque keyboard music. Many musicologists would argue that Bach's piece should be performed with steady rhythm, flat dynamics, and detached phrasing—probably at a slow tempo, given the nature of the allemande as a dance. We wanted to see whether such stylistic features matter in consumers' aesthetic appreciation of the music and, if so, how. Toward the end of answering these questions, 16 subjects listened to the 16 recorded performances in random orders and rated them on 38 adjectival scales that represented various *perceptions* (complexity, activity, novelty, expressiveness) as well as *affect* or attitude toward the listening experience (pleasing, enjoyable, good, beautiful). A path analysis suggested the pattern of relationships shown in Figure 3.2. This diagram indicates that affect responds positively to such perceptions as activity, complexity, and expressiveness but negatively to perceived novelty. Meanwhile, the perceptions themselves reflect the four musical features in a manner such that perceived novelty depends primarily on a rubato rhythm; activity on a fast tempo; complexity on a fast tempo, varied dynamics, and legato phrasing; and expressiveness on legato phrasing and a fast tempo. Furthermore, a fast tempo exerts a positive influence on affect above and beyond that accounted for by the intervening effects of the various perceptions. In short, the stylistic features of interest do make a difference in determining aesthetic appreciation, although the relationships involved appear more complex than those implied by most musicologists. Specifically, the model explains about half the variance in evaluative judgment (multiple $R = 0.73$) via a causal structure in which features determine perceptions that, in turn, influence affect. These results support the importance of the stylistic features of interest, but not in the manner prescribed by musicology. Rather, contrary to recommended performance practice, listeners responded most favorably to a fast tempo, varied dynamics, and legato phrasing. As the old saying goes, consumers may not know much about art, but they know what they like.

Neopositivistic Macroscopic
Consumer Research on Communication

Second, I turned increasingly toward studies that were more macroscopic in conceptualization but still just as neopositivistic in methodology as before. In other words, I began to explore survey approaches for investigating communication phenomena in such areas as listening preferences for different artists on the radio, attitudes of record buyers toward various jazz musicians, patterns of media consumption that change from one situational context to

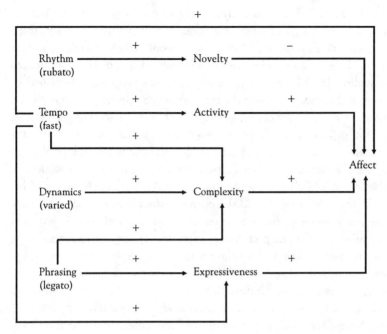

Figure 3.2. Path Analysis of How Features and Perceptions Determine Affective Responses to a Piece by Bach

another, and audience tastes that cluster together in various areas of enter-tainment and the arts. Aspects of this work often carried some managerial relevance to problems in radio programming, record producing, and media marketing (again, for reviews, see Holbrook, 1987e, 1987g).

One example occurred in a study done with the help of another MBA student, Douglas Holloway, in which we examined the preferences of jazz listeners toward various artists played by a local all-jazz radio station—namely, WRVR in New York, once the city's only 24-hour-a-day jazz station until a change of call letters and musical format (first to country, then to easy listening) struck it down (Holbrook & Holloway, 1984; Holbrook & Huber, 1979b). With the help of WRVR's program manager (Dennis Waters), we mailed questionnaires to 1,000 addressees who had volunteered their names for this purpose, receiving replies from a sample of 327 respondents. The questionnaire collected preference ratings on each respondent's enjoyment of 59 jazz artists whom WRVR frequently included on its list of featured performers. Preferences were correlated among artists and across respondents to obtain a matrix of intercorrelations in which musicians with strong associations tended to be liked by the same people. These correlations were transformed into distance measures and submitted to a metric multidimensional scaling (MDS) by using a computational procedure described by Holbrook and Lehmann (1981). Briefly, this MDS routine positions objects with stronger positive associations closer together in a space and places those with less positive or more negative associations farther apart in such a way as to maximize the correspondence between the input psychological proximities and the geometric distances in the resulting spatial representation. In the case of the WRVR data, a two-dimensional solution achieved a fit between the input proximities and the output distances of $r = .79$. This two-dimensional preference space appears in Figure 3.3 and suggests two key factors underlying the jazz preferences expressed by our respondents.

First, the horizontal axis separates the more commercial artists on the left (Grover Washington, Roy Ayers, Bob James) from the more purist musicians on the right (Lester Young, Clifford Brown, Zoot Sims). Second, a distinction appears vertically between the more familiar recording stars at the top (Ray Charles, Miles Davis, Louis Armstrong) and the more esoteric performers at the bottom (Sun Ra, Marion Brown, Hampton Hawes). The proximities of the musicians in the space carry clear implications for which tastes cluster together in the preference patterns of the WRVR audience. Thus, preferences for such musicians as Maynard Ferguson, Quincy Jones, Freddie Hubbard, Donald Byrd, and Herbie Hancock (all in the upper left-hand corner) tend to hang together, as do those for Bill Evans, Lee Konitz, Art Pepper, Gerry Mulligan, and Zoot Sims (all in the lower right).

Furthermore, our data show that relative preferences for these two clusters of musicians were associated with lower versus higher education, respectively ($r = .73$). Hence, a jazz station that wanted to attract listeners of higher socioeconomic status might have considered playing the latter group of artists. As it happened, WRVR aspired to reach a more general audience by programming musicians from all sectors of the preference space. Its program manager therefore adopted a circular pattern for constructing the playlist. In such a progression, a recording by Miles Davis might precede one by Duke Ellington, to be followed by Charlie Parker, Clifford Brown, Paul Desmond, Jim Hall, Phil Woods, Keith Jarrett, David Sanborn, Chick Corea, Hubert Laws, Grover Washington, George Benson, Freddie Hubbard, Maynard Ferguson, and so on in an order that would preserve affective con-

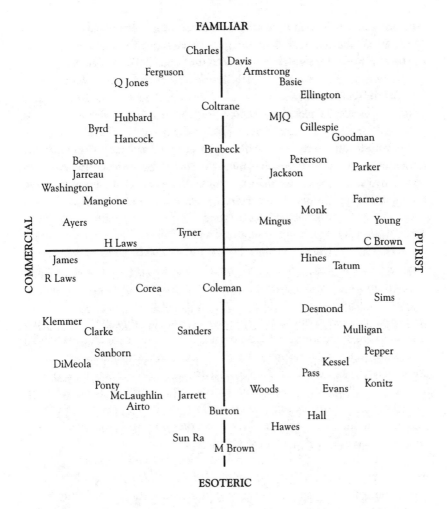

Figure 3.3. MDS Preference Space for 59 Jazz Musicians Based on the Survey of WRVR Listeners

SOURCE: From Holbrook and Holloway (1984), p. 65. Adapted with permission.

tinuity between successive selections as much as possible while still rotating through the space every hour or so. The logic was that listeners who like one artist would stay tuned for the next, thus minimizing dial spinning that might have been inspired by the station's jumping from one preference cluster to another. Unfortunately, WRVR's top management made their change in musical format before this plausible assumption could be tested empirically. The station's fans went to bed one night listening to the city's greatest gift to jazz and woke up the next morning to the sounds of Conway Twitty.

Interpretive Microscopic
Consumer Research on Communication

But third, during the mid-1980s, my work moved beyond the conventional neopositivistic approach toward the greater use of interpretive methods. Here, as the term *interpretive* implies, I have found myself engaged in attempts to understand the meanings of various acts of communication. Thus, at the microscopic level concerned with relatively narrow spheres of application, I have sometimes analyzed single works of art such as motion pictures (*Out of Africa, Gremlins,* or *Two for the Road*), plays (Tina Howe's *Painting Churches* or *Coastal Disturbances*), epic poems (*The Odyssey* or *The Aeneid*), novels (*Pamela* or *Ulysses*), and even popular songs (David Frishberg's "Matty," "The Dear Departed Past," or "Do You Miss New York?"). Such studies of communication are interpretive in the sense that they draw on the *theory of signs* ("semiotics" or "semiology") and pursue concerns associated with *understanding the meaning of a text* ("hermeneutics"). They are microscopic in that they examine the intricate *internal aspects* of an artwork that enable it to illuminate phenomena pertinent to consumer behavior or to everyday life by using *consumption symbolism* to convey part of the artistic meaning and its relevance to the human condition (for a detailed review and lengthy references to this work, see Holbrook & Hirschman, 1993).

Here, I might mention one such semiological analysis that is especially close to my heart because it was, for me, the first. Again, the study in question benefited from insights contributed by an MBA student at Columbia— namely, Mark Grayson, who came to my marketing class after earning his bachelor's degree in English at Harvard College. Mark suggested to me that he would like to do an independent study project. When I asked him what topic he envisioned, he replied, "Something involving films, but *not* based on data from experiments or surveys." When I probed further, he mentioned his hope of pursuing some sort of interpretive analysis along the lines of what one might find in literary criticism, his area of expertise.

I should emphasize that, at the time, Mark's proposal departed dramatically from the accepted neopositivistic canons of the day. Nonetheless, I let his idea percolate in my unconscious for about a month or so while I wondered what to do with it. Finally, on a cold day in December 1985, I experienced an epiphany or moment of revelation comparable to the flashes of insight that sometimes are referred to—after the famous story of Archimedes in the bathtub—as "eureka experiences" (Koestler, 1964). My wife, Sally, and I had gone to see the new film *Out of Africa*. As I sat in the dark theater, I suddenly realized that the creators of this motion picture had molded many of its multiple meanings from their use of *consumption symbolism* or *symbolic consumer behavior*—that is, from the way characters such as Karen Blixen (Meryl Streep) and Denys Finch-Hatton (Robert Redford) acquired, used, and disposed of everyday consumer products. The precise instant that this power of symbolic consumption to shape artistic meaning dawned on me occurred at the point in the film when Karen works on unpacking the various cherished possessions that she has brought from her native Denmark and opens the box containing her precious cuckoo clock.

I now believe that this episode in the film serves as what Auerbach (1969) called an *Ansatzpunkt* or a "point of departure" for the exploration of its multiple meanings. Drawing on such a point of departure, the entire interpretive analysis of an artwork sometimes unfolds from just one crucial passage, scene, or detail that, like a DNA molecule or a hologram, seems to contain the code for implications that extend throughout the entire work of art. Thus, a small specimen can provide the key basis for an elaborated understanding of the remaining text. Indeed, such an *Ansatzpunkt* can radiate outward, shedding light on the overall work to further its hermeneutic exegesis in a manner that Auerbach (1953), among others, demonstrated over and over.

For the particular point of departure that commanded my attention in *Out of Africa*, the cuckoo clock unpacked by Karen Blixen reflects the extreme gulf separating the Western European society that she has left from the African culture to which she has come. Immediately, as a token of this cultural gap, Karen's otherwise steel-nerved manservant, Farah, blinks at the cuckoo with an expression of utter amazement. Soon, the local Kikuyu children gather to watch the clock with an attitude of eager anticipation and of subsequent astonishment when finally the little bird chirps its bizarre message and they run with delighted giggles back to their more familiar native habitat. Later, near the end of the film, as Karen tries to prepare Farah for her imminent return to Denmark, she puts a tag on the same cuckoo clock to ready it for inclusion in the yard sale that represents her financial and emotional ruin via the humiliating disposition of her precious belongings. At the conclusion of this sad task, she asks the loyal but mournful Farah to take the timepiece outside to be sold. Ultimately, the camera focuses on the forlorn cuckoo clock—so freighted with significance and now a poignant emblem of the rift about to reopen between the two poles of Karen's cultural experience with her disappointed return to Western civilization and the lonely abandonment of her African home. In effect, European patterns of consumption have once again driven their wedge between the two cultures.

Mark Grayson and I explored this and other aspects of the consumption symbolism in *Out of Africa* at some length to construct a reading of the film that ultimately appeared in the *Journal of Consumer Research* (Holbrook & Grayson, 1986). For reasons explored later in the book—especially in Chapter 7—it would be fair to say that the passage of our paper through the review process of this journal and into print did not occur without difficulty. Indeed, the advent of interpretive approaches in consumer research posed a great threat for reviewers wedded to the conventional neopositivistic methods. Ultimately, however, this particular story had a happy but ironic ending.

Mark Grayson sat one day in the office of my colleague down the hall, talking about his plans for taking her consumer-behavior class. She described its content and, as a way of indicating the sort of research underlying the material in the course, held up a copy of *JCR* that had just arrived in her mail. Mark asked, with a sweet innocence that belied his own excitement, "Oh, is that the issue that includes my article on the semiology of symbolic consumer behavior in *Out of Africa?*"

It was.

Interpretive Macroscopic
Consumer Research on Communication

Fourth, I have also felt increasingly inclined to broaden my horizons to consider the effects of communication at the societal level. Hence, like others, I sometimes have moved in the direction of a focus that I would characterize as *interpretive* (seeking understanding) and *macroscopic* (directed toward a comprehension of broader implications for the culture of consumption in which we live). This impulse has led to my dialogue with Rick Pollay (1986) on the social effects of advertising (Holbrook, 1987c), to my work with Beth Hirschman suggesting that all consumer behavior might fruitfully be regarded as a text or discourse that invites interpretive analysis (Hirschman & Holbrook, 1992), to my efforts toward satisfying my friends at the Marketing Science Institute by specifying the managerial relevance in the semiology of consumption symbolism (Holbrook & Hirschman, 1993), to my critique of television game shows from the viewpoint of cultural studies (Holbrook, 1993a), to my exploration of ethical issues in consumer research (Holbrook, 1994b), and to my marketing-related reflections on the meaning of postmodernism (Holbrook, 1994e).

One theme that runs throughout this comparatively recent stream of more interpretive and macroscopic studies concerns the role that the media in general and advertising in particular play in shaping the consciousness of American consumers engaged as participants in the *culture of consumption* or what I call the "W.I.M.P. culture"—wherein W stands for Western-White, I for individualistic-imperialistic, M for materialistic-militaristic, and P for Protestant-paternalistic-and-profit-oriented (Holbrook, 1994e). I originally addressed this issue when my friend Rick Pollay kindly invited me to write a reply to his own piece on the unintended consequences of advertising (Pollay, 1986). In that article, Pollay represented the "conventional wisdom" or "prevailing opinion" espoused by various social critics as arguing that advertising trivializes reality, distorts societal values, engenders dangerous or debilitating emotions, and thereby produces unintended consequences that offer due cause for alarm. Toward the goal of defending the role of advertising against these attacks, I replied by suggesting that the arguments cited by Pollay "adopt a tacit view of advertising as a *monolithic institution* that somehow . . . acts in concert to pursue certain shared ends via a set of common means" (Holbrook, 1987c, p. 96) and that these views accuse advertising of pandering to a mass audience by means of insipid jingles, slogans, or stereotypes; of manipulating social values toward the embrace of greed, sloth, pride, lust, or a few other deadly sins; and of fostering unhealthy emotions that impede rationality to replace reason with fear, guilt, self-contempt, or cynicism (pp. 96-98).

Against such claims, I argued that "most of the institutions involved in advertising appear on closer examination to be bastions of pluralism, characterized by in-fighting, checks and balances, and various other contrapuntal tendencies" (p. 98) so that these particularistic or atomistic tendencies lead toward the cultivation of select and often highly sophisticated taste segments via the design of differentiated appeals presented in beautifully crafted vignettes; toward the reflection of such wholesome social values as sociability, affection, generosity, ecumenism, personal enrichment, or temperance; and toward the encouragement of essentially rational behavior based on brand-related differential advantages or on such healthy emotions as joyfulness, gratitude, or love (pp. 98-102).

But, having thus spent the force of my general disagreements with Pollay's broad claims concerning the evils of commercial communication, I can now report that further reflection has led me to agree with many of the points he makes when applied to specific cases of media-related phenomena that seem to command our attention. For example, I can think of no more glaring example of pandering to the lowest common denominator in greed, envy, selfishness, and lust than one encounters when watching the daytime television game shows in general and *The Price Is Right* in particular. My book on this topic regards the TV game shows as manifesting an ethos of consumption via the celebration of merchandise amidst an overt obeisance to the mandate of materialism (Holbrook, 1993a). In particular, my close reading of the longest running and most successful exemplar—*The Price Is Right*—views this program as a formulaic reenactment and ritualistic validation of consumption-oriented possessiveness that reflects, reinforces, or even enshrines the obsession that many modern consumers feel with merchandise valued almost for its own sake, beyond any need or even capacity to use it, as a kind of disembodied target of misdirected desire. Foremost among the features of this game show that, in sympathy with many feminist critics, I find most repugnant, one encounters the many heavy-handed ways in which it stereotypes and demeans the role of women as consumers in this society. In this, the program's host—Bob Barker—serves not only as MC (master of ceremonies) but also as MCP (male chauvinist pig). He routinely insults his predominantly female guests and treats the women who demonstrate the prizes for public delectation as just one more type of merchandise on display (otherwise known as "My Lovelies" or "Barker's Beauties"). In this connection, previous to the appearance of my book, no regular participant on the show commanded more attention than the "Lovely Dian" (Dian Parkinson), who regularly appeared in skimpy negligees, skintight swimsuits, and other cleavage-revealing garments uniquely well-tailored to the objective of inspiring lewd comments and double entendres from Barker himself. Indeed, after resigning from her role on *The Price Is Right*, Parkinson sued Barker for sexual harassment.

In fairness to the confused sensibilities of male viewers, one should note that Dian Parkinson gave every indication of participating willingly and even eagerly in her own sexual stereotyping. Thus, she took pains to display her patented moves whenever possible, as in the suggestive gesture whereby she leans over to flaunt the majesty of her bustline while blowing friendly kisses at the audience. Moreover, Dian appeared conspicuously and, one assumes, voluntarily in an eye-catching array of voluptuous nude poses featured in the December 1991 issue of *Playboy* (Wayda, 1991). It would be hypocritical of me to pretend that I did not enjoy Dian's public unveiling. I did. Furthermore, when Dian's *Celebrity Centerfold* videotape subsequently appeared just in time for the Christmas 1993 season, I immediately added it to my collection (Playboy Home Video, 1993). My point, however, is that, given such complicity in her own treatment as a sex object, it would be hard to make a case for Dian Parkinson as a Champion of Feminism.

❏ *An Elephant's Faithful*

In sum, as I hope to have demonstrated by the examples described here, most of what I do stems from an abiding interest in communication and thereby illustrates the main theme of this chapter—namely, how one consumer researcher departed from an early preoccupation with studies of decisions to buy goods or services and moved in the direction of investigating the consumption of entertainment, the arts, advertising, and the media. Yet, I am painfully aware that others in the field could find many exceptions to this general direction; and if one prizes a cohesive research program, such lapses must count as weaknesses. Hence, reminiscent of the legendary consumer nondurable produced by Procter & Gamble, I can claim a purity level of no more than 99 and 44/100 percent. Like Ivory soap, I hope to float. But, unlike Horton's miraculous progeny, I certainly do not have wings.

So, I speak not vainly of accomplishments, but hopefully and humbly of aspirations. In this connection, we can all dream of flying. For this is the ultimate moral not only of the legends concerning Charlie Parker, or Bird, but also of the story by Dr. Seuss about the wonderful Horton. By virtue of this elephant's remarkable ability to strive steadfastly in one single-minded struggle, his caring nurturance triumphs over Mayzie bird's lazy nature. Horton's patience, persistence, and perseverance transform the creature that finally hatches into a creation that reflects his own true spirit.

We cannot take this message literally, for as scientists, we know that nurture cannot change nature; environmental experience cannot alter genetics; and learning cannot reverse biology. But as poets, we can interpret the myth of Horton figuratively as a symbolic representation of the rewards that come from remaining true to one's purpose and from keeping one's promises to oneself.

By investing all of our patience, persistence, and perseverance in a program of research, we can hope to exert an effect on nature—in the sense that we as researchers might change the nature of research in some field such as consumer behavior. We can hope that the passionately committed hatching of our most precious ideas can permit them—birdlike, but also with elephantine resolve—to amaze the world by taking wing. In short, we can aspire to experience the joyous moment of insight and discovery that eventually may reward our efforts to emulate Horton's memorable motto:

> I meant what I said
> And I said what I meant. . . .
> An elephant's faithful
> One hundred per cent.

❏ Note

1. From *Horton Hatches the Egg* by Dr. Seuss.™ Copyright © 1940 and renewed 1968 by Dr. Seuss Enterprises, L.P. Reprinted by permission of Random House, Inc.

WHAT IS
CONSUMER RESEARCH?

I, long before the blissful hour arrives,
Would chant, in lonely peace, the spousal verse
Of this great consummation.
   —*William Wordsworth (1814/1948),*
    "The Recluse," p. 278

❏ *Introduction*

Still Stuck on Neopositivistic
Managerially Relevant Studies of Decisions to Buy

 In Chapter 3, I discussed a shift in the prevailing direction of consumer research from a narrow focus on goods and services to a broader inclusion of other product categories. Yet, while moving me in the direction of work on communication in general and on consumer aesthetics in particular, my Hortonesque adventures began from the traditional vantage point of neopositivistic managerially relevant studies of decisions to buy (Statement 3 in Figure 1.3 from Chapter 1). Like most of my colleagues, I still thought of the consumer primarily as a purchaser who makes buying decisions based on brand choices. In my expanded consideration of communication and products related to the arts and entertainment, those brand choices might refer to pop singers, jazz musicians, or classical pianists; but my emphasis still reflected the conventional wisdom that regarded the consumer as a buyer.

From the dominant perspective of managerial relevance, this preoccupation with buying decisions made perfect sense. Marketing managers want research that improves their job performance by increasing profits. Profits hinge on sales. Sales depend on market share. Market share results from purchasing behavior. And purchasing behavior reflects brand choices. Hence, serving managers implies building buyer-behavior choice models. Q.E.D. End of story.

Early Teaching

Thus, when I taught my first class in consumer behavior during the summer of 1975, it seemed natural to begin by telling the students that they should regard the title for this course as something of a misnomer because, although it implied an interest in consumption, we would deal primarily with buying. At the time, brainwashed by the entrenched force of current thinking on the subject, I thought that this focus on buying, rather than on consuming—on purchase decisions rather than on consumption activities, on choosing rather than on using—was entirely fitting, proper, and natural. Comfortingly enough, everyone in the field of consumer research appeared to agree on this doctrine. Only later did I realize we were dead wrong.

This chapter begins the story (continued in Chapter 5) of how we as consumer researchers moved toward a broader study of the consumption experience by abandoning our preoccupation with buying behavior to embrace a view closer to that represented by Statements 4 and 5 in Figure 1.3 from Chapter 1: Scientific Research Is Neopositivistic Managerially Relevant Studies.

❑ *The Consumption Experience*

Inklings

I owe the realization of a need for this change in how consumer researchers view the consumer to my friend Elizabeth Carter Caldwell Hirschman—otherwise known as Beth. During the late 1970s and early

1980s, Beth taught marketing at New York University. But although I worked at the Columbia Business School (only a short subway ride uptown), I had to travel all the way to San Francisco to meet my colleague from NYU.

This meeting occurred in the fall of 1979 when we both attended a conference of the Association for Consumer Research (chaired by Jerry Olson) for which we both had organized special topic sessions. My session dealt with consumer aesthetics (Holbrook, 1980); Beth's focused on understanding style and taste and included presentations on the future of aesthetic criteria (Wallendorf, 1980), on measuring consumer tastes in popular music (Shulman, 1980), and on layers of meaning (Hirschman, 1980). Naturally, given my own interests in studies of aesthetics and the arts, I attended Beth's session with eager anticipation.

Imagine my surprise when it turned out that her talk consisted largely of criticizing *me*. Briefly, it seems that Hirschman (1980) took exception to my attempts to isolate the effects of perceptions or beliefs from those of affect or preferences (Holbrook & Huber, 1979a); she also objected to my efforts to treat factual and evaluative message content as separable (Holbrook, 1978). In short, Beth's point was that Morris had tended to pull apart things that should go together. To quote William Wordsworth's poem "The Tables Turned" (1798/1948, p. 189) on this theme:

> Sweet is the lore which Nature brings;
> Our meddling intellect
> Misshapes the beauteous forms of things —
> We murder to dissect.

From the perspective of her focus on aesthetic layers of meaning, Beth was quite right. So I tried not to take offense at her criticisms. Like any assistant professor struggling for recognition in an overpopulated field of academicians and a crowded marketplace of ideas, I was happy just to hear my name mentioned and to see it spelled correctly. Like a cat who senses the presence of an ailurophobe and thereupon directs all of its efforts toward the goal of sitting on that person's lap, Morris tried to make friends.

After the session, I went up and introduced myself to Beth. We agreed that our interests overlapped considerably and that we should get to know each other better after we returned to New York. So we exchanged addresses.

I told her I lived on the Upper West Side at 140 Riverside Drive. She told me she lived next door.

Only in Manhattan must one travel thousands of miles to meet one's friendly neighbors. Nonetheless, for me, the encounter was blessed. I soon found myself collaborating with a colleague of boundless energy and impassioned insights, attuned with extraordinary sensitivity to the hedonic and aesthetic nuances of the human condition. In short, Beth Hirschman explored the meanings of consumption in the daily lives of consumers in ways I had never seen or imagined before. She opened new vistas in a previously unexplored world of consumption experience.

Beth and I began our work together by organizing a conference held in May 1980 at New York University (Hirschman & Holbrook, 1981). The conference dealt with the general topic of symbolic consumer behavior and was sponsored jointly by NYU's Institute of Retail Management and the Association for Consumer Research. At this gathering, several distinguished consumer researchers presented papers on symbolic consumption and consumer aesthetics. For example, Rebecca Holman spoke on apparel as communication, a topic with direct links to Dawn Mello's talk on haute couture. Leon Schiffman and Steven Schnarrs examined the consumption of historical romance novels from the viewpoint of consumer aesthetics in popular literature. Although neither symbolic consumption nor consumer aesthetics was an altogether new topic, the conference provided an opportunity, for the first time, to assemble those with congenial interests in these areas of consumer research.

Experience

Meanwhile, as these activities brought me into closer contact with Hirschman, a new view of the consumer began to emerge. Briefly, we found ourselves thinking of consumers less as buyers and more as people who engage in consumption. We shifted our focus from purchase decisions to *consumption activities*, from choosing to *using*, from buying to *consuming*.

As with any conceptual development, this shift in perspective had roots in the earlier work of others. Had we known the literature better, we could have found clear anticipations of our viewpoint, traced obvious parallels with earlier writings, and done more to acknowledge the contributions of, among others, Wroe Alderson (1957), Harper Boyd and Sid Levy (1963),

Jack Jacoby (1975, 1978), and Walter Woods (1981). Our early failure to credit these intellectual predecessors in enough detail resulted from simple ignorance.

Nevertheless, as I have already suggested, ours was an ignorance pervasive in the field as a whole—a conspiracy of silence on the subject of consumption that, we thought with growing confidence, invited some vigorous dissent. This dissent emerged in views shared by Beth and Morris that gave birth to two papers. The first delved into the hedonic aspects of consumer behavior and emphasized the role played by the multisensory, imaginative, and emotional aspects of product usage, such as those found in smelling flowers, in daydreaming while doing one's homework, or in reacting joyously when one's favorite team wins the Super Bowl (Hirschman & Holbrook, 1982). The second emphasized neglected aspects of the consumption experience as a source of consumer "fantasies, feelings, and fun"—as in thoughts entertained when anticipating one's next vacation, anxiety over whether one's car will start on the morning after a blizzard, or the thrill of beating one's neighbors in a set of mixed doubles (Holbrook & Hirschman, 1982). In particular, the latter way of regarding "the experiential aspects of consumption" focused on a series of systematic contrasts between the older decision-oriented perspective and the emerging experiential view.

Styles of Presentation

The contrast between the writing styles in which these two articles were presented says something instructive about the differences in scholarly temperament between their respective first authors at the time. Beth's version covered a lot of ground, with racy illustrations and vaulting leaps of imaginative insight to make connections between various facets of hedonic gratification (Hirschman & Holbrook, 1982). True to his grounding in the more traditional approach, Morris pursued a format that followed a tighter structure—some might say a more "uptight" form—and imposed a rigid organization on the material (Holbrook & Hirschman, 1982). This need for order surfaced most clearly in a diagram that made a series of comparisons between the decision-oriented and experiential views. With some changes to bring it up to date, several omissions to streamline it a bit, and what I hope are a few artistic improvements, that diagram reappears here as Figure 4.1 and prepares the way to a more detailed discussion in the following section.

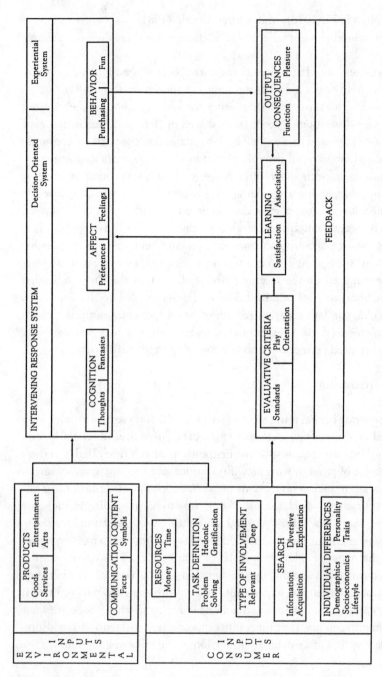

Figure 4.1. Contrasts Between the Decision-Oriented and Experiential Views of Consumer Behavior

SOURCE: From "The Experiential Aspects of Consumption: Consumer Fantasies, Feelings, and Fun," by M. B. Holbrook and E. C. Hirschman (1982), Journal of Consumer Research, 9, p. 133. Published by University of Chicago Press. Copyright © Journal of Consumer Research, Inc., 1982. Adapted with permission.

Contrasting Views

One key point to notice in Figure 4.1 is that the figure draws heavily on the sort of boxes-and-arrows model of cognition → affect → behavior or C-A-B developed by John Howard and others (as discussed in Chapter 2). This representation of the consumer appears in the upper right-hand corner under the heading "Intervening Response System," which refers to the consumer responses that mediate between various sorts of inputs and outputs. As shown on the left of the diagram, the inputs include those from the environment, such as the products themselves (e.g., toothpaste, ballet performances) and various types of marketing-related communications (e.g., information from package labels, symbolic meanings from television commercials featuring tough football players or sexy glamour queens). The inputs also encompass aspects of the consumers themselves involving the resources they bring to the purchase or consumption situation, how they define their task or search for a solution, and what sorts of personal characteristics make them tick. Meanwhile, at the bottom of the diagram, the outputs occur in the form of consequences that produce feedback effects on subsequent consumer behavior—as when satisfaction with the brand purchased reinforces this behavior to create brand loyalty (e.g., the habitual choice of Coke, rather than Pepsi) or when aspects of consumption are so frequently paired in experience that they become associated in the consumer's mind (e.g., the link in memory between Energizer batteries and the indefatigable rabbit).

Most important, numerous left|right comparisons portray the distinction between the decision-oriented focus on buying (left) and the more experiential emphasis on consuming (right). These contrasts represent the essence of the key distinction drawn by Figure 4.1 and summarize the bases for the shift that has occurred in my own work from a more decision-oriented to a more experiential view of consumer research.

Environmental Inputs

Among environmental inputs, as noted in Chapter 3, the types of *products* studied by researchers shift from *goods and services* (e.g., deodorant, fast-food restaurants) to *entertainment and the arts* (e.g., television soap operas, jazz recordings). Also, the *communication content* of interest changes from objective or denotative *facts* (e.g., calories per can for a soft drink, miles per gallon for a car) to subjective or connotative *symbols* (e.g., meanings associated with the Marlboro Man or conveyed by the clothing that adorns the heroine of a film) (Hirschman & Holbrook, 1981).

Consumer Inputs

Meanwhile, among consumer inputs, the emphasis on *resources* shifts from *money* to *time*, as in the difference between studies of spending patterns and those focused on leisure activities (Unger & Kernan, 1983). Perspectives on *task definition*—that is, the goals or objectives pursued by the consumer— open to include not only the more restricted types of *problem solving* involved in brand choice but also the more open-ended *hedonic gratification* that accompanies recreational pastimes, artistic activities, and aesthetic experience (Hirschman & Holbrook, 1982). *Type of involvement* expands from its narrow focus on the elaboration of *relevant* thoughts, as in the listing of counterarguments to an advertising message, to embrace more powerful aspects of *deep* involvement as shown by connoisseurs, collectors, hobbyists, aficionados, or fans (Bloch & Bruce, 1984; Holbrook, 1987a). *Search* by the consumer now refers not only to decision-oriented *information acquisition* (e.g., talking with friends or reading *Consumer Reports*) but also to broader types of *diversive exploration* like those associated with artistic endeavor and play (e.g., when doing watercolors for fun or reading for pleasure) (Berlyne, 1960, 1971, 1974). *Individual differences* on such frequently studied general customer characteristics as *demographics, socioeconomics*, and *lifestyle* are supplemented by *personality traits* such as romanticism/classicism (Holbrook & Corfman, 1985; Holbrook & Olney, in press), visualizing/verbalizing tendency (Holbrook, 1986a; Holbrook, Chestnut, Oliva, & Greenleaf, 1984), and nostalgia proneness (Holbrook, 1993c, 1994d). (For a review of the last-mentioned developments, see Holbrook, 1993d; Holbrook & Schindler, 1991.)

Intervening Response System

As noted earlier, the intervening response system contains the basic building blocks of the aforementioned C-A-B model. Here, *cognition* expands to include not only *thoughts* (knowledge or beliefs about a product or brand) but also *fantasies* (imagery or daydreams in which the mind wanders along various paths of free association). *Affect* moves beyond simple attitudes or unidimensional *preferences* (e.g., liking Crest better than Colgate) to embrace a broad multidimensional array of emotions or *feelings* (e.g., joy when hearing the Finale to Beethoven's *Ninth Symphony*, sorrow when viewing the evening news about war or crime in the streets, anger when watching Rush Limbaugh, disgust when listening to Howard Stern, fear when contemplating yeast infections, love when Bill Cosby walks down the aisle at the Inaugural Celebration while carrying Dizzy Gillespie's trumpet). And *behavior* encompasses not only the traditional focus on buying choices or *purchasing* decisions (what consumers do at the cash register) but also an expanded concern for usage activities or *fun* (e.g., how they play with their new roller blades when they get them home).

Feedback

Finally, in traditional models, a feedback loop occurs in which learning depends on a comparison between *output consequences* and *evaluative criteria* that, if favorable, produces *satisfaction* to reinforce *learning*. In this traditional view, the performance of a product or how it *functions* in use is compared with a set of expectations or *standards* derived from a task or work orientation to determine the resulting level of customer *satisfaction*. High satisfaction results in *learning* according to the model of operant or instrumental conditioning, in which reinforced or rewarded behavior tends to be repeated. This learning feeds back to build habitual *preferences* consistent with brand loyalty.

By contrast, the experiential view suggests that outputs in the form of *pleasure* are organized by a *play orientation* into patterns of *association* that depend on respondent or classical conditioning wherein, when objects are frequently paired together, each comes to evoke responses formerly associated with the other in such a way that associations due to the frequent pairing of, say, Michelin tires and beautiful babies might cause Michelin eventually to evoke *feelings* of love and protectiveness normally associated with babies but not necessarily with tires. (On the other hand, babies might begin to remind one of round rubber objects, but that is another story.)

Ontological Crisis

The paradigmatic shift suggested by the broadened sphere of concerns displayed in Figure 4.1 raised a whole new set of questions not previously entertained by researchers working in the area of consumer behavior. In the work by Hirschman and Holbrook, these questions reoriented the focus of Beth and Morris toward the consumption experience (as opposed to the buying decision). Several consumer researchers now began to direct their attention toward the fantasies, feelings, and fun that accompany the consumption of video games, music, television, and a host of other experientially oriented products.

But such mini-revolutions in thinking did not come cheap. Rather, they entailed the burden of plunging some consumer researchers (including me) into an ontological crisis—that is, into a turmoil of doubts concerning what is meant by the term *consumer research* or questions about the nature of research on consumer behavior. For the first time since its relatively recent birth—even while it still remained an adolescent—people working in the discipline had begun to raise perplexing issues concerning the defining characteristics of consumer research. For the first time, some consumer researchers had begun to wonder whether they could define this field of inquiry in a convincing manner. For the first time, some had begun to ask the potentially embarrassing question that gives this chapter its title—namely, What is consumer research? And, for the first time, facing this question confronted many consumer researchers with an intoxicating but somewhat unpleasant sense of existential angst. The still-unfinished task of this chapter is to rise to this ontological challenge by attempting to provide a satisfactory account of consumer research that answers or at least addresses the fundamental question, What is consumer research? while simultaneously incorporating the essence of the experiential perspective just described.

❑ What Is Consumer Research?

The developments in the field of consumer research just described culminated in a crisis of identity in which the discipline came to embrace a variety of topics once thought too arcane or abstruse for studies devoted to understanding consumption. For example, instances of this trend from the mid- to late 1980s include articles on consuming rituals (whereby, for example, people bathe, groom, and perfume themselves ceremonially); consumer aesthetics (which explores the determinants of appreciative responses to art and entertainment); styles of research (from the more scientistic to the more humanistic); primitive aspects of consumption (as when phenomena found in developed societies parallel those typical of primal cultures); language in popular American novels (the ubiquitous mention of brand names being a case in point); play as a consumption experience (as when one responds emotionally while participating in a video game); consumption symbolism (cinematic and theatrical); the contribution of literary criticism (via the application of genre analysis to the case of advertising); dramaturgical aspects of consuming roles (as when people use their clothing as costumes, possessions as props, or home as a stage); impulsive or compulsive buying (whereby one might not only make an unplanned or irrational purchase but also pay for it with a credit card that one cannot afford); feminist insights (related especially to perspectives on consuming that tend to get neglected by a patriarchal neopositivistic scientific orientation); and introspective approaches to consumer research (of which this book aspires to be an example). Although a relevant content analysis of the consumer-behavior literature by Helgeson, Kluge, Mager, and Taylor (1984) came too early to reveal these developments clearly, the trend appears with full force to anyone who directs even a cursory glance at the tables of contents found in the *Journal of Consumer Research* or ACR's *Advances in Consumer Research* published between, say, 1982 and 1990. More and more, the perspectives of an increasingly diverse range of disciplines crept into the field of consumer research. This proliferation of disciplinary perspectives raised some important conceptual issues.

Toward a Definition

In defining consumer research, I incorporate various suggestions aimed at broadening the concept of consumer behavior to include not only acquisition but also usage and disposition activities (Jacoby, 1975, 1978; Sheth, 1982); at extending the view of products to embrace not only traditional durable and nondurable goods but also other more intangible services, ideas, and events (Kotler, 1972; Kotler & Levy, 1969); and—above all—at emphasizing the role of hedonic responses as part of the consumption experience (e.g., in my work with Beth Hirschman, mentioned earlier).

Specifically, I propose a definition of consumer research based on the following key points:

1. Consumer research studies *consumer behavior.*
2. Consumer behavior entails *consumption.*

3. Consumption involves the acquisition, usage, and disposition of *products*.

4. Products are goods, services, ideas, events, or any other entities that can be acquired, used, or disposed of in ways that potentially provide *value*.

5. Value is a type of *experience* that occurs for some living organism when a goal is attained, a need is fulfilled, or a want is satisfied.

6. Such an achievement, fulfillment, or satisfaction achieves *consummation*.

7. The process of consummation is therefore the fundamental subject for *consumer research*.

The Role of Consummation

From this argument, it follows that *consumer research* refers to the *study of consummation* in all of its many aspects. Consummations of one sort or another are what all humans and therefore all consumers seek. Consummation—attaining *customer value* or achieving *satisfaction*—thereby designates the central core of the concept of consumer research.

This view suggests that consumer research stands on its own as a separate discipline and borrows from other established disciplines no more nor less than they, in turn, borrow from one another. Accordingly, in what follows, I briefly review what I regard as some primary contributions made by other disciplines to the study of consumer behavior.

❑ The Role of Other Disciplines

In summarizing the role of other disciplines, I make no pretense of providing complete coverage of the field. Rather, I focus on what strikes me as the major or most useful concept(s) contributed by each parent discipline. I thus offer an inevitably simplified and idiosyncratic view, but one that I hope captures some of the landmarks that serve as underpinnings for consumer research.

The broad outline for this discussion, as shown by Table 4.1, stems from the concept of value in acquisition, usage, and disposition. This table isolates the primary contributions from macroeconomics, microeconomics, psychology, sociology, anthropology, philosophy, and the humanities by indicating where they have exerted their greatest impacts on consumer research. I address each, in turn, paying particular attention to apparent gaps left by each contributory discipline to be filled by other fields of inquiry.

—— **TABLE 4.1** ————————————————————————————————————
Examples of Primary Contributions From Various Disciplines to the
Study of Consumer Behavior

Field of Inquiry	Value	in	Acquisition,	Usage,	and	Disposition
Macroeconomics	—		aggregate spending	—		—
Microeconomics	—		product purchases	—		—
Psychology	—		brand choice	—		—
Sociology	—		—	role-playing; leisure activities		—
Anthropology	—		the shopping experience	rituals, ceremonies, traditions, collections; consumption symbolism, semiotics		gift giving; garbology
Philosophy	reasoned action; consumer misbehavior		—	—		—
Humanities	consumer aesthetics; stories, analogies, imagery, metaphors		entertainment and the arts; leisure activities	appreciative reactions; emotions; intrinsic value		durability: collecting and nostalgia

Macroeconomics

In the first row and second column of Table 4.1, the field of macroeconomics makes its major contribution to the understanding of acquisition, as represented by a nation's aggregate spending behavior. From this perspective, spending for consumption is what remains after subtracting (a) government purchases of goods and services, (b) gross private domestic investment, and (c) net exports from gross national product. Conversely, from the viewpoint of the national income accounts, *consumption* is *disposable personal income* less *savings* (Dornbusch & Fischer, 1984; Lipsey & Steiner, 1969).

This macroeconomic focus on aggregate spending obviously provides a woefully incomplete account of consumer behavior in general or the consumption experience in particular. It tells little about usage or disposition, as opposed to acquisition. Once a money exchange for goods or services occurs, the macroeconomist cares little about what happens to those products.

Furthermore, macroeconomics remains silent on many forms of consumption, such as housework or other services produced in the home, leisure activities that occur outside the marketplace, goods exchanged in gray-market or bartering relationships, or products consumed but treated as expenses in legitimate business transactions as in the case of the infamous three-martini lunch. In other words, when you mop the floor or play Frisbee with your golden retriever on the beach or take a client to the Four Seasons, your lusty consumption activities escape the attention of the macroeconomist.

Perhaps most seriously, macroeconomics focuses on the quantitative, easily measured aspects of market exchanges while ignoring their more qualitative psychic and social benefits or costs (Scitovsky, 1976; Tucker, 1974). If the deflated price in constant dollars of the compact disc by Natalie Cole that you buy today equals that of the 33 rpm album by her father, Nat, that your parents bought 40 years ago, the musical value must be comparable, right? Wrong! (By the way, the price of musical recordings in deflated dollars is one of the few areas in the economy where real costs actually have declined over the past half-century, but one would have to be tone deaf to conclude that their value has increased. Compare, for example, Kenny G with Benny G—especially when the latter was accompanied by Teddy Wilson, Gene Krupa, and Lionel Hampton. Or contemplate the almost perverse manner in which New Age music mimics what people used to ridicule as Muzak.)

Finally, macroeconomic indicators say little about the process of choice among individual product categories. But, although the macroeconomist does not seem to care very much whether consumers spend their money for butter or guns or roses, this issue provides a major topic for the treatment of consumption in microeconomics.

Microeconomics

In the next row of Table 4.1, microeconomics attempts to explain the allocation of income among product categories (Henderson & Quandt, 1958). Its classic formulations via (a) marginal utility theory (Marshall,

1920), (b) indifference curves (Hicks, 1946), or (c) revealed preferences (Samuelson, 1948) achieve increasingly parsimonious explanations of the downward-sloping demand curve and various income effects on purchases in a particular product class. From whichever of these three vantage points you choose to employ, microeconomics tells you that—with rare departures that need not trouble us here—as price falls, quantity purchased increases.

This microeconomic approach accounts for product purchases only by virtue of taking as givens the tastes that explain acquisition behavior by determining the shapes of indifference curves or "isopreference" contours—that is, the trade-offs among goods that people regard as leaving them equally well off. Microeconomists do not care why you might trade two 1957 Joe Adcock baseball cards for one 1953 Jackie Robinson, but only that you would make such an exchange if an additional penny were thrown into the bargain. Thus, they relegate the responsibility for investigating such tastes to other disciplines—the unfortunate catch being that other disciplines also generally fail to make such inquiries (Douglas, 1979).

Moreover, with rare exceptions such as those found in the "new home economics" (Becker, 1976), microeconomics says little about the investment of time, energy, and other scarce resources that occurs in a household's usage and disposition of various product classes as diverse as television sets and sports equipment (Bellante & Foster, 1984; Nickols & Fox, 1983) or that appears in other social exchange processes (Brinberg & Wood, 1983; Sherry, 1983). With the conspicuous exception of the Nobel laureate Gary Becker (1976), most microeconomists have forgotten the truism "Time is money."

Furthermore, with another partial exception regarding those who have focused on an analysis of the role played by the underlying characteristics of goods (Lancaster, 1971, 1974; Ratchford, 1975, 1979), microeconomics neglects choices at the level of the brand, rather than the product. Most microeconomists do not seem to care whether the consumer drinks Pepsi or Diet Coke, let alone Diet Coke with or without caffeine. This problem of brand choice, however, has received illumination from the work of psychologists.

Psychology

As further shown in Table 4.1, psychology has contributed models well suited to handling the phenomenon of choice among brands. Of particular value in this respect have been the multiattribute attitude models (Ajzen &

Fishbein, 1980; Fishbein & Ajzen, 1975) and multidimensional joint spaces (Carroll, 1972; Kruskal & Wish, 1978) used by consumer researchers to account for the formation of preferences among brands via (compositional) linear compensatory models (Ryan & Bonfield, 1975; Wilkie & Pessemier, 1973), via (decompositional) conjoint analysis and ideal point formulations (Green & Carmone, 1970; Green & Srinivasan, 1978; Pessemier, 1977), or via some (integrative) combination of the two (Holbrook, 1981; Huber, 1975; Neslin, 1981; Tybout & Hauser, 1981). I presented examples of such models in Chapter 3 as illustrations of the micro and macro neopositivistic approaches to research on communication. Detailed accounts appear in virtually every textbook on marketing research and consumer behavior.

As described in Chapter 3, I have devoted a major part of my career to developing and testing such models, initially in connection with ordinary consumer products and later in the area of consumer aesthetics. However, most such formulations could, in essence, be boiled down to the almost alarmingly simple but fundamental proposition that the more your brand possesses the levels of various features desired by some consumer, the more this consumer will perceive your brand to possess the right amounts of those attributes and therefore will tend to like your brand. If people want singers who wear their underwear on the outside of their clothing and if Madonna wears her wardrobe inside out, people will like Madonna. It's that simple. And if the reader finds this logic amazingly obvious, I shall not disagree. But sometimes, what seems obvious to ordinary people can entertain social scientists for years. Or decades.

For all of its merits, the work derived from psychological models—including other, more ambitious information-processing or decision-making frameworks not discussed here (Bettman, 1979; Wright, 1975)—illuminates *acquisition* via *brand choice* far more than usage or disposition behavior. Showing that people choose Miller Lite because they think it tastes great and is less filling does not tell much about how these party animals behave when they are chugging down the stuff or whether they recycle their aluminum cans. Of course, the relevant choice models could be applied to partying (usage) or recycling (disposition). For example, to paraphrase Cyndi Lauper, if "girls" do indeed "just want to have fun" and if these girls perceive partying as the quickest route to having fun, then these girls surely will party all night long, perhaps with green hair or shaved heads. Moreover, deeper insights into various facets of this partying activity could doubtless result from the adoption of a more microscopic level of analysis. But such applications have not constituted the conventional concerns of the decision theorists in consumer research.

Furthermore—with rare exceptions such as that represented by the normative component that incorporates the effects of social influence into the multiattribute attitude model (Fishbein & Ajzen, 1975; Miniard & Cohen, 1983)—the typical psychological treatment does relatively little to place brand preferences into the social context that includes ongoing interpersonal activities and shared symbolic meanings. For example, sometimes one drinks Bordeaux Cabernet Sauvignon—when what one really prefers is Gallo Hearty Burgundy—largely because one wants to impress one's date. Sometimes, one assumes, girls in general and Cyndi Lauper disciples in particular decide to get head-to-toe tattoos or to wear rings in their noses largely because of the effect they believe such fashion statements will have on their friends. These more social concerns have been addressed by contributors from sociology and anthropology whose studies have focused on various aspects of product usage and disposition.

Sociology

The sociological perspective in consumer research has considered the interpersonal context in which consumption activities are embedded (e.g., Reingen, Foster, Brown, & Seidman, 1984; Solomon, 1983). This framework has proven especially fruitful in addressing problems raised by product usage in the third column of Table 4.1. Sociologists, it seems, see people as operating within the context of the shared consumption experiences that shape their lives.

Thus, sociological concepts of *conspicuous consumption* (Veblen, 1899/ 1967) and *role performance* (Goffman, 1959) view everyday consumer products as overt marks of social status and as dramaturgical aids—props, costumes, stage sets, or scenery—whereby people define and display the self-concepts they wish to communicate to themselves and to others (Belk, Bahn, & Mayer, 1982; Bloch, 1982; Holman, 1981; Kehret-Ward & Yalch, 1984; Murray, 1980; Sirgy, 1982; Solomon, 1983). In the dramaturgical view, quite literally, "all the world's a stage" and all the people "merely players." From this perspective, as social actors, consumers use products to support the roles they perform in their interpersonal relations and to reflect their own personal identities. For example, at Harvard College for many decades, the true initiates—aspirants to membership in the intellectual community—carried green book bags. Not brief cases (which might have protected valuables from damage due to bumping or dropping). Not canvas carriers (which might have been fitted with convenient straps to permit easy carrying). But always green book bags—usually slung over the shoulder in a manner that (with enough books inside the bag) could dig a painful groove in the flesh adjacent to the collar bone. During the early 1960s, the Harvard undergraduates who lived in Dunster House used to amuse themselves by predicting which pedestrians emerging from the married students' dorm would turn left to cross the bridge over the Charles River toward the Business School, as opposed to right toward the Yard, where the classes in liberal arts took place. The ones carrying green book bags always turned right toward Enlightenment. The ones with leather attaché cases invariably veered left, like lemmings, toward the Charles.

Others taking a sociological perspective have explored patterns of primarily social activities that cluster together as uses for leisure time (Hawes, Talarzyk, & Blackwell, 1975; Unger & Kernan, 1983). For example, Holbrook and Lehmann (1981) reanalyzed some data collected by Market Facts to show that those who often go camping also frequently go boating, swimming, hunting, hiking, jogging, and walking; similarly, those who habitually play cards also like to entertain friends, drink, and watch sports on television. Potentially, the latter become couch potatoes—so named because, like spuds, they are "tubers"—that is, devoted to the "boob tube."

Thus, two key contributions from sociology that help explain product usage stem from research on role playing or dramaturgy and on patterns of leisure activities. These usage-related themes, however, do suggest the need for a complementary focus on product disposition (what happens to products after they are used), which, in turn, raises further questions about the meanings of products (the symbolic significance that causes some to be stored carefully in the attic and others to be thrown carelessly into the garbage). Such issues have increasingly concerned those who study consumption from the perspective of anthropology.

Anthropology

Anthropological studies have made valuable contributions to the understanding of product disposition (under the last column of Table 4.1). For example, several researchers have studied *gift giving,* a process wherein one person's disposition simultaneously becomes another's acquisition (Sherry, 1983). Sometimes, whole chains of gifting develop, as in the case of the legendary 50-year-old fruitcakes that have circulated at Christmastime among families from one generation to the next.

At a more mundane level of product disposal, *garbological research* examines people's discardings to draw conclusions about differences in their product acquisition and usage behavior (Wallendorf & Reilly, 1983). Several years ago, for example, I read that someone in Greenwich Village had made a career of studying the contents of Bob Dylan's trash can. In work with primates, this focus on disposition extends to the detailed analysis of their feces (Goodall, 1971). Although this use of excrement has not yet become a popular technique in research on human consumers, one should not rule out the potential for such investigations in the future, perhaps by those committed to "naturalistic methods" in pursuit of "a fresh way of acquiring knowledge about consumers and fresh perspectives about the domain and nature of consumer behavior" (Belk, 1991, p. 1). Meanwhile, this possibility does highlight the close parallels increasingly recognized (as in this book) between consumption by animals and people (Oliver, 1984) and by consumers in primal and civilized societies (Hirschman, 1985a).

Further contributions from anthropology to the understanding of product usage concern the study of those artifacts that consumers do not discard but that instead become part of consumption *rituals,* such as bathing or grooming (Rook, 1985); family *ceremonies,* such as those held at Thanksgiving, Christmas, Passover, or Easter (Wallendorf & Arnould, 1991); ancestral *traditions,* such as those involving legends or mythology (Hirschman, 1987; Levy, 1981); or *collections* of such objects as baseball cards, stamps, coins, or musical recordings (Belk, Wallendorf, Sherry, & Holbrook, 1991; Belk, Wallendorf, Sherry, Holbrook, & Roberts, 1988). Indeed, most products carry *symbolic meanings* that define, communicate, and solidify the owner's or user's place in the social system (Douglas, 1979; Levy, 1959). Such social meanings can be addressed from the viewpoint of consumption symbolism or *semiotics* (Holbrook & Hirschman, 1993). For example, articles of clothing and grooming habits serve as signs in a language that permits the encoding or decoding of status- or personality-related information (Barthes, 1983; Holman, 1980; Lurie, 1981). Ponder, for example, the calculations that one undertakes in choosing a suit of clothes to wear on one's next job interview (Solomon & Anand, 1985). When making such symbolic gestures, every detail matters—from the color of one's shirt or blouse to the scent of one's perfume or aftershave. As the saying goes, "Clothes make the (wo)man"—or with more Machiavellian intent, "Dress for success."

Furthermore, this focus on clothing and fashion has encouraged an awakened recognition of the *shopping experience* as itself an important hedonic aspect of the consumer's acquisition behavior (Donovan & Rossiter, 1982; Fraser, 1985). In this light, it makes sense to regard the giant Mall of America in Bloomington, Minnesota, as an overgrown amusement park (complete with the world's largest indoor roller coaster and other amazing recreational adventures) or Bloomingdale's department store (New York City) as a form of theater (perhaps, one sometimes senses, a theater of the absurd).

However, despite their obvious importance in the daily lives of consumers, the aforementioned questions of ritual, ancestral, mythological, symbolic, or semiotic meaning imply a context of social conformity and therefore tend to neglect the deviance from norms or departures from ethical codes that generally are viewed as problems of morality. Interest in such ethical questions encourages one to look for potential contributions from the domain of philosophy.

Philosophy

As yet, the general philosophical tradition has contributed relatively little to the study of consumer behavior. One possible approach might look to the philosophy of action, or *praxeology* (Anscombe, 1957; Goldman, 1970; Von Wright, 1983) and might apply the concept of rational explanations for buying behavior (O'Shaughnessy, 1987) to construct a consumer theory of *reasoned action* (Ajzen & Fishbein, 1980; Oliver & Bearden, 1985; Shimp & Kavas, 1984). Thus, drawing on praxeology, O'Shaughnessy (1987) attempts to explain why people buy. Such a rational or reasons-based approach, however, stops short of fully exploring the aforementioned problems of deviance and departures from moral codes (Cooper-Martin & Holbrook, 1993; Holbrook, 1986b, 1987d, 1994b).

To address the latter phenomena, one might profitably borrow from ethics to conceptualize morality in consumption and thereby to address the phenomenon of consumer *mis*behavior. Indeed, the untapped potential for research on consumer misbehavior boggles the mind. Without plunging into the distinctions and niceties involved in defining misbehavior, it appears clear that many widespread consumer activities constitute violations of societal norms or breaches of ethical codes that consumer researchers perhaps would prefer to ignore. Among these, I would include *immorality* (e.g., committing adultery, polluting the environment, overindulging); *illegality* (e.g., robbing a bank, cheating on income taxes, speeding on the highway, parking in front of a hydrant); *irrationality* (e.g., gambling compulsively, shopping until you drop, superstitious dressing, making an impulse purchase); and *irregularity* (e.g., transsexuality, psychotic hallucinations, a neurotic preoccupation with cleanliness, dressing unfashionably).

Although some limited study has been devoted to such topics as compulsive shopping (O'Guinn & Faber, 1989), impulse purchases (Rook, 1987), addictions (Hirschman, 1991), and freaks (Fitzsimons, Block, & Holbrook, 1993), most aspects of consumer misbehavior have received relatively little attention from consumer researchers. Clearly, some examples—such as armed robbery or arson—may deeply offend many people's sensibilities. One might prefer not to think of grand larceny or insider trading as forms of consumption. Nevertheless, as widespread (if regrettable) occurrences, such consumption phenomena deserve full exploration within the purview of consumer research, a point to which I return in Chapter 5.

More generally, as discussed in Chapter 7, the broadened perspectives borrowed from the philosophy of science now infusing consumer research have opened the way to a wider range of less conventional and less neopositivistic approaches (Olson, 1982). Such *postpositivistic* or "postmodern" outlooks (Sherry, 1991) have emphasized a focus on theory development within the context of discovery along the lines emphasized in Chapter 2 (Deshpande, 1983); a view of theory justification as relativistic and constructionistic in sympathy with arguments to be made in Chapter 7 (Peter & Olson, 1983); a consequent interest in the history and sociology of science consistent with the plan for this book announced in Chapter 1 (Anderson, 1983, 1986); and, most of all, a pluralistic approach to the philosophy of science in consumer research (Hirschman & Holbrook, 1992). These departures from the traditional hypothetico-deductive method have also included movements toward encompassing the humanities.

Humanities

As a former English major in college, I was shocked and disappointed to discover, around 1965, how little the humanities had penetrated the study of consumption. With their eagerness to achieve scientific status, consumer researchers seemed to have eschewed all forms of knowledge that might smack of humanistic inclinations. In this flight from human studies, any sort of scientistic empiricism—no matter how trivial its intent or how flawed its execution—earned higher honors in the discipline than even the most profound interpretive insights into the study of consumption. However, the situation has at last begun to change.

The humanities have started to sneak into consumer research in a variety of ways that may help deepen the understanding of value in acquisition, usage, and disposition (Hirschman, 1985b, 1986a; Holbrook et al., 1989). To illustrate briefly by drawing on just one author's work—namely, my own—I would cite the following examples from the last row of Table 4.1:

1. The broadening of acquisition to include the consumption of free goods that primarily involve the investment of time expenditures—such as *entertainment and the arts* (Holbrook & Zirlin, 1985) or other *leisure activities* (Holbrook & Lehmann, 1981)

2. The extension of usage to encompass wider spheres of *appreciative* reactions with strong *emotional content* or other types of *intrinsic value* (Holbrook, O'Shaughnessy, & Bell, 1990)

3. The deepening of disposition to address neglected issues concerning the nature of *durability* in consumption (Holbrook, 1986d), as in the phenomena associated with *collecting* (Belk et al., 1988; Belk et al., 1991) or with various aspects of *nostalgia* (Holbrook, 1993c, 1993d, 1994d; Holbrook & Schindler, 1989, 1991, 1994a, 1994b; Schindler & Holbrook, 1993)

Furthermore, several authors have suggested that art objects, when interpreted for their substantive content, may themselves provide direct insights into consumption phenomena. In this vein, for example, Douglas (1979) uses the novels of Henry James to explore consumer symbolism; Schudson (1984) draws on Dreiser's *Sister Carrie* to illustrate the role of materialism in consumer behavior; Holbrook (1991c) traces the role of symbolic consumption in narratives as diverse as Homer's *Odyssey* and Joyce's *Ulysses*. As any student of literature knows, there are countless ways to read a poem or novel. One way to interpret such a work focuses on its symbolic consumer behavior—that is, the meanings carried by the consumption experiences portrayed. Thus, when James Joyce (1922/1986) describes Leopold Bloom fixing breakfast for his wife, Molly, the author embeds a host of references to his protagonist's disappointed love life and stalled career in the advertising business into the context of the everyday consumer activities at hand. Here and throughout the book, Bloom's constant references to sausages in general and to "Plumtree's potted meat" in particular create a cumulative impression that pervades the narrative:

> Plumtree's Potted Meat serves as a metaphor for a phallus (sausage, the meat), a vagina (a vessel, the pot), and sexual fruition (the tree, the plum). . . . Metaphorically, Bloom's pot (Molly's vagina) lacks meat (Bloom's penis) so that his home remains incomplete (empty of sexual intercourse). This painful imagery haunts Bloom all day. (Holbrook & Hirschman, 1993, p. 215)

In short, one responds to Bloom, in part, on the basis of what and how he consumes.

Turning to popular culture, Hirschman (1987) explicates the mythical meanings of films that have achieved the greatest box office success, such as *E.T.* and *Star Wars;* Holbrook and Grayson (1986) discuss the importance of symbolic consumption for the development of plot and character in the movie *Out of Africa;* O'Guinn, Lee, and Faber (1986) analyze the role of motion pictures and television in consumer acculturation; and Stern (1989) explores literary approaches to the analysis of meaning in advertisements. Ultimately, Hirschman and Holbrook (1992) suggest that all consumer behavior might be regarded as a text in search of interpretation.

Meanwhile, pursuing more neopositivistic routes, others have used quantitative *content analyses* to address themes relevant to consumption found in comic strips (Kassarjian, 1983; Spiggle, 1985), novels (Friedman, 1985), and advertising (Belk & Pollay, 1985; Pollay, 1985). For example, Friedman (1991) has provided instructive data on the frequencies with which various brand names appear in novels, plays, hit songs, and so on.

More generally, the humanities may play a role in consumer research by supplying stories, analogies, imagery, and other metaphors that help inform or clarify one's sense of who one is and one's vision of where one is going. This humanistic impulse appears in the metaphorical character of the introspective chapters contained in this book. The method of subjective personal introspection pursued here draws on the humanities as its fundamental source of inspiration.

❏ *Toward Consumer Research*

Eclecticism

My cursory account of the primary contributions from various disciplines to the study of consumer behavior has necessarily been quite selective. Nevertheless, it should be evident that various widely differing scientific and scholarly specialties have contributed to the development of consumer research, each filling in gaps left by the others. During its history, consumer research has adopted an eclectic multidisciplinary stance. Indeed, the great landmark contributions to theory in the study of consumer behavior—such as those by Howard (1963a, 1963b), Nicosia (1966), Engel et al. (1968), Howard and Sheth (1969), and their various colleagues—have been emphatically ecumenical in spirit and integrative in nature, drawing on a number of areas of inquiry. One applauds this eclecticism (Lutz, 1989) even while wondering whether the field might not move ahead faster were consumer researchers to seek their own independent status as a unique discipline (Belk, 1986). In this light, I find it instructive to contrast consumer research with marketing research.

The Debate

Much debate has focused on the similarities and differences between consumer research and marketing research. My position holds that *consumer research* involves the study of consumption as the central focus pursued *for its own sake*, whereas *marketing research*, among other things, involves the study of customers in a manner intended to be *managerially relevant* (Holbrook, 1985a, 1985b, 1986f, 1989a). This distinction and the accompanying debate entertains us further in Chapters 6 and 9.

However valid my own opinion, these issues highlight two important facts of life for consumer researchers. First, the debate itself suggests that, overall, one can point to little agreement on what is meant by consumer research. In a sense, consumer researchers share no consensus about what they denote by the term that defines their field of inquiry. Second, my own conclusion—reinforced by other participants in the debate, such as Anderson (1983), Hirschman (1986b), and Wallendorf (1985)—suggests the need to ground consumer research in a central preoccupation with consumption, independent of any relevance that subject might carry for marketing managers or, indeed, for any other external interests. These two considerations combine to argue for a redefinition of the field.

Consummation

As indicated previously, the early 1980s saw consumer research extending beyond its initially restricted focus on buying and embracing a larger sphere of issues associated with *consuming* in general (acquiring, using, disposing) and with *consumption experiences* in particular. This evolution in thinking demands a recognition of these expanded horizons in the way consumer researchers define their area of study.

I therefore have urged my fellow consumer researchers to regard the discipline as one that takes consumption as its central focus and that consequently examines all facets of the value potentially provided by the experiences that occur when some living organism acquires, uses, or disposes of any product that might achieve a goal, fulfill a need, or satisfy a want. In short, consumer research encompasses virtually all human activities regarded from the viewpoint of consummation.

I regard this inclusiveness as a strength, rather than a liability. From my perspective, almost everything one does involves consumption:

> People get up in the morning, start consuming the moment their toes touch the carpet, allocate their time to various consumption activities throughout the day, and continue consuming until they finally drift off to sleep at night, after which they confine their consumption mostly to dreams, pajamas, and bed linens. (Holbrook, 1985b, p. 146)

In other words, people's lives comprise one constant and continual (though not always successful) quest for consummation.

What does or should distinguish consumer research from those other fields previously mentioned is its conscious focus on consummatory behavior. *Consummatory behavior* involves activities aimed at achieving goals, fulfilling needs, or satisfying wants: running a mile in less than 10 minutes, eating a hamburger, listening to Ella Fitzgerald. In short, these activities entail processes wherein consumers seek, reach, and surpass consummation. And, speaking of consummation, one should not forget that making love is also a quintessential form of consumer behavior in the sense that it involves time-using activities aimed at achieving pleasure. Or joy.

One might therefore expect that consumer researchers would readily accept consummation as their central focus and therefore that, in this respect, someone who preached that message would find him- or herself in good company, surrounded by supportive spirits. But in that expectation, one would be disappointed.

A Lonely Peace

Recall the three lines from Wordsworth's "The Recluse" that serve as an epigraph for this chapter. At this point, some earlier lines will prove quite instructive:

> Paradise, and groves
> Elysian, Fortunate Fields—like those of old
> Sought in the Atlantic Main—why should they be
> A history only of departed things,
> Or a mere fiction of what never was?
> For the discerning intellect of Man,
> When wedded to this goodly universe
> In love and holy passion, shall find these
> A simple produce of the common day.
> —I, long before the blissful hour arrives,
> Would chant, in lonely peace, the spousal verse
> Of this great consummation.
> —Wordsworth, 1814/1948, p. 277

As suggested in these lines, the focus on consummation has died away, leaving those of us who would sing its praises feeling somewhat "lonely"—in at least two senses.

First, figuratively, the world has fallen from the State of Bliss in which Adam and Eve's sole task was to enjoy pleasant forms of consumption. In *Paradise Lost*, John Milton (1674/1957) told this story with a power never matched:

> So hand in hand they pass'd, the loveliest pair
> That ever since in love's imbraces met,
> *Adam* the goodliest man of men since born
> His Sons, the fairest of her Daughters *Eve*.
> Under a tuft of shade that on a green

Stood whispering soft, by a fresh Fountain side
They sat them down and after no more toil
Of thir sweet Gard'ning labor than suffic'd
To recommend cool *Zephyr*, and made ease
More easy, wholesome thirst and appetite
More grateful, to thir Supper Fruits they fell,
Nectarine Fruits which the compliant boughs
Yielded them, side-long as they sat recline
On the soft downy Bank damaskt with flow'rs:
The savory pulp they chew, and in the rind
Still as they thirsted scoop the brimming stream;
Nor gentle purpose, nor endearing smiles
Wanted, nor youthful dalliance as beseems
Fair couple, linkt in happy nuptial League
Alone as they. (Book IV, lines 321-340)

In contrast to this sweet life in Paradise, modern consumers face pains and difficulties imposed by prices and budget constraints, by scarcities of time and materials, by questions of propriety and morality, by possible safety hazards and physical dangers, by deceptive advertising and media clutter, and by an existential angst in choosing among products, none of which are perfect.

Second, in an academic world dominated by marketing researchers preoccupied with buying, as opposed to consuming, consumer researchers face a lonely battle if they elect to sing about the tarnished vestiges of the perfect consumption that characterized lost innocence. Those departed and maybe fictitious pleasures involved pure and blissful consummation. What remains in the human condition is an imperfect and tainted world in which consumers can only strive to surmount their constant barriers to fulfillment. To focus on this neglected quest—to deal single-mindedly with the nature of value in acquiring, using, and disposing—takes courage worthy of Wordsworth's (1918/1948, p. 278) brave Romantic cry:

I sing:—"fit audience let me find though few!"
So prayed, more gaining than he asked, the bard —
In holiest mood. . . .
—I, long before the blissful hour arrives,
Would chant, in lonely peace, the spousal verse
Of this great consummation.

Notice that the word *spousal* operates here in two senses. Literally, it means "nuptial" and suggests the nearly sexual energy with which the poet is married to his consummatory vision of paradisal fulfillment. Furthermore, it suggests the cognate "espouse," whose associations convey the sense of "supporting a cause." The proposed redefinition of consumer research as the study of consummation is such a cause. As implied by Wordsworth's reference to a "lonely" peace, this cause might require running against the grain of conventional thinking in relative isolation—at least for a while.

The Common Day

Wordsworth's message is one of hope based on "the heroic dimensions of common life, and the grandeur of the ordinary" (Abrams, 1963, p. 69). In his tour de force *Natural Supernaturalism*, Abrams (1971) takes Wordsworth in general and the aforementioned fragment from "The Recluse" in particular as his touchstone for romanticism. Indeed, his entire book emerges from an unfolding of the meaning to be found in Wordsworth's poem viewed as "the manifesto of a central Romantic enterprise" (p. 14).

Abrams (1971) interprets Wordsworth's fragment along lines close to those I have already suggested:

> The vision is that of the awesome depths and height of the human mind, and of the power of that mind as in itself adequate, by consummating a holy marriage with the external universe, to create out of the world of all of us, in a quotidian and recurrent miracle, a new world which is the equivalent of paradise. (p. 28)

According to Abrams, this vision represents the essence of the romantic consciousness as "a secularized form of devotional experience" (p. 65) founded on a "general tendency . . . to humanize the divine" (p. 68)—hence, his title *Natural Supernaturalism*. Here, the key metaphor involves a spiritual journey or quest in search of an apocalypse within as "a personal and inner experience, not a generic and outer event" (p. 50): "The restored paradise of the Apocalypse will not be a location outside this world to which we will be transferred after death; it will be this world itself, as experienced by our redeemed and glorified senses in our earthly existence" (p. 53). Thus, in romanticism, a theme of spiritual search at least as old as the *Confessions* of St. Augustine (c. 400/1961, p. 83) is transformed into a secular context based on an interpretation of the "book of nature" (rather than the Bible) as its supreme text (p. 104) and rooted humanistically in "the Mind of Man" (p. 94). Here, the focus is on overcoming "sorrow," "suffering," and "the agonies of the human condition" (p. 443) through "the deliverance of mind and imagination . . . so that they may transform the dull and lifeless world into a new world instinct with the life and joy it reciprocates with the per-ceiving mind" (p. 431): "And the norm of life is joy—by which is meant not that joy is the standard state of man, but that joy is what man is born for" (p. 431).

Ordinary Consumption

A century after Wordsworth, a comparable celebration appeared in the poem "Sunday Morning," by Wallace Stevens (1961). This piece evokes the sublunary joys and everyday pleasures experienced in

> Complacencies of the peignoir, and late
> Coffee and oranges in a sunny chair,
> And the green freedom of a cockatoo . . .
> The pungent oranges and bright, green wings.

Set on a day of the week that might otherwise stir associations concerning the meaning of religion and the role of the Deity, this poem turns instead to an evocation of ordinary consumption. It asks a question, central to Abrams's view of romanticism—"Where, then, is paradise?"—and answers it in terms closely tied to those of Wordsworth's "great consummation":

> There is not any haunt of prophecy . . .
> . . . that has endured
> As April's green endures; or will endure
> Like her remembrance of awakened birds,
> Or her desire for June and evening, tipped
> By the consummation of the swallow's wings.

As Abrams suggests, "Stevens represents the musing in solitude of a modern woman as she savors the luxuries of her Sunday breakfast in a brilliant . . . setting of sun, rug, coffee and oranges, and a green cockatoo" and thereby repeats the Wordsworthian, romantic theme of consummation in "a union with the common earth" (Abrams, 1971, p. 70):

Deer walk upon our mountains, and the quail
Whistle about us their spontaneous cries;
Sweet berries ripen in the wilderness;
And, in the isolation of the sky,
At evening, casual flocks of pigeons make
Ambiguous undulations as they sink,
Downward to darkness, on extended wings.[1]

The Spousal Verse

Only a tiny fragment remains as Wordsworth's "The Recluse"—what Frye (1963) calls "one great flash of vision" (p. 18). This is the passage in which Wordsworth so passionately celebrates the ordinary consumption experiences found in everyday life and drawn from what he calls the "simple produce of the common day."

Let us take this indeed reclusive but hopeful snatch of poetry as a bright omen. Let us interpret its sole, stubborn survival as a sign that speaks through the centuries and that signals a need to ground consumer research in its true foundation, the study of consumption and of the processes wherein the acquisition, usage, and disposition of all kinds of products potentially provide value by achieving human goals, fulfilling human needs, and satisfying human wants. In short, let us join with Wordsworth to chant, in lonely peace, the spousal verse of this great consummation.

❑ Note

1. From *Collected Poems* by Wallace Stevens. Copyright © 1923 and renewed 1951 by Wallace Stevens. Reprinted by permission of Alfred A. Knopf, Inc. and Faber and Faber Ltd.

O, CONSUMER, HOW YOU'VE CHANGED

Some Radical Reflections on Gorillas, Pets, and the Roots of Consumption

Novelists, dramatists and biographers had always been satisfied to exhibit people's motives, thoughts, perturbations and habits by describing their doings, sayings, and imaginings, their grimaces, gestures and tones of voice. In concentrating on what Jane Austen concentrated on, psychologists began to find that these were, after all, the stuff and not the mere trappings of their subjects. . . . Man need not be degraded to a machine. . . . He might, after all, be a sort of animal, namely, a higher mammal.

—Gilbert Ryle (1949),
The Concept of Mind, p. 328

Let us not be scared by the bogey of anthropomorphism into the arms of the spectre of Cartesian mechanism. It is not anthropomorphism to believe that man and the higher animals have much in common so far as instinct and emotion are concerned, but an acknowledgment of truth scientifically demonstrated.

—Edward A. Armstrong (1963),
A Study of Bird Song, p. 195

❏ Introduction: From Experience to Emotions

In the previous chapter, the reader saw the conception of consumer research shift some distance from the study of buying to the study of consuming. Specifically, during the early 1980s, the conventional concern for

107

decisions to buy, prevalent during the 1960s and 1970s, gradually gave way to an expanded interest in the consumption experience. In short, as the narrow decision-oriented view yielded in some circles to a broadened experiential perspective, many consumer researchers began to dwell on various aspects of consumer fantasies, feelings, and fun.

Even people like Jim Bettman—a master of the decision-oriented approach to modeling buyer choices—showed some recognition of this shift in the research agenda. Thus, in a panel discussion at one conference, Jim acknowledged the new focus on what he called "the soft underbelly of consumer research." The operative word here is *soft*, as in "soft" versus "hard" sciences. Around the same time, at a cocktail party during the Summer Educators' Conference of the American Marketing Association in 1982, Jim passed me a bowl of mixed nuts with the comment, "Here, Morris, have some fantasies, feelings, and fun." Jim's joke registered a growing acceptance of the fact that the world of consumer research, however "nutty," had fundamentally changed.

This emergence of an experiential perspective raised a whole new set of concerns. Of particular significance, the study of emotional responses associated with the consumption experience—the *feelings* in "fantasies, feelings, and fun"—now loomed as an important but neglected topic. In this chapter, I explore this and related aspects of the experiential perspective (as usual, with the help of animal metaphors) by addressing the theme "O, Consumer, How You've Changed" and by drawing on stories about animals, pets, and people to arrive at "Some Radical Reflections on the Roots of Consumption." With some suggestive anecdotes, I develop 10 propositions on the nature and role of the consumption experience and on the importance of certain experiential aspects of consumer behavior—especially the role of emotions— that deserve increased attention. These propositions are "radical" in the sense that they go back to the "roots" of consumer behavior—that is, to the value provided by the services obtained via consumption experiences. The metaphorical content of my stories offers one window on this neglected reality.

❑ Consuming Animals

Koko and All Ball

Once upon a time, actually in 1985 at the Gorilla Foundation in California, there lived a 13-year-old, 230-pound ape named Koko, surely one of the world's most educated, loved, and celebrated pongids. As described in the book by Patterson and Linden (1981), Koko spoke to her trainers in American Sign Language (ASL), using her hands to encode a vocabulary of more than 500 words. Having become quite sophisticated in her capacity to communicate in this manner, this talented primate one day greeted her keepers with the announcement that she wanted them to bring her something to play with—namely, a cat (Patterson, 1985).

Koko's trainers responded by giving their intelligent anthropoid a small kitten without a tail. Koko named this kitten All Ball and spoke about it in such phrases as "Koko Love Visit Ball." As seen in Figure 5.1, the gorilla and the kitten played together long and happily, with Koko displaying highly developed qualities of tenderness and affection (Vessels, 1985).

This playful friendship ended prematurely, however, when All Ball wandered away and was killed by a car. When Koko's keepers broke the news that All Ball had died, Koko showed obvious and painful symptoms of extreme grief, mourning her loss in an anguished expression of the most profound sadness (Hackett, 1985). As described by Penny Patterson (1985): "I went to Koko at once. I told her that Ball had been hit by a car; she would not see him again. . . . Ten minutes later, I heard Koko cry. It was her distress call—a loud, long series of high-pitched hoots" (p. 24). Fortunately for Patterson's ego, Koko just cried mournfully, rather than use her finely tuned skills in American Sign Language to express the obvious conclusion: "Penny Stupid Put Ball Street Dead."

Despite this touching incident, good reasons exist for remaining skeptical on the question of whether animals in general and apes in particular can learn a human language (Sebeok, 1981; Sebeok & Umiker-Sebeok, 1981; Terrace, 1985). However, no one questions that animals can communicate with people via the interspecies use of signs (Sebeok, 1981). Furthermore, what they communicate in this fashion is a wide range of wants and emotions, many of which people can also recognize in themselves.

In other words, animals experience wants and feelings closely related to those found in human consumers. Not coincidentally, Koko's typical day is a veritable festival of consumption activities (Patterson & Linden, 1981): breakfast, housecleaning, schoolwork, play, snack, more lessons, lunch, more play and instruction and snacks, dinner, dessert, entertainment, toothbrushing, bedtime. About the only difference between Koko and a human child in these respects is that Koko does not say her prayers (yet). Thus, Koko's activities closely parallel the experiences involved in human consumption. In that sense, Koko becomes a metaphor—a metaphor for consumer behavior.

Figure 5.1. Koko and All Ball
SOURCE: From Holbrook (1987d), p. 156. Reprinted with permission.

In sum, I regard Koko as a metaphorical consumer—far more human in her thoughts, emotions, activities, and values than the reductionistic decision-making, brand-choosing automatons that most consumer researchers (myself included) studied during the 1960s and 1970s. Koko's story continues a movement begun when ethologists recognized insight in the behavior of their problem-solving apes (Köhler, 1925) and declared that no atomistic, behavioristic, or other reductive explanation could adequately account for such displays of intelligence and primal creativity (Koestler, 1964).

Koko provides anecdotal evidence—often the most persuasive kind—that animals (at least semiotically sophisticated primates) engage in complex consumption experiences characterized by *fantasies* (imagining and requesting a cat), *feelings* (love for the kitten and grief over its death), and *fun* (the enjoyment of games and other playful activities). Clearly, Koko consumed the services provided by All Ball as a kind of living toy. Just as clearly, All Ball participated in a reciprocal consumption experience centered around those curious and sensuous proclivities for which cats are justly famous. Together, the kitten and the gorilla remind us that animals display complex behaviors not easily explained by the kinds of conventional choice models, decision theories, or other information-processing accounts I described earlier when discussing the traditional boxes-and-arrows approaches.

If we as researchers grant this status to animals, then surely we must acknowledge that humans, too, pursue consumption experiences not well handled by any sort of reductionistic formulation. If animals display such apparent examples of fantasies, feelings, and fun in their consumption activities, we cannot plausibly deny these phenomena in the case of human consumers. Yet, it appears that much conventional consumer research did verge on such denials and thereby tolerated wide gaps in our understanding of the consumption experience.

Consumption and Pets

In the traditional model of the consumer as a cognitively guided decision maker who makes purchases based on choices among available brands, researchers often overlooked fundamental consumption phenomena of intuitively obvious importance. The flavor of this neglect appeared in an experience with a paper that I coauthored with Bill Moore on evaluating household pets—specifically, dogs (Moore & Holbrook, 1982). In the lengthy review process that preceded eventual publication, Bill and I were surprised to learn that some of our colleagues did not regard pet ownership as a viable example of consumer behavior.

This denial flies in the face of well-established findings on the psychological importance of domestic animals as nearly full-fledged members of the family (Hickrod & Schmitt, 1982; Horn & Meer, 1984; Tucker, 1967). As in the case of Koko, a pet's death may create nearly unbearable emotional consequences for its owners:

> Loss of a pet is often agonizing, akin to the loss of a close friend or relative. . . . Many people go through an agonizing separation when they lose a pet. . . . Characteristic symptoms include depression, anger, guilt, apathy, loss of appetite, loneliness, sleeplessness, numbness, periods of intense anxiety and episodes of crying. (Brody, 1985, p. C8)[1]

Grief due to the death of a pet opens the way to expensive pet-loss counseling services (Brody, 1985) and costly burial plots in pet cemeteries (Haitch, 1985)—not to mention a potential for the dastardly consumer frauds sometimes reported in the news media. These and other lucrative business opportunities have not escaped the attention of real-world marketers:

> There are about 98 million dogs and cats in the United States, a number greater than the human population of all but seven nations. Well over half of America's households are home to a furred, finned or feathered friend of some kind. Those pets are the foundation of an $8.5 billion-a-year industry that translates peoples' love for animals into profits. . . . As Leslie B. Charm, president and chief executive officer of Docktor Pet Centers, puts it, "The company philosophy recognizes that its business is predicated on 'selling love,' but that does not obfuscate the profit motive." (Lefferts, 1985, p. F15)[2]

Indeed, in terms of shelf space, pet supplies are the single largest product category in the typical supermarket (Meer, 1984). And Socks—the current presidential cat—has become a national celebrity.

Yet, until some recent work by Beth Hirschman (1994), we as consumer researchers have typically resisted the acknowledgment of such consumption phenomena. Apparently, the nature of consumption experiences that appear so obvious in the case of Koko may elude our grasp in the case of human consumers. Perhaps the traditional decision-making models have prevented us from recognizing such phenomena at our own level on the evolutionary ladder. Whatever the reason for their neglect, such consumption experiences deserve our full attention but cannot be adequately represented by conventional cognitive, rational, decision-oriented buyer-behavior models (including, no doubt, those studied by Moore and Holbrook, 1982).

A Think Piece

A vivid illustration, still couched within the framework of pet consumption, appeared in a play by Jules Feiffer entitled *A Think Piece*, whose characters and plot might almost have been designed to demonstrate the point argued here. In this play, Betty Castle (the female protagonist) appears as a feelingful person, governed by her rather volatile emotions, with a "passion" for shopping but an inability to make decisions about the trivia that crowd her daily life. By contrast, her husband, Gordon (a teacher, what else?), maintains a cool rationality governed by logic and intellect, thereby embodying the conventional view of the consumer as an almost computerlike decision maker. When, in an emotional frenzy bordering on hysteria, Betty assassinates the beloved family dog (Zero) by dropping it from the window of the Castles' high-rise apartment, all Gordon can do is sadly to repeat his stereotypical diagnosis: "Dumb, dumb, . . . dumb."

Besides illustrating that humans (Feiffer's female protagonist, Betty) can sometimes act with less gentleness and affection than gorillas (our own heroine, Koko), *A Think Piece* represents a complex consumption experience (Betty's frantic anger at the hapless family pet) while satirizing the futile attempt of cognitively oriented decision models to explain such phenomena (Gordon's diagnostically inadequate "dumb, dumb, . . . dumb"). Obviously, the wife's treatment of Zero is far worse than "dumb." It is appalling and, on the night I saw the play, elicited a horrified gasp from the audience. But, however unsavory, Betty's cruelty reminds us as researchers how much happens in consumer behavior that eludes our conventional decision-oriented models and methods. For example, powerful emotions of anger or rage might lead to mistreating the family pet. Our job is to try to recapture some of these missing ingredients of consumption. For that, the experiential perspective becomes indispensable.

❏ Toward a Radical View of Consumer Research

Mouselab

Great thinkers of every age have tended to view human behavior as analogous to the machine or mechanical device of which they feel proudest. Impressed by big ships, Homer and Virgil saw life for Odysseus and Aeneas as something like a boat ride. In the Age of Enlightenment, to Descartes or Newton the world appeared to work a bit like a giant clock. For Freud, human psyches resembled the dynamic hydraulic systems of indoor plumbing. Today, those inclined toward a mechanistic view see a person as a walking-and-talking analogy to the computer.

In consumer research, as already noted, my hero, John Howard, got this mechanistic ball rolling by borrowing Herbert Simon's decision-flow models—based on diagrams of computer programs—to construct boxes-and-arrows representations of how buyers make brand choices. This approach reached even more elaborate stages of complexity and refinement in the subsequent work by Jim Bettman, who began by using comparable decision networks to explain consumer choices (Bettman, 1970) and who later based his overview of the consumer on a computerlike logical-flow diagram (Bettman, 1979).

This tendency to view the consumer as an information-processing machine for making decisions has led to the development of the so-called Mouselab located at Duke University (Bettman, Johnson, & Payne, 1991). Here, the term *Mouselab* does not imply that the consumer resembles a poor lost laboratory mouse wandering helplessly in the Maze of Existence while searching pathetically for food or some other form of consummation; rather, it refers to an electronic gadget, a peripheral device linked to a personal computer by which subjects signal the information they wish to acquire and indicate their decisions concerning brand choices on the screens of the PCs to which their computer mice are attached. Metaphorically, Mouselab registers the manner in which subjects play the Electronic Game of Life.

The digital magnetic traces left by these interactions between consumers and machines enable the Mouselab researchers to draw inferences concerning the consumer's short-term memory capacity (similar to a computer's random access memory or RAM); long-term memory capacity (analogous to a computer's hard disk); information-processing algorithms or decision heuristics (comparable to software); and choice mechanisms that guide the formation of purchase intentions (all with direct analogies in the world of computers). Thus, Mouselab uses machines to treat consumers like machines. The scenario that unfolds resembles that of two computers playing chess with each other. In short, as the current variation of the age-old metaphor for People as Machines, Mouselab conveys a view of the Consumer as a Computer.

Mousetrap

Clearly, those who espouse the experiential view have moved away from the conventional conceptualization of the consumer as a logic-chopping engine and would tend to describe Mouselab as something closer to a "mousetrap." From the experiential vantage point, it might seem as if the proponents of Mouselab have fallen into a logical trap (confusing the metaphor of human-as-machine with reality), have entrapped consumers in their mistake (by forcing them to behave like computers), and have snuffed out the life from their objects of study (by converting people into robotlike, decision-making automatons). Mousetrap turns living consumers into electronic zombies programmed to make purchase choices in their lifelessly ratiocinated efforts to be smart shoppers.

Focusing on consumption experiences in general and on consumer emotions in particular, those who support the experiential perspective reject the view of consumers as machines or computers. To them, the consumer looks like a flesh-and-blood creature or an animal—specifically, a living and breathing member of the species *Homo sapiens*. Thus, in ways not appreciated by the proponents of computer models, the Consumer is a Human Being.

The Radical Premise

The proposed experiential view of consumer behavior strikes me as "radical" in the same sense that a radish is a "radical" plant: specifically, it has roots.

In this connection, the first dictionary definition of *radical* is "of or growing *from a root* of a plant." The second is "of or relating to the *origin: fundamental.*" Only at the third definition does one encounter the currently popular but historically more recent meaning, "marked by a considerable departure from the usual . . . *extreme*" (all from *Merriam-Webster's Collegiate Dictionary*, 1993, p. 963, italics added).

Obviously, a concept can be radical in the original senses of that term by (a) stemming from the roots and (b) building on the foundations of a phenomenon without being (c) strange or bizarre. Similarly, my proposal for revisions in our approach to consumer research can be termed radical in the senses that it (a) returns to the roots of consumption and (b) explores the fundamentals of consumer behavior. It is extreme only in the sense that it

(c) does depart from the conventional wisdom (the decision orientation) by getting back to basics (the consumption experience).

As earlier practitioners of consumer research fully recognized, consumer behavior rests on *value*, and all customer value inheres in the consumption *experience* (Holbrook, 1986a, 1987d, 1987h, 1993b, 1994a; Holbrook & Corfman, 1985). For example, in an early book on consumer behavior, Ruby Turner Morris (1941) anticipated the dependence of customer value on the experiences that goods provide:

> The emphasis . . . is upon the *services* of goods, not upon the goods themselves. Wants should be thought of not as desires for goods—but rather for the events which the possession of them makes possible. . . . Goods are wanted because they are capable of performing services—favorable events which occur at a point in time. (pp. 136-137)

Abbott (1955) extended the implications of this view by suggesting that the *services of products* satisfy wants by providing consumption experiences:

> The thesis . . . may be stated quite simply. What people really desire are *not products* but *satisfying experiences*. Experiences are attained through activities. In order that activities may be carried out, physical objects or the services of human beings are usually needed. Here lies the connecting link between man's inner world and the outer world of economic activity. People want products because they want the *experience-bringing services* which they hope the products will render. (p. 40, italics added)

Thus, an emphasis on the consumption experience—far from being anything esoteric or strange—is actually something reassuringly basic, resoundingly fundamental, and (therefore) befittingly radical. In advocating fuller recognition of the experiential viewpoint, we as researchers return to the roots of the discipline and revive a focus that used to seem obvious but that all but disappeared behind the onslaught of the decision-oriented perspective.

The Importance of Consumption

The urgency of this project appears with particular force if one ponders the importance of consumption in one's daily life. In *Thought and Action*, Hampshire (1982) establishes consumption as central to the apprehension of reality. Specifically, he argues that (1) apprehension of reality depends on language and (2) language reflects the nature of consummation or consumption. In his words,

> (1) A language is always a means of singling out . . . certain elements of experience and reality as subjects which can be referred to again and again. . . . Reality and experience cannot be thought about unless we have rules that correlate particular groups of signs with particular recurrent elements in reality and experience. (p. 11)

> (2) In any natural language the objects of reference primitively chosen will be persisting things, differentiated into kinds, at least in part, by their usefulness in serving different but constant, human needs; . . . that is, anything that can be used to serve exactly the same human need will count as the same kind of thing. (p. 21)

In other words, our needs as consumers and their gratification in consumption shape the language that, in the manner suggested by the linguist Benjamin Lee Whorf (1956), mediates our experience of reality. Simply put, the nature of consummation dictates what objects will have the same names; for example, those objects called "food" are things that stop us from being hungry. And those names direct our attention and thereby help construct the reality that we experience; for example, we come to know that merchants sell food at supermarkets, but not at hardware stores.

Perhaps the importance of this Whorfian phenomenon explains why Koko seems like such a prototypical consumer. At least figuratively, Koko has learned to talk in her prehensile sign vocabulary (ASL) and now speaks the language of consumption (fantasies-feelings-fun) by which one defines one's own reality. Clearly, consumer researchers must construct the tenets of consumer research—that is, the theories used to study consumption phenomena—to reflect that reality as experienced through the language of consumer behavior. Like Koko, consumer researchers must learn to communicate by means of the appropriate signs.

Shortcomings of the Conventional Wisdom

When we as researchers turn to the economic, psychological, sociological, anthropological, and philosophical principles generally taken to account for consumer behavior (as summarized in Chapter 4), we find a rather restricted and even impoverished perspective on the web of life that pervades consumption phenomena.

- ❏ *Economists* view consumers as rational decision makers solving a problem in constrained utility maximization: Purchase the combination of products that maximizes overall utility subject to an income-based budget constraint (e.g., Henderson & Quandt, 1958).
- ❏ *Psychologists* propose multiattribute attitude models in which beliefs about probabilistic means-ends relations or *expectancies* (E_i) are weighted by the evaluation of ends or *values* (V_i) and summed across relevant dimensions or *attributes* to explain the *intentions* (I) that guide purchase *behavior* (B): $\Sigma(E_i \cdot V_i) \rightarrow I \rightarrow B$ (e.g., Fishbein & Ajzen, 1975).
- ❏ *Sociologists* study action systems from a similar viewpoint: People do (read "buy") what they believe will satisfy their wants (e.g., Parsons, 1937).
- ❏ *Philosophers* develop parallel concepts in the theory of action or *praxeology*, which holds that *beliefs* and *wants* provide *reasons* to explain the *intentions* that guide *behavior* according to a kind of practical syllogism: Wanting Y and believing that doing X will achieve Y, taken together, imply doing X (e.g., Anscombe, 1957; Goldman, 1970; Hampshire, 1982).

Thus, from all of these perspectives, *if* (a) I *want* to look beautiful and *if* (b) I *believe* that buying Revlon lipstick will make me look beautiful, *then* (c) I *buy* Revlon lipstick. Or *if* (a) I *want* to impress my boss and *if* (b) I *believe* that wearing my Armani suit will impress my boss, *then* (c) I *wear* my Armani suit. In short, *if* (a) I have a *want* and *if* (b) I hold the *belief* that buying some brand will satisfy that want, *then* (c) I *buy* that brand.

Although seldom juxtaposed in explicit comparisons, these conventional perspectives from the various disciplines share a focus on rational, rule-following, purposive action. They thereby explain much that is important in consumer behavior, especially purchase decisions or brand choices, while leaving much else that is equally important unexplained or even unexamined. In other words, they account, in part, for why I buy Skippy instead of Jiff—perhaps because I prefer Skippy's taste, consistency, or price. But they do not comment on the *emotional significance* of eating peanut butter—charged as this food is with meaningful recollections of childhood, home, and loved ones from years gone by. For some people, peanut butter evokes memories of their youth and precipitates instant waves of nostalgia that guide the consumption experience. How well some people remember coming home after school—hungry, greedy—and making themselves a peanut-butter-and-jelly sandwich to tide them over until dinnertime. And if their mothers fed them Skippy then, they probably want Skippy now. Not to mention Welch's grape jelly or Smucker's strawberry preserves. If the decision-oriented perspective ignores all of this—and it does—then how can one enthusiastically subscribe to that approach?

In fairness, one must admit that conventional decision-oriented models do account well for those aspects of consumer behavior that are (a) *easiest* to explain (e.g., brand choice, as opposed to product usage), (b) most important to *practical* marketing applications (e.g., the firm's market share, as opposed to a society's quality of life), and (c) most *trivial* in terms of human happiness (e.g., buying, as opposed to consuming). But when we contemplate using such logically tight analytic schemes to address consumption phenomena as emotionally complex as loving a cuddly pet, admiring a charismatic political leader, enjoying a family vacation, appreciating the awesome grandeur of Bruckner's Seventh Symphony, or even wolfing down a peanut-butter-and-jelly sandwich, we as researchers must ask which of the models shown in Figure 5.2 better represents the consumption experience.

❑ Some Lessons From Pets

Speaking eloquently, if metaphorically, for the fundamental importance of consumption experiences in the lives of consumers, Koko and Zero have much to teach us as researchers in response to the question just raised. I pause, therefore, to take stock of 10 lessons extracted from the shift toward an experiential view, as illustrated by these two anecdotal stories about the consumption of pets.

Consuming Versus Buying

First, both Koko in California and Betty Castle in Feiffer's play set in New York City engage in consuming, as opposed to buying, behavior (Alderson, 1957). This realization reinforces the call for more work on consumption activities versus purchasing decisions (Holbrook & Hirschman, 1982). Along similar lines, as noted earlier, Jacoby (1975, 1978) and Sheth (1982) have distinguished among acquisition, consumption, and disposition phe-

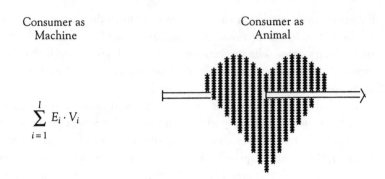

Consumer as
Machine

Consumer as
Animal

$$\sum_{i=1}^{I} E_i \cdot V_i$$

Figure 5.2. Alternative Models of the Consumption Experience
SOURCE: From Holbrook (1987d), p. 163. Adapted with permission.

nomena and have suggested that we as researchers ignore the latter two categories only at our peril. The fact that both Koko's All Ball and Betty's Zero represent particularly unfortunate examples of product disposal only serves to reinforce this point. In ASL, "Betty Bad Drop Zero Dead."

Consumption Experiences Versus Purchase Decisions

Second, both anecdotes indicate that *consumption is an experience, rather than a decision.* They thereby remind us that our economic, psychological, sociological, and philosophical theories of utility-maximizing, reasoned, purposive, and intentional actions may represent only a small subset of the relevant consumption experiences. For example, Koko's feelings of love and grief (mourning the loss of her kitten) or Betty's expression of discontent and rage (killing the family dog) are aspects of consumption that can never be captured adequately by a decision-making framework.

Product Usage Versus Brand Choice

Third, both Koko and Betty engage in product usage, rather than brand choice. In both cases, the primary selective process concerns the allocation of resources (money, time, ability, effort) among products, rather than among brands: walking the family dog versus cooking dinner, or playing with the kitten versus eating a banana. I have argued elsewhere that too little consumer research involves macrolevel analysis across products, as opposed to microlevel analysis across brands (Holbrook, Lehmann, & O'Shaughnessy, 1986). The former across-products perspective appears more central to questions about how people organize the activities that shape their lives as consumers. The essence of the consumption experience depends less on whether one chooses Miller or Budweiser, Marlboros or Camels, and *Penthouse* or *Playboy* than on whether one indulges in guzzling beer, smoking cigarettes, and reading soft-core pornography in the first place. From this perspective, selecting Skippy versus Jiff matters less than eating peanut-butter-and-jelly instead of cheese-and-crackers.

Intangible Services Versus Tangible Goods

Fourth, both stories about pet consumption focus attention on consuming intangible services, as opposed to tangible goods. Kittens and dogs provide value via the services they render as pets. But the same truth applies to all instances of consumption—whether of tangible or intangible products, whether in fact or in imagination. As previously mentioned, *nothing can yield value except through the experience of its services* (Abbott, 1955; Morris, 1941). The only difference (in this respect) between a kitten and a banana lies in the durability of the services available. The banana is called a "nondurable" because its ability to provide hunger-satisfying services does not last very long. By contrast, a kitten may offer its service of companionship for 15 or even 20 years.

Durables Versus Nondurables

Thus, fifth, both anecdotes call attention to products whose ability to perform want-satisfying services lasted more briefly than expected. They thereby remind us of the distinction between durables and nondurables. *Durability* might be defined as the length of time over which a product (a good, a service, an event, or an idea) performs the services that yield its characteristic value. This perspective uncovers two important points that appear to have attracted little attention (Holbrook, 1986d, 1987d).

First, the distinction between nondurable and durable goods (e.g., a graham cracker vs. a lawn mower) is mirrored by analogous but seldom-noted contrasts between nondurable and durable services (e.g., dry cleaning vs. cosmetic surgery), between nondurable and durable events (e.g., a rock concert vs. a wedding ceremony), and between nondurable and durable ideas (e.g., a political campaign speech vs. a folktale). These distinctions refer to the time span of a consumer-product interaction that produces valued benefits in the form of consumption experiences. These experiences vary in longevity for intangible services, events, and ideas, just as they do for more tangible manufactured goods. Clearly, for some cases, one does expect the relevant experiences to last indefinitely, as in the case of a marriage ('til death do us part) or cosmetic surgery (where one tends to become upset if one's face-lift falls) or folktales (which one can tell and retell around the campfire after a hard day of hunting bison with a club).

Second, durability in tangibles and intangibles covers a relevant range far broader than that normally considered. For example, we as researchers might define levels of durability on a logarithmic scale as

    (1) less than a second (nano-durables)
    (2) under a minute (antidurables)
    (3) under an hour (nondurables)
    (4) under a day (faux-durables)
    (5) under a week (hypodurables)
    (6) under a month (infradurables)
    (7) under 1 year (subdurables)
    (8) under 10 years (quasi-durables)
    (9) under 100 years (mere durables)
    (10) under 1,000 years (extradurables)
    (11) under 10,000 years (ultradurables)
    (12) under 100,000 years (maxi-durables)
    (13) under 1 million years (superdurables)
    (14) under 1 billion years (hyperdurables)
    (15) billions of years (megadurables)

I have christened this scale the Milky Way Scale because it is anchored by the Milky Way candy bar at one end (consumption time = a few seconds) and by the Milky Way galaxy at the other extreme (consumption time = eons).

Most available consumer research purporting to study durables has dealt with the *hypodurables* in category 5 (e.g., panty hose, collapsible umbrellas), the *infradurables* in category 6 (e.g., cigarette lighters, potted plants), the *subdurables* in category 7 (e.g., clothing, light bulbs), the *quasi-durables* in category 8 (e.g., automobiles, household appliances), or the *mere durables* in category 9 (e.g., houses, furniture). I suggest that consumer researchers should study the cases of durability that occur among the *extra-*, *ultra-*, *maxi-*, *super-*, *hyper-*, and *megadurables* in categories 10 to 15, wherein the goods, services, events, and ideas in question render their value over a period of hundreds, thousands, millions, or even billions of years (e.g., the Statue of Liberty, a Stradivarius violin, the Declaration of Independence, *Hamlet*, Greek sculpture, the Bible, the Grand Canyon, the Big Dipper, the Sun, the Deity).

As one example, businesses often emulate the old Polaroid commercials by trying to sell consumers a "piece of the sun." The marketing of Halley's comet that occurred when it traveled through the night skies during the mid-1980s offers a spectacular case in point. In the year of the comet, telescope sales doubled, thanks to a big push from telescope marketers (Geist, 1985). (In New York City, this trend also helped create a secondary market for Venetian blinds.)

Similar phenomena of durability surround the consumption of artworks whose appreciation may endure for centuries and beyond. People continue to celebrate the works of Bach 300 years after his birth and those of Mozart 200 years after his death. Soon, people shall doubtless turn their attention to Brahms, who died in 1897. Yet, we as researchers lack a full understanding of these consumption events, especially with respect to the question of what makes such products endure. Surely, such endurance bears some relation to spiritual and aesthetic value (Meyer, 1956, 1967). Yet, just as surely, we have not yet come close to unraveling the mysteries of aesthetics and spirituality. Hence, such issues await and even demand investigation. And a closer examination of such true durability may shed light on the importance of less dramatic differences in longevity at the lower end of the durability continuum.

Time, Energy, and Ability Versus Money

Sixth, in terms of resource allocation, both Koko and Betty Castle engage primarily in the investment of time, energy, and ability (animate resources) as opposed to money (inanimate resources) in their respective consumption experiences (cf. Alderson, 1957, p. 286). Progress has been made toward treating time, energy, and ability as key animate resources allocated by consumers among consumption activities (Holbrook & Lehmann 1981; Unger & Kernan, 1983). For example, Becker (1976) regards time and consumer goods as key inputs into the household's production function, and this contribution recently helped win him the Nobel Prize in economics. More generally, when we as people consume, we expend part of our life force or psychic energy (Csikszentmihalyi & Rochberg-Halton, 1981). Thus, the resources that we allocate among various consuming activities or devote to different consumption experiences are *living* resources. Playing tennis requires not only shoes, balls, rackets, a court, and some decent weather, but also one or three partners and about 60 to 90 minutes of time. Golf requires not only shoes, balls, clubs, a few hundred acres of prime real estate, and a cart to ride in, but also a morning or afternoon to waste. In short, if time is money, all consumption reduces to the expenditure of time (the ultimate scarce resource). This point appears clearly in the activities of the penniless Koko, whose time, energy, and effort are all she has to spend.

Multifaceted Emotions Versus Simple Affect

Seventh, both Koko and Betty Castle remind us that the consumption experience contains multifaceted emotional components that extend far beyond simple affect. Traditionally, consumer researchers treated affect as a unidimensional continuum that extends from positive to negative, from pro to con, from favorable to unfavorable, from good to bad, from approach to avoidance, or from liking to disliking. Even those who have undertaken more ambitious treatments of affect have tended to retain aspects of this unidimensional view, especially if they come from a cognitivist decision-oriented background (Cohen & Areni, 1991).

Yet, this historically prevailing conception of affect appears unnecessarily restrictive. Thus, in accord with the emerging experiential perspective, I have argued for replacing the unidimensional concept of affect narrowly conceived with a broader multifaceted concept of emotion (Holbrook, 1986c; Holbrook & O'Shaughnessy, 1984). Specifically, beginning in the mid-1980s, I have maintained that consumer emotions range over a wide variety of types (e.g., joy, sadness, love, hate, anger, fear, pleasure, arousal, surprise, disgust). Drawing on the extensive research by psychologists and on more recent studies by those interested in consumer behavior, I have suggested that emotional responses involve at least four mutually interdependent components:

1. Physiological responses (e.g., brain waves, pupil dilation, facial muscles, heart beat, sweat glands)
2. Cognitive interpretations (e.g., attributing one's sensations to a precipitating event)
3. Phenomenological feelings (e.g., the subjective experience of one's affective state via a lump in the throat, a tingle in the back of the neck, a sinking heart, a visceral knot)
4. Behavioral expressions (e.g., body language such as an embrace or an obscene gesture)

For example, anger might involve (1) increased blood pressure, (2) attribution of this response to the fact that one's toaster oven has malfunctioned and burned the croissants, (3) visceral sensations in the pit of one's stomach, and (4) a frown. Or sadness might entail (1) a decreased pulse rate, (2) blaming one's state on the loss of one's favorite fountain pen, (3) a dull fuzziness in the head, and (4) shedding a few tears.

These aspects of responding, interpreting, feeling, and expressing appear to interact in a reverberating network of interrelationships with no necessary causal priority among its constituent parts (Denzin, 1984; Giorgi, 1970). Hence, all subcomponents are equally important to the overall emotional experience. The most visible manifestations to an external observer, however, are the behavioral expressions that involve such overt signals as body postures, nonverbal gestures, and facial mien (Cacioppo, Losch, Tassinary, & Petty, 1986). In other words, to express emotions, we as people slouch or stand up straight, we make a fist or cross our arms, we wave or give someone the finger, we scowl or smile, and we speak tenderly or in a harsh tone. Ultimately, we write books.

Behavioral expression performs an important communicative function that, as in the case of artistic creativity, may itself serve as a purpose for the consumption experience (Holbrook & Zirlin, 1985). Such expressive consumption reaches its apotheosis in the dance (Highwater, 1981; Ruesch & Kees, 1956). For example, at a performance in honor of Bishop Desmond M. Tutu, I once saw Welcome Msomi and the Izulu Dance Theatre execute an ecstatic outpouring of physical movement that could not be seen as anything other than an exultant expression and consumption of pure joy. In another context, King and Straub (1984) make a similar point when they describe some classically trained ballet dancers practicing in a studio:

> Their faces ran with sweat. Their leotards were wet with sweat. The room, as large and airy as it was, stank of sweat. . . . Most of all he remembered their expressions—all that exhausted concentration, all that pain . . . but transcending the pain, . . . he had seen joy. Joy was unmistakably what that look was. . . . Joy. . . . Joy, he thought again. . . . Joy. . . . And . . . that feeling of joy remained, like a rainbow inside his head. (pp. 192-193)

Consumer Misbehavior Versus Behavior

Eighth, my animal examples mimic the fact that many consumer activities fall outside the bounds of conventional personal or social norms and therefore are labeled as consumer misbehavior, as opposed to consumer behavior. In Chapter 4, I distinguished among immoral, illegal, irrational, and irregular aspects of consumption. Here, these distinctions matter less than the broader recognition that such forms of unethical, unlawful, foolish, or deviant consumer behavior exist widely but receive scant notice from our discipline (Cooper-Martin & Holbrook, 1993; Holbrook, 1986b, 1994b).

For example, drug addicts (immorality), criminals (illegality), gamblers (irrationality), and transvestites (irregularity) represent exaggerated forms of extremely common consumer "misbehaviors"—namely, overeating, speeding on the highway, playing bingo, and dressing out of fashion. Yet, with such rare exceptions as the aforementioned work on compulsive shopping (O'Guinn & Faber, 1989), on impulse buying (Rook, 1987), on addiction (Hirschman, 1991), on freaks (Fitzsimons et al., 1993), and on a broad range of ethical and unethical consumption (Cooper-Martin & Holbrook, 1993) consumer researchers have granted the various types of consumer misbehavior very little systematic attention.

Why have we as consumer researchers turned our backs on such important and widespread phenomena? I suspect it is because consumer misbehavior makes us rather uncomfortable. For example, to acknowledge that robbing banks or embezzling money from the pension fund is just one more type of consumption might seem to degrade the discipline a bit. In other words, researchers seem to respond to consumer misbehavior with an almost prissy aversion—as if to hope that, by ignoring it, they can make it go away.

The Whole Versus Its Parts

Ninth, by recalling the work in Gestalt psychology, Koko evokes an awareness of the mutual interdependency among consumption phenomena. Like any gestalt, the consumption experience is a complex whole that cannot meaningfully be decomposed into isolated parts. Thus, one may define the consumption experience as a gestalt that results from a complex system of mutually overlapping interrelationships in constant reciprocal interaction with personal, environmental, and situational inputs (Hirschman & Holbrook, 1986).

Hirschman and Holbrook (1986) distinguish among four components of the consumption experience: thought, emotion, activity, and value. These components closely resemble the standard repertoire of key variables in the C-A-B-S formulation: cognition (thought), affect (emotion), behavior (activity), and satisfaction (value). However, besides modifying our conceptualization of these components somewhat as already described in Chapter 4, Hirschman and I borrow from Kurt Lewin (1936, 1951) to suggest that thought, emotion, activity, and value may best be regarded as interdependent regions of the life space and may be represented most clearly by a schema—often referred to as a "Venn diagram"—showing all possible intersections of these components as overlapping subregions of the psychological field into which a person can move at any time. A revised version of this diagram appears in Figure 5.3.

Among other things, this view of overlapping regions questions our ability to construct a clear causal model of the consumption experience. In this sense, the boxes-and-arrows formulations typical of the traditional decision-oriented approach and illustrated in Chapter 2 appear doomed to fail when applied to the experiential perspective. Rather, "like other aspects of human behavior, the consumption experience is a complex concatenation, a network, a web, an organic whole, a dynamic unity, a reverberating system of mutually overlapping interdependencies" (Hirschman & Holbrook, 1986, p. 236).

Marketing Managers Versus Consumers

Finally, I can find virtually no managerial relevance or any other practical implications in either the story of Koko and All Ball or the tale of Betty and Zero. Rather, in both anecdotes, the issues of concern spring from the

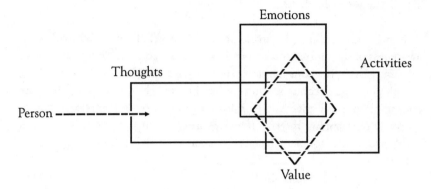

Figure 5.3. The Consumer's Life Space

interests of the consumers themselves and not from those of any marketing managers who might wish to benefit from, improve on, or otherwise alter the nature of their consumption experiences.

This nonpragmatic aspect of my animal stories coincides with my predilection for viewing consumer research as an end in itself pursued for its own sake without regard to any benefits that it might bestow on marketing practitioners or other applications-oriented users. Although I find this orientation salutary and recommend it to all researchers temperamentally capable of accepting it, I shall save it for more extended treatments in Chapters 6 and 9.

❏ *Telling Stories*

Conceptual Humanism

The 10 preceding lessons from pets suggest the need for a radically revised view of the consumption experience—one that makes room for a more refined treatment of emotional components, as well as the other experiential aspects just described. Together, these 10 reorientations apply to both substantive and methodological issues. Substantively, they suggest that consumption experiences result from the investment of living resources in the usage of products and involve complex reverberating networks of such components as thought, emotion, activity, and value. Furthermore, methodologically, they imply the need for more eclectic, creative, diverse, or even deviant pathways to theory development and for more introspective, phenomenological, qualitative, or self-expressive approaches to validation (Fennell, 1985; Thompson, Locander, & Pollio, 1989).

Beth Hirschman (1985b) has drawn on work by Mitroff and Kilmann (1978) to describe four alternative styles of consumer research:

1. Analytical science (based on sensing and thinking)
2. Particular humanism (based on sensing and feeling)
3. Conceptual theory (based on intuiting and thinking)
4. Conceptual humanism (based on intuiting and feeling)

Beth's example of the fourth style—conceptual humanism—was none other than Morris the Cat.

As noted in Chapter 1, being pigeonholed or put into a box tends to make even a conceptually humanistic cat quite uncomfortable. Indeed, Morris believes that each of the styles of research just mentioned has its place in the creation and validation of theory concerning consumer behavior. And over the years, each has characterized various facets of my own work, as well as that of others. As argued by Hirschman (1985b), however, to advance the development of theory on the consumption experience (especially its emotional components), I have sometimes inclined toward the style of research known as *conceptual humanism*, or what Hirschman and Holbrook (1986) call "introspective self-cultivation" and what in Chapters 1 and 7, I call "subjective personal introspection."

Conceptual humanism involves the extensive use of subjective, personal, introspective material and often proceeds via the construction of anecdotes, analogies, or metaphors. In short, conceptual humanism relies heavily on *telling stories*—that is, "telling" both in the sense of recounting tales and in the sense that these narratives are meaningful by virtue of their richness in personal references, their metaphorical content, and their resonance in human lives (Mitroff & Kilmann, 1978). This focus accords with an increased interest in the role of metaphors in science (Jones, 1982) and philosophy (Lakoff & Johnson, 1980), and it uses stories as one potential path toward knowledge.

In short, conceptual humanism prizes the use of stories and related narrative forms to uncover the meanings of everyday experience. For example, Hunter (1983) suggests that

> When we wish to communicate . . . we tell a story of some sort. These are revelatory stories which disclose to us the meaning of our existence and experience in new and regenerative ways. Story is the language of the spirit. If we are to escape both sterile positivism and solipsistic subjectivism we must address ourselves to the issues of the *truth* and the *effectiveness* . . . of revelatory stories. (p. 3)

Lewin (1936) agrees that narrative accounts can often reveal otherwise inaccessible complexities of mutually interdependent psychological processes:

> The most complete and concrete descriptions of situations are those which writers such as Dostoyevski have given us. These descriptions have attained what the statistical characterizations have most notably lacked, namely, a picture that shows in a definite way how the different facts in an individual's environment are related to each other and to the individual himself. (p. 13)

As prophesied by Hirschman (1985b), consumer researchers began to emphasize the role of telling stories during the mid- to late 1980s. For example, Holbrook et al. (1989) endorsed the merits of storytelling, tying this narrative approach to the work of such psychologists as Bruner (1986) in his *Actual Minds: Possible Worlds*, such sociologists as Brown (1977) in his *Poetic for Sociology*, and such anthropologists as Geertz (1988) in his *Works and Lives: The Anthropologist as Author*. As summarized by Schweder (1988), Geertz suggests that "a great ethnography is not simply a compilation of facts; it is an imaginative way of seeing through experience" (p. 13):

> According to Mr. Geertz, ethnographic reality does not exist apart from our literary versions of it. . . . The appreciation of Mr. Geertz's brilliant writing is much like the appreciation of a brilliant metaphor. Both suffer from explication; something inevitably gets lost in translation. (p. 13)[3]

In this spirit, John Sherry (1991)—trained as an anthropologist but writing as a consumer researcher—has challenged his colleagues as follows:

> Are there consumer researchers among us who are able to write novels based upon their research? . . . Might not such novels be as readily aspired to as

exemplars as are the natural science treatises that are our current models? . . . Who is it among us, writer of the occasional poem or short story, who might be turned toward the illumination of consumer behavior? (p. 571)

John Sherry has moved partway toward answering his own questions by collaborating recently with Fuat Fırat to edit two special issues of the *International Journal of Research in Marketing* devoted to "postmodern" consumer research and including poems by both George Zinkhan and John himself, as well as my own narrative essay about New York City (Holbrook, 1994c). This essay is entitled "Loving and Hating New York: Some Reflections on the Big Apple"; it begins in song and ends in wonder.

Although Hirschman (1985b) has offered some pertinent examples in her provocative account of the four styles, the use of stories in consumer research is not yet well understood or fully accepted. Rather than attempt an abstract explication, I provide some brief stories as illustrations here and later. I begin by retelling a short narrative that I wrote one sunny morning in May 1984. It focuses on the consumption experiences and emotional responses of a consumer researcher as he begins his workday. Somewhat autobiographically, in tune with my own feelings surrounding the development of the experiential view advanced in Chapters 4 and 5, it is called "I Awake."

❏ I Awake

I awake. My first conscious thoughts concern the double ugliness of the rough sound emanating from the Sony clock radio purposely placed on the other side of the nearby bookcase so as to force me eventually to leave my warm bed to turn it off—once ugly because that sound has shattered the peaceful tranquility of my gentle slumber and twice ugly because the Sony now plays Willie Nelson's unconscionably syrupy version of "Stardust" embellished by harsh sibilant scratching noises that the *High Fidelity* I was reading last night attributes to multipath distortion caused by reflections of the FM signal off New York's high-rise buildings. One such edifice looms above me, and as if by Divine calculation, bright rays from the newly risen sun strike one of its windows at precisely the right angle to glint cruelly into my half-cracked eyes while I inwardly gather my strength in preparation for the aural assault soon to be mounted by the Sunbeam electric clock also positioned beyond my arm's reach and carefully set to lag 5 minutes behind the radio. Willie has stopped singing by now, thank God, and the comparatively cheerful sounds of Roberta Flack and Peabo Bryson have just started when the buzzer itself begins to wail. Sally moans in dormant rebellion from her fetal position on the wrinkled sheets beside me, pulling the softly odored comforter even more tightly around her face until only her nose pokes through.

I summon the courage necessary for my most heroic deed of the day. Suddenly, in one well-practiced and nearly continuous motion, I leap from the covers, press the switch that silences the Sunbeam's grating alarm, shuffle my feet into a pair of leather slippers that I have been cultivating since the seventh grade, click off the loud fan that we run all night to drown out street noises, flip the button that mercifully relieves Roberta, Peabo, and the Sony of their multipath burden, and appear before my own eyes stark naked in the mirror over the bathroom sink.

Here, I commence the rituals that members of my family refer to as my "ablutions." Their execution requires only a few moments, but they proceed according to a fixed routine so rigid that Sally, a psychotherapist, labels them "compulsive" and almost clinically "obsessive." Once begun, my ceremony of cleansing and anointment deviates from its ineluctable course for no force on earth, save perhaps an insufficient supply of Crest or Mennen. First, I splash warm water on my bristly cheeks and chin, wincing when the temperature suddenly changes from warm to scalding and making my 2,683rd mental note to ask the super to fix the faucet. Next, I apply a liberal quantity of lime-scented and -flavored Edge shaving gel, congratulating myself on the discovery of this miraculous face-preserving ointment that daily saves me from the painful bloodletting suffered with urbane equanimity by Cary Grant in Monday night's rerun of *Mr. Blandings Builds His Dream House*. In contrast to Cary's ordeal, my slippery face slides uneventfully under the smooth strokes of my Gillette Atra until I note with satisfaction the almost babylike perfection of the finished results. Still moist from rinsing off the Edge, I squeeze a generous dollop of mint-flavored Crest onto my medium-hard Colgate toothbrush and then let my mechanical wrist-flicking and arm-bending technique take over while I inspect with disapproval the sparse patch of straggling growth that barely adorns the top of my high and shining forehead. After automatically slurping, swishing, spitting, and drying, I brush these forlorn locks in a few brisk gestures that manage to impose order on every pathetic one of them with the expenditure of only a few seconds' time and energy.

Finally, I come to the cherished moment in which I wipe a little squirt of Mennen Afta on my newly razored skin, rejoicing in its balmlike powers.

Now it is time to dress. I march to my closet, and because I shall work at home today, I abandon my process of sartorial choice to whim and reckless impulse. Of course, I do not deviate from my standard practice of pulling on size 32 Jockey shorts and gray cotton socks because I long ago discovered, first, my acute sensitivity to even the tiniest variations in underwear design and, second, the happy maxim that virtually any combination of shoes and pants interacts harmoniously with charcoal-colored hosiery. Capitalizing on this reassuring principle, I force my way into a tight pair of faded Levi's (which I momentarily suspect of belonging to my slender 15-year-old son, Chris), climb into a lavender polo shirt (which, for some reason, features a blue pig standing on the very spot where an alligator is supposed to reside), and slip into my trusted Weejuns (acquired in high school and now so nicked and scuffed that they rival my ancient slippers in venerability).

I barely avoid stepping on Quarter, the cat, who lolls playfully on his back in the foyer (specifically, on that narrow portion of the hardwood floor through which all traffic must pass), and plod into the kitchen where, with practiced expertise, I fill the kettle with cool water, set the gas burner ablaze under it, and dole out Zabar's coffee grounds into the filter paper at the top of an incriminatingly stained Melitta pot. In this enterprise, I maintain an incorruptible compromise exactly halfway between the amount of grounds preferred by Sally and by me (as gauged by my Prufrockian coffee measure); like Solomon, I believe that fairness must decide all such questions.

Justice must also prevail in issues concerning the morning juice, a matter toward which I now direct my full concentration. Through careful experimentation and empirical study, I have determined that (a) orange juice is too sour, (b) apple juice is too sweet, (c) Chris, my growing son, can consume either beverage with approximately twice the speed empowered to me, and (d) Sally's consumption of fruit juice cannot be detected by even the most unobtrusive measurement (though she does occasionally eat a kiwi fruit or two). Careful balancing of the scales of justice therefore demands that I purchase huge quantities of both orange and apple juice, that I mix small amounts of each into a combined potion (which I call "orple" juice and which, thankfully, Chris would not touch with a broom handle even if such life-and-death concerns as his next Genesis record were at stake), and that I consign the remainder of the Tropicana and the Motts to Chris for purposes of immediate disposal in huge Herculean gulps while I take dainty sips of my special concoction.

The first such sip of orple washes down my daily vitamin pill, which I rather casually select as the most general-purpose specimen to be found in the three-tiered array of bottles that Sally uses to support her $70-a-month vitamin habit. Such monetary thoughts even now flood my mind as she bustles cheerfully into the kitchen and announces with enormous enthusiasm her revelation that, before 7:00 a.m. on weekdays, one can call Italy at only $1.85 for the first 3 minutes and, further, that she has just put this telephonic privilege to excellent use by direct-dialing Porto Venere and locating a hotel room that we can inhabit next summer for only 280,000 lire per night (meals included).

I suppress my reflex question concerning the exchange rate between lire and dollars and opt instead for imploring her to stop using her fingers to remove the surface raisins from the box of raisin bran before passing it to me. After finally securing what is left of the Kellogg's, I pour some rather flaky cereal into a small plastic bowl and flood it in a bath of low-fat milk.

My use of this dairy product represents still one more compromise that attains nearly rabbinical wisdom in its careful balance of equity and fairness. I prefer skimmed; Chris prefers homogenized; so we all drink 2% low-fat— except, of course, Sally, who hates all milk, as reflected perhaps by her small-boned stature. I infer her disproportionally dainty size from the impression that her body seems too tiny to contain her huge spirit—particularly, this morning, her boundless enthusiasm for travel to such places as Italy and (I now learn with growing financial apprehension) Switzerland.

Carrying my freshly brewed cup of mocha/Colombian blend, I stumble toward my study. I execute one more precarious pirouette around Quarter (still spread across the foyer floor) and, finally, sit before my big, white, glass-topped desk. I reach for a Kleenex and blow my nose lustily (for the cat exacerbates my aching allergies). I switch on the 100-watt GE bulb in my yellow-shaded antique brass lamp (for the sky has grown dark, and it has begun to rain). I remove my Sheaffer fine-tipped fountain pen and two pieces of Eaton's Berkshire bond from my drawer and place them on the desk in front of me (for I think I should write something about consumer behavior today).

The blank expanse of white pages on white desk stares up at me expectantly. I wait for a profound thought about consumer behavior to occur to me. Suddenly, it comes.

Like everyone else in this world, I am a consumer. I climbed out of bed exactly one half-hour ago, and already I have spent 29 minutes and 36 seconds engaged in various consumption experiences. Allowing 6 hours for sleep (during which consumption is reduced, though not altogether stopped), I shall spend about 18 hours consuming today. In my 40 years, this kind of behavior has added up to about 262,800 hours of consumption experiences. Surely, I should by now be an expert on consumption. If I had one lira for every hour I've spent consuming, we could spend a night in the Italian hotel to which Sally at this moment busily writes a letter requesting a reservation.

Then why do I feel so ignorant about consumer behavior? Perhaps it is because consumer researchers seem to ignore the experiential phenomena through which I have been living. I glance nervously at my shelves of periodicals and journals, all neatly arranged in chronological order. A pale brown section containing 40 issues of the *Journal of Consumer Research* nestles among the other multicolored bindings. I notice absentmindedly how the lettering changed from black to brown in 1977 and the cover from tan to beige in 1983. I ponder the mystery of these alterations. I think about all the models of brand choice and buying behavior that these wise pages contain. I wonder dreamily where the flesh-and-blood consumer hides amid all this talk of product adoption and purchasing decisions.

This thought seizes me now. My demon has called me. My muse has spoken. I begin to write. I am awake.

Interpretation

Interested readers might amuse themselves by interpreting "I Awake" for the light that it might shed on the nature of consumption as portrayed in this chapter. I confine my own comments simply to noting that the story does appear to offer examples of the 10 points mentioned earlier.

Consuming Versus Buying. In "I Awake," the speaker refers to a complex series of consumption experiences packed into a half-hour time span. No real buying behavior occurs—only the consuming of objects bought earlier (shaving gel, toothpaste, coffee) or of services provided for free (by family members, by Quarter the cat).

Consumption Experiences Versus Purchase Decisions. The relevant consumption experiences take the form of fantasies (daydreaming about Cary Grant), feelings (embarrassment over the ill-fitting jeans), and fun (swinging into the breakfast routine).

Product Usage Versus Brand Choice. Although some brand names do appear (Sunbeam, Crest, Mennen, Edge, Atra), most of the emphasis in this story concerns the speaker's expenditure of time on various consumption activities—for example, the ceremonies of washing and dressing or the ordeal of starting the day's work. Although he mentions Tropicana and Motts, one understands that he could just as easily manufacture orple from, say, Minute Maid and Dole. Furthermore, when he refers to milk, the important differences lie between homogenized, skimmed, and 2% low-fat—not between Sealtest, Borden's, and Elmhurst Dairy.

Intangible Services Versus Tangible Goods. Much of the consumer satisfaction described in the story reflects its characters' experience of such intangible services as travel (fantasizing about a trip to Italy or Switzerland) or companionship (the ever-present cat in the hallway).

Durables Versus Nondurables. The speaker's attention gravitates toward the durable, as opposed to nondurable, end of the consumption spectrum. Thus, he expresses some displeasure with certain quasi-durables (the music of Willie Nelson and the wail of the alarm clock), positively nostalgic feelings toward some mere durables that he has owned since childhood (leather slippers and Weejun loafers), and an ambivalent attitude toward at least one mega-durable (the sun). Furthermore, even the true nondurables found in the story (shaving balm, orange juice) are associated with consuming rituals (morning ablutions, breakfast) that endure and that thereby provide their relevant customer value—as quasi-durable services—over a lengthy period of time. Implicitly, the speaker is concerned with how the memory of orple remains even after young Chris has grown up and moved to a home of his own. Similarly and reflexively, as represented by the "wise pages" in those old copies of the *Journal of Consumer Research,* no one writes a scholarly paper, much less a story, without hoping that its message will endure.

Time, Energy, and Ability Versus Money. Except for the speaker's preoccupation with his wife Sally's expensive travel plans, most of the story concerns the investment of time and energy needed to move him from his cozy bed to his intimidating desk. For example, eating breakfast is a social activity that requires a few inputs of coffee, juice, and cereal plus significant amounts of three people's time (not to mention the services of Quarter the cat, whose influence pervades the story, even as he sprawls peacefully across the floor in the foyer).

Multifaceted Emotions Versus Simple Affect. Despite its mundane setting, this story conjures up some fairly strong emotions that surround the consumption experiences described: fatigue and discomfort on arising early, sensuous pleasures of the morning ablutions, family love at the breakfast table, dread of the blank paper on the big white desk. These emotions weave together in the story—fugue-like—as they do in our lives as consumers.

Consumer Misbehavior Versus Behavior. Although the speaker manages mostly to avoid immorality and illegality in this particular tale, his consumption of orple certainly verges on irregularity. And what could one say to dispute the irrationality of a person with bad allergies who insists on owning and loving a cat?

The Whole Versus Its Parts. The story gives some sense of how consumption experiences fit into a holistic pattern, rather than lend themselves to isolation for segregated scrutiny. One cannot make sense of the author's preferences for Mennen Afta outside the overall context of the interrelated grooming and shaving activities at whose conclusion it provides the final soothing balm.

Marketing Managers Versus Consumers. Finally, the speaker in "I Awake" focuses on consumption experiences regarded as worthy of consideration for their own sake as everyday life-filling aspects of the human condition and without regard for any opportunities that they might offer to profit-motivated marketing managers. If marketing managers can find a way to capitalize on this story of Mennen, Quarter, Tropicana, and old copies of JCR—first tan, then beige (later gray, now white)—such business opportunities are of no concern to the speaker, whose preoccupation rests with the power of these objects to evoke comfort, love, contentment, and anxiety, respectively, and with how these feelings fit into his existence as a consumer.

Predictive Validity

Practitioners of the neopositivistic methods described earlier pride themselves on their ability to support hypotheses generated from their theories by establishing their predictive validity—that is, their ability to forecast outcomes when tested against empirical data. I would not claim any such lofty corroboration for the truths found in the story "I Awake." Yet, I cannot resist sharing a passage written by my son, Chris, on an application for graduate school roughly 10 years after I wrote "I Awake" (which he has never seen). It comes from his longer response to one of those inane questions that university administrators delight in putting on application forms. Even when wrenched from context, it seems to recall themes found in this chapter generally and in "I Awake" especially:

> I was sitting in the living room of my parents' apartment on Manhattan's Upper West Side. My parents had gone away for the weekend, and I had come to feed the cat on a Saturday afternoon. I had expected to open up a can of low fat, nondairy, California cat food . . ., clean the litter, and leave in time to grab some coffee at a nearby Hungarian pastry shop before sundown. . . . But after feeding the cat, I didn't leave. . . . The cat was curled up on a pillow, compact as a pill box, making it difficult to tell where his tail began and ended. He was eighteen years old—I had grown up with him—and he was dying. I sat with him there, in a room that had . . . been remodeled since I had moved out of my parents' home, and I thought of my life while growing up in that apartment—of playing with the cat when he was ten pounds heavier, of the old sepia carpet in the living room . . ., of my old room—and of how all those footprints were vanishing from my world. . . . That afternoon stays with me. It seeps into the arabesques of my life and illuminates them, showing me what I no longer have, what I've gained, and what has never left me.

These recollections by my son, Chris, echo the essence of "I Awake" better than any further exegesis by me could possibly manage. They contribute a touch of what my neopositivistic friends would call "intersubjective validity"—that is, the support of one subject's observations by those of another. They reflect aspects of consumer behavior that were found in the activities of Koko the gorilla and that pervade daily experience of the human condition.

❏ Conclusion

In Chapters 4 and 5, I have attempted to justify the radical shift in consumer research away from the decision orientation and back to the roots of experiential consumption. Reflections on those issues, as inspired by some stories about pet consumption, have suggested that the conventional models and methods do not adequately encompass the full range of phenomena relevant to the consumption experience. They cannot represent the grief-stricken misery of the poor whimpering gorilla (Koko) or the hysterical cruelty of the dog owner (Betty Castle) in Feiffer's play (*Think Piece*). Nor can they capture the essence of a sunny morning with a green parrot in the imagination of Wallace Stevens or of daybreak in a kitchen near Quarter the cat.

I therefore have proposed—and where possible, attempted to achieve—an expansion of consumer research to reflect a fuller treatment of

consuming (vs. buying)

experiencing (vs. deciding)

using products (vs. choosing brands)

intangible services, events, and ideas (vs. tangible goods)

more durable products (vs. sub- or quasi-durables)

expenditures of *time, energy, and ability* (vs. money)

multifaceted emotional components (vs. narrowly defined affect)

consumer mis*behavior* (vs. behavior)

mutually interdependent wholes or gestalts (vs. their individual elements)

intrinsically motivated concern with consumption *for its own sake* (vs. extrinsically motivated managerial relevance)

Furthermore, I have introduced a methodological theme to be developed more fully in Chapter 7—namely, the greater reliance on storytelling and other aspects of conceptual humanism (as opposed to the various neopositivistic dictates of the hypothetico-deductive approach) as one route to a more complete understanding of the consumption experience. I have illustrated this narrative approach in a brief story called "I Awake"; further examples appear in the chapters that follow.

❑ *Epilogue*

As I write these words, on what happens to be the officially proclaimed coldest day in New York City since the 1880s, the wind howls outside my window, blowing frozen gusts against the trembling panes and leaving a solid crust of white ice crystals on the inside. Contrasting vividly with the scene in "I Awake," this wintry picture evokes an image of the cold analytic light under which consumer researchers have so often scrutinized their subject. In attempting to meet the neopositivistic prescriptions imposed by the hypothetico-deductive method, researchers have often worked in the name of dispassionate detachment to shed a chilly illumination on the decision-oriented phenomena under study but have too seldom admired the rainbow of feelings and appreciative responses that pervade all consumption experience.

Through the frost that blurs the frozen scrutiny under which researchers have generally regarded the consumer, we as researchers search for a glimpse of the warm-blooded consumption experience in our vision of Koko in her cage. We seek the variegated, suggestive spectacle of this massive but gentle gorilla who tickles her playful kitten.

O, Koko, how you consume!

O, Consumer, How You've Changed!

❑ Notes

1. Brody (1985), p. C8. Copyright © 1985 by The New York Times Company. Reprinted by permission.

2. Lefferts (1985), p. F15. Copyright © 1985 by The New York Times Company. Reprinted by permission.

3. Schweder (1988), p. 13. Copyright © 1988 by The New York Times Company. Reprinted by permission.

WHITHER
CONSUMER RESEARCH?

Some Pastoral Reflections on
Bears, Baltimore, Baseball, and
Resurrecting the Study of Consumption

I'd be pretty dumb if all of a sudden I started being something I'm not.
—*Yogi Berra, quoted in Clark (1984), p. 6*[1]

Against the rules, yes, Boo Boo. But I am a nonconformist bear.
—*Yogi Bear, quoted in Clark (1984), p. 6*[2]

Morry . . . an old guard . . . came to us in Junior Kindergarten. . . . Moe is
the class' leading non-conformist. . . . Favorite class is English. . . . Illustrious
Ledger Editor who writes unprintable, flaming editorials. . . . Often referred
to as Turtle. . . . Is looking east to Harvard.
—*Milwaukee Country Day School (1961),*
The Arrow, High School Yearbook

❑ Introduction

The Managerial Shibboleth

As seen in the previous two chapters, developments during the early
1980s pushed consumer researchers toward a broader focus on the consumption experience in general (Chapter 4) and on the role of consumer emotions

141

in particular (Chapter 5). By the mid-1980s, some workers in the field had jettisoned enough of the traditional baggage so that, for them, consumer research could have been characterized succinctly as Statement 5 in Figure 1.3 from Chapter 1: Scientific Research Is Neopositivistic Managerially Relevant Studies. Here, one might think of the magic words "Managerially Relevant" as a kind of shibboleth—that is, a phrase that one repeats to signal one's unquestioned loyalty to a group or cause.

At the same time, the emerging concern for emotional experience, especially when coupled with an interest in the consumer aesthetics of entertainment and the arts, tended to encourage consumer research of dubious practical import to most marketing managers. For example, studies on perceptual and affective responses to music often prompted comments about the absence of obvious ways marketers could use our findings. Gradually, increased tension developed between traditionalists who espoused the cause of managerial relevance and those who had embarked on new approaches toward the study of consumption. The latter believed that such studies were important and that a pressure toward banausic purposes would only stifle scholarly and scientific progress. Yet, thus far, few were willing to disregard the notion of practical applicability for marketing managers—few, that is, except Robert Ferber.

Bob Ferber's Vision

I first met Bob Ferber—a small, white-haired, dapper gent of enormous energy and famous perspicacity—in 1975 when he chaired a conference on the state of the art in consumer research. Held in Lake Geneva, Wisconsin, and sponsored by the National Science Foundation (NSF), this symposium brought together prominent scholars from all parts of the consumer research field and from a number of closely related disciplines. I joined this distinguished company only because Bob Ferber had invited John Howard to discuss the area of consumer nondurables (e.g., coffee, toothpaste, detergent), and John Howard had generously asked me to serve as his coauthor.

This invitation coincided with my first year as a teacher on the Columbia Business School's marketing faculty. I had been hired to occupy a "tenure-track" position that almost everybody thought should not be filled by one of Columbia's own graduates (to avoid potential "intellectual incest"). Furthermore, most of my senior colleagues apparently believed that the research from my dissertation (*A Study of Communication in Advertising*) was too convoluted or even irrelevant to the real world. Hence, as a budding teacher, I sensed a need to convince my superiors that I could do something practical or useful.

John Howard and I produced a lengthy manuscript on the consumption of nondurables that ultimately appeared, after considerable editing, as a chapter in Bob Ferber's book (Holbrook & Howard, 1977). When we presented the original voluminous version at Ferber's NSF conference, I felt pleased at how we had managed to weave together the references to studies of consumption with those from the area of marketing management. Hence, a few weeks later, I experienced total astonishment when we received Ferber's instructions for condensation and revision—mostly requests to remove "all that stuff about implications for marketing managers" (or words to that effect). At the time, this editorial stance against managerial relevance struck me as preposterous. I now see it as the essence of scholarly wisdom and scientific integrity.

For the rest of the 1970s, as editor for the *Journal of Consumer Research*, Ferber built on this vision by opening the journal to multidisciplinary contributions without concern about their implications for marketing management as long as they increased understanding of the consumer. Indeed, Ferber's openness in this direction helped inspire the development of the experiential perspective. In the fall of 1981, Beth Hirschman and I had just received encouraging feedback from Ferber on our "fantasies, feelings, and fun" paper when we sadly learned that, after a sudden illness, he had passed away. Besides the loss of a friend, his untimely death introduced considerable confusion into the editorial process at JCR. When it finally appeared, more than a year later, our paper on the consumption experience bore the marks of four JCR editors (Holbrook & Hirschman, 1982).

Not everyone agreed with Ferber's openness to research on consumers without regard to implications for marketing management. Indeed, most consumer researchers—still echoing the aforementioned shibboleth—tended (sometimes rather vehemently) to disagree. One such staunch advocate for the traditional viewpoint in favor of managerial relevance was my friend and fellow New Yorker, Jack Jacoby.

Jack Jacoby's Perspective

Jack Jacoby—one of the true pioneers in the field of consumer research (mostly from the perspective of the decision-oriented focus)—received his doctorate in psychology, taught that subject at Purdue University during the 1970s, and then moved in the early 1980s to New York University as the director of NYU's Institute for Retail Management (IRM). Jacoby does much business consulting and expert legal testimony for a variety of prestigious corporate clients and governmental agencies. Furthermore, he believes that such an anchoring in marketing applications in the context of real-world practice leads to more insightful, more useful consumer research.

Thus, when Beth Hirschman and I chaired the conference of the Association for Consumer Research in 1984, we invited Jack Jacoby to put together a special topic session in the form of a debate on the role of contacts with marketing practitioners and the merits of forming consulting relationships entitled "The Vices and Virtues of Being Relevant." Ultimately, Jacoby assembled a panel featuring three consumer researchers from each side of this debate on the appropriate interface between consumer researchers and marketing managers: Jagdish Sheth and Jerry Wind (speaking on the "virtues of consulting"); Jim Bettman and Russell Belk (on the "vices of consulting"); Jacoby himself (proconsulting); and Morris the Cat (anticonsulting).

The discussion ranged far beyond the issue of consulting per se and extended into many aspects of the basic question: Should the concerns of marketing managers and other practitioners shape the scholarly and scientific priorities of consumer researchers? Given the participants' strong feelings, it should have surprised no one that the ensuing debate literally shook the rafters. After the dust had settled, Jack Jacoby and I stood arm in arm and smiling. But, to put it mildly, we had not exactly resolved the issues raised by the special topic session (Jacoby, 1985a, 1985b).

In the process, I had learned something important about myself. I had learned that, as a consumer researcher in the years following my exposure to the priorities set by Bob Ferber, I had grown committed to a lack of concern for the practical, the useful, and the managerially relevant. I had—first, by temperament, and second, by conviction—grown dedicated to a kind of consumer research that is intentionally impractical, useless, and managerially a-relevant (not primarily focused on relevance to marketing).

Temperament, Convictions, and Consequences

Here, I wish to explain various outcomes of this branching away from the doctrine of "neopositivistic managerially relevant studies"—a branch that budded under the tutelage of Bob Ferber during the late 1970s, that flowered in the mid-1980s for Morris the Cat, and that subsequently blossomed for a number of other consumer researchers who appear to agree with Morris and who have offered some moral support. In describing this shift away from managerial relevance, I discuss, first, how it reflects my own basic *temperament*; second, why it supports my personal *convictions*; and, third, what I anticipate as its *consequences* for the direction of consumer research in the years ahead—in other words, "Whither Consumer Research?"

❏ *Temperament*

The Poetics of Morris the Cat

In Eugene O'Neill's (1957) *A Touch of the Poet*, Sarah describes Simon in words that ring profoundly true in the heart of an old English major from Harvard:

> Oh, he isn't like . . . anyone else at all. He's a born dreamer. . . . He wanted to get away from his father's business, where he worked for a year after he graduated from Harvard College, because he didn't like being in trade. (act 1)
>
> And he said he . . . was a failure at what he'd hoped he could be, a poet. So I kissed him and told him he was too a poet . . . and it was what I loved most about him. (Act 4)[3]

In college, I experienced a phenomenon that has since been confirmed by psychologists studying intrinsic motivation—namely, that attaching an extrinsic reward (say, grades) to some activity that might otherwise be pursued for its own sake (say, the reading of English literature) can erode the whole basis for its value with disastrous consequences (say, a thorough distaste for literary studies). Accordingly, I turned to the study of a subject ostensibly less prone to the criterion of intrinsic value—namely, business.

In the course of studying business, however, I learned gratefully that one aspect of that field does possess intrinsic value for me. Specifically, the phenomena of consumer behavior strike me as worth exploring in their own right. For me, consumer research is an end in itself—its own reward—and not just a means to somebody else's ends or the achievement of some ulterior purpose. By temperament, I resist the intrusion of managerial usefulness, marketing applications, consulting opportunities, or other ways to turn consumer research into an extrinsically motivated enterprise.

I noted in Chapter 2 that art and aesthetics provide close parallels to the development of theory in consumer research. Another such parallel concerns the possible intrusion and distorting influence of commercialism.

Commercialism: The Consumer Researcher Visits Radio City

I once attended the performance of a spectacle aptly entitled "Gotta Getaway!" at New York's Radio City Music Hall. Everything about this show seemed calculated to appeal to the broadest possible audience. It included a star singer, acrobats, magicians, trained animals, and a pipe organ of staggering sonic capabilities. But most of all, it displayed the nonpareil Rockettes—that high-kicking chorus of 32 dancing beauties who pranced through their famous routine carrying torches and sporting costumes designed to match the garments worn by the Statue of Liberty.

Judging from the enthusiastic response of the packed Music Hall, the audience loved this performance. Apparently, only I experienced discomfort. This discomfort stemmed from my irresistible inclination, as I sat there watching the dancers and daydreaming in the dark, to compare this exhibition of mass appeal to the role of commercialism in consumer research.

High Culture and Popular Culture in Consumer Research

In describing the activities of artists and craftspeople, social scientists portray a continuum from high to popular culture. One extreme concerns Art with a capital A; it is produced by artists pursuing creative ends for their own sake and is appreciated by those with acquired knowledge and developed taste. The other extreme concerns entertainment with a small e; it is produced by professionals who hope to win mass acceptance and achieve commercial success by appealing to the common denominator in shared tastes.

Sociologists such as Gans (1974) follow this distinction with an immediate disclaimer against *elitism*. We do not mean, they insist, that high culture or art is "better" than popular culture or entertainment. One person's enjoyment is just as valid as another's. All we claim, they say, is that one type of appreciation requires effort and training, whereas the other is easily accessible. The former appeals to people with the ability and willingness to deal with complexity, whereas the latter attracts those with unrefined tastes and a confirmed intolerance for ambiguity. But according to those opposed to elitism, is the former therefore better than the latter? Certainly not.

Just as in the contrast between high and popular culture, the distinction in consumer research between academicians and practitioners or between scholarship and consulting again raises the dread specter of elitism. Who can say that research motivated by intellectual curiosity is in any sense better than that motivated by managerial relevance? How dare anyone prefer the scholarly and academic to the practical and useful? Why would we elevate pure research above marketing application?

One answer to these familiar charges of elitism follows directly from my earlier analogy between consumer research and artistic creativity. Like a work of art, a piece of consumer research may be relatively great and enduring, or it may be comparatively shallow and short lived. Just as in the arts, this difference often hinges on a distinction between the pursuit of the work for its own sake and the pursuit of commercial success for the sake of money.

Consider what happens when artists forsake their purest creative visions and turn instead toward attempts to reach a larger audience by trading artistic integrity and aesthetic value for the advantages of easy execution and immediate accessibility. Recall, for example, the deterioration of gifted jazz musicians such as Wes Montgomery or Herbie Hancock who have diluted their styles to seek mass appeal.

Like many artists, Mahalia Jackson faced a choice about where to aim on the cultural continuum. She could continue devoting her life to the art of singing gospel music, or she could make the executives at her record company very happy by recording some pop tunes. Mahalia Jackson told the marketing practitioners to leave her alone. She followed her own artistic vision.

Analogously, however difficult the course might seem, consumer researchers should move away from a preoccupation with practicality toward concerns worth pursuing for their own sake. This theme has often been treated metaphorically as the difference between talking and singing or between walking and dancing. However wistfully, we as researchers want our research not merely to walk and talk; we want it to sing and dance.

The Dancer and the Dance

Similar imagery recurs ubiquitously in the Fred Astaire movies. In Cole Porter's *Silk Stockings* (1957), for example, Cyd Charisse as Ninotchka represents cold, hard, rigid technocratic dogma. Ninotchka is a Russian agent who initially concentrates on inspecting factories and power plants and who demeans music as merely "necessary for parades." Fred Astaire was never more artistic, graceful, and eloquent than when teaching Ninotchka how to dance. And Cyd Charisse was never more glorious than in the intimately choreographed scene in which she pulls on her first pair of stockings and dances around her boudoir.

In vivid contrast, stocking and dancing imagery also pervades Josef von Sternberg's *The Blue Angel* (1930). In this powerfully distressing film, the heartless cabaret performer Lola Lola (played by Marlene Dietrich) uses her stockings as one unseemly tool to win the affections of Professor Immanuel Rath (Emil Jennings). Lola is a real operator—self-interested, glamorous, enticing. She already knows how to sing and dance, as indicated by the constant repetition of her sultry torch song "Falling in Love Again." Indeed, in a cruel role reversal, she teaches the professor to perform and forces him to dress in a clown's costume and to stand upon the stage, crowing like a rooster while a magician breaks eggs on his bald head and humiliates him in front of his fellow professors, his former students, the assistant mayor, the local shopkeepers, and other townspeople who once held him in respect. This barnyard imitation—this tragic music-hall dance, this supplication to the local businessmen—conveys Professor Rath's debasement and embodies the sacrifice of everything he had valued. Early in the film, the professor showed indignant outrage when he found one of his students looking at risqué photographs of Lola Lola. Now, after himself falling under Lola's spell, he reaches his nadir when he hawks these same dirty pictures to an unruly and abusive nightclub audience. "How's business?" asks Lola. "Only sold two cards," he complains, ". . . ignorant crowd." "I live off that 'ignorant crowd,' " she protests. "Better," he replies, "to die like a dog than to live like that."

The clear analogy with consumer research will not escape the reader. Specifically, when we as researchers pursue our own truest concerns, like Fred Astaire we dance with the angels. When we obey only the dictates of marketing managers, primarily pursuing monetary gain, we wallow with Professor Rath. As he ignominiously crows like a rooster upon the stage, Professor Rath implicitly offers his obeisance to commercialism.

Which type of character does the consumer researcher aspire to be—Emil Jennings as the professor who chases the cruel and sordid but eminently businesslike Lola or Fred Astaire as the dancer who miraculously transforms the coldly technocratic Ninotchka into a warm and loving paramour? After her transformation, Ninotchka rejects her absurd Russian comrades and delivers some lines that suggest an answer based on the privileging of beauty over utility: "For the first time in my life, I looked at something and thought, 'How beautiful' instead of 'How useful.' . . . Let *them* settle their business, and *we* will get back to beautiful things."

In sum, our research resembles a dance. We can pursue knowledge like beauty for its own sake and soar like Nureyev or Baryshnikov in their primes; or we can wrap our feet in utilitarian slippers of lead. Whichever path we choose—the road more or less traveled—we become part of what we do. We assume the characteristics of our research focus. To paraphrase an old saying: "Wherever you go in life, that's where you'll be."

Such thoughts and feelings concerned William Butler Yeats in his poem "Among School Children." He saw the interconnectedness and unity of things—as in the leaf, blossom, and trunk or "bole" of a tree—and evoked the process by which we become what we do:

> Labour is blossoming or dancing where
> The body is not bruised to pleasure soul,
> Nor beauty born out of its own despair,
> Nor blear-eyed wisdom out of midnight oil.
> O chestnut-tree, great-rooted blossomer,
> Are you the leaf, the blossom or the bole?
> O body swayed to music, O brightening glance,
> How can we know the dancer from the dance?
>
> —Yeats, 1928/1956,
> "Among School Children"

❏ Convictions

The Three Bears

When first voiced publicly in the mid-1980s, the sentiments expressed in the preceding section on "temperament" failed to endear me to my colleagues of a more banausic bent. Their negative reaction was nothing, however, compared with the brouhaha that developed over my contribution to the aforementioned ACR session on the virtues and vices of consulting. I intended this paper—"Why Business Is Bad for Consumer Research" (Holbrook, 1985b)—as a statement of the extreme position opposed to closer ties between consumer researchers and marketing managers (as advocated by Jack Jacoby, Jagdish Sheth, and Jerry Wind). In retrospect, however, it appears that the passions arising from my poetic temperament led me to an overdramatic or hyperbolic use of language that distracted readers from my central argument.

In what follows, I review my convictions concerning the possible dangers inherent in close ties between consumer researchers and marketing managers. Specifically, I emphasize three aspects of business that appear to threaten consumer research and that I sometimes refer to as "the three bears."

Why Business Is Bad for Consumer Research

As mentioned previously, consumer researchers have too often put the cart before the horse by dwelling on the study of buying, as opposed to consuming. This point was emphasized long ago by Jack Jacoby (1978) when he lamented, "Most definitions of consumer behavior shackle us by confining attention to purchase. . . . Consumption must be given greater salience and be more tightly integrated with the existing consumer behavior" (p. 94). Similarly, Jagdish Sheth (1982) has also suggested that "we still need more research . . . in the non-decision-making domains of . . . consumption life styles . . . and consumption life cycle . . . and consumer satisfaction" (pp. 13-15).

As the reader will suspect, I concurred wholeheartedly at the time with Jacoby's and Sheth's conclusions. Furthermore, I would concede that, during the ensuing decade, thanks in part to their encouragement, the focus of our discipline has shifted a bit toward tempering the traditional decision-oriented view with an admixture of the experiential perspective recommended in the two previous chapters. However, despite some efforts toward integrating these potentially complementary ways of looking at consumption (Holbrook et al., 1990), consumer researchers have still not achieved an equitable balance.

More fundamentally, Jacoby and Sheth have adumbrated some key unanswered questions:

Why do such problems with consumer research exist?

Why have consumer researchers typically focused on purchase decisions while screening out consumption experiences?

Why have consumer researchers energetically pursued what is conceptually less important (buying) while ignoring what is conceptually more important (consuming)?

I believe that at least three factors related to the influence of business interests on consumer research—which I refer to affectionately as "the three bears"—threaten to misdirect our focus and thereby help account for what is wrong:

1. A basic misconception of the nature of business
2. Domination of consumer research by the managerial perspective
3. The distorting influence of executive teaching, business consulting, industrial partners, and corporate sponsorship

Each of these three bears, unleashed by the business community on the fledgling discipline of consumer research, deserves detailed scrutiny.

Bear #1: A Basic
Misconception of the Nature of Business

Roughly 90% of academics considering themselves consumer researchers come from business schools. This pervasiveness of the business orientation would present no major problem were it not for the tendency of people in business schools to subscribe to a basic misconception of the nature of business. In brief, too many of us think of the word *business* as synonymous with "profit-oriented corporate management." This view diverges from the truth, however, and introduces a serious bias into our research activities.

Businesses always involve interrelations between managers and customers. It follows that anyone seeking to understand business had better study the behavior of both managers and customers. Furthermore, no cogent reason appears to exist for claiming that one is more important than the other. Hence, researchers should study the behavior of managers and customers in roughly equal measure.

Yet, the curriculum of a typical business school lists courses devoted almost entirely to managerial behavior. In such areas as finance, accounting, business law, organizational behavior, industrial relations, management science, banking, and even corporate strategy, one seldom takes the behavior of customers explicitly into account. Even so-called marketing courses in advertising, sales, product management, or marketing planning often are preoccupied with the actions of business managers. Only a handful of courses in marketing strategy, market research, or buyer behavior maintain a consistent focus on the customer. And of those few available courses that do single out the consumer, most adopt a managerial perspective that asks, essentially, "How can businesspeople use consumers to make money?"

We might calculate, without fear of exaggeration, that the typical business school faculty member devotes over 99% of his or her attention to managers and less than 1% to consumers. This means that, collectively, those who work in business schools invest virtually all of their intellectual resources in studying only half of the problem. Hence, they misconstrue the central topic that they purport to investigate—namely, business. They scrutinize the behavior of managers down to the finest detail but pretty much ignore the consumers, who constitute the other half of business life.

Bear #2: Domination of Consumer Research by the Managerial Perspective

Second, even when we occasionally have dared to look directly at consumer behavior, most of our research efforts have aspired to some sort of managerial relevance. Specifically, consumer researchers have typically tried to cater directly to the interests of marketing managers, focusing on things that matter to managers, such as purchasing decisions, buying commitments, and brand choices. These phenomena happen in the stores, affect cash register activity at the checkout counter, show up in the UPC scanner data, affect the firm's bottom line, and therefore prove endlessly fascinating to anyone who embraces the managerial perspective. For example, as Geraldine Fennell (1982) correctly noted, "Marketing management's essential question is: What should we do to ensure that our brand is selected over competition?" (p. 8).

The potentially repressive effects of an inflated concern for managerial relevance occupies my attention at some length in Chapter 9. Here, however, I should mention an experience that occurred during the mid-1980s when I spoke to some colleagues in the Marketing Department at a major business school and urged the importance of studying consumption in general and its emotional aspects in particular. These marketing scholars saw little merit in my argument until I reluctantly added the consideration that emotional responses to a product might exert favorable feedback effects via purchase satisfaction to reinforce subsequent buying behavior. This insistence on relevance to brand choice reflects the managerial perspective with a vengeance. But the need to invoke it as support for my claims made me feel like a sellout.

In directing attention away from consumption phenomena and toward buying behavior, managerialism departs from scholarly concerns and moves toward the kind of crass commercialism lamented earlier. Managerialism rejects Sir Edmund Hillary's worthy reason for climbing a mountain ("because it's there") in favor of Willie Sutton's sordid rationale for robbing banks ("because that's where the money is").

I have observed among my colleagues and business contacts that those most ardently addicted to the managerial view often show a commensurate fascination with the sport of football. Accordingly, I have devised an analogy that speaks directly to these football fanciers in their own terms. Specifically, the extreme managerial perspective resembles a theory of football that focuses primarily on the kickoff. Someone holding such a view notes that the game begins with a kick. Hey, so the kickoff must be really important. Then some things happen on the field that we don't care about very much. Then, if all goes well, we get another kickoff. And so we proceed—from one kickoff to the next.

Similarly, managerialists might note that the buyer begins by making a trial purchase. This purchase "kicks off" some other things that happen (consumption experiences) that do not interest managerialists very much (daydreams, emotional responses, aesthetic appreciation). Then, if all goes well, we get a repeat purchase—that is, another kickoff for a subsequent round of consumption activities. And so, as before, we proceed from one purchase to the next.

This view constitutes a terrible theory of football but an even worse theory of consumer behavior. Indeed, researchers will never fully understand consumer behavior until they escape from the misleading sway of the managerial perspective. This perspective channels attention toward only those aspects of consumer behavior that affect the firm's market share—the effect of advertising dollars on brand loyalty, the impact of promotional expenditures on sales volume, and the role of prices in determining market demand. Yet, most consumption activities would deserve study even if they exerted no impact at all on business profitability.

Think about it.

As noted earlier, people get up in the morning, start consuming the moment their toes touch the carpet, allocate their time to various consumption activities throughout the day, and continue consuming until they finally drift off to sleep at night, after which they confine their consumption mostly to dreams, pajamas, and bed linens. In short, daily living consists mostly of consumption experiences. Such experiences determine people's happiness, their well-being, their quality of life. Clearly, they merit investigation even where they are of no particular interest to business managers. By comparison—face it—the managerial perspective is restrictive, one-sided, and incomplete.

> Bear #3: The Distorting Influence of Executive Teaching,
> Business Consulting, Industrial Partners, and Corporate Sponsorship

Third, business interests sometimes mislead by masquerading as an ally to the study of consumption. Here, they act as a sort of wolf- or (to preserve my metaphor) bear-in-sheep's-clothing. I refer to the many cases in which essentially management-targeted academic activities are touted on the basis of their claimed potential payoff in research opportunities. Variants that I have personally observed on innumerable occasions include the following:

1. Consumer researchers should engage in *executive teaching* to help get "tuned in" to the important issues of consumer research.
2. Consumer researchers should do *business consulting* to obtain data leading to publishable findings on real-world consumer problems.
3. Consumer researchers should seek *industrial partners* to provide funding for joint work on consumer-related issues.
4. Consumer researchers should solicit *corporate sponsorship* to support worthwhile scholarly activities.

These four arguments ring through business schools so constantly that many people may not have given them careful scrutiny. Let us therefore examine each of these time-honored but potentially distorting influences.

Executive Teaching and the Spirit of Anti-Intellectualism. For many years— roughly from 1975 to 1990—I followed the example of my colleagues and mentors on the business faculty by engaging in a certain amount of executive teaching in my school's management-training programs. One incentive that sustained my efforts in the executive classroom came from continued assurances by my senior colleagues that this experience would help me uncover insights into potentially fruitful areas of consumer research. After giving this promise every possible chance to reach fulfillment, I can now attest that it appears fundamentally incorrect. My labors in the vineyards of management training have left me highly skeptical that this activity leads to important new directions for consumer research.

More than a half-century ago, in a prophetic book called *The Higher Learning in America*, that curmudgeonly genius Thorstein Veblen (1918/ 1954) developed a merciless caricature of what he saw as the business-person's inveterate anti-intellectualism: "The businessmen of this country, as a class, are of a notably conservative habit of mind. . . . The spirit of American business is a spirit of quietism, caution, compromise, collusion, and chicane[ry]" (pp. 69-70). Veblen's querulous tone does not necessarily negate the validity of his observations. He saw business executives as the avatars of conformity and self-interest, in whose cost-benefit analyses of mental exertion intellectual curiosity loses every time:

> Now, in that hard and fast body of aphoristic wisdom that commands the faith of the business community there is comprised the conviction that learning is of no use in business. This conviction is, further, backed up and coloured with the tenet . . . that what is of no use in business is not worth while. (p. 73)

Indeed, business executives tend to approach training programs with a resolute bias against scholarship and science. For them, *academic, theoretical, conceptual,* and *intellectual curiosity* are words of opprobrium. Until recently, this attitude had mercifully failed to penetrate the ivied walls of the university classroom. But during the early 1990s, the tide may have begun to turn. Recently, two former undergraduate accounting majors from Wharton who had moved to my school for their MBAs informed me that my class on consumer research was so "theoretical" that neither it nor I belonged in a business school. This perspective suggests that, in an age of recession with its resulting underemployment of the post-baby-boomers, the business-person's conventional mind-set might prove dangerously portable. Veblen, of course, anticipated all this:

> The technologist and the professional man are, like other men of affairs, necessarily and habitually impatient of any scientific or scholarly work that does not obviously lend itself to some practical use. . . . And the two unite with the business-man at large in repudiating whatever does not look directly to such a utilitarian outcome. (1918/1954, p. 30)

Thus, from Veblen's righteous viewpoint, "the training that comes of experience in business must . . . be held to unfit men for scholarly and scientific pursuits" (pp. 75-76).

Similarly, in his judicious study *The Academic Ethic*, Edward Shils (1983), from the University of Chicago, contends, "The charge that universities are ivory towers has been . . . made from the . . . standpoint of the 'practical man,' usually the businessman, who could not see the point of intellectual activities which did not show a profit or which did not contribute directly to industrial and agricultural production" (p. 17). Given this attitude, it follows that anything of a scholarly or scientific nature presented to business executives must be sugar-coated and disguised as knowledge that is practical in an immediately gratifying way. This happens despite a recognition that "It is not an obligation of a teacher to please his students; the attempt to please the students often gives rise to supine and degrading flattery without intellectual substance" (Shils, 1983, p. 46).

The viewpoint that typifies the marketing practitioner receives its quintessential statement in a letter that I received during the mid-1980s from a top executive at one of the major packaged goods companies: "If the graduates I have seen from virtually all business schools do have a shortcoming, it's their lack of understanding that success in business requires more than thinking. . . . It requires action." Such an easy dissociation between thought and action manages to imply that somehow the latter can and should exist without the former. This disturbing impression gains reinforcement from *Usable Knowledge*, a book by Lindblom and Cohen (1979), who suggest that, as a problem-solving technique, thinking may have its limits:

> Our interest is in . . . an alternative to understanding, thought, or analysis. . . .
> Tossing a coin is . . . a simple form of action rather than thought. It reaches an outcome. It solves the problem. . . . And it may do so faster, no more fallibly, and no less efficiently than can an analyzed solution. (p. 21)
> . . . If coin tossing can produce an answer to a practical problem, so can reading the entrails of fowls. (p. 24)

As a symptom of what happens when usability serves as the standard for knowledge and when practicality substitutes for understanding, this statement speaks for itself.

Business Consulting and the Abandonment of Joy. Those who argue for linkages between consumer researchers and marketing managers frequently ex-
tol the benefits from engaging in various forms of business consulting (which
for our purposes also includes comparable work for government agencies,
lawyers, or various nonprofit institutions). For example, Jack Jacoby (1985b)
mentions that consulting activities may extend our thinking, may influence
other scholars, may prompt additional studies, may help disseminate knowledge, may shape a framework in which to test new ideas, may provide data
otherwise unobtainable, and—in general—may expand our intellectual
horizons in countless ways. No doubt Jacoby himself has benefited from these
advantages and has turned them to good purpose in his own work and teaching, but I do not believe that others can reasonably hope to be so fortunate.

The reason for my skepticism arises from the fact that the typical consulting climate differs from the atmosphere needed to foster dedicated scholarship or scientific commitment. These differences include divergences in time
perspective (short- vs. long-run), objectives (profit-oriented vs. intellectual), commitment (shifting vs. enduring), interpersonal relations (hierar-
chical vs. egalitarian), and concern for privacy (secret vs. public).

Thus, Hyde (1983) distinguishes between *work* (time-pressured, paid, and
determined from outside) and *labor* (self-paced, unpaid, and guided from
within). Hyde draws on Hagstrom's (1965) analysis of scientific research as
a form of gift giving wherein the scientist contributes new knowledge in return for scholarly recognition as opposed to money: "Manuscripts for which
the scientific authors do receive financial payments such as textbooks and
popularizations, are . . . held in much lower esteem than articles containing
original research results" (Hagstrom, 1965, p. 13).

True, even devout scholars must feed and clothe their families, and consulting may put food on the table. In this connection, most universities
(mine included) have adopted formal policies permitting such consulting activities, provided they do not divert too much faculty time—say, no more
than 1 day a week (Goodell, 1968, p. 33). Notice, however, that if teaching
takes 2 days and other administrative duties 1 day a week, then consultants
who follow such guidelines spend at least half of their available research time
on outside consulting work.

From the perspective adopted here, consulting betrays the spirit of consumer research by converting a potential scientific gift into a marketable

commodity. Under a consulting relationship, knowledge becomes property. Thus, when he was president of Yale University, A. Bartlett Giamatti (1983) made this distinction quite explicitly: "The basic difference between universities and industries [is]. . . the academic imperative to seek knowledge objectively and to share it openly and freely; and the industrial imperative to garner a profit, which frequently creates the incentive to treat knowledge as private property" (p. 5).

This proprietary status of consulting constantly tempts executives to enshroud such information beneath a veil of secrecy. Virtually everyone agrees, however, that "secrecy conflicts . . . with the norms of free communication in science" (Hagstrom, 1965, p. 88). For Shils (1983),

> The obligation to knowledge is met through . . . "open" publication; secrecy is alien to the . . . university. . . . The general obligation is to undertake research which is publishable. . . . If all of the results of the scientist's research emerging from the particular project are to be kept secret, then he should not seek to do that kind of research in his capacity as a member of a university. (pp. 43, 60-61)

In academic circles, stories circulate about researchers prevented from publishing potentially important findings because of their proprietary nature. In consulting relationships, questions arise about whether to keep research secret lest competitors use proprietary findings to their own advantage. But the need for secrecy looms large only when research is *extrinsically motivated* (as a means to solving managerial problems). By contrast, I believe that consumer research prospers best when it is *intrinsically motivated* (pursued for its own sake).

If consumer research offers intrinsic value (as an end in itself), no one should object to publishing it because it should serve no particular managerial purpose. Hassles over secrecy, therefore, signal the presence of utilitarian or banausic, as opposed to scientific or scholarly, value in a piece of consumer research. Hence, consumer researchers should not be rallying for the right to *publish* research that has *practical value* to competitors; rather, they should be fighting for the freedom to *conduct* research that has *no practical use* to any marketing manager.

But why, the reader might wonder, do I come down so strongly on the side of basic, pure, enlightened science, as opposed to applied, practical, engineered technology? The reason, quite simply, is that I believe—rather passionately—that the former leads more directly to the advancement of knowledge in consumer research (as it does in most other scientific and scholarly pursuits). Whether readers agree with other assertions I make will largely depend on whether they buy this particular premise.

In distinguishing between science and technology, Michael Polanyi (1958) describes "a gap . . . between two kinds of knowledge . . . one derived from an acknowledged purpose, the other unrelated to any such purpose" (p. 175). Similarly, Veblen (1918/1954) distinguished between "material expediency" and "idle curiosity" (p. 27). Thus, the distinction between consumer research and consulting simply mirrors the more general contrast between "pure science" and "applied research" (Brooks, 1978, p. 182) or between "knowledge for its own sake" and "social usefulness" (Holton, 1978, p. 232).

To probe the advantages of basic science or pure scholarship over applied research, it helps to review some relevant facets in the development of the American university. As portrayed by Derek Bok (1982), then president of Harvard, this academic institution has emerged from a combination of three intellectual streams: first, the British emphasis on the moral preparation of gentlemen; second, the German research orientation; and third, the Yankee ideal of usefulness and pragmatism. Clark Kerr (1982, p. 9), the former head of Berkeley, traced British or humanist traditions back to Plato's Academy ("devoted to truth largely for its own sake"), the German or scientific traditions to the Pythagoreans ("concerned, among other things, with mathematics and astronomy"), and the Yankee or professional traditions to the Sophists ("who taught rhetoric and other useful skills").

Hence, on the university campus, the clash in consumer research between pure and applied studies reflects a broader contrast between the Germanic scientific ideal versus the American pragmatism:

> In one view, . . . inquiry should be allowed to push against any of the frontiers of knowledge, and not merely along that border where material benefits were promised. . . . In the second view, research was a public service that originated in a client's need and ended in a client's satisfaction. (Metzger, 1955, pp. 107-108)

Obviously, the three orientations just described—British, German, and Yankee—present a choice of goals that every researcher working within the university must face. It would be presumptuous of me to prescribe a set of values for others. Indeed, I am totally committed to the pluralistic ideal of encouraging each consumer researcher to adopt whatever approach feels most comfortable (Hirschman & Holbrook, 1992). But, just as obviously, it would be hypocritical to hide my own values behind a veil of relativism. Hence, I concede without apology that I personally favor the British-Platonic-scholarly and German-Pythagorean-scientific ideal, also sometimes referred to as *Wissenschaft* (Kerr, 1982, p. 4): "The very notion of *Wissenschaft* . . . signified a dedicated, sanctified pursuit . . . not the study of things for their immediate utilities, but the morally imperative study of things for themselves and for their ultimate meanings" (Metzger, 1955, p. 99). This tradition of Wissenschaft takes *disinterested inquiry*—that is, study motivated by intellectual curiosity, rather than by material gain—as a kind of sacred trust. It asks not what knowledge can do for me, but rather what I can do for knowledge. In other words, this tradition prizes knowledge as "its own reward" (Kerr, 1982, p. 3), "for its own sake" (Low, 1983, p. 69), with "a value in itself, apart from any use to which it is put" (Shils, 1983, p. 3).

Because of its intrinsically motivated nature, the pursuit of science and scholarship for their own sakes entails a type of value closely associated with *play*. Like leisure pursuits, "Research is in many ways a kind of game, a puzzle-solving operation in which the solution of the puzzle is its own reward" (Hagstrom, 1965, p. 16). Via imaginative acts, "mathematics creates the objects of its own discourse . . . in the very course of playing the game" (Polanyi, 1958, p. 186).

Analogies between science and play resemble those between research and artistic creativity, as in Bronowski's (1965) insistence that "there is a likeness between the creative acts of the mind in art and in science" (p. 7):

> In science and in the arts the sense of freedom which the creative man feels in his work derives from what I have earlier called the poetic element in it: the uninhibited activity of exploring the medium for its own sake, and discovering as if in play what can be done with it. . . . Pure science is (like art) a form of play. (p. 76)

Max Weber (1919/1946) spoke of science in terms of this "*inward* calling," "strange intoxication," "passion," "enthusiasm," "inspiration," "frenzy," and "passionate devotion" (pp. 134-136). Similarly, Metzger (1955) proclaimed "the passion for truth" (p. 92), whereas Broad and Wade (1982) averred that "researchers believe passionately in their work" (p. 216).

Where does this passion come from? One answer often voiced by dedicated scientists themselves is: *joy.* Thus, for example, Polanyi (1958) attributes the crucial energizing element to "the overwhelming elation felt by scientists at the moment of discovery" (p. 134). In other words, what sustains scientists and scholars is neither the money they earn nor the fame they gain, but the occasional sense of joyous discovery—that rare moment of fulfillment that somehow manages to make everything else seem worthwhile.

References to the intrinsically motivated, playful aspects of scientific activity run rampant in the stories told by various contributors to the volume *The Joys of Research* (Shropshire, 1981), reaching perhaps their most deeply felt expression when the biophysicist Rosalyn Yalow (1981) evokes an excitement bordering on ecstasy or rapture: "I'm a scientist because even at this stage I love investigation. Even after the Nobel Prize, the biggest thrill is to go to my laboratory and hope that that day I will know something nobody ever knew before" (p. 115).

Could anyone abjure this dream of joyous discovery in order to chase the banausic benefits stemming from pragmatic usefulness? Could anyone reject pure knowledge sought for its own sake and argue instead for the comparative merits of practitioner-oriented consulting?

You bet.

Many people wear the hats of business executives, marketing managers, and academic consultants. Collectively, such folks criticize pure research for its lack of relevance to real-world problems, echoing the familiar complaint to the effect that "basic scientific research has [too often] been conducted as an end in itself, with the result that the practical aspects that could be of great benefit to the public have been obscured or lost" (Hutt, 1978, p. 160). In *Usable Knowledge*, Lindblom and Cohen (1979) articulate the same view:

> In some preliminary studies, we have interrogated willing social scientists on their rationales for project choice. The justification of their projects appeals not to developed knowledge of how or when social science is or is not useful, but simply to judgments about the "importance" of the problem to be studied. . . . Judgment about the importance of a problem is a naive and wholly indefensible guide to research priorities. (pp. 87-88)

Many universities and, within them, virtually all schools of business have bought this type of utilitarian argument hook, line, and sinker. For example, Ben-David (1972) describes this pragmatic influence as follows: "The

contemporary idea of . . . applied research arose at the American universities
. . . because there was . . . an actual or potential demand for services in some
vaguely and unscientifically defined field of interest (such as . . . business
management)" (pp. 101-102). This perspective reflects the Yankee tradition
of vocational education evinced by Benjamin Franklin when he tried to
dedicate the University of Pennsylvania to "a *more useful* culture of young
minds" (quoted by Kerr, 1982, p. 12).

That Yankee spirit survives and repeatedly puts those who support the
pursuit of knowledge for its own sake on the defensive by favoring the esca-
lation of marketing consultancy in consumer research. Indeed, the elevation
of practical relevance above knowledge as an end in itself constitutes the
apotheosis of Yankee know-how.

The intellectual heirs of Yankee practicality who engage so enthusiastically in consulting activities have every right to do their own work as they
see fit. But in my view, their rights stop short of forcing their pragmatic perspective on others, as they have so often tried to do by imposing the standard
of Yankee utility on those of us who prefer to answer a call to more basic, less
applied consumer research.

In challenging the Yankee ethos, I lean toward what Bok (1982) labeled
the claims of the "traditionalists" that "many professors spend too much of
their time consulting with corporations or advising government officials on
specific policy issues" (p. 68). Along these traditionalist lines, Giamatti
(1983) asserted that "the constant challenge for the university is to know in
clear and principled terms how to cherish learning, and its pursuit" (p. 9).
Hagstrom (1965) favored "the elaboration of theories that are of no use
whatever in daily life" (p. 9). Shils (1983) ruled out usefulness as a proper
academic incentive and regarded consulting activities askance:

> The prospective "users" of knowledge . . . invite academics to do research
> designed for immediate practical use, alongside or instead of concentrating on
> the advancement of fundamental knowledge. . . . It is not that all these services
> are . . . despicable. . . . Nevertheless, they extend the nonintellectual pre-
> occupations of the university and they are distractions from its central respon-
> sibilities for teaching and discovery. (pp. 18-20)

Putting the case in its strongest terms, Giamatti concluded that "when a
professor decides to take substantial . . . managerial responsibility for the
success of a company, he likely would best serve the university by relin-

quishing tenure and assuming adjunct status" ("Corporate/University Ties," 1983, p. 32).

Long ago, Veblen (1918/1954) had made a very similar point in two very different ways—the first nice, the second nasty. First—in words that anticipated the reasonable arguments of Bok, Hagstrom, Shils, and Giamatti— Veblen said: "A university is an endowed institution of culture. . . . This work has no business value. . . . Indeed, it is a fairly safe test; work that has a commercial value does not belong in the university" (p. 151). Second—in a way that captured some sense of his righteous passion—he also said:

> Intimate association with . . . "utilitarians" unavoidably has its corrupting effect on the scientists and scholars, and induces in them also something of the same bias toward "practical" results in their own work. . . . The university of medieval and early modern times, that is to say the barbarian university, was necessarily given over to the pragmatic, utilitarian disciplines, since that is the nature of barbarism. . . . The barbarian culture is pragmatic, utilitarian, worldly wise, and its learning partakes of the same complexion. The barbarian, late or early, is typically an unmitigated pragmatist. (pp. 31-34)

Industrial Partners and the Forfeit of Academic Freedom. Another oft-heard argument on behalf of consumer researchers forming closer ties with marketing managers stems from the claim that industrial partners would provide funding for cooperative endeavors. Those holding this view assume that their mutual interest in learning more about the customer will channel money from industrial partners in directions that will lead to a growth in knowledge. However, in my view (one not widely shared by others in the business school community), such industrial partnerships place an unacceptable strain on academic freedom.

I must begin with a few words on behalf of academic freedom and on the importance of unfettered free inquiry in general and in the conduct of consumer research in particular. The literature on academic freedom suggests that we as teachers should never make the mistake of taking intellectual liberty for granted. Thus, Hofstadter (1955) and Metzger (1955)—chronicling the slow, arduous, and often painful development of academic freedom in the American university—clearly indicate that, like democracy, intellectual liberty requires vigilant protection.

American educators, it appears, believe that intellectual liberty is a fundamental requirement for science and scholarship. They do not believe that liberty is sort of nice but that it is okay to sell oneself into intellectual slavery if one wishes. They believe that freedom is the sine qua non. Period.

And they say so at every opportunity.

Yet, unfortunately, proclaiming the virtues of free inquiry does not necessarily safeguard its attainment or guarantee its achievement. Free inquiry exists only where the course of research reflects impulses arising from within the university, as opposed to forces exerted from outside. As several contributors to *Limits of Scientific Inquiry* (Holton & Morison, 1978) made clear, certain restrictions on academic freedom must be set where harmful externalities threaten the welfare of uninformed subjects, innocent bystanders, or the general society. One must regulate research on nuclear reactors, for example, if they are liable to blow up a major city or on genetic engineering if it runs the risk of unleashing a dangerous mutation. But Nelkin (1978) argues convincingly that the idea of free inquiry must be jealously guarded by the continual efforts of scientists and scholars to oppose external pressures through perpetual negotiations in which they resist all forms of external control. Thus, as suggested by Brooks (1978), scientists and scholars must know where they stand in the perennial conflict between internal imperatives (the "best science") and external pressures ("less good science") in setting research priorities.

Most academic researchers have reacted with undisguised horror to any perceived threats to their academic freedom, regarding intellectual liberty as a nonnegotiable precondition for the advancement of knowledge:

> In science, there is no substitute for independence. . . . Dissent is the native activity of the scientist. . . . Dissent is not itself an end; it . . . is the mark of freedom. . . . No one can be a scientist, even in private, if he does not have independence of observation and of thought. (Bronowski, 1965, pp. 61-62)

Furthermore, academic administrators have stood united in their determination to guard the sacred status of academic freedom (Giamatti, 1983; Low, 1983). Bok (1982) declared that the "critical element is an environment of freedom in which professors can do their work without constraints or external direction" and abhorred any "imposition of restraints on the kinds of ideas and hypotheses that scholars can publicly entertain" (pp. 19-20).

But despite all of these good intentions, various threats to academic freedom have arisen with disturbing regularity. Most recently, as federal funding began to dry up during the Reagan years, universities looked elsewhere for financial support so that industrial partnerships came to play a larger role than ever before, particularly in such areas of innovative technology as genetic engineering and computer sciences. Hence, as widely reported by such concerned publications as *Chemical and Engineering News* ("Corporate/University Ties," 1983; "Kennedy," 1982; "University/Industry Ties," 1982), the relationship between industry and academia in joint ventures and cooperative research emerged as a threat to academic freedom. Some critics expressed a concern that "as the ties between universities and industries grow increasingly closer, a balance must be struck between the intellectual independence of the scientist [in] the university and the industrial desire for commercial opportunity" (Gore, 1983, p. 125). Such concerns were greatly exacerbated by the rather aggressive attitude displayed by some industrial partners and voiced rather blatantly by Thomas Kiley (1983) of Genentech: "Make no mistake about it: for-profit corporations are, by definition, not in business to give away money. Where they provide money for research, they invariably do so in order to gain competitive advantage" (p. 63).

Faced with this set of issues with respect to industrial-academic partnerships, university presidents voiced their concern. Loudly. For example, a conference held at Pajaro Dunes and attended by the presidents of Harvard, Stanford, MIT, Cal Tech, and the University of California (Rosenzweig, 1983) pondered the ties between business and academia: "Attractive as these relationships are, they present a host of problems. The most important of these . . . is the potential distortion such relationships may cause to academic objectives" ("University/Industry Ties," 1982, p. 4). Several of these presidents acknowledged a fear that "as the university moves closer to a partnership with industry, . . . the university inevitably relinquishes some of its unique capabilities for unrestricted exploratory research and freedom of action" (Fusfeld, 1983, p. 18). In the words of the old aphorism, "He who pays the piper calls the tune." Indeed, this truism was captured humorously in a limerick quoted by Kerr (1982, p. 69):

> There was a young lady from Kent
> Who said that she knew what it meant
> When men took her to dine,
> Gave her cocktails and wine;
> She knew what it meant—but she went.

Perhaps most saliently, in his book *Beyond the Ivory Tower*, Bok (1982) presented the troublesome issues raised by industrial partnerships: "Few people

would welcome a situation in which academic scientists did not simply consider which potential problems for research were most intellectually challenging and important but were influenced by powerful extraneous factors,
such as the prospect of large financial rewards" (p. 149). Yes, we can almost
hear old Thorstein Veblen saying, "I told you so." Veblen (1918/1954) could
find no words adequate to expressing the horror with which he regarded the
subservience of scholarly and scientific objectives to business interests: "If
. . . business principles were quite free to work out their logical consequences
. . ., the outcome [w]ould be to put the pursuit of knowledge definitely in
abeyance within the university, and to substitute for that objective something for which the language hitherto lacks a designation" (pp. 170-171).
For our purposes, the key question is what this unnameable threat implies for
the conduct of consumer research. As I argued in the mid-1980s and would
argue all the more vehemently today, industrial partnerships potentially pose
dangers to consumer research even more serious than the commentaries by university administrators have acknowledged. But these threats have been resolutely
ignored in accordance with what I call the "business school blind spot."

Corporate Sponsorship and the Business School Blind Spot. Although university
presidents have agonized over the potential problems posed by industrial
partnerships, business school deans and marketing professors have remained
remarkably untroubled by these potential dangers. Indeed, to anyone concerned about the cause of academic freedom, the lack of interest in such
issues displayed by the faculties of business schools appears nothing short of
astonishing. One never hears of a business school administration expressing
concern because its faculty members spend too much of their time on executive teaching, consulting, industry-funded grants, or other corporation-
sponsored research. It never seems to occur to anyone that the possible
biases resulting from corporate sponsorship might affect research conducted
in a business school or might distort research priorities. Business schools
have adopted a simple, tacit rule for dealing with these dangers: No one
notices.

Might such a bias or distortion beset corporate-sponsored consumer research conducted by marketing professors? The answer, I believe, is deci-
sively yes. It might. Although I do not have definitive proof that such
distortions have commonly occurred, I suggest that business school communities should at least show some concern for this potential problem. They
should at least ask whether intellectual integrity in research is threatened by

letting industry pay for it. They should at least wonder whether academic freedom is compromised by permitting practitioners to shape the directions for inquiry. And consumer researchers should at least reflect on whether they might be restricted by confining their attention to issues that happen to interest marketing managers. They should at least think about the possible connection between accepting money from industry and warping their intellectual priorities as consumer researchers.

As one salient example, if I am correct in arguing that consumer researchers have emphasized the importance of (managerially relevant) buying decisions at the expense of neglecting the role of (phenomenologically significant) consumption experiences, then one need not wonder whether corporate sponsorship might distort research priorities. It already has done exactly that.

With the general growth of industrial partnerships in the university community, members of other disciplines have found out what happens when they let profit-oriented corporate managers intrude into the research process. And they do not like it. As soon as business sidles up to science, one hears complaints from researchers about interference with their intellectual integrity. Yet, in my experience, one seldom hears such complaints voiced in the context of business schools. Apparently, like fish in water, we have so long been submerged under the influence of business sponsorship that we do not even notice it anymore. The good news about living underwater is that the water disappears. The bad news is that we drown.

As Edward R. Murrow pointed out, "The obscure we see eventually, the completely apparent takes longer" (quoted by Ray & Myers, 1986, p. 65). In my view, the way business interests exert their power to distort consumer research is most insidious precisely because no one seems to notice that this power exists. In particular, I fear that a corporate sponsor's apparent hands-off posture may lull the consumer researcher into a false sense of academic freedom. As Hofstadter (1955) insisted long ago, an undetected interference with free inquiry is the most threatening of all.

If members of other disciplines worry so much about the intrusion of business into their research, why do consumer researchers not share this concern? Some might reply that, because business schools study business, it is acceptable for their research directions to be guided by business interests. But I find this logic unpersuasive. Ichthyologists study fish, but we do not recommend to them that they should set their research agendas by asking the advice of sharks.

Others might argue that there is nothing wrong with being reasonably flexible and bending research interests a little to suit the needs of business sponsors. But very quickly, "bent" becomes "biased"; "biased" becomes "distorted"; and "distorted" becomes "warped." Can those who try to address managerially relevant aspects of consumer behavior assert truthfully that business interests play no role in shaping their choice of topics? And if such influences do occur, can they sincerely claim the advantages of intellectual liberty?

As I contemplate this danger, I feel like a character from an old horror movie who sees the monster coming and who screams a warning but who is ignored. During the past decade, many have listened, but just as many have turned a deaf ear.

Thus, consumer researchers swim in the tide of corporate sponsorship without really noticing the ebb and flow of the invisible currents that steer them. But occasionally, as in *Jaws*, some otherwise unseen dark force lunges to the surface where it can be regarded with due terror. For example, I recall a meeting in which the representative of a large computer manufacturer offered to lend personal computers to the members of our Marketing Division (in hopes that we would, in turn, influence our students to prefer that brand of equipment), but only if we would promise to provide certain "deliverables," such as marketable software that the company could sell for profit (just one of numerous shortsighted strategies that have since plunged that particular company into deep financial difficulty).

I recall as well a dismal session with members of a giant food conglomerate (since acquired in a corporate takeover) in which sponsorship of consumer research that cut across product lines received the cold shoulder because it extended beyond the bounds of any one division's accountability (so that no one brand manager would be able to claim credit).

Finally, I recall an admission by the director of a major research-funding institute that the relevant corporate donors want "marketing relevant" research and that work on such aspects of consumer behavior as the ethics of irregular, irrational, illegal, or immoral consumption would not interest them.

This last experience proved prophetic. Several years later, I participated in a conference on advertising, sponsored by the Marketing Science Institute (MSI) and attended by many researchers and managers from industry:

> The question of whether anyone wanted to focus on issues of social responsibility was raised. If the mass audience is having their emotions manipulated,

it tends to raise questions of societal impacts. . . . In general, there was relatively little interest among the group members in studying the societal effects of emotional advertising. (Holbrook, 1991a, p. 50)

This amoral stance appears to characterize MSI, which seems to feel no hesitation in publicizing its attitude. Thus does the business perspective blind itself to the distorting nature of its own effects.

The fact that the attempts of those in business to steer consumer research are usually subtle, well intentioned, and friendly only makes them more dangerous. For example, I once participated on a committee charged with developing proposals for research on consumer durables to be funded by several sponsoring corporations represented by various committee members. As a basis for encouraging the development of research ideas, one member (who worked for a major retailing chain) suggested the following definition of *consumer durables:* "an infrequently purchased product (or major component of a product) which is not changed in size, shape, or content by normal use and requires an outside or self-contained source of power in order to function." This definition contains some obvious logical flaws and inconsistencies. First, some durables may be frequently purchased (e.g., books, recordings), whereas some nondurables may be bought infrequently (e.g., caviar, snails). Second, durables may change their size or shape during consumption (e.g., houseplants, mobile sculptures, model airplanes). Third, some durables fail to require an external or internal source of power (e.g., furniture, works of art). In short, the proposed definition clearly fails to describe consumer durables. What it does describe, beyond doubt, is household appliances. Hence and most problematic, the proposed definition stemmed from a perspective that implicitly guided research toward issues of particular concern to the spokesperson from appliance retailing. The definition therefore attempted to steer science toward pursuing company-oriented ends. And it did so in a way hidden from the academic researchers whose work might have been directed by its distorting influence.

Denouement: The Three Bears Return

From all of these considerations, it follows that consumer researchers should refrain from selling their energies to the highest corporate bidders. They should instead stubbornly pursue those aspects of consumer behavior that they find interesting as ends in themselves. In short, they should insist on maintaining their right to intellectual liberty and academic freedom.

Some might argue that, because it neglects the grim realities of funding in academic institutions, my position is impractical. To these critics, I reply: Hallelujah. I certainly hope that I am being not only impractical but also nonfunctional, antibanausic, and useless. Otherwise, how could I insist on the merits of intrinsically motivated inquiry? How could I suggest that consumer research should be a playful, creative activity?

In short, I suggest that consumer researchers should react with dismay to any attempt by marketing practitioners or other business executives to set their research priorities. In the story of my "three bears," I have implicitly identified the role of pure consumer research with that of the sweet and fair-haired Goldilocks. Unfortunately, my version of this fable, intended as a warning against what I regard as pernicious pressures to achieve managerial relevance in research on consumer behavior, lacks the happy ending that we heard as children, in which Goldilocks escapes and the bears never see her again (Lothrop, Lee & Shepard Books, 1982). My version culminates in a more frightening but more realistic denouement: "When the bears returned to the cottage from their day in the woods, they found Goldilocks peacefully asleep. . . . They immediately did what any self-respecting bears would do. They killed her on the spot" (Holbrook, 1985b, p. 154).

❑ Consequences

Consumer Research Reconsidered

A year after the debate just described, Beth Hirschman and I organized another special topic session for the 1985 conference of the Association for Consumer Research, entitled "Whither ACR?" In serving as conference chairman, Rich Lutz (1985) had provided the central topic for the session when he issued a call for papers that revived the debate concerning the managerial relevance of consumer research and that suggested members of ACR should move in the "direction" of "more systematic attention" to "the effects of marketing activities on consumers" (p. 5).

As indicated in the preceding sections, I could not disagree more strongly with this claim by Lutz. Given the stature of Lutz in the profession, his clarion "call for papers" trumpeted one more victory for those favoring the cause of managerial relevance and signaled one more setback for those concerned with arguing on behalf of basic consumer research pursued for its own sake.

I therefore aimed my paper for the special ACR session at the doctrine of managerial relevance as revived by Lutz (1985). But I had learned the previous year that speaking my mind directly would only get me into trouble; hence, I went underground—or, more precisely, underwater. I disguised the thrust of my message in a way that still allowed me to pursue my thoughts on the threat to consumer research from the ethos of managerial relevance. In short, I broke from the conventions of discourse in our field by drawing on the tradition of pastoral elegy (Holbrook, 1986f). Specifically, as a frame for my comments on "Whither ACR?" I drew on John Milton's *Lycidas* (1637/ 1957).

> Yet once more, O ye laurels, and once more,
> Ye myrtles brown, with ivy never sere,
> I come to pluck your berries harsh and crude,
> And with forced fingers rude
> Shatter your leaves before the mellowing year.
> Bitter constraint, and sad occasion dear,
> Compels me to disturb your season due. (ll. 1-7)

Lycidas Is Dead

In short, to convey how I feel about managerial relevance, I drew on a mournful story, but one that has a hopeful resolution, in which the poet "bewails a learned Friend, unfortunately drowned . . . on the Irish Seas."

> For Lycidas is dead, dead ere his prime,
> Young Lycidas, and hath not left his peer.
> Who would not sing for Lycidas? He knew
> himself to sing, and build the lofty rhyme.
> He must not float upon his watery bier
> Unwept, and welter to the parching wind,
> Without the meed of some melodious tear. (ll. 6-14)

I took Lycidas as my symbol for the potential premature demise of consumer research—Lycidas, the marvelous shepherd boy who has "sunk . . . beneath the watery floor" (l. 167). This oceanic image recalls my earlier comparison of commercialization and overzealous managerial relevance to swimming like a fish in water. Furthermore, Milton's poem contains plentiful water-and-light, sea-and-sun imagery. In this spirit, I recall a story about the sun—in this case, the *Baltimore Sun,* that town's daily newspaper—that my mother-in-law used to tell when remembering a friend named Miss Lee.

Hattie Pays for the Baltimore Sun

Once upon a time, Miss Lee moved from her home on a plantation near Charlottesville to the city of Baltimore. Miss Lee had grown up in patrician luxury, surrounded by crops, servants, and the good things in life. In her later years, she moved with her devoted housekeeper, Hattie, to a small apartment near her doctor in the big city. Miss Lee enjoyed the cultural stimulation of the urban environment, but Hattie found it more difficult to adapt. Finally, one day, the newspaper boy's asking to be paid for delivery of the paper pushed Hattie over the edge. She came bursting into Miss Lee's bedroom in tears and cried:

> O, Miss Lee, I can't stand it no more. Back home, when I needed eggs, I just went to the hen house and grabbed up a few; now I need to place an order with the poultry man and wait 2 days. Back home, when I wanted milk, I could just go out to the barn and get me some from the cow; now I have to call the dairy company and pay them to come and bring it. Back home, when I had to fix vegetables for supper, I could just go out to the garden and pull some up right out of the ground; now I have to carry a shopping basket and a pocketbook full of money all the way down to the grocery store. And now—Lord, Lord— there's a boy down there at the front door who says he's here to collect for the sun.

At one level, Hattie failed to recognize that the sun in question was a newspaper and not the big star in our solar system. But, at a much more profound level, Hattie had intuitively grasped one key issue better than do many consumer researchers. Hattie understood, metaphorically, that consumers want to enjoy the sunshine and that marketers want to collect for the sun; that is, consumers want to consume and marketers want to charge them money for their consumption experiences. In other words, Hattie sensed the contrast that underlies the fundamental difference between marketing and consumer research.

As Hattie grasped, the consumer's perspective centers in consumption experiences; presumably, consumer research should reflect those interests.

By contrast, marketing research reflects the marketing manager's concern for buying decisions. Hence, consumer research and marketing research differ fundamentally in orientation.

I like marketing. If I did not, I could not have stood up and taught it for a living. I want the companies whose stocks I own to practice good marketing management and to make lots of money. I want my students to go out and become good marketers, to succeed on the job, to thrive, and to prosper. So I have spent many of my waking hours thinking about marketing, trying to teach MBAs what I know about the formulation of marketing strategy, and contemplating the solution of marketing problems. But although I deeply believe that marketing is worthwhile, I must admit that many of us in marketing are in the position of trying to collect for the sun. Therefore, our concerns as marketers contrast with those that matter to consumers.

As Levitt (1960, 1962) has taught so well, I recognize that marketing often involves a large component of customer orientation and, therefore, that any decent piece of consumer research may eventually be relevant to some marketer somewhere or somehow. But as Levitt's critics have insistently pointed out, customer orientation must be tempered by some concern for the firm's skills, strengths, capabilities, resources, costs, and other internal constraints so that, ultimately, we arrive at what is sometimes called the profit orientation, the survival orientation, or the "marketing orientation" (in the truest sense of that much-abused term).

Accordingly, the research intended to serve this marketing orientation by focusing on the firm's profitability differs fundamentally from consumer research. In short, consumer research emerges from the perspective of the *value-seeking consumer*, whereas marketing research adopts the orientation of the *profit-seeking marketing manager*.

> Where were ye, Nymphs, when the remorseless deep
> Closed o'er the head of your loved Lycidas? (ll. 50-51)

Siren Songs

In his call for papers, Lutz (1985) proposed that "ACR has lost some of the 'excitement' which was characteristic of the organization during the 1970's," suggested that "the pendulum has perhaps swung too far in the direction of broadening consumer research," argued that "what the field needs is more systematic attention to the 'core' of the domain rather than its fringes," specified that "the core of the domain of consumer behavior rests both empirically and definitionally on the effects of marketing activities on consumers," and prescribed a "remedy" based on studying "the effects of marketing variables on consumer behavior" (p. 5).

This back-to-the-core theme was soon reiterated by Rich Yalch (1985) in his departing editorial for the *ACR Newsletter*:

> At present . . . the need for variety characteristic of cognitively complex individuals seems to be motivating radical proposals for how the discipline should approach consumer research. . . . My concern is that younger, impressionable members of the discipline might mistake the leaders' temporary disinterest with the discipline's core areas of research and fascination with the fringe areas as evidence of a major paradigm shift. . . . However, . . . the focus will remain on the purchase behavior of the "shopper" in the household for common consumer goods and services. (p. 2)

From my perspective—especially with the benefit of hindsight—these polemics by Rich Lutz and Rich Yalch constitute an "Embarrassment of Riches." It now seems clear that these two scholars had been listening to the same muse—one that issued bad advice.

> But now my oat proceeds,
> And listens to the Herald of the Sea,
> That came in Neptune's plea.
> He asked the waves, and asked the felon winds,
> What hard mishap hath doomed this gentle swain? (ll. 88-92)

In my admittedly idiosyncratic view, three sirens of the deep had been calling to the two ACR leaders (who, unlike the crew of Odysseus, had not remembered to put wax in their ears before they went sailing). Lutz (1985) described these three siren songs quite specifically as his three major assumptions:

1. ACR was conceived of, founded by, and continues to be dominated by marketing academics (approximately 80% of the current membership).
2. Consumers would have little to "consume" were it not for the activities of marketers.
3. It is entirely possible to conduct scholarly, scientific research on the effects of marketing variables on consumers. (p. 5)

All three assumptions strike me as either untenable or irrelevant to the issues at hand.

First, although the perspective of marketing management may once have dominated consumer research and still may threaten to exert an untoward degree of influence, there is no good reason why it must continue to do so. Furthermore, many (probably including Rich Lutz) think that the participation in consumer research of representatives from other disciplines deserves expansion, not contraction. Seeking a hard-core marketing focus for the field of consumer research hardly seems likely to foster that end.

Second, as vividly articulated earlier by Hattie, we should avoid the assumption that consumption depends exclusively or even largely on the activities of marketers. Basking in the sunshine that falls for free on Gainesville, his home, Rich Lutz cannot plausibly believe that consumers would have little to consume without marketing.

Third, although scholarly work on marketing variables is indubitably "possible," it does not necessarily follow that it is "fundamental" to consumer research or that such a focus should be proclaimed as our guiding light. Indeed, scientific progress often moves fastest when it remains relatively independent from the pressures of various interest groups. Perhaps I may further clarify this last point by turning to an analogy drawn from another pastoral source—an interest I share with Rich Lutz—namely, baseball.

> For we were nursed upon the self-same hill,
> Fed the same flock, by fountain, shade, and rill;
> Together both, ere the high lawns appeared
> Under the opening eyelids of the Morn,
> We drove a-field. . . . (ll. 23-27)

The Consumer Researcher Plays Left Field

In a classic comedy sketch, George Carlin (1975; personal communication, 1994) contrasts the sports of football and baseball. As he emphasizes, "Baseball and football are the two most popular spectator sports in this country. And, as such, it seems to me they ought to be able to tell us something about ourselves; about our values or national character and maybe how those values have changed over the last hundred years. For that reason, I enjoy comparing baseball and football" (G. Carlin, personal communication,

1994). In this comparison, football emerges as pragmatic, tough-minded, and rapacious; baseball as fun, tenderhearted, and gentle:

Baseball is a 19th-century game.
Football is a 20th-century technological struggle.

Baseball is played on a diamond, in a park! The baseball park!
Football is played on a gridiron, in a stadium, sometimes called Soldier Field, or
    War Memorial Stadium.

Baseball begins in the spring, the season of new life.
Football begins in the fall, when everything is dying.

In football, you wear a helmet.
In baseball, you wear a cap.

Football is concerned with downs. "What down is it?"
Baseball is concerned with ups. "Who's up? Are you up? I'm not up. *He's* up!"

In football, you receive a penalty.
In baseball, you make an error. "Whoops!"

In football, the specialist comes in to kick.
In baseball, the specialist comes in to relieve somebody.

Football has hitting, clipping, spearing, piling on, personal fouls, late hitting, and
    unnecessary roughness.
Baseball has the sacrifice.

Football is played in any kind of weather: rain, snow, sleet, hail, fog . . . can't
    see the game, don't know if there *is* a game going on; mud on the field,
    can't read the uniforms, can't read the yard markers, the struggle will con-
    tinue!
In baseball, if it rains, we don't go out to play. "I can't go out! It's raining out!"

Baseball has the 7th-inning stretch.
Football has the 2-minute warning.

Baseball has no time limit; "We don't know when it's gonna end!"
Football is rigidly timed, and it will end, "even if we have to go to sudden death."

In baseball, during the game, in the stands, there's a kind of picnic feeling. Emo-
    tions may run high or low, but there's not that much unpleasantness.

> In football, during the game, in the stands, you can be sure that at least 27 times you were perfectly capable of taking the life of a fellow human being.

And finally, the objectives of the two games are completely different:

> In football, the object is for the quarterback, otherwise known as the field general, to be on target with his aerial assault, riddling the defense by hitting his receivers with deadly accuracy, in spite of the blitz, even if he has to use the shotgun. With short bullet passes and long bombs, he marches his troops into enemy territory, balancing this aerial assault with a sustained ground attack which punches holes in the enemy's defensive line.

> In baseball, the object is to go home! And to be safe! "I hope I'll be safe at home!" (G. Carlin, personal communication, 1994; Reprinted with permission)

George Carlin's contrast vividly undercuts the analogy frequently drawn between business and football. Business does not really resemble a football game, after all. In football, the purpose is to bash, battle, and bruise the opponent into oblivion. Clearly, football, with its intent on destruction, resembles not business, but war. Hence, the business strategists who dwell excessively on football and military analogies pursue the wrong metaphor.

Rather, business is like a baseball game in which the sphere of action at any moment includes a batter, a pitcher, a catcher, some other fielders, and maybe some base runners. In football, there is no meaningful analogy to the customer. In baseball, the batter corresponds to the business customer. The pitcher parallels the salesperson. The catcher resembles the marketing manager. And the consumer researcher plays left field.

Consider, first, the batter. The batter stands at home plate and waits for his pitch. He is a discriminating customer. He does not want to expend his resources on a bad product. But, when he sees an offering he likes, he swings with it—or at least *at* it.

Meanwhile, the pitcher is a salesperson—making a "pitch" in the sense exposed by Levitt's (1960, 1962) celebrated critique of the selling orientation. The pitcher wants to persuade the batter to swing at a bad pitch. His art is deception, misrepresentation, and chicanery. As the consumer of pitches, the batter's best interests are directly antithetical to those of the pitcher.

I do not suggest that all or even most real-world salespeople behave in the product-oriented manner of Levitt's selling orientation. But some do. And we as researchers should not blind ourselves to that fact either. Nor should we blithely assume that, as marketing manager, the catcher always strives to keep the pitcher honest.

Meanwhile, the consumer researcher resembles an outfielder. As a scientist interested in explanation (why or how might the batter swing at the next pitch) and prediction (when and where will a fly ball come floating into the outfield), he or she focuses primarily on the customer. Watching the batter—stance, swing, how the ball leaves the bat, where the ball travels—becomes the chief preoccupation.

The outfielder is also an artist. He plays the key role in one of the most beautiful and awe-inspiring moments in all sports. I refer to the towering fly ball—majestic in its soaring freedom, seemingly unfettered in its flight, apparently capable of a path that might take it anywhere but that almost magically just happens to take it into the tiny pocket of the fielder's extended glove. Thus, the outfielder participates in a visual phenomenon that seems at once entirely surprising, yet somehow completely inevitable. Just as an artist reconciles departure from structure or draws order out of chaos, the outfielder turns tension into resolution. In this capacity (recall Chapter 2), the outfielder resembles the consumer researcher engaged in theory development. And the motivation is essentially similar: joyful exploration of a phenomenon found fascinating, namely the batter's manner of consuming the product delivered by the pitcher.

So, when one says, colloquially, that an idea "comes out of left field," one refers to something unexpected, divergent, or even wildly improbable that somehow magically fits. The liberating sense of fun in the old Von Tilzer and Norworth song suggests the playfulness that informs all truly creative activity:

> Take me out to the ball game;
> Take me out to the crowd.
> Buy me some peanuts and Crackerjacks;
> I don't care if I never come back.

Many people have found—and sometimes lost—this feeling in baseball:

> I lost interest in spectator sports the day the Dodgers left Brooklyn, which was also the day I became a cynic. . . . The Dodgers were the good guys in the terrible fight against hate and racism, and they seemed to say, somehow, that

Brooklyn was a more humane, liberal and moral place than, say, St. Louis. They deserved our loyalty. Then one day they moved to Los Angeles for something as trivial as money. I have never again been to a professional sports event. (Reinhold, 1984, p. 38)[4]

Reinhold's description of how he felt when the Dodgers left New York for California reminds me of the way the Yankee fans responded to Reggie Jackson 20 years later. Jackson was a power slugger from Babe Ruth's hit-a-home-run-or-strike-out school of batsmanship, but he would shy away from running into the fence when chasing a fly ball, would complain if asked to play the role of designated hitter so as to let a more dependable fielder occupy right field, and would still demand ever-higher salaries. Reggie finished by getting traded to the California Angels and by leaving the many Yankee fans in a state of disenchantment. Similar disillusionment may afflict those who take a cool, detached look at the role of the managerial perspective in consumer research.

> Ay me! whilst thee the shores and sounding seas
> Wash far away, where'er thy bones are hurled;
> Whether beyond the stormy Hebrides,
> Where thou perhaps under the whelming tide
> Visit'st the bottom of the monstrous world. . . .
> Look *home*ward, *Angel*, now, and melt with *ruth*
> And, O ye dolphins, waft the hapless youth.
> (ll. 154-164, italics added).

Sweet Lou Comes Home

My own greatest baseball hero has been Sweet Lou Piniella, left fielder for the New York Yankees during the last 10 years of his career. Other players have been fleeter of foot (Mays), stronger in muscle power (Snider), higher in batting average (Aaron), longer lasting in their careers (Winfield), and vastly better paid (Tartabull). But Sweet Lou was the quintessential baseball hero. With his square jaw, steady gaze, and incredibly smooth swing, he resembled the prototypical ballplayer. And, in spirit and love for the game, he approached the Platonic ideal.

Lou would play in pain. Lou would cheerfully crash into the fence in pursuit of a fly ball. Lou would line that clutch single over the shortstop's head, time after time. Lou never hassled anybody about his salary. He simply took all the risks and tried with all his heart because he loved to play the game. As he approached the plate, the fans would begin a chorus of "Looo-oooo-oooo-oooo!" The fans loved Lou because Lou loved baseball. In a radio interview just after his final game, he declared: "It's been a lot of fun. It really has. . . . It's been a thrill. . . . I enjoyed it. I had goosebumps out there the whole day. . . . I play the game with emotion. . . . The fun I've had playing baseball will be with me the rest of my life."

This moment did not mean the end of Sweet Lou's career in baseball. A short time later, on Lou Piniella Day at Yankee Stadium, he told his fans, "This is not a farewell, this is only a hello. . . . The good thing is that I'm not going anywhere." Indeed, in one way or another—first as batting coach, then as manager for the Yankees, and later as manager for the Reds and the Mariners—he has remained part of the game. He has stayed close to the heart of baseball, where he belongs. Far from fading into oblivion, Sweet Lou has definitely come home.

> Weep no more, woeful shepherds, weep no more,
> For Lycidas, your sorrow, is not dead,
> Sunk though he be beneath the watery floor.
> So sinks the day-star in the ocean bed,
> And yet anon repairs his drooping head,
> And tricks his beams, and with new-spangled ore
> Flames in the forehead of the morning sky. (ll. 165-171)

The Shepherds Weep No More

My story needs a hopeful ending. I have contemplated Hattie and the Baltimore sun, Sweet Lou Piniella in left field, and the consumer researcher as Lycidas sunk beneath the watery floor of managerial relevance. All three metaphors permit optimistic resolutions. The sun sinks, but rises again tomorrow morning. Sweet Lou retires but comes home as a successful manager of baseball teams. Lycidas dies but can himself be brought back to life.

> Now, Lycidas, the shepherds weep no more;
> Henceforth thou art the Genius of the shore,
> In thy large recompense, and shalt be good
> To all that wander in that perilous flood. (ll. 182-185)

In response to the question, "Whither consumer research?" the members of the discipline have a choice. Figuratively, they can resurrect Lycidas or bury him under the sea. They can celebrate the homecoming of Sweet Lou Piniella or can root for some overpaid California slugger to milk his team for an even higher salary. They can aim to bring daylight back into the field or can simply announce that they are here to collect for the sun. Conversely, they can strive for managerial relevance to win big consulting fees and research grants or can try hard merely because they love to play the game of consumer research.

As I have tried to show, some consumer researchers have chosen the path toward resurrection, sweetness, and light. They have come home to a focus on the consumer (not marketing management) as central to their concerns. They have scraped away the barnacles of utilitarian concerns, have escaped the perilous flood of managerial relevance, and have explored fresh woods or new pastures by developing approaches to the study of consumption that they see as intrinsically worthwhile and even joyful.

> Thus sang the uncouth swain to th' oaks and rills,
> While the still morn went out with sandals grey:
> He touched the tender stops of various quills,
> With eager thought warbling his Doric lay;
> And now the sun had stretched out all the hills,
> And now was dropped into the western bay;
> At last he rose, and twitched his mantle blue:
> To-morrow to fresh woods, and pastures new. (ll. 186-193)

❏ Notes

1. Quote from Yogi Berra reprinted by permission.

2. Copyright © 1995 Hanna-Barbera Productions, Inc. All rights reserved.

3. Quoted from O'Neill, E. (1957). *A Touch of the Poet.* Copyright © 1957 Vintage Books. Reprinted with permission.

4. Reinhold (1984), p. 38. Copyright © 1984 by The New York Times Company. Reprinted by permission.

ROMANTICISM, SUBJECTIVE PERSONAL INTROSPECTION, AND MORRIS THE EPICUREAN

I Am an Animal

Not the fruit of experience, but experience itself, is the end. . . . To burn always with this hard, gemlike flame, to maintain this ecstasy, is success . . . on this short day of frost and sun.

—Walter Pater (1873/1947),
"Conclusion to The Renaissance," p. 573

A kind of writing has developed which is neither the evaluation of the relative merits of literary productions, nor intellectual history, nor moral philosophy, nor epistemology, nor social prophecy, but all these things mingled together into a new genre. . . . The aim is to understand, not to judge. The hope is that if one understands enough poems, enough religions, enough societies, enough philosophies, one will have made oneself into something worth one's own understanding.

—Richard Rorty (1982),
Consequences of Pragmatism, p. 66

❏ Introduction

The Neopositivistic Mainstream

Prior to the mid-1980s, conventional research on consumer behavior had held fast to two basic tenets that served as the twin towers where members

182

of the field found their axiological and methodological homes. Tower 1 embodied our *axiology*—that is, our concept of value, based on the aims of the discipline—and erected its gleaming facade on a foundation of managerial relevance. Tower 2 embodied our philosophy of science and endorsed a neopositivistic perspective, which served as a methodological constraint on anyone wishing to undertake the study of consumption.

But during the mid-1980s, as I described in the previous chapter, members of the old guard in consumer research watched with horror as Tower 1 came tumbling down. Various free-spirited individuals had torn away the managerial bulwark of the discipline and had proclaimed the "irrelevance of relevance" as a goal in studies of consumption. Many traditionalists took refuge in Tower 2—namely, in a neopositivistic philosophy of science built on the hypothetico-deductive method.

As the received view in marketing and consumer research (e.g., Hunt, 1983), the *hypothetico-deductive approach* assumed that a researcher begins with some general theory concerning the phenomenon of interest. From this general theory, hypotheses are deduced of the form: $X \rightarrow Y$ (in the presence of Z). The researcher then devises operational measures of X, Y, and Z; collects data in a situation where X (and perhaps Z) can be systematically manipulated or observed to vary; and then tests the hypothesis that $X \rightarrow Y$ (given Z). If the data support the hypothesis, then the underlying theory is "corroborated" in the sense that it is *not falsified* (Popper, 1959/1968). If not, then the theory must be revised and submitted to further testing, and thus to possible further refutation, followed by possible further revision. Thus does science move forward under the banner of hypothetico-deductive *falsificationism*.

Around 1985, most consumer researchers found their methodological home in hypothetico-deductive falsificationism according to the credo that "Scientific Research Is Neopositivistic Studies" (Statement 6 in Figure 1.3 from Chapter 1). This neopositivistic fortress was constructed upon various assumptions related to *epistemology* (the nature of knowledge), *axiology* (the nature and types of value underlying research), *ontology* (the nature of reality), *internal validity* (the demonstration of causality), and *external validity* (the generalizability of findings from one to another domain of interest). These key neopositivistic assumptions can be stated as follows (Hunt, 1983; Lincoln & Guba, 1985):

1. *Epistemology*. According to the Cartesian dualism between Mind and Body, a split occurs between Subject (inward consciousness) and Object (outward

reality). Objective *knowledge* is achieved when the inward Subject attains an accurate representation of the outward Object.

2. *Axiology.* Successful research must be *value free* in the sense that the researcher's own aims, goals, motivations, preferences, wants, or needs must not intrude. Rather, the researcher must remain detached and divorced from self-interest.

3. *Ontology.* One *reality* exists. Our job is to know it. We thereby attain Truth (with a capital *T*).

4. *Internal Validity.* Within experimental research—the preferred neopositivistic methodology—the justification of a causal interpretation requires ruling out alternative hypotheses. If researchers can control for all other factors while showing that changes in X precede changes in Y, then they may claim that they have demonstrated *causality* and thereby attained internal validity.

5. *External Validity.* But the goal is to achieve *nomothetic* knowledge—that is, findings *generalizable* to a broader context. In other words, showing that $X \rightarrow Y$ (given Z) becomes increasingly important as Z encompasses a wider range of situations and populations. From this neopositivistic perspective, good consumer research explains not just one consumer under certain limited conditions but rather a whole market at large. We aim not only for Truth but also for Universal Truth.

All of this roughly summarizes the conventional beliefs subscribed to by the neopositivistic consumer researcher holed up in Tower 2 in 1985, feeling momentarily safe but already secretly threatened. Various postpositivistic warriors had begun to chip away at the foundations of the neopositivistic fortress. By the early 1990s, the intellectual bastion of neopositivism in consumer research would be seriously undermined.

New Assumptions

Who leveled the tower of neopositivism in our discipline? Who persuaded us to shorten the traditional credo by one more crucial notch in our thinking until it became "Scientific Research Is Studies" (Statement 7 in Figure 1.3 from Chapter 1)?

Many people played major roles in the transformation currently under consideration. For example, as noted in Chapter 1, a watershed issue of the *Journal of Marketing* appeared in 1983, with critical contributions by Rohit Deshpande (1983), by Paul Anderson (1983), and especially by Paul Peter and Jerry Olson (1983), who espoused relativism in the philosophy of science, turned around the old troubling question, "Is marketing a science?" and instead raised the more fundamental issue, "Is science marketing?" This brilliant piece drew on the broad attack against the neopositivistic philosophy of science waged by such thinkers as Thomas Kuhn, Paul Feyerabend, Michael Polanyi, and Richard Rorty and geared toward the need for revisions in our neopositivistic credo. These shifts led toward replacing the neopositivistic tenets with a new set of assumptions, along the following lines:

1. *Epistemology.* Knowledge results not from a subject coming to know an object to attain "objectivity," but rather in a *subject-object interaction* validated by a conversation with other subjects so as to achieve, at best, intersubjectivity (agreement among people).

2. *Axiology.* Research can never be value free but must always reflect the *value judgments* of the investigator concerning what topics are interesting, what approaches worthwhile, and what results important. Here, the best we can hope for is that researchers make their values explicit and reveal any personal biases so that readers of their work can take these into account.

3. *Ontology.* If knowledge involves a subject-object interaction validated intersubjectively, then no one Truth exists. Rather, *many truths* exist within various scientific communities pursuing *different paradigms* (different frameworks of rules and commitments concerning concepts, methods, and aims). These paradigms may achieve internally consistent visions of truth within scientific communities, but they may clash or (more accurately) be incommensurable (not capable of comparison) between communities with alternative paradigms. Hence, there is not one Truth (with a capital *T*), but rather many truths (with a small *t* and an *s*) in the world of consumer research.

4. *Internal Validity.* Any phenomenon is determined by so many mutually dependent factors that *clear causal effects can never be established.* Hence, causality does not exist in the sense pursued by neopositivists. Rather, consumer behavior entails a complex tangle of intertwining forces, interdependent facets, and reciprocally connected factors related to the consumption experience.

5. *External Validity.* As a result, a researcher would be fortunate to gain *idiographic understanding* of selected individuals—that is, partial insight into one or a few cases, as opposed to nomothetic knowledge of universals. Hence, a consumer researcher should be content to seek understanding in one or a few cases of consumption, rather than vainly attempt to comprehend whole markets or entire societies.

These departures from conventional wisdom have been variously referred to as "postpositivistic" or "postmodern" (Sherry, 1991), but here generally will be called "interpretive." Breakthrough moments for the penetration of interpretive approaches into consumer research included key contributions on *semiotics* by David Mick (1986) and *alternative paths to knowledge* by Hudson and Ozanne (1988). About the same time, I had an exceptionally gifted student named Mark Grayson, who wanted to work on some critical analysis of film and who thereby nudged me in the direction of pursuing what started as a semiological interpretation of the movie *Out of Africa* and later became a stream of studies on the role of consumption symbolism in understanding works of art and entertainment (Holbrook & Grayson, 1986). Comparable approaches were pursued by, among others, Beth Hirschman (1987) and were greatly encouraged by a colloquium on semiotics in marketing held at Northwestern University and organized by Jean Umiker-Sebeok (1987). Ultimately, the viability of these interpretive approaches gained official recognition by the Association for Consumer Research in the form of a volume edited by Beth Hirschman (1989), *Interpretive Consumer Research*, with contributions by, among others, Julie Ozanne, Laurie Anderson (Hudson), Paul Anderson, Paul Peter, Jerry Olson, Barbara Stern, David Mick, Ed McQuarrie, Priscilla LaBarbera, John Sherry, and Grant McCracken. Later, thanks again to helpful support from Jean Umiker-Sebeok and her husband, Tom Sebeok, the progress in this area of interpretive research was further consolidated by an overview of semiological approaches to the interpretation of symbolic consumer behavior in both popular culture and the arts entitled *The Semiotics of Consumption* (Holbrook & Hirschman, 1993).

So, which of all these people deserves primary credit for moving the field of consumer research in the direction of a greater emphasis on interpretive approaches? The answer, I believe, lies in the name of a person not mentioned thus far in Chapter 7: John O'Shaughnessy.

John O'Shaughnessy

From the time he joined the faculty of the Columbia Business School in the mid-1960s, John O'Shaughnessy has devoted his academic life to relentlessly studying the philosophy of science and its relevance to research in marketing and consumer behavior. For 25 years, with an unbounded scholarly dedication, John has roamed the libraries and corridors of the university, making friends with such important thinkers as Ernest Nagel and Arthur Danto from the Philosophy Department and devouring the relevant literature on the philosophy of science. My innumerable conversations with John have often begun with his saying something like, "Did I tell you that I've been reading an interesting book?" (a rhetorical question) and have usually ended in my dawning recognition that the encounter between this man and the philosophical literature would someday change the course of consumer research forever.

These changes took many years to reach their ultimate fruition. An essentially private person, John did not attend many conferences or cater to the review process at our major journals. Rather, John quietly toiled away on his life's work and waited patiently for the recognition from consumer researchers that finally emerged in the late 1980s when he published *Why People Buy* (O'Shaughnessy, 1987). Regarding verbal protocols collected from consumers as a text requiring interpretation, this work applied hermeneutic methods comparable to those used in literary criticism to an understanding of the rules and reasons underlying consumption-related behavior. Inspired by John during these years, I acquired enough rudimentary knowledge of the relevant concepts to permit me to coauthor a summary of the hermeneutic approach to interpreting consumption via what we called "the linguistic turn" in marketing research (O'Shaughnessy & Holbrook, 1988) and to draw on John's shared wisdom in developing a defense of "The Need for an Interpretive Approach to Studying Consumption Behavior" (Holbrook & O'Shaughnessy, 1988) against attacks by some of the neopositivistic critics (Calder & Tybout, 1987). Meanwhile, John has continued to pursue his penetrating excursions into the philosophy of science. These have resulted in what I believe will become the definitive treatment connecting the philosophy of science to consumer research—namely, John's major work, *Explaining Buyer Behavior: Central Concepts and Philosophy of Science Issues* (O'Shaughnessy, 1992).

Deeply influenced by John O'Shaughnessy's acceptance of interpretive approaches in general and hermeneutic exegesis in particular, I have moved in three closely related directions. The first, described in Chapter 3, drew on the semiological analysis of symbolic consumption in works of art or entertainment and, when integrated with a parallel series of studies by Beth Hirschman, led to *The Semiotics of Consumption* (Holbrook & Hirschman, 1993).

Second, the hermeneutic approach espoused by John O'Shaughnessy and others taught Beth and me to regard consumer behavior as a text that invites interpretive analysis (Ricoeur, 1976, 1981). Our book on this theme, subtitled *The Study of Consumption as Text,* adopts a resolutely pluralistic stance toward methods in consumer research and supports the use of diverse approaches ranging from the most neopositivistic at one extreme to the most postpositivistic at the other. This pluralism or eclecticism explains the book's main title: *Postmodern Consumer Research* (Hirschman & Holbrook, 1992).

A third and somewhat more extreme aspect of the same general trends surfaced late in the 1980s as I directed my attention toward a previously neglected approach to the study of consumption—namely, an approach that focused introspectively on my own consumption experiences. Specifically, this approach regards one's own consumption experiences as a possible window on the human condition, conducts a sort of "participant observation" on one's own life as a consumer, and produces autoethnographic essays based on a type of systematic self-reflection that I refer to as *subjective personal introspection.*

Preview

In this chapter, I develop this theme of self-reflection on the consumption experience in the form of essays based on subjective personal introspection. This emphasis recalls Walter Pater's vivid insistence—as quoted in the epigraph to this chapter—on "experience itself" as "the end" (1873/1947, p. 573). Furthermore, this emphasis resonates with the romantic spirit; it accepts the gift of subjective intuitions, personal revelations, and introspective insights; and it celebrates the essay as a kind of writing that Richard Rorty (1982)—in the second epigraph to this chapter—has characterized as "a new genre" aimed at developing oneself into "something worth one's own understanding" (p. 66).

This chapter moves reflexively (as an essay-on-essays) toward the closer embrace of such a romantic, introspective, experiential approach to studying consumer behavior. In general, I argue for the potential usefulness-meaningfulness-and-validity of subjective personal introspection in advancing the aims-concepts-and-methods of consumer research. Toward this end, I begin by tracing the romantic literary background of the introspective essay. I then plead the case for subjective personal introspection and provide examples of introspective approaches taken by such great consumption-obsessed authors as Michel de Montaigne and Walter Pater, followed by an example drawn from my own life as a consumer. I conclude that, although any approach has its limitations, subjective personal introspection may contribute valuably to the study of experiential consumption.

Thus, in a sense, this chapter provides a cornerstone for the book. In my attempt to justify the role of systematic self-reflection, I aspire to a degree of reflexivity one level higher than that pursued elsewhere in the book. In other words, I present an essay on the essay—that is, *a self-reflective experience in self-reflection*. I hope that, in the process, I provide a justification for the approach to consumer research that emerged in the late 1980s, that I illustrate later in a self-analysis entitled "I Am an Animal," and that I call subjective personal introspection.

❑ Romanticism

Campbell's Romantic View of Consumption

In *The Romantic Ethic and the Spirit of Modern Consumerism*, Colin Campbell (1987) argues that the success of the Industrial Revolution (which required a "demand" adequate to absorbing capitalism's "supply") depended on the development of a culture of consumption. In Campbell's view, this "spirit of consumerism" arose from the awakening of an essentially romantic ethos (associated with an emphasis on hedonic gratification) among consumers in 18th-century Western Europe generally and England in particular.

Campbell supports this argument with considerable sophistication and vigor. Briefly, he suggests that (a) we lack and therefore need an adequate theory of consumer behavior, (b) such a theory would view consumption as essentially hedonic in nature, (c) such a hedonic view rests on a fundamentally romantic ethos, and (d) the appropriate romantic ethos emerged historically from internal forces working within Protestant Puritanism. (Note that Campbell's title plays on Weber's classic *The Protestant Ethic and the Spirit of Capitalism*.)

Summary of Campbell's Argument

Because of their crucial role in Campbell's worldview and their relevance to the theme of this chapter, each of the four points just mentioned deserves a short summary.

The Lack of and Need for Adequate Theory. Campbell suggests that our ability to understand modern consumption suffers from the absence of a suitable theory of consumer behavior: "No satisfactory account of modern consumer behavior exists" (1987, p. 36). From this vantage point, Campbell calls for "the development of a satisfactory overall theory of consumer behavior" (p. 41). His own solution involves a theory couched in the terms of hedonism.

The View of Consumption as Essentially Hedonic. To explain consumption, Campbell proposes that "a theory of modern hedonistic conduct can indeed account for the distinctive features of modern consumer behavior" (p. 7). He anchors his concept of hedonism in "enjoyment of the pleasurable dimension of an experience" (p. 59) so that "the primary object is to squeeze as much of the quality of pleasure as one can from all those sensations which one actually experiences during the course of the process of living" (p. 69). This hedonic orientation goes beyond sensations as the source of pleasure to embrace the role of emotions in the consumption experience—intense joy, for example. Hence, pleasurable consumption results from the emotional significance of the products consumed: "Individuals do not so much seek satisfaction from products, as pleasure from the self-illusory experiences which they construct from their associated meanings" (p. 89). In other words, consumer products promote daydreams, fantasies, and other imaginative experiences that provide key sources of hedonic gratification in emotional response: "Individuals employ their imaginative and creative powers to construct mental images which they consume for the intrinsic pleasure they provide, a practice best described as day-dreaming or fantasizing" (p. 77). "Thus fantasizing is fundamentally a form of hedonism" (p. 81).

The Romantic Sources of Hedonism. Campbell traces the hedonic nature of modern consumption to the romantic ethos that developed generally in 18th-century Western Europe and particularly in England. He characterizes romanticism as a "mode of feeling" (p. 181) in which "imagination became the most significant and prized of personal qualities" (p. 193). This romantic ethos emphasizes the links among imagination, beauty, and pleasure so that "the imagination and the experiencing of pleasure became largely commensurate" (p. 193). Hence, in Campbell's view, hedonism, romanticism, and modern consumption have converged via their common pursuit of pleasure resulting from the imaginative evocation of emotional experience:

> The romantic ideal . . . functioned to stimulate and legitimate that form of autonomous, self-illusory hedonism which underlies modern consumer behavior. . . . More specifically, Romanticism . . . legitimates the search for pleasure as good in itself. . . . Romanticism has served to provide ethical support for that restless and continuous pattern of consumption which so distinguishes the behavior of modern man. (pp. 200-201)

The Emergence of Romanticism From Puritanism. Perhaps more controversially, Campbell finds the sources of the romantic ethic in certain aspects of Protestantism. Thus, he suggests that the romantic worldview emerged from tendencies latent within Puritanism itself:

> What needs to be asserted most forcibly is that there existed within Protestantism, and even within that especially harsh and vigorous branch of it known as Puritanism, two major strands of thought . . . and that whilst the former subsequently evolved into rationalism and utilitarianism, the latter developed into Sentimentalism and Romanticism. (p. 219)

This latter development resulted from "a 'taste' for the strong meat of powerful religious emotion" (p. 134) characteristic of the Puritans and might be compared suggestively with the ecstatic raptures that typify certain contemporary evangelical, charismatic, and revivalist sects. According to Campbell, such tendencies toward the cultivation of religious emotions paved the way for romanticism and thereby encouraged the emergence of consumption habits that built the consumer demand necessary to accommodate the supply of products unleashed by Weber's "spirit of capitalism." In this sense, the romantic and Protestant ethics provided mutually reinforcing tendencies that combined to ensure the success of the Industrial Revolution.

Points of Disagreement With Campbell's View

Although admiring the force of Campbell's account, I do disagree with some aspects of the four major theses just described.

The Lack of and Need for Adequate Theory. I cannot agree that no adequate theory of consumer behavior exists. Rather, the relevant theories had appeared long before Campbell's book, though he had not managed to find them. Understandably, as a sociologist, he drew his references almost entirely from the social sciences and the humanities, rather than from the discipline of consumer research itself. Hence, his book does not reflect the rather extensive conceptual and empirical work available in the *Journal of Consumer Research, Advances in Consumer Research, Psychology & Marketing,* the *Journal of Marketing Research,* or innumerable other publications by consumer researchers.

The View of Consumption as Essentially Hedonic. In this abundant consumer-research literature, Campbell could have found some helpful support for his theory of hedonic consumption. Specifically, Hirschman and Holbrook (1982) had called attention to some emerging concepts, methods, and propositions relevant to hedonic consumption. Furthermore, in work that reinforces Campbell's emphasis on daydreams and the imagination, Holbrook and Hirschman (1982) had discussed the experiential aspects of consumption: "consumer fantasies, feelings, and fun." This work had led to a stream of research exploring the emotional, symbolic, and aesthetic aspects of consumer behavior. Meanwhile, several other consumer researchers (literally too numerous to mention) had explored these and related issues. All of this suggests that Campbell unintentionally exaggerated the depths of ignorance to which he consigned the state of knowledge concerning consumer behavior.

The Romantic Sources of Hedonism. Although I agree with Campbell's emphasis on the need to devote greater attention to the romantic aspects of consumption (Holbrook, 1991c; Holbrook & Corfman, 1985; Holbrook & Hirschman, 1993; Holbrook & Olney, in press), I would suggest that romanticism characterizes only some—not all—aspects of consumption and typifies consumers to varying degrees, some more than others. In other words, I believe that both classical and romantic tendencies—that is, both thoughts and feelings, both reasons and emotions, both actions and reactions—coexist within the typical consumption experience and pervade the behavior of the typical consumer so that they tend always to be mingled or "compresent" in a kind of "mixed bag" (Holbrook et al., 1990). In other words, people *think* about which amusement park will produce the most *fun;* they *decide* which videotape will provide the greatest *enjoyment;* they *choose* which flavor of ice cream will bring the most *pleasure.* Campbell allows for this possibility when he acknowledges that the Protestant and romantic ethics are "complementary rather than contradictory" (1987, p. 223).

The Emergence of Romanticism From Puritanism. Campbell provides just one partial account for the emergence of romanticism. However, one should certainly consider such additional factors as the reaction against neoclassicism (Abrams, 1953), the medieval revival (Beers, 1968), disillusionment over the French Revolution (Abrams, 1971), and the Eastern influences associated with the so-called oriental renaissance (Schwab, 1984). At best, Campbell's preoccupation with the evolution of Puritanism as the source of the romantic ethic appears incomplete.

Points of Agreement With Campbell's View

Having raised these caveats concerning Campbell's (1987) portrayal of romanticism in consumption, I hasten to add that I basically support the general outlines of his position and take him to be the leading authority on this theme. I agree, for example, with Campbell's conception of consumption as "processes through which economic resources are used up . . . in the satisfaction of human wants" and with his additional comment that "human beings may, however, also obtain gratification from activities which do not, in any conventional economic sense, involve the use of resources at all (except those of time and human energy), such as the appreciation of natural beauty or the enjoyment of friendship" (p. 38). Also, I concur with the importance that Campbell attaches to the hedonic or experiential aspects of consumption, to their anchoring in romanticism, to the resulting roles of such emotions as joy and sorrow, and to the consequent emphasis accorded to the "aesthetic dimension of experience" (p. 67). Furthermore, I endorse Campbell's method of drawing on examples from such literary figures as Virginia Woolf, Jane Austen, Samuel Johnson, Jean-Jacques Rousseau, William Wordsworth, and D. H. Lawrence—to name only a few of the many references that borrow from the humanities to illustrate points of relevance to the social sciences. In all of these ways, Campbell has provided support for this essay addressing the influence of romanticism on the role of subjective personal introspection in providing accounts of experiential consumption.

Romanticism in the Lives of Consumers

My focus on romanticism differs somewhat from Campbell's and recalls the earlier discussion of Wordsworth in Chapter 4. Specifically, I argue that romanticism influences the lives of consumers, not so much by accounting for *why* people buy (romanticism → hedonism → consumer demand → buying behavior) as by helping to enrich the *experiences* that surround *consumption* activities (romanticism → experiential consumption → emotional responses → pleasure). By suggesting a characterization of consumer behavior in terms of its experiential content in general or its joys and sorrows in particular, romanticism opens multiple windows on the nature of the human condition. Although often mixed with classicism (as previously noted), romanticism pervades consumer behavior to its very core and finds one key unifying theme in the experiential aspects of acquiring, using, and disposing of products (goods, services, ideas, events)—in short, in the joys and sorrows of consumption. Furthermore, this theme invites exploration via deeply self-reflective subjective personal introspection.

Before urging these points at greater length, I address the question of what I mean by romanticism. This definitional task poses a genuine challenge, for numerous views on the nature of romanticism have coexisted, each with some claim to credence.

Romantic and classical temperaments appear, to varying degrees, in all human endeavors so that one finds romantic tendencies mixed into the works of all eras—from Greek epics to modern poetry. Although a particular period (say, the late 18th and early 19th centuries) adopts the romantic perspective to an unusually high degree, it appears at other times and places as well. Thus, near the end of the 19th century, Walter Pater (1876/1947) argued that "the romantic spirit is, in reality, an ever-present, an enduring principle" (p. 584). Indeed, to varying degrees throughout history, romanticism has pervaded a broad range of human experience. Beyond this ecumenical point, however, one finds much diversity in the various formulations employed to capture the essence of romanticism. I first distinguish between *eclectic* and *global* views before isolating the specific version of the latter that we rely on here.

Eclectic Views of Romanticism

Eclectic views of romanticism tend to generate lengthy enumerations of characteristics presumed to typify the romantic temperament. For example, in *Zen and the Art of Motorcycle Maintenance*, Robert Pirsig (1974) divides human understanding into two kinds—romantic and classical—by using a list of modifiers:

> The romantic mode is primarily inspirational, imaginative, creative, intuitive. Feelings rather than facts predominate. . . . It proceeds by feeling, intuition and esthetic conscience. . . . The classic style is straightforward, unadorned, unemotional, economical and carefully proportioned. Its purpose is . . . to bring order out of chaos. . . . Everything is under control. (pp. 66-67)

The split between classicism and romanticism is a familiar theme in the study of philosophy (Jenkins, 1962). Thus, in the literature on aesthetics, Harold Osborne (1970) describes classicism as involving harmony, composition, proportion, correctness, completeness, convincingness of representation, skill, craft, rules, and methods. By contrast, Osborne sees romanticism as involving "genius, creative imagination, originality, expression, . . . emotion, and sentiment" and "a special emphasis on the affective and emotional aspects of experience" (pp. 193-194).

Osborne's treatment accords well with the viewpoint of literary critics (Frye, 1963). For example, M. H. Abrams (1953) sees romanticism as spontaneous, expressive, personal, lyrical, subjective, inspired, passionate, demonic, sublime, and imaginative.

More generally, Jamake Highwater (1981) notes the affinity of the romantic sensibility to the primal mind and its reverence for the natural, the intuitive, the emotional, and the visionary—as opposed to the mechanical, the linear, the reasoned, and the literal.

Similarly, in the philosophical literature, Crane Brinton (1967) describes romanticism as "a very complex syndrome of 'biases' in the direction of . . . intuition, spirit, sensibility, imagination, faith, the unmeasurable, the infinite, the wordless . . . the vicarious adventure of fantasy" (pp. 206-209). To this, Robert Nozick (1981) adds his identification of romanticism with "overcoming obstacles, breaking bonds, powerful irrational emotions, titanic struggle, . . . the dynamic process of transcending limits" (p. 613).

In sum, the eclectic view generally regards the romantic as sensitive, emotional, intuitive, chaotic, and free-spirited, while seeing the classicist as purposive, reasonable, realistic, orderly, and controlled. These listlike characterizations differ in spirit from attempts by other authors who provide more global perspectives on the nature of romanticism.

Global Views of Romanticism

Walter Pater

In his article on the classic and romantic, Walter Pater (1876/1947) cited Stendhal's sweeping characterization of romanticism and classicism as embodied by literary works that give the greatest possible pleasure to oneself and to one's grandparents, respectively. Pater saw romanticism as a tendency, rather than a period, and based his own generalization on the concept of "strange beauty" (p. 585): "It is the addition of strangeness to beauty, that constitutes the romantic character in art; and the desire of beauty being a fixed element in every artistic organization, it is the addition of curiosity to this desire of beauty, that constitutes the romantic temper" (p. 584). Pater suggested that the Middle Ages exert a romantic fascination because of their tendency to illustrate this combination of "curiosity and the love of beauty" (p. 585).

Henry Beers

Working at the end of the 19th century, Henry Beers (1899/1968) agreed with Pater in seeing romanticism as a tendency, rather than as a period, but saw its essence as limited in scope to a reverence for things medieval: "Romanticism . . . means the reproduction in modern art or literature of the life and thought of the Middle Ages" (p. 2). Beers went on to characterize the medieval poets as "marked by an excess of sentiment, by overlavish decoration, a strong sense of color and a feeble sense of form, an attention to detail, at the cost of the main impression, and a consequent tendency to run into the exaggerated, the fantastic, and the grotesque" (p. 4). This list verges on the enumerative approach discussed earlier. But generally, in what is actually a strongly unified treatment, Beers stuck quite close to his avowed emphasis on the Middle Ages: "The history of romanticism . . . is little else than a record of the steps by which . . . new features of that vast and complicated scheme of things which we loosely call the Middle Ages were brought to light and made available as literary material" (p. 189).

Jacques Barzun

Another global view of romanticism appears in Jacques Barzun's *Classic, Romantic, and Modern* (1943/1975). Writing during World War II, Barzun rejected a stereotypical list of identifiable romantic characteristics (p. 13) and instead identified a more basic unifying romantic theme—the desire to solve a dominant problem creatively—found most conspicuously at the end of the 18th century because of the need for reconstruction in the wake of the French Revolution: "The dominant problem . . . was to create a new world on the ruins of the old. The French Revolution and Napoleon had made a clean sweep. . . . The next generation must build or perish. Whence we conclude that romanticism is first of all constructive and creative" (p. 14). Barzun also emphasized, however, that this worldview extends beyond the time period commonly called "romantic" and embraces broader aspects of the human condition—in particular, "the contrast between man's greatness and man's wretchedness; man's power and man's misery" (p. 16). In this view, Goethe's *Faust* is the "bible of Romanticism" (p. 8); Rousseau in his *Confessions* is its prophet (p. 20): "Survival . . . suggests that the first law of the universe is not thought but action. As Goethe has Faust say, 'In the beginning was'—not the Word, or Thought, but 'the Deed' " (p. 77). Hence, Barzun found essential romanticism in a chronicle of great deeds such as Homer's *Odyssey* (p. 67) and in Byron's contention that "the goal of life is not happiness . . . but activity" (p. 77):

> *Faust* is rightly supposed to be the gospel of the romantic life. . . . The crisis consists in rejecting, with full risks, the inherited modes of experience and taking up activity as the path to new ones. . . . The romantic apostles of Faustian striving . . . could only admire an active greatness. . . . The goal and the reward were . . . won by striving. (pp. 87-93)

Along these lines, Barzun attempted to focus his own emphasis on the creative *act* of (re)*construction.*

M. H. Abrams

M. H. Abrams (1971) has linked romanticism to a comparable focus on the themes of reconciliation, reunion, and return. I have described Abrams's view in Chapter 4 and shall not repeat that discussion here.

René Wellek

Writing at mid-century, René Wellek (1955) saw romanticism as a reaction against neoclassicism: "We can speak of a general European romantic movement . . . as . . . a revolt against neoclassicism, which meant a rejection of the Latin tradition and the adoption of a view of poetry centered on the expression and communication of emotion" (pp. 2-3). Wellek traced this tendency through the work of such literary critics as Shelley, Wordsworth, and Coleridge. One might summarize Wellek's principal theme by attending briefly to his characterization of Coleridge, who rejected the neoclassical unities of time, space, and action, replacing them with a holistic view of the artwork. This criterion of wholeness countenanced Coleridge's celebration of the imagination as a unifying force that achieves "the reconciliation of opposite or discordant qualities" (p. 186) and supported his emphasis on the role of feeling (p. 163) wherein "poetry must be passion" (p. 167).

Frank Kermode

Another global view of romanticism appears in work by Frank Kermode (1957), roughly contemporaneous with that of Wellek. Drawing on Coleridge and the English tradition, Kermode sees romanticism as involving the interplay of joy and suffering associated with Keats: "Some difference in the artist gives him access to . . . joy. . . . But the power of joy being possible only to a profound 'organic sensibility,' a man who experiences it will also suffer exceptionally. He must be lonely, haunted, victimized, devoted to suffering rather than action" (p. 6). Kermode contends that "this association of suffering and joy . . . is at the root of Romantic thought" (p. 10) and offers the odes by Coleridge ("Dejection") and Keats ("On Melancholy") as the *loci classici* for this viewpoint:

> O pure heart! thou needs't not ask of me
> What this strong music in the soul may be!
> What, and wherein it doth exist,
> This light, this glory, this fair luminous mist,
> This beautiful and beauty-making power.
> Joy, virtuous lady! Joy that ne'er was given,
> Save to the pure, and in their purest hour.
>   —Coleridge, 1802/1948, p. 178

> She dwells with Beauty—Beauty that must die;
> And Joy, whose hand is ever at his lips
> Bidding adieu; and aching Pleasure nigh,
> Turning to poison while the bee-mouth sips:

Aye, in the very temple of Delight
Veiled Melancholy has her sovran shrine,
Though seen of none save him whose strenuous tongue
Can burst Joy's grape against his palate fine;
His soul shall taste the sadness of her might,
And be among her cloudy trophies hung.

                                        —Keats, 1820/1948, p. 821

This commingling in art of joy and suffering extends into the 20th century in the work of a poet such as Yeats, whose "Adam's Curse" commemorates the romantic truism that

. . . 'To be born woman is to know —
Although they do not talk of it at school —
That we must labour to be beautiful.'
I said: 'It's certain there is no fine thing
Since Adam's fall but needs much labouring. . . .'

                                        —Yeats, 1904/1956, p. 78

Northrop Frye

A final global view of romanticism, offered by Northrop Frye (1968), gravitates toward Wellek's and Kermode's emphases on the commingling of joy and sorrow. Specifically, Frye suggests that "the central theme of Romanticism is that of the attaining of an expanded consciousness" (p. 42). For him, as for Abrams (1971), this pervasive theme stems from the romantic awareness of "the fall of man" as a state in which "a sense of an original identity between the individual man and nature has been lost" (p. 17):

Man has "fallen," not so much into sin as into . . . self-consciousness, into his present subject-object relation to nature, where, because his consciousness is what separates him from nature, the primary conscious feeling is one of separation. The alienated man cut off from nature by his consciousness is the Romantic equivalent of post-Edenic Adam. (pp. 17-18)

Given this predicament, romantic poets tend to see themselves as heroes of a quest seeking "a nature who reveals herself only to the individual" via "an expanded consciousness": "The great Romantic theme is the attaining of an apocalyptic vision by a fallen but potentially regenerate mind" (pp. 37-38). Frye finds this theme ubiquitous in such figures as Goethe's Faust, Byron's

Childe Harold, Coleridge's Ancient Mariner, Shelley's Wandering Jew, and especially the narrator of Rousseau's archetypal *Confessions*. Such works replace the "up" and "down" movement of imagery (from heaven to hell) with an opposition between "within" and "without" (from subject to object) (p. 47). Thus, romanticism points to "two kinds of reality"—the "reality out there" (known to science and reason) and the "reality that we bring into being through an act of creation" (known to subjective experience) (p. 125). Hence, Keats tends to identify truth with beauty ("Ode on a Grecian Urn" and "Endymion") and their experience with joy (p. 127). His famous phrase—"O for a life of sensations rather than of thoughts"—prompts the following gloss by Frye: "O for a life in which thoughts have the immediacy of sensations, instead of a life in which sensations are as unsubstantial as thoughts" (p. 152). In such a world—as seen already in the "Ode on Melancholy"—"sadness" and "sorrow" commingle inextricably with "Delight" and "Joy" to create the "aching Pleasure" of a "Beauty that must die" as the essence of human experience (p. 153).

❏ Subjective Personal Introspection

From Romanticism to Introspection in Consumer Research

In what follows, I pursue a view—close to that offered by Frye and comparable to those of Pater, Kermode, or Abrams—in which the consumer researcher engages in a quest to seek the essence of joyful or sorrowful consumption experiences through an expanded consciousness attained by means of subjective personal introspection. This view borrows from the romantic ideal of the independent, insightful, inspired individual who explores imaginative visions via the inner reality revealed by deep self-reflection. In short, I argue for subjective personal introspection as an approach potentially useful to consumer researchers willing to undertake autoethnography on themselves via a romantic kind of participant observation in their own lives. (For comparable examples of autoethnography applied to consumer behavior, see the account of learning to play jazz piano by Sudnow, 1978, and the work on the consumption of pets by Sanders, 1990.)

Although the terms *subjective*, *personal*, and *introspective* overlap partially in meaning, they also carry somewhat different senses. Specifically, according to *Merriam-Webster's Collegiate Dictionary* (1993), *subjective* means "modified or affected by . . . experience, or background" (p. 1172). *Personal* means "relating to an individual or an individual's character, conduct, motives, or private affairs" (p. 867). And *introspection* means "an examination of one's own thoughts and feelings" (p. 615). Hence, subjective personal introspection implies an examination of one's own individual mental experiences. In essence—following the romantic ethos—I advocate experiential, private self-reflection on joys and sorrows related to consumption and found in one's own everyday participation in the human condition.

Going Against the Grain

As might be expected, the proposed move toward a greater reliance on subjective personal introspection, which began with some work by Holbrook (1986e, 1987a, 1988a, 1988b) and gradually gained some support from others (Gould, 1991), has encountered stiff resistance from the ranks of mainstream consumer researchers. Indeed, a debate has raged within consumer research between such *neopositivists* as Calder and Tybout (1987), Hunt (1983), and Leong (1985) and such *interpretivists* as Hirschman (1986a), Holbrook and O'Shaughnessy (1988), and Hudson and Ozanne (1988). Rather than accept subjective personal introspection as a valid source of knowledge, neopositivists have preached against what they regard as an "anarchy of self-indulgence and paroxysms of self-expression" (Calder & Tybout, 1987, p. 139). Meanwhile, even those more inclined toward relativism (Muncy & Fisk, 1987) have tended to relegate private experiential self-reflection to the role of theory development within the context of discovery (Deshpande, 1983).

Such consumer researchers as Peter and Olson (1983) or Anderson (1986), however, have emphasized the importance of persuading others as the basis for building a *social consensus* to support a given approach or hypothesis. This focus on intersubjective agreement reflects the spirit of much postmodern thought: Emphasizing *rhetoric* (various means of persuasion), it appears to open the door—a least a crack—to accepting the potential validity of one's own subjective personal introspection.

Toward a Defense of Subjective Personal Introspection

It would require a prohibitively lengthy philosophical investigation to attempt a full-fledged defense of introspective approaches to acquiring knowledge. With the increasingly common denial of the distinction between subject and object (Bernstein, 1971, 1983), arguments on behalf of subjectivity might seem almost beside the point. However, the postmodern flight from a *correspondence theory* of truth (in which mind mirrors nature) toward an epistemology based on *consensus* (arrived at through a communal conversation) does appear to leave some room for arguments drawn from subjective personal introspection to play a role in the intersubjective validation of shared knowledge (Rorty, 1979, 1982). In other words, if intersubjective validity requires interpersonal consensus, I can use self-reflections on my own private consumption experiences to convince others to accept the truth of some piece of knowledge about consumer behavior in which I happen to believe.

The neopositivistic distinction originally made by Reichenbach (1938) between the *context of discovery* (theory development) and *the context of justification* (hypothesis testing), especially when coupled with a widespread abandonment of once-popular introspective accounts (Bazerman, 1987) and a prevalent distrust of introspection among modern psychologists (Carlston, 1987), has generally restricted the use of introspective methods to the realm of concept generation (Scheffler, 1982). According to this view, introspection belongs to the process of formulating hypotheses, which then require testing by more rigorous procedures.

In the postmodern critique, however, this familiar neopositivistic distinction between discovery and justification has tended to break down (Kordig, 1978; Nelson, 1987a; Scheffler, 1982). In the words of Kuhn (1970b): "There are always at least some good reasons for each possible choice. Considerations relevant to the context of discovery are then relevant to justification as well" (p. 328). In particular, one finds a growing recognition that justification may itself depend, in part, on subjective factors (p. 329). According to this view, subjective personal introspection may play a role not only in the initial insights of discovery but also in building the ultimate consensus that strengthens interpretive validation.

Beginning with Martin Heidegger, philosophers have increasingly challenged the meaningfulness of Descartes' dualistic split between subject and object (Guignon, 1983). Heidegger's struggle to overcome the Cartesian dualism has led ultimately to the influential work of Richard Rorty (1979, 1982). Drawing not only on Heidegger but also on Wittgenstein and Dewey, Rorty argues that the gap between subject and object—between mind and matter, between self and other—is a pseudo-problem that encourages a misleading *correspondence theory* of knowledge. In this troublesome correspondence theory, the mind behaves like a mirror, seeking to attain an accurate reflection of objective reality in subjective consciousness—hence, Rorty's title *Philosophy and the Mirror of Nature* (1979). But more than three centuries of post-Cartesian debate have shattered the mirror metaphor of correspondence theory. Hence, following Thomas Kuhn (1970b, 1977), Rorty espouses a community-based view of knowledge as (a) *social* in character and (b) dependent on the *shared rules, group norms,* and *linguistic habits* of humans engaged in a *discourse* or *conversation.* Kuhn (1977) sees science as a group product generated by a *scientific community* bound together by a *common language* (p. xxii). Elsewhere, he elaborates:

> If I were writing my book again now, I would . . . begin by discussing the community structure of science. . . . Community structure is a topic . . . which . . . has recently become a major concern. . . . Groups like these should, I suggest, be regarded as the units which produce scientific knowledge. . . . Science is . . . the only activity . . . in which each community is its own exclusive audience and judge. (Kuhn, 1970a, pp. 252-254)

Similarly, Bernstein (1971) regards knowledge as *social* in character and as based on *shared norms:* "The conception of reality . . . essentially involves the notion of a COMMUNITY" (p. 176). If anything, Rorty (1982) goes even farther toward shifting his emphasis to the importance of a *conversation* among the members of a *linguistic community:*

> Pragmatism . . . is the doctrine that there are no constraints on inquiry save conversational ones . . . only those . . . constraints provided by the remarks of our fellow-inquirers. . . . The pragmatist tells us that it is useless to hope that objects will constrain us to believe the truth about them. . . . In the end, the pragmatists tell us, what matters is our loyalty to other human beings clinging together against the dark. (pp. 165-166)

Such attempts to circumvent the subject-object dichotomy via an emphasis on communal standards of truth entail the abandonment of hopes for an unachievable objectivity and the embrace of aspirations toward *intersubjective validity* (the achievement of consensus): "An attempt to go beyond the subject/object distinction . . . seeks to place itself at the center of experience [where] the truth it seeks belongs not to the order of objectivity but to that of intersubjectivity" (Megill, 1985, p. 201). In this connection, even

Karl Popper (1959/1968) tended to define objectivity as synonymous with *intersubjective* testability so that "the *objectivity* of scientific statements lies in the fact that they can be *inter-subjectively tested*" (p. 44). More recent thinkers, moving still more vehemently in this direction, have bolstered the aforementioned shift from a more neopositivistic toward a more interpretivistic philosophy of science. Thus, Wayne Booth (1974) assumes that "validity or falsehood is . . . established communally, in some kind of intersubjective agreement" (p. 119). Richard Rorty (1987) praises "the new fuzziness" (p. 51) in which "objectivity is intersubjectivity" (p. 42):

> The "new fuzziness" . . . is an attempt to blur just those distinctions between the objective and the subjective and between fact and value which the critical conception of rationality has developed. We fuzzies would like to substitute the idea of "unforced agreement" for that of "objectivity." . . . We would like to disabuse social scientists and humanists of the idea that there is something called "scientific status" which is a desirable goal. . . . There is no point in assigning degrees of "objectivity." . . . For the presence of unforced agreement . . . gives us everything in the way of "objective truth" which one could possibly want: namely, intersubjective agreement. (pp. 41-42)

From the perspective just described, *any* means toward building intersubjective agreement may play a role in establishing communitywide, shared versions of truth. Thus, for Paul Feyerabend (1982), science depends on *persuasion*. This view alerts us as researchers to the importance of the art of persuasion or *rhetoric* (Burke, 1969). For example, Wayne Booth's (1974) conception of "man as a rhetorical animal" (p. 137) leads toward a "consensus" theory of science (pp. 109-112) based on "communal validation" (p. 146), or what Berger and Luckmann (1966) call the "social construction of reality." Hence, such works as the volume edited by Nelson, Megill, and McCloskey (1987) emphasize linkages among what might be called the "four C's" in postmodern philosophies of science: (a) *communication* (rhetorical content), (b) *constructivism* (socially and linguistically constructed reality), (c) *community* (shared conventions, conversations, and construals), and (d) *consensus* (convergence of convictions). As summarized by Nelson (1987b),

> By rhetorics, I mean . . . the substantive, expressive, and persuasive talk needed for communication among humans. . . . Rhetoric must play a legitimate

role in collective inquiry of any kind. . . . Rhetoric of inquiry concerns the interaction of communication and inquiry. It studies the reasoning of scholars in research communities. . . . It endeavors to learn how reason is rhetorical and how recognition of this should alter inquiry. . . . Rhetoric of inquiry intends to help scholars improve the rhetoric—and therefore the content, as well as the reception—of their research. . . . It accommodates studies of the many shared but often unarticulated features of human communication in scholarship. (pp. 202-206)

In a similar vein, Donald McCloskey (1985) has emphasized the role of rhetoric as it affects scientific discourse in economics: "Rhetoric does not claim to provide a new methodology, and therefore does not provide formulas for scientific advance. It does not believe that science advances by formula. It believes that science advances by healthy conversation" (p. 174).

Accompanying this concern for the role of rhetoric, one finds an increasing acceptance of *pluralism*. Thus, Booth (1974) expresses "confidence in a multiplicity of ways of knowing" (p. 99). Nelson (1987a) regards rhetoric as the "postmodern epistemology" (p. 408) and argues that "the challenge is to pluralize it" (p. 414). Bernstein (1971) endorses "the manifest pluralism of contemporary philosophy" (p. 7). And Rorty (1982) proclaims, "We should let a hundred flowers bloom" (pp. 218-219).

The foregoing considerations establish some opportunity for the role of subjective personal introspection as an alternative path to knowledge. Put simply, self-reflection on private experiences may provide material that will help convince one's audience about the merits of one's insights, the universality of one's feelings, or the validity of one's own experiential reality. Rhetorically, the introspective essay may play the role of a persuasive communication. For example, Booth (1974) emphasizes the rhetorical power of stories and suggests that "narrative embodiment often does in fact strengthen persuasion" (p. 181)—an argument that supports the persuasiveness of the introspective essay:

Any literal statement of message loses the special kind of knowing that the stories offer. . . . The only discursive treatises that seem to rival narrative in this kind of adequacy are those which, like Pascal's *Pensées*, make narrative heroes out of their authors. It is the passion of Pascal we read for, the arguments almost becoming characters in his drama. . . . The rhetoric of narration provides one way of knowing that can never be achieved by "the rhetoric of science." (pp. 186-187)

Similarly, in economics, McCloskey (1985) claims that "introspections, even if imprecise, can be better than regression estimates infected with misspecifications and errors in the variables" (p. 45):

> Economists pointlessly limit themselves to "objective" facts. The modernist notion is that common sense is nonsense, that knowledge must somehow be objective, not *verstehen* or introspection. But, to repeat, we have much at our disposal about ourselves as economic molecules, if we would examine the grounds for assent. (p. 181)

In the postmodern view, this push toward introspection returns the self-observer to human concerns with inwardness, self-consciousness, and passionate feelings. On this theme, Bernstein (1971) suggests that the task of "man" is to become human:

> His task as a human being is not to "think" himself out of this condition: such an attempt is pathetic and comic. His task is to *become* an existing human being, and this means to become subjective, not objective, to passionately appropriate and identify himself with the existential possibilities that confront him. (p. 114)

Long ago, Nietzsche made a similar comment concerning the role of personal experience: "We others who thirst for reason want to look our experiences as straight in the eye as if they represented a scientific experiment" (quoted by Kaufman, 1974, p. 116).

Some Intuitive Support

The preceding commentary has presented scholarly arguments for the shift from a more traditional, neopositivistic approach toward a more interpretive approach to consumer research in general and toward the greater reliance on subjective personal introspection in particular. The important point is that strong philosophical arguments support the role of subjective personal introspection in science generally and in consumer research specifically. Thus, in moving from more neopositivistic studies toward more interpretive self-reflections on my own private consumption experiences, I believe that I have not simply leapt off an epistemological cliff into the bottomless chasm of unforgivable solipsism nor entered the twilight zone of ultimate narcissism; rather, I have followed the postmodern philosophical temper of the times into an acceptance of interpretive approaches, moving past the interpretivism of semiology and hermeneutics into the private self-reflective experiences uncovered by subjective personal introspection.

Nevertheless, it might help to provide additional intuitive or anecdotal support for the position at which I have now arrived. I therefore present two essentially metaphorical arguments on behalf of subjective personal introspection. I call these, respectively, (a) "I Am a Camera" and (b) "The Ultimate Participant Observation."

I Am a Camera

First, faith in the validity of subjective personal introspection rests on a principle analogous to that which works toward the assumed accuracy of images produced by a camera. Here, note the comments on photography in *Romanticism and Realism* by Charles Rosen and Henri Zerner (1984):

> That photography not only does not, but cannot, lie is a matter of belief, an article of faith. . . . Our belief guarantees its authenticity; to put it simply, we tend to adhere unquestioningly to the conviction that the photographic image is of something that was actually in front of the camera, in a necessary and deducible relation to it; we tend to trust the camera more than our own eyes. . . . Photographic vision has become a primary metaphor for objective truth. (pp. 107-108)

Quite obviously, although the camera itself does not lie, the people who use cameras can, of course, employ them deceptively for the purpose of telling falsehoods. Clearly, photographers can crop a picture, doctor the negative, or aim the camera at such an angle as to misrepresent reality. Indeed, in a sense, any photograph reflects a point of view and thereby embodies a form of distortion. But this is not the issue presently at stake; rather, the key issue involves the sense in which one says colloquially that "the camera does not lie" or believes the proverbial promise: "See yourself as others see you."

Essentially, a photograph is the product of a socially constructed apparatus:

1. As a community, we agree on certain laws of physics and chemistry concerning the behavior of light, how it is refracted by a glass lens, and how it affects certain silver halide emulsions.
2. Collectively, we build a device that transmits light in a certain way to a certain chemically coated strip of film.
3. We use agreed-on procedures to develop this film according to certain carefully specified conventions.
4. Voila! We obtain a photographic image that, we agree, represents reality in a manner about which there exists a high degree of social consensus.

In other words, we "know" that the photo represents "reality" insofar as that reality corresponds to the implementation of certain chemical reactions and optical principles about which we all agree. Thus, this phenomenon depends on "the way a photograph is made . . . the mechanical apparatus and chemical processes that largely replace the decisions and judgments of the picture maker" (Rosen & Zerner, 1984, p. 108).

In a sense, subjective personal introspection represents a similar sort of phenomenon. Of course, like a camera, introspection can be used for the purpose of misrepresentation, deception, or distortion; but that is still not the point. Rather, the point again concerns the role of social construction.

1. As a society, we agree on certain overall principles of education and on the inculcation of certain broad values.
2. Collectively, we raise children to share certain presuppositions and beliefs as a basis for conceiving the world.
3. We monitor these conceptions as they mature developmentally, making certain adjustments deemed socially necessary.
4. Voila! We thereby produce private experiential impressions that we as a society have some reason to trust, precisely because we as a society have played such a major role in creating the human instrument that registers them.

In other words, we "know" that introspection represents "reality" insofar as that reality reflects certain habits of thought about which we all agree. Thus, this phenomenon depends on the role of rules or codes as a basis for the communication or conversations via which we establish conventions:

> The world that each of us experiences has been, of necessity, pre-encoded for us. . . . What we learn is not the world but particular codes into which it has been structured so that we may "share" our experiences of it. The world into

which every infant is born and into which every child is socialized is not a "natural" world. It is a world that has been invented—construed—so that *we* might inhabit it. (Thayer, 1982, p. 30)

For these reasons, I believe that society has some reason to trust subjective personal introspections of the human mind in general and of my own mind in particular, precisely because those introspections belong to an instrument for recording and decoding that society itself has built:

> Theories precede facts; we have to have theories in order to know what facts to look for . . . and thus the interpretation . . . precedes the perception. . . . The world we observe is a world that pre-exists for us, in the structures or sign-systems of which we are in turn creations—properties of the cultures within which we have been in-formed. (Thayer, 1982, p. 37)

The Ultimate Participant Observation

As a second intuitive basis for my faith in the power of subjective personal introspection to provide insights into experiential consumption, various researchers devoted to naturalistic inquiry have expressed support for participant observation as a route to in-depth understanding (Lincoln & Guba, 1985). In a sense, research via subjective personal introspection represents the ultimate realization of this method in which one merges with the phenomenon under investigation by conducting participant observation on one's own life. For example, Danny Jorgensen (1989) attests to the advantages of relying on an intimate familiarity with the insider's life experiences:

> One of the principal advantages of participating while observing . . . is the possibility of experiencing the world of daily life as an insider. Sometimes this only can be accomplished by becoming the phenomenon and experiencing it existentially. (pp. 62-63)
> Personal experience derived from direct participation in the insiders' world is an extremely valuable source of information. . . . As a researcher, you should be properly critical of personal experience—just like any other information. Yet your experiences—because they are your experiences—are subject to even more critical examination than the experiences of other members. (p. 93)

In subjective personal introspection, one reports events and interprets meanings in which one has experienced intimate involvement, to the greatest extent possible, since birth. Reviving arguments articulated by C. Wright

Mills (1959) in *The Sociological Imagination,* Norman Denzin (1989) has emphasized the power of this imaginative absorption in one's subject matter wherein "the researcher with the sociological imagination uses his or her life experiences as topics of inquiry" (p. 48). In Denzin's words, social scientists should "self-consciously make their own experience part of their research" (p. 49): "Researchers are advised to study those areas of social life where they have some intimate familiarity. By doing so, he or she can draw upon the stock of knowledge that has been built up out of previous life experiences" (p. 108).

Participant self-observation also offers certain clear advantages of a practical nature. One need not spend a lengthy time in the field nor confront strange or dangerous surroundings. One need not struggle over the problem of communicating in another language or travel long distances to find a suitable research site. One need not labor to obtain the approval of a human subjects committee or wrestle with difficult ethical problems concerning the violation of an informant's privacy.

In short, one commits oneself to an honest exploration of one's own subjective personal introspections in order to reveal one's own private, self-reflective experiences. One commits oneself to a systematic self-examination, to a searching exploration of whatever feelings and beliefs one holds to be sincere and true.

Science and Introspection

I now wish to build on the various arguments just presented by showing that subjective personal introspection can reveal worthwhile knowledge concerning consumer behavior. Whether such knowledge is "scientific" or not depends on how one defines "science." If one adopts the definition favored by some neopositivists, the answer is probably no. If one accepts the more relativistic criteria suggested by contemporary interpretivists, the answer might under some conditions become yes.

As already indicated, consumer research has moved increasingly toward a greater acceptance of interpretive methods. From this perspective, we as researchers have witnessed a slightly more tolerant openness to approaches such as subjective personal introspection in studies of consumer behavior. Thus, I now wish to provide some historical examples to support my claim that the aims, concepts, and methods of introspective research on consumption experiences may make useful, meaningful, and valid contributions to consumer research.

Things to Come

Toward that end, I discuss (a) the background of introspection as a style of thinking and (b) the essay as a form for writing about introspection. I then point out cases in which the introspective essay has attained triumphant levels of insight by celebrating the achievements of Michel de Montaigne and Walter Pater. Here, the "validity" at stake is intersubjective instead of objective in nature. Informed by private experiential self-reflection, the introspective essay attempts to achieve a deep probing of the human condition and pursues broad suggestiveness, as opposed to narrow empiricism. Bathed in the ethos of romanticism, it aspires to an exaltation of ecstatic experience, rather than a resignation to inhibited rationality. In this, it moves toward the celebratory Wordsworthian vision of consumer behavior as consummation. Aware of suffering, it moves toward joy.

❏ The Background of Subjective Personal Introspection: Michel de Montaigne and Walter Pater

From Ancient to Modern

To introspect, one must have the sense of a self that one can introspect *into*. The ancients (as revealed in the Homeric epics) lacked any such clear sense of self (Davy, 1978) and greeted "every morning as if it were the first day of their lives" (Auerbach, 1953, p. 12). In the words of Gray (1985), "Homer's . . . warriors don't . . . learn by experience" (p. 18). On this theme, Jaynes (1976) hypothesizes that the ancient Greeks had no sense of consciousness and, as a result, did not engage in introspection:

> What is mind in *The Iliad*? . . . The answer is disturbingly interesting. There is in general no consciousness in *The Iliad*. (p. 69)
> The characters in *The Iliad* do not sit down and think out what to do. They have no conscious minds as we say we have, and certainly no introspections. (p. 72)

> Iliadic man did not have subjectivity as do we; he had no awareness of his awareness of the world, no internal mind-space to introspect upon. (p. 75)

In sum, it appears that consciousness and therefore introspection are relatively recent human inventions, only two thousand years older than, say, the fax machine or the cellular telephone. Something like our modern conception of consciousness emerged with the Socratic Greeks but probably did not approach our current sense of personal selfhood until the Enlightenment, as exemplified by the chasm that René Descartes (1641/1986) opened between body and soul, between mind and matter, between subject and object, or between self and other (Campbell, 1984).

I propose to look to a period just before the emergence of the Cartesian dualism, circa 1640. Anticipating this cataclysmic philosophical development, Michel de Montaigne (1533-1592) had written his memorable collection of self-reflective introspections, giving birth to the concept of the *personal essay.*

Michel de Montaigne

Although we might trace the origins of Montaigne's approach to such intensely personal works as the spiritual revelations of St. Augustine (circa 400), whose *Confessions* (c. 400/1961) reflect his transformation from "a great sinner" to "a great saint" (Pine-Coffin, 1961, p. 11), it is generally agreed that Montaigne virtually invented the modern essay form. The term *essay* itself comes from the French *essai,* meaning "an attempt," a "trial," or a "test." In his essays, Montaigne attempted to construct a self-analysis, a self-portrait, or an "introspective study of human nature and human conduct" (Frame, 1958, p. v) by using what Auerbach (1953) describes as "a method of self-auscultation, of the observation of one's own inner movements" (p. 297). In this, Montaigne showed some affinity for what more contemporary thinkers might call the "personal construction of reality" (Hirschman & Holbrook, 1992):

> Montaigne writes essays about his own life, and . . . one of his main activities is . . . "essaying": testing and tasting one's own life while experiencing it, thinking about it and recording the thoughts. . . . The essay is a sample of the self as it is involved in this complex of activities. (Good, 1988, p. 32)

Montaigne's preoccupation with the self does not imply, however, any self-centered flight into solipsism or egocentrism; rather, he aimed to use his self-discoveries as a window through which to observe the human condition, believing that his method of introspection could "illuminate the general conditions of human existence" (Auerbach, 1953, p. 309). All of this appears in the famous passage taken by Auerbach (1953) as his *Ansatzpunkt* or point of departure (Auerbach, 1969):

> I set forth a humble and inglorious life; that does not matter. . . . Each man bears the entire form of man's estate. . . . Authors communicate with the people by some special extrinsic mark; I am the first to do so by my entire being, as Michel de Montaigne. . . . If the world complains that I speak too much of myself, I complain that it does not even think of itself. . . . At least I have one thing according to the rules: that no man ever treated a subject he knew and understood better than I do the subject I have undertaken; and that in this I am the most learned man alive. (Montaigne, 1595/1958, p. 611)

Here, we find Montaigne's claim to be the first to speak entirely of himself, the rationale that his fidelity and sincerity ensure a complete understanding of his subject matter, and his belief that this subject matter leads toward a fuller comprehension of humanity because "each man bears the entire form of man's estate." In Auerbach's (1953) view, this passage provides a complete justification for the *Essays*: "If every man affords material and occasion enough for the development of the [sic] complete moral philosophy, then a precise and sincere self-analysis of any random individual is directly justified" (p. 297).

Montaigne's Essays

In the essays themselves, one finds a wealth of personal revelations combined with the keen insights of an inquiring mind. Significantly for our purposes as researchers, many of these introspective observations concern themselves with aspects of consumer behavior. In an early essay called "Of Custom . . . ," Montaigne addresses the local norms that people take for granted as part of their immediate social environment: "The principal effect of the power of custom is to seize and ensnare us in such a way that it is hardly within our power to get ourselves back out of its grip and return into ourselves to reflect and reason about its ordinances" (p. 83). Elsewhere, he gives examples of wonderfully bizarre consumption habits, many of them doubtlessly apocryphal in origin or even invented by his own fertile imagination, but used tellingly to provide vivid instances of his point that different cultures produce dramatically different modes of consumer behavior, all of which appear perfectly normal in the societies where they flourish:

> There are countries where, except for his wife and children, no one speaks to the king except through a tube. . . . There are places where there are public brothels of males, and even marriages between them; where the women go to war alongside their husbands, and take their place not only in the combat but also in command. Where they not only wear rings on the nose, lips, cheeks, and toes, but also have very heavy gold rods thrust through their breasts and buttocks. Where in eating they wipe their fingers on their thighs, on the pouch of their genitals, and on the soles of their feet. (p. 80)

In some of these passages, Montaigne sounds like an impressionable voyeur who has overdosed on too many *National Geographics*. But often, he shines the light of his introspective relativism onto the foibles of his own society. One illustration that still carries some weight for today's Western consumers concerns the pocket handkerchief, about which Montaigne tells the following charming story:

> One French gentleman always used to blow his nose in his hand, a thing very repugnant to our practice. Defending his action against this reproach . . ., he asked me what privilege this dirty excrement had that we should prepare a fine delicate piece of linen to receive it, and then, what is more, wrap it up and carry it carefully on us; for that should be much more horrifying and nauseating than to see it dropped in any old place, as we do all other excrements. I found that what he said was not entirely without reason; and habit had led me not to perceive the strangeness of this action. (p. 80)

Montaigne's Epicureanism

Montaigne was increasingly preoccupied with local customs as he moved through philosophical phases of stoicism and skepticism toward a more Epicurean focus on the nature of his own private experience (Frame, 1958, p. xii). *Epicureanism*—the philosophical basis for Montaigne's later essays—is characterized by two important beliefs: first, the incontestability of immediate experience; second, the identification of good and evil with pleasure and pain, respectively (De Lacy, 1967, p. 3).

Montaigne's later, more Epicurean essays draw deeply on personal experiences in general and on consumption experiences in particular. As noted by Good (1988), "Experience is the unifying idea: His last and perhaps his greatest essay is 'On Experience.' . . . Here the experience of essaying and the essaying of experience are given their fullest treatment" (p. 37). The following statements offer a pastiche taken from the first 10 pages of Montaigne's essay on experience and reveal his commitment to self-examination:

> There is no desire more natural than the desire for knowledge. We try all the ways that can lead us to it. When reason fails us, we use experience. (p. 815)
> I study myself more than any other subject. That is my metaphysics, that is my physics. (p. 821)
> I would rather be an authority on myself than on Cicero. In the experience I have of myself I find enough to make me wise, if I were a good scholar. (p. 822)
> It is from my experience that I affirm . . . the school of the world. (p. 824)

This relentless focus on personal experience in the "school of the world" leads Montaigne inevitably toward a preoccupation with his own habits of consumption: "Montaigne gives us the smallest details of his existence, his habits of eating, sleeping, defecating, exercising, love-making, talking, and reading. . . . Montaigne's project . . . has the cumulative all-inclusive form of experience itself" (Good, 1988, p. 42). In passing, Montaigne reveals innumerable details (sometimes more than we really want to know) about his favorite foods (meats, melons, and sauces); his dislike for a stuffy or smokey atmosphere (which makes him feel weak and heavy); his nocturnal habits (sleeping alone and well covered up); his fondness for scratching (especially his ears, which itch on the inside); his kidney stones (whose voiding is sweet); and even his own slovenly table manners ("I often bite my tongue and sometimes my fingers, in my haste," p. 848).

All of this self-revelation hinges, of course, on the Epicurean ideal of pursuing one's pleasures and avoiding as many pains as possible. At one point, Montaigne produces the following product-filled, preference-based, pleasure-oriented, experience-packed celebration of his own consumption habits:

> I cannot, without an effort, sleep by day, or eat between meals, or breakfast, or go to bed without a long interval, of about three full hours, after supper, or make a child except before going to sleep, or make one standing up, or endure my sweat, or quench my thirst with pure water or pure wine, or remain

bareheaded for long, or have my hair cut after dinner; and I would feel as uncomfortable without my gloves as without my shirt, or without washing when I leave the table or get up in the morning, or without canopy and curtains for my bed, as I would be without really necessary things. I could dine without a tablecloth; but very uncomfortably without a clean napkin, German fashion; I soil napkins more than they or the Italians do, and make little use of spoon or fork. (p. 830)[1]

Clearly, in Montaigne, we encounter a man who believes that, in describing his consumption experiences, he describes himself and, in a sense, portrays all humankind. As noted by Thomas (1979), the miracle is that, by dwelling on himself as revealed through his own consumer behavior, Montaigne manages to put readers in touch with the essence of the human condition:

> He is resolved from the first page to tell you absolutely everything about himself, and so he does. (p. 121)
> To be sure, he does go on and on about himself, but that self turns out to be the reader's self as well. . . . You lean forward in your chair, and he begins to tell you what it is like to be a human being. (Thomas, 1979, p. 122)

From Montaigne to Pater

Michel de Montaigne's essays have inspired countless subsequent attempts in closely related genres. Among other effects, Montaigne's creations have reached across a span of more than 400 years to play a role in shaping this book. Indeed, they have led toward this book's reliance on the introspective essay, as well as this chapter's advocacy of subjective personal introspection. To put it mildly, I regard Montaigne as my master. And, in this, I find myself in the good company of many other authors.

In general, Graham Good (1988) describes the essay as "a commentary which has broken free . . . to become self-contained and *sui generis*" (p. 3):

> The essay offers personal experience. . . . Ultimately, the essayist's authority is not his learning, but his experience. . . . The essay lets its discourse take the shape of experience. . . . The essay offers knowledge of the moment . . . where self and object reciprocally clarify and define each other. . . . The essay stays closer to the individual's self-experience than any other form except the diary. (pp. 5-8)
> The heart of the essay as a form is this moment . . . where the self finds a pattern in the world and the world finds a pattern in the self. This moment is

> . . . a spontaneous, unpredictable discovery. . . . Self and object are configured in a mutually illuminating way. . . . The essay aims to inspire confidence . . . by its capacity to record the particulars of experiences and responses accurately *as particulars*. The essay is an act of personal witness. (pp. 22-23)

Following Montaigne, the self-reflective discoveries of the essayist often refer to consumption experiences and other aspects of consumer behavior. For example, Grant McCracken (1988) recounts how Diderot (1713-1784) discovered the importance of consistency among products that cohere in a pattern of consumption and described this phenomenon in his essay "Regrets on Parting With My Old Dressing Gown" (Diderot, c. 1760/1964). In honor of Diderot, McCracken (1988) refers to cultural consistencies, correspondences, and complementarities among today's goods—the sense in which a BMW car, a Rolex watch, and a Mont Blanc pen "go together"—as "Diderot Unities and the Diderot Effect" (pp. 118-129).

In another set of personal *Confessions* written by an almost exact contemporary of Diderot, Jean-Jacques Rousseau (1712-1778) declared his intention "to display to my kind a portrait in every way true to nature" wherein "the man I shall portray will be myself" (1782/1933, p. 17). Essentially an exercise in telling "the story of his feelings, and of what they led him to do" (Cohen, 1933, p. 9), Rousseau's focus helped prepare the way for the Romantics. Paradoxically, Rousseau began his autobiographical revelations by declaring that he had "resolved on an enterprise which has no precedent, and which, once complete, will have no imitator" (p. 17). Yet, the *Confessions* doubtless reflected the influence not only of St. Augustine but also of Montaigne. Furthermore, countless authors have followed Rousseau by detailing their own emotional and intellectual experiences. These have included Goethe, Tolstoy, J. S. Mill, Ruskin, Trollope, Gide, Proust, Dickens, and Joyce (Cohen, 1933, p. 7). A century after Rousseau, this distinguished company was joined by the illustrious Walter Pater (1839-1894).

Walter Pater

Another hero of the essay form, Walter Pater (1873/1947) explicitly acknowledged the influence of Rousseau's *Confessions* in reaching his own conclusions on the preeminent importance of seeking and finding "intellectual excitement," especially in his appreciation of the arts:

For our one chance lies in . . . getting as many pulsations as possible into the given time. Great passions may give us this quickened sense of life, ecstasy and sorrow of love, the various forms of enthusiastic activity, disinterested or otherwise, which come naturally to many of us. Only be sure it is passion—that it does yield you this fruit of a quickened, multiplied consciousness. Of this wisdom, the poetic passion, the desire of beauty, the love of art for art's sake, has most; for art comes to you professing frankly to give nothing but the highest quality to your moments as they pass, and simply for those moments' sake. (p. 575)

Pater's chief literary accomplishment lay in his development of the intro-spective essay in which he revealed "his power to paint evocative pictures of moments of intense experience in finely wrought, decorative prose" (Schaper, 1967, p. 56). Recalling Montaigne, Pater subscribed to a kind of intellectually rarefied Epicureanism—a dedication to the joys of consumption—which surfaced most clearly in the "Conclusion" to his book *The Renaissance,* wherein he vividly proclaimed his guiding concern for seeking pleasure in experiences pursued for their own sake (Alston, 1967, p. 347). In this "Conclusion," whence came my epigraph for this chapter, Pater (1873/1947) gave passionate expression to his conviction that the Good Life entails a cultivated appreciation of the beautiful and the profound in the immediacy of sensory and especially aesthetic experience pursued as an end in itself:

At first sight experience seems to bury us under a flood of external objects. . . . But when reflexion begins to act upon those objects . . . each object is loosed into a group of impressions . . . impressions unstable, flickering, inconsistent, which burn and are extinguished with our consciousness of them. . . . Experi-ence, already reduced to a swarm of impressions, is ringed round for each one of us by that thick wall of personality through which no real voice has ever pierced. . . . Every one of those impressions is the impression of the individual in his isolation. . . . Not the fruit of experience, but *experience itself, is the end.* . . . *To burn always with this hard, gemlike flame, to maintain this ecstasy, is success in life.* . . . *Not to discriminate . . . is, on this short day of frost and sun, to sleep before evening.* With this sense of the splendour of our experience and of its awful brevity, gathering all we are into one desperate effort to see and touch, we shall hardly have time to make theories. . . . The theory or idea or system which requires of us the sacrifice of any part of this experience . . . has no real claim upon us. (pp. 573-574, italics added)

Although one should properly interpret this famous and stirring passage as a vivid expression of the Epicurean "desire for a refined type of happiness which is the reward of the cultured man who can take pleasure in the joys of the mind" (Winn, 1962, p. 93), Pater's contemporaries tended to misconstrue his "Conclusion" as an outpouring of vulgar hedonism in the mode of "eat and drink for tomorrow we die" (Levey, 1985, p. 20). To discourage such misimpressions, Pater removed his magnificent "Conclusion" from the second edition of *The Renaissance*. Furthermore, for the purpose of dealing more fully with the issues raised by this misunderstanding, Pater (1885) wrote his masterpiece—*Marius the Epicurean*.

Marius the Epicurean

On the surface, as an example of historical fiction, *Marius the Epicurean* presents the story of a young Roman's intellectual education, spiritual awakening, religious conversion, and premature death in the time of Marcus Aurelius (roughly A.D. 161-180). Yet, a broad critical consensus generally agrees that *Marius* conveys an essentially autobiographical and idiosyncratic outlook—impressionistic and confessional in its tone, personal and self-reflective in its approach (Levey, 1985). Above all, Pater adopts an introspective focus and turns it onto the nature of subjective experience. Thus, according to Levey (1985), "the most significant and fundamental similarity between Pater and his fictional character lies proclaimed already on the title-page in the use of the words 'the Epicurean' to describe Marius" (p. 19).

Actually, Pater portrays the early education of Marius as Cyrenaic, rather than Epicurean. Another form of hedonistic philosophy, Cyrenaicism shared certain beliefs with Epicureanism—namely, that (a) "only active physical sensations . . . were sure guides and criteria for action" and (b) "the particular sensation of pleasure of the moment was . . . the only good desirable for its own sake, and the criterion of right and wrong" (Kidd, 1967, p. 286). For a while, oriented toward the joys of consumption, Marius embraces these simple doctrines of Cyrenaicism:

> He was ready now to concede, somewhat more easily than others, the first point of his new lesson, that the individual is to himself the measure of all things, and to rely on the exclusive certainty to himself of his own impressions. . . . And for a time Marius lived much, mentally, in the . . . philosophy of pleasure. . . . It became the stimulus towards every kind of activity, and prompted a perpetual, inextinguishable thirst after experience. . . . Our knowledge is limited to what we feel, he reflected: we need no proof that we feel. . . . How natural the determination to rely exclusively upon the phenomena of the

senses. . . . He would be sent back, sooner or later, to experience, to the world of concrete impressions, to things as they may be seen, heard, felt by him: but with a wonderful machinery of observation, and free from the tyranny of mere theories. (Pater, 1885/1985, pp. 110-115)

Such passages as this sound very much like the earlier "Conclusion." Yet, in *Marius*, Pater took pains to answer his critics. Thus, Pater insisted that the Epicureanism of Marius moved beyond simple Cyrenaicism or vulgar hedonism to focus on the pleasures of the mind via the cultivation of the intellect's capacity for aesthetic experience and other refined sensibilities:

With this view he would demand culture . . . or, in other words, a wide, a complete, education . . . directed especially to the expansion and refinement of the power of reception; of those powers, above all, which are immediately relative to fleeting phenomena, the powers of emotion and sense. In such an education, an "aesthetic" education, as it might now be termed, and certainly occupied very largely with those aspects of things which affect us pleasurably through sensation, art, of course, including all the inner sorts of literature, would have a great part to play. . . . Such manner of life might come even to seem a kind of religion—an inward, visionary, mystic piety, or religion, by virtue of its effort to live days "lovely and pleasant" in themselves, here and now, and with an all-sufficiency of well-being in the immediate sense of the object contemplated. . . . In this way, the true aesthetic culture would be realizable as a new form of the contemplative life. (Pater, 1885/1985, pp. 117-118)

Here, *Marius* elaborates the true message of the "Conclusion" by pushing Epicureanism in the direction of the contemplative life dedicated to a cultivated appreciation of beauty and a refined sensitivity to feeling. Near the end, Marius reflects back on his life's experiences as "the unbroken placidity of contemplation" in which "all its movement had been inward; movement of observation only, or even of pure meditation" (p. 288). Ultimately, for Marius as for Pater, this perspective justifies a kind of purified Epicureanism in a manner that puts it permanently beyond the reach of critical attacks on vulgar hedonism:

His deeper wisdom had ever been . . . to use life, not as the means to some problematic end, but, as far as might be, from hour to *dying* hour, an end in itself—a kind of music, all-sufficing to the duly trained ear. . . . The vision of men and things, actually revealed to him on his way through the world, had developed, with a wonderful largeness, the faculties to which it addressed itself, his general capacity of vision; and in that too was a success. . . . Throughout that elaborate and lifelong education of his receptive powers, he had ever kept in view the purpose of preparing himself towards possible further revelation some day—towards some ampler vision, which should take up into itself and explain this world's delightful shows, as the scattered fragments of a poetry, till then but half-understood, might be taken up into the text of a lost epic, recovered at last. (Pater, 1885/1985, p. 294)

By treating "this world's delightful shows" as "fragments of poetry" from a larger "text," through the penetrating vision of Marius, Pater gives intensely vivid impressionistic accounts of various consumption experiences that might well interest consumer researchers who have turned their attention to hedonic consumer behavior or experiential consumption.

Consider, for example, the following three intensely rich descriptions of (a) a sailing expedition, (b) an evening supper, and (c) the decor of a house.

[A.] Flavian and Marius sailed further than they had ever done before to a wild spot on the bay. . . . In the absolute transparency of the air on this gracious day, an infinitude of detail from sea and shore reached the eye with sparkling clearness, as the two lads sped rapidly over the waves. . . . They reached land at last. The coral fishers had spread their nets on the sands, with a tumble-down of quaint, many-hued treasures, below a little shrine of Venus, fluttering and gay with the scarves and napkins and gilded shells which these people had offered to the image. (p. 95)

[B.] The room in which he sat down to supper, unlike the ordinary Roman inns at that day, was trim and sweet. The firelight danced cheerfully upon the polished, three-wicked *lucernae* burning cleanly with the best oil, upon the white-washed walls, and the bunches of scarlet carnations set in glass goblets. The white wine of the place put before him, of the true colour and flavour of the grape, and with a ring of delicate foam as it mounted in the cup, had a reviving edge or freshness he had found in no other wine. (p. 128)

[C.] The fragments of older architecture, the mosaics, the spiral columns, the precious corner-stones of immemorial building, had put on, by such juxta-position, a new and singular expressiveness, an air of grave thought, of an intellectual purpose, in itself, aesthetically, very seductive. Lastly, herb and tree had taken possession, spreading their seed-bells and light branches, just astir in the trembling air, above the ancient garden-wall, against the wide realms of sunset. (Pater, 1885/1985, p. 228)

These brief excerpts demonstrate vividly that, in Pater's Epicureanism, one dwells in a world of deeply felt and intensely appreciated consumption experience.

Furthermore, Pater's concentration on such imaginative details of consumption experience is no mere accident of literary style. For example, one theme in *Marius* concerns what Pater calls "the sentiment of home" (p. 59). Very early in the book, he crowns a beautifully rich description of his hero's childhood villa with a memorable whiff of olfactory imagery: "Even on summer nights the air there had always a motion in it, and drove the scent of the new-mown hay along all the passages of the house" (p. 47). Toward the end of the story, as Marius lies ill and dying in a strange bed, he recaptures his sense of home via a telling repetition of this vivid sensory impression:

> Even during those nights of delirium he had felt the scent of new-mown hay pleasantly, with a dim sense for a moment that he was lying safe in his old home. The sunlight lay clear beyond the open door; and the sounds of the cattle reached him softly from the green places around. (p. 292)

I find Pater's deep autobiographical and impressionistic introspections inspiring. Hence, my admiration for Pater's attempts to capture the essence of life via intensely felt subjective accounts of personal consumption experiences has encouraged my effort to reflect the spirit of his insights in my own introspective essays and in part of this chapter's self-reflective title—meant as a homage to Walter Pater—"Morris the Epicurean."

❑ Morris the Epicurean and the ACR Trilogy

Old Cat, New Tricks

During the late 1980s—recalling Pater's approach—Morris the Cat became Morris the Epicurean. In this spirit, he created three introspective essays that drew heavily on self-reflections concerning his own private consumption experiences. At the time, these exercises in subjective personal introspection represented extreme departures from the neopositivistic norms that had so strongly dominated consumer research. With some trepidation, Morris presented each of them at conferences of the Association for Consumer Research (ACR) in 1985, 1986, and 1987. I call them my "ACR trilogy" (Holbrook, 1986e, 1987a, 1988b).

Epicurean in intent, these essays explored closely interrelated aspects of my own private, self-reflective experiences. All three dealt, in some sense, with my own responses to works of art by addressing the pervasive role of music in my world, the importance of various decorative artifacts in establishing my sense of home, and the meanings of collections of artworks in our family life. Together, these essays reflect a subjective personal introspective approach; they investigate questions raised by my interest in the nature of experiential consumption.

The three introspective essays in my ACR trilogy were published in the conference proceedings entitled *Advances in Consumer Research* as "I'm Hip: An Autobiographical Account of Some Musical Consumption Experiences" (1986e); "An Audiovisual Inventory of Some Fanatic Consumer Behavior: The 25-Cent Tour of a Jazz Collector's Home" (1987a); and "Steps Toward a Psychoanalytic Interpretation of Consumption: A Meta-Meta-Meta-Analysis of Some Issues Raised by the Consumer Behavior Odyssey" (1988b). The third of these essays—loaded with the animal imagery so characteristic of this book, largely reworked, and greatly expanded—appeared as "The Psychoanalytic Interpretation of Consumer Research" (Holbrook, 1988a) and is discussed here in detail under the chapter's subtitle "I Am an Animal." But first, I offer a brief summary of the ACR trilogy with reference to three important and recurrent themes: music, home, and collections.

Music

Certain phenomena raise questions difficult to address by conventional approaches to consumer research, and such issues often turn out to rank high in importance. It follows that these substantively important consumption experiences invite investigation by new or divergent approaches—for example, those that draw heavily on subjective personal introspection.

One case in point, explored more frequently in recent years, concerns *consumer aesthetics*. Yet, as noted in Chapter 3, most researchers have used a neopositivistic approach that has failed to uncover many of the essential meanings of music and other artworks in people's lives.

Two essays in my ACR trilogy ("I'm Hip" and "The 25-Cent Tour") explore the meaning of music and of objects connected with music in my own life as a consumer. I believe that these self-reflections indicate how subjective personal introspection can begin to uncover the deep meanings that underlie consumption experiences. To the best of my knowledge, "I'm Hip" was the first time that anyone in our field had attempted this approach. A much-expanded version of this essay entertains us further in Chapter 10.

Home

The self-reflections in "The 25-Cent Tour" and "I Am an Animal" also bear directly on the manner in which my wife, Sally, and I have assembled collections of artworks that establish our sense of home. These essays document some ways in which we fill our homes with objects that resonate with meaning in our lives as consumers. In both of these explorations, I offer detailed autoethnographic inventories of our cherished possessions and explore the themes that give these objects symbolic meanings in our living space.

Collections

Finally, all three parts of the ACR trilogy describe extended collections of objects that cluster together to embody the meanings central to my own identity. Thus, "I'm Hip" and "The 25-Cent Tour" dwell on my collection of musical artifacts—especially my array of jazz recordings and related paraphernalia. The meanings associated with these "musifacts" are certainly deeply felt, but not secret or otherwise inaccessible. By contrast, "I Am an Animal" explores more buried, unconscious meanings associated with a collection of visual artworks from our weekend house in Pennsylvania (and echoed at our apartment in New York City). Here, the interpretation draws on self-reflective insights gained from a 5-year Freudian psychoanalysis. Hence, in "Animal," the material grows even more deeply subjective, personal, and introspective.

Illustration

It seems to me that the general approach described in this chapter and the specific considerations just raised with respect to the ACR trilogy beg for some sort of detailed illustration in the form of a concrete example. Here, I must ask myself an important question: If I really do believe in the approach that I call subjective personal introspection, then why not go all the way? Why not bare my soul? Why not tell my secrets? Why not risk embarrassing myself for the sake of science? Why not continue the metaphorical character of this book by revealing to the world what it doubtless already suspects? So, all right, already. Here it is—my illustration of subjective personal introspection and, simultaneously, my confession: *I Am an Animal*.

❑ *I Am an Animal*

Background

This essay grew out of a widely celebrated project known as the Consumer-Behavior Odyssey, in which I participated for 2 weeks during the summer of 1986. On this "odyssey," several consumer researchers lived in a gigantic recreational vehicle; drove this RV from California to Connecticut; practiced some homegrown ethnography by interviewing informants at flea markets, county fairs, fat farms, shopping malls, circuses, and other consumption-oriented venues; shot countless photographs and videotapes of these encounters; and publicized their own adventures extensively (Belk, 1991; Connors, 1986; Wallendorf & Belk, 1987). As defenders of a new approach to consumer research, some members of the odyssey adopted a rigidity of procedure that has ruffled a few feathers. My own somewhat disenchanted reaction emerged from experiences that occurred when the odyssey came to visit *my* house and proceeded to use *me* as an informant.

Specifically, members of the Consumer-Behavior Odyssey raised some questions about my own consumption by explicating my family's collection of artworks that represent animals and related motifs. To challenge their conclusions, I draw on insights gained from 5 years of psychoanalysis to search for meaning in four especially vivid childhood memories and in a phobia whose manifest content appears to have condensed the latent structure of these memories.

The Odyssey Visits the Poconos

On a hill high in the Pocono Mountains, located about 5 miles southwest of Lord's Valley, Pennsylvania, and surrounded by woods filled with deer, raccoons, and even bears, sits a small gray house that my wife, Sally, and I use for retreats from the noise and bustle of the big city. During the summer of 1986, this house received visits from two sets of guests. The first was a hoard of insects, rodents, and other vermin who had taken advantage of our prolonged absence during the spring to invade our home. The second was a group of researchers and friends from the Consumer-Behavior Odyssey.

In late June, about 3 weeks before the scheduled arrival of my colleagues, Sally and I drove to the house to prepare it for their occupancy. There, to our horror, we discovered a rampant infestation of household pests that included daddy longlegs, ants, flying insects, and field mice who had moved inside for the winter months.

Feeling struck by all seven plagues simultaneously, I immediately acquired a massive collection of ant traps, mousetraps, bee poison, rat poison, and other pesticides. I stored this potent arsenal in a bookcase near the front door and employed it relentlessly to attack the legions of intruders that had invaded our living quarters. Eventually, my labors as an exterminator more or less rid the house of pests and prepared it for the advent of a new set of visitors.

To my chagrin, the first thing the Odysseans noticed on entering our house was my assortment of pesticides. One Odyssean immediately spread out my arsenal on the floor and began photographing it, gleefully announcing that this would serve as a wonderful example for his marketing class. Meanwhile, Russell Belk's field notes for August 7 reveal that he, too, was forcefully struck by the same symptoms of the infestation:

> Morris . . . relates his great mice hunt and ant eradication. . . . Morris also talks about disposal of mice, their stupidity, and the possibility that they mourn. Earlier discussion indicated that it was mouse droppings that most annoyed Morris. Their dead bodies also horrify him, so he picks them up with tongs and throws them away still in their traps. They are then thrown away in the garbage. Neither Morris nor son Chris ever had rodents as pets.

My efforts to explain the need for all of the pesticides proved futile. No amount of vivid detail could convince the Odysseans that I had not over-reacted to the pest problem. Even my scariest story about finding a dead mouse in one of their beds won no converts to my point of view.

All of this left me with a certain sense of frustration, reflected in my log entry for Thursday, July 31:

My Odyssey friends have found my concerns with pest control to be scream-ingly funny. This, after I got bitten by wasps from head to foot to protect them against the vicious dangers of the hornet's nest that I discovered only inches away from where they have been parking their van. This, after I have coura-geously gone on rat patrol after rat patrol, trapping and killing at least 30 or 40 of the nasty little rodents, sometimes up to 8 or 9 a day.

The Odyssean Interpretation

On the last day of the odyssey visit, the time came for me to serve as an informant and for Russell Belk and Melanie Wallendorf to take the photo-graphs that have since won our house a featured role in their videotape (Wallendorf & Belk, 1987).

My role as informant surfaced on the evening of Thursday, August 7, as documented in my log for that day:

> While I have some beer and peanuts, Russ and Melanie interview me about the house. Russ . . . seems to be working on a theme that has to do with symbolic hunting. Evidence in support of this theme includes the artistic animals scattered around the house, the longbow on the wall, and plentiful supplies of anti-mouse and -ant devices. . . . I re-explain the household pest problem as best I can. Amazingly, to me, they *still* think I am overreacting. Maybe I should have just left that dead mouse in Jeff's bed.

The Odysseans interpreted the contents of our house as revealing an unconscious Morris-as-Great-White-Hunter theme, with the pesticides and a longbow proving my murderous intent against members of the animal kingdom large or small and with our collection of art objects serving as symbolic trophies metaphorically equivalent to an array of moose heads, deer antlers, stuffed owls, and mounted fish.

For example, Belk's field notes for August 7 document the artistic con-tents of the house as follows:

> Morris says he collects little except photos, books, music, and stuff that hangs on the walls (art). . . . The decoration includes 2 batiks . . . one (hated) sea horse, turtle, and fish, one of a parrot from Grand Cayman; a pottery parrot from Cozumel, a Mexican bird design rug, a Mexican papier mâché brightly painted owl; a pink flamingo . . .; a plastic cat; an African lion wool hanging . . .; an African-looking/wood-looking "antelope" carving (really plaster) pur-chased in Scranton; and a bow of painted and laminated wood (bought for

$2.50 at a flea market last year). . . . Together with the predominant poisons and traps for ants, mice, and wasps, this portrays Morris symbolically as a great white hunter.

This interpretation found its way into the script for the Consumer-Behavior Odyssey's official videotape:

Everywhere we looked was another artistic representation of an animal, even though the owner claimed never to have intended such a theme. There was also a decorative archery bow, suggesting a hunter prepared to dominate intruding animals. And in all parts of the house and cabinets, we found a potent arsenal of poisons and traps for use against animal or insect intruders whether they walked, flew, or crawled into his territory. *Again the owner cited seemingly pragmatic reasons for this arsenal, but the evidence suggested he had made a fetish of gaining dominion over the animal kingdom* [italics added].

Displayed at schools around the country by members of the odyssey, the videocassette containing this interpretation quickly achieved a considerable amount of exposure. Indeed, when one of Columbia's job recruits came to our home for cocktails, the first thing he said was, "Gee, this place looks familiar." This celebrity soon led me to wonder whether I enjoyed being portrayed as a would-be murderer of innocent animals.

I must admit that, although I do not consciously regard myself as a predator, our collected artistic artifacts do seem, on the surface, to support the Great-White-Hunter thesis. At the time of the odyssey, our Pennsylvania living room did actually contain the following objects:

1. A bright green papier-mâché owl from Mexico
2. Two framed cloth prints from Grand Cayman (one of a parrot, the other including a fish, a turtle, and a sea horse)
3. An African wall hanging that features a lion's head (with a shaggy mane made out of yarn)
4. A small wall hanging with a stylized profile of a bird from Mexico
5. A small black pottery bird from Mexico
6. A yellow plastic cat
7. A reproduced African carving of an antelope head
8. A plastic pink flamingo
9. A small hand-painted abstract portrait of a brown cat

10. A colored print of two abstract but clearly animate forms
11. A macramé owl
12. A green laminated bow (without string or arrows)

As already noted, our living room also housed a cabinet filled with products for exterminating household pests. The plentitude of these pesticides bolstered the apparent case for my harmful intentions against members of the animal kingdom. The plentitude of these pesticides bolstered the apparent case for my harmful intentions against members of the animal kingdom. Actually, these products had been there for only about a month. Indeed, our need for them had grown directly from my having postponed their use for so long. I do not consciously enjoy slaughtering defenseless little creatures.

But, as also explained, the Odysseans never fully comprehended the urgency of the mass extermination that had immediately preceded their arrival. Hence, I believe that they misinterpreted the meaning of the pesticide arsenal, incorrectly assuming it to be a permanent feature of our living space. Actually, these products had been there for only about a month. Indeed, our need for them had grown directly from my having postponed their use for so long. I do not consciously enjoy slaughtering defenseless little creatures.

Nevertheless, I do agree that the art objects seem to reflect a coherent theme, featuring multiple references to members of the animal kingdom. In retrospect, the unconscious nature of this theme appears quite striking. Our country house harbors numerous artistic objects carrying a pervasive animal motif that I had never consciously noticed. What does this mean? Do the artworks symbolically represent a powerful, repressed hunting instinct? Do they serve as metaphorical trophies? Have I figuratively slain a group of surrogate dragons?

Despite the considerable amount of surface detail mustered in its defense, the Morris-as-Great-White-Hunter interpretation felt wrong to me. In this connection, I believe that understanding consumption patterns revealed by field notes or other naturalistic methods may require moving to a deeper level of analysis. Such questions, initially raised by the Odysseans, have haunted me and have sent me on a different kind of odyssey through the back pages of my mind.

Psychoanalytic Interpretation of the Pocono Artwork

I intend no sweeping judgments on the methods of naturalistic inquiry as represented by the general orientation of the Consumer-Behavior Odyssey. I wish merely to suggest that naturalistic inquiry *may* raise neglected psychoanalytic questions that it cannot necessarily answer without the supplementary use of deeper insights from more clinical approaches. In this connection, Freud's *Interpretation of Dreams* (1900/1965) draws an explicit link between repressed childhood urges and Homer's epic:

> The[re] may . . . be wishes of the past which have been abandoned, overlaid and repressed, and to which we have to attribute some sort of continued existence. . . . They are not dead in our sense of the word but only like the shades in the Odyssey, which awoke to some sort of life as soon as they had tasted blood. (p. 282)

Interpreting the meaning of the art objects in our Pocono home, the Odysseans had found the built-in contradiction between the collection of animal art and the arsenal of weapons but had failed to notice that it was indeed a contradiction. This incompatibility between valuing and destroying animals—buried in the text of our household consumption—poses a challenge for interpretation. I believe, with Leo Bersani (1986), that such a challenge yields to the interpretive insights gained through psychoanalysis.

Memories

My 5 years of psychoanalysis—four sessions a week on the couch, from 1974 to 1978—have begun to recede from my everyday awareness, but several insights still remain that seem to shed some light on my consumption of art as interpreted by the Consumer-Behavior Odyssey. Specifically, I believe that four childhood memories and an early phobia bear directly on my unconscious reasons for our collection of animal-related artworks. (Here, I refer only to *my* unconscious motivations, not Sally's. This appears valid because we have a long-standing agreement not to display anything in our shared space unless we both want it there.)

The relevant childhood memories extend back to my earliest years when, just after my birth in Milwaukee, Wisconsin, my mother took me to Montgomery, Alabama, to live with my grandmother while we all waited for my father to come back from World War II. Never having seen my father, I was surrounded by affectionate females—my mother, my grandmother, my nurse, a young aunt, and a few other women. Collectively, these people made sure that my many needs and wants were fully satisfied. Few tiny boys can ever have had it so good. This paradise continued for almost 2 years.

Memory One

It is a warm, sunny day in the country at a place near Montgomery called Verbena. I am playing on a porch near the kitchen, crawling on the gray wood floorboards. Near the railing, insects buzz around the tall bushes in the flower bed where my mother likes to garden. She stands at a distance on the other side of the yard. I pull myself up on the white porch railing and peak over the top. She does not see me; so I stumble in the general direction of my good friend, Chimmey, the large golden collie that belongs to my aunt. Chimmey stands in the shade, hungrily eating his lunch from a tin plate. I lurch up to him and throw my infant arms around his huge furry neck in a big baby hug that I have repeated countless times before, always with gratifying results.

My next experience is one of utter . . . surprise. Rustling skirts emerge from all the doorways with access onto the porch. My mother rushes toward me from across the yard. To my alarm, I hear myself screaming. I see red goo on the front of my clean, fresh, white suit. Women's voices cry out. I grasp that something very bad must have happened.

In retrospect, I know that Chimmey has bit me, taking a large chunk out of my right cheek. I am rushed to the doctor, who stitches up the gaping wound and applies an enormous bandage. Everyone feels very distressed about all this—I because I have been scared half out of my wits by Chimmey's sudden attack; Chimmey because, after merciless scolding, he senses that he has made a Big Mistake; and all the women because tomorrow my father will be coming home from the war to get a first glimpse of his bouncing baby boy, whose face is now covered by gauze and adhesive tape.

Memory Two

It is another warm, sunny day in Alabama. I stand with my mother and grandmother on the station platform to meet the train that will bring my father home. My right cheek is covered by a thick white bandage, but in my excitement, I have forgotten all about that. The train is very late. As we wait by the railroad tracks for what seems like an eternity, my excitement mounts. Any moment, my father will arrive. I am filled with eager enthusiasm. Everyone has told me, over and over, how wonderful it will be.

At last, a steam locomotive appears in the distance, moving very slowly, its headlights blazing. It creeps down the tracks and finally stops in front of us. From the other end of the train, one lone passenger descends—a tall, red-headed, freckled man wearing an Army uniform. Someone pushes me gently from behind and whispers, "Go to him."

I run down the platform past several Pullman cars to the place where my father stands with his suitcases. Swiftly, he bends down and grabs me in his arms. He lifts me up and hugs me tightly and rubs his face against my left cheek. I feel a sharp, burning pain where his rough 2-days' growth of whiskers scratches my tender skin. In my anguish of surprise, I shriek and then struggle to hold back enormous sobs that threaten to pour out of me.

Soon, my mother reaches us and takes me in her arms, trying to comfort me while I whimper. My father looks first puzzled, then angry. I sense that I have spoiled the family reunion.

With the resilience of childhood, my wounded sensibilities associated with the whisker scratches heal quickly. My father treats me with great love, though he does occasionally tend to lose his temper, sometimes when I least expect it. The dog bite on my other cheek takes longer to mend. Eventually, it becomes a cute dimple that endears me all the more to the Matrons of Montgomery.

Meanwhile, my father has taken my mother away for a month's vacation in northern Wisconsin, leaving me behind. A month feels like a very long time to a small boy.

Not long after these episodes, we move back to Milwaukee. While my mother searches for a place to live and my father resumes his medical practice, we stay for a time with my other grandparents. Here, I sleep in a crib next to the bed of my nurse, Teenie.

Memory Three

When I open my eyes, the cold, gray light of a Midwestern dawn filters through the tall, narrow windows on the side of the room opposite my crib. I stand and peer over the railing at Teenie, peacefully asleep in the bed next to mine. Then, with well-practiced skill, I pull myself up on the railing and swing my right knee over the top. From there, I tumble out of the crib, dropping gently onto the soft blankets at the foot of Teenie's bed. She stirs wearily and takes me under her covers. I feel warm, cozy, and safe as I again drift back to sleep.

When we move into our new house, I get my own room, like a big boy. But Teenie now sleeps in another room on the third floor.

By the age of 4, I have turned my private space into a listening booth. My most favorite plaything is my 78 rpm phonograph, and I have already begun my career as a collector of recordings. I sit with this machine for hours on end, spinning shellac disks and singing along with people like Uncle Don and Uncle Remus. I treat each fragile record with enormous care and master the delicate equipment so well that I earn the right to operate my parents' phonograph in the living room.

Memory Four

I sit alone on the floor in the living room and sift through a stack of phonograph albums, most of which I know by heart. I discover one that I have not heard before. I cannot read yet, but I can see the picture of a small boy and some animals on its cover.

Expecting to hear something like *Br'er Rabbit* or *Babar*, I put this recording on the record player. Immediately, I am plunged into the terrifying story *Peter and the Wolf*. I find the narrator's tale and Prokofiev's music so frightening that I literally do not have the courage to approach the phonograph close enough to turn it off. Instead, I flee to the kitchen to find Teenie. I shut the door to avoid hearing the dread events unfolding in the living room. When I am sure that the piece has ended, I ask Teenie to come with me while I put away the record albums. Teenie helps me. She is my friend.

(Recently, I found the original album of *Peter and the Wolf* in the basement of my parents' new house in Milwaukee. It features Serge Koussevitzky leading the Boston Symphony Orchestra on the RCA Victor Red Seal label. The cover shows little Peter dressed in a cute red suit, a very frightening wolf with his tongue hanging out as he chases a duck that tries in vain to fly away, and *another* picture of the same wolf with a rope around his neck and a silhouette of the unlucky bird in his stomach. I brought this dread object back to New York City with me. Now, almost 50 years after I first heard it, the record album still makes me shudder slightly every time I look at it.)

The Wolf Phobia

At about the age of 4, I developed a phobia that lasted for at least a year. Every evening, even in the coldest weather, my parents insisted on opening my bedroom window to let in some fresh air. From this ritual, I conceived the fantasy that, each night, a ferocious wolf climbed through the open window into my room. If my face was hidden beneath the covers, this wolf would leave me unharmed and go away. If, by contrast, the wolf could see my head poking out, he would bite it off and murder me on the spot. Needless to say, I always slept with my head under the covers.

Interpretation

The foregoing memories and phobia—especially the connections among them—emerged into consciousness during my 5-year psychoanalysis. I have therefore literally spent years working on an interpretation of these materials. Although their implications extend into many areas of my life and psyche, here I explore only those associations of direct relevance to my consumption of the collected artistic objects described earlier.

It seems evident that my early upbringing among my mother, Teenie, and the other women of Montgomery would have encouraged the development of Oedipal urges and other infantile sexual attachments. I was literally surrounded by several lonely women whose men had gone off to war and whose attentions doubtless combined to make Little Master Morris the most spoiled child in the state of Alabama. In this situation, I enjoyed an infantile bliss that lasted until the return of my father.

This paternal return is indelibly linked—in both time and imagery—with Chimmey's terrifying attack. The bite on the cheek parallels the scratches from my father's beard; dog's hairy muzzle parallels my dad's rough whiskers. The two events are further associated by my utter surprise on both occasions—a surprise repeated later at moments when my father would unexpectedly lose his temper over seemingly trivial offenses.

One dared not imagine consciously what reaction might greet a nontrivial offense—say, an offense like the classic Freudian Oedipal predicament of loving the mother and wanting to banish the father so as to gain her undiluted attention. Yet, inevitably, the return of his father can only have filled little Morris with unconscious rage over suddenly having to share the affections of his mother—a fury intensified immediately by her month-long absence and later by the removing of his surrogate mother to a different room.

Guilt over such unconscious rage causes one to anticipate punishment. Faced with Oedipal longings, the male child tends to develop unconscious fears of castration at the hands of the father. The endangerment of Peter (a clear phallic reference) by the Wolf (a clear association with Chimmey and, from there, to my father) fit all too neatly into this overdetermined pattern of latent mental connections. Not long after the scary episode with *Peter and the Wolf*, the phobia appeared as a displacement of these unconscious thoughts and impulses.

Thus interpreted, my reconstructed memories and phobia seem to carry the latent meaning that, from my viewpoint as a child of 4, my only safety lay under the covers (with a surrogate mother) and that if I ventured to poke out my head (Peter, the penis) in the direction of my Oedipal longings (my real mother), a vicious creature (the wolf substituting for my father) would amputate it (with all the unexpected fury of an angry collie).

How, the reader might be wondering, does this pattern of latent associations connect with the artistic objects in our Pennsylvania home?

Evidence

In the context of the childhood memories and phobia just described, the artworks that so fascinated my friends on the Consumer-Behavior Odyssey carry two striking features.

First, at least half of the artistic objects refer to birds (numbers 1, 2, 4, 5, 8, and 11 in the preceding list). Birds, of course, are characterized by bills, by beaks, and (in the case of the family Picidae) by peckers—that is, by clear phallic associations. These phallic connections are echoed by the plastic cat's upright tail, the antelope's horns, the brown cat's contour, and the lion's shaggy mane. If we recall that, in the story about Peter, the wolf eats a duck but is ultimately captured with the help of a bird, we might infer that this art collection serves symbolically as a sort of sanctuary. Figuratively, as a grand resolution of castration anxiety, the Pocono home gives the birds and other phallic references shelter—metaphoric protection against wolves. Indeed, in this light, the pesticides could also be interpreted as an expression of the desire to ward off evil intruders.

Second, another striking feature of the artistic objects in Pennsylvania is that they lack any emblem of a wolf. Apparently, I had successfully banished this frightening creature from the region that protects my assortment of phallic images. Yet, I could not help wondering what had happened to this most terrifying symbol. Where had the wolf gone? Did he no longer haunt me? Or had he simply sneaked off to lurk in some other corner of my world?

Figure 7.1. Author's View of Appel's *I Am an Animal*
SOURCE: From Holbrook (1988a), p. 167. Reprinted with permission.

While I pondered these questions, I sat in my familiar study in our apartment in New York City. Suddenly, I experienced what can only be described as a moment of epiphany involving a profound shock of recognition. As I looked up from my desk toward the wall facing me, I found—staring me in the face—the large apparition of a wolf.

No hallucination, the wolf appeared in a big, abstract, brightly colored lithograph by Karel Appel that adorns the wall opposite my desk. The first time I saw it, in Chicago during my impoverished student days in the early 1970s, I loved it on sight. After a modest improvement in our finances, Sally and I tracked it down and bought it. With the exceptions of our car, our house, and our apartment, it became our single largest purchase. Its title—chosen prophetically by Appel to describe the inner life of Morris the Cat—is *I Am an Animal*. My drawing of this animal appears in Figure 7.1.

Appel's form is abstract enough to be interpreted as almost any four-footed creature: a dog, a cat, a fox, a raccoon, or even a cow. I now realize, however, that for me it represents a wolf. Everything is there—the pointed ears, the beady eyes, the quivering nostrils, the extended tongue, the menacing jaw—in short, pure panting lupinity.

Why, then, do I regard this work of art with such affection? The answer seems to be that it converts the menacing wolf theme into happy, playful comedy—an endearingly funny beast with purple legs, a green neck, and a blue-orange-and-lavender face. By transforming the latent terror of the wolf image into this acceptable—even lovable—manifest content, the artwork evokes a feeling of mastery over the libidinous wishes and unconscious fears displaced onto the wolf metaphor. In a sense, the lithograph delights by reminding me unconsciously that—although "I am an animal" and, indeed, we are all animals—we can tame our horrific and forbidden repressed urges by the re-creation of meaning through processes analogous to the conception of an artwork. Thus, artistic consumption can sublimate our most threatening wishes and can ventilate our deepest fears. The evidence, if we choose to find it, hangs on our walls, sits on our bookshelves, and resounds in our ears.

Corroborations

One could ask how I might possibly *corroborate* such an interpretation. Does it represent a kernel of truth capable of attaining some degree of intersubjective validity? Or is it just a self-fulfilling prophecy based on selecting evidence to support my own pet theory? The answer, I believe, draws on several sources of support—all of them bolstering the interpretation just offered.

Clinical Corroboration

One source of corroboration comes from the psychoanalyst who worked with me for 5 years. In a letter expressing general agreement with the interpretation described here, she reminded me of a black bird that I had given her because of its associations with a nursery rhyme that had played a key role in my analysis. I had completely forgotten this gift and the related rhyme, but it came flooding back with unmistakable relevance:

> Sing a song of sixpence,
> Pocket full of rye;
> Four and twenty blackbirds,
> Baked in a pie;

> When the pie was opened,
> The birds began to sing;
> Wasn't that a dainty dish
> To set before a king?
>
> The king was in his counting house
> Counting out his money;
> The queen was in the parlor
> Eating bread and honey;
> The maid was in the garden
> Hanging out the clothes,
> Along came a blackbird,
> And snipped off her nose.

Clearly, for Morris, this verse represents key members of his nuclear family—not only the father (a king, trying hard to earn a living) and the mother (a queen, enjoying the finer things of life), but also the nurse (a maid, hanging out the wash). The unfortunate episode with the nose again reflects typical childhood castration anxieties—where, in this case, the blackbird (which is itself a phallic symbol) retaliates with a vengeance.

The central wish fulfillment, however, appears in the first stanza. Here, one learns that the nursery rhyme concerns a large number of birds, thereby mirroring the Pocono art collection. As in *Peter and the Wolf*, these phallic symbols are again threatened, this time with the danger of being cooked alive. Thus, the 24 birds are baked in a pie. But—miraculously—they are saved (like the duck in the wolf's stomach).

For me, *black*birds in this nursery rhyme also carry strong associations with the expressiveness of certain favorite African American jazz musicians and singers (e.g., Charlie "Bird" Parker, as discussed in Chapter 2). At the literal level, this poem frees the birds and they begin to sing. Figuratively, the repressions are lifted, and the meanings of the bird imagery with all of its Oedipal associations begin to emerge into consciousness.

Contextual Corroboration

Another psychoanalyst who has often visited our apartment in New York concurred generally with the preceding interpretation and called my attention to additional evidence presented by the artworks contained in our city dwelling. My subsequent inventory of the artistic objects in our apartment supports her suggestion. As she anticipated, consistent with the Pocono art collection, phallic animal imagery abounds:

A pencil sketch of three naked ladies with grotesquely distended necks

A large green papier-mâché parrot with a bright yellow beak

An aquatint by Picasso, featuring a man with a beard from which emerges a long pipe or cigar

A small pottery owl

A glazed clay cat face with long, thick whiskers

A tiny metal rocking horse with a long, thin neck

A large plaster giraffe

A ceramic tile depicting a yellow rooster, a red cow, and a black bull with long horns

A wooden rabbit with huge, erect ears

Birds and cows in two small prints

An Egyptian cat with pointed ears

A double-headed clay sculpture of a monster with a face where its tail should be

A Man Ray lithograph of a centaur holding both its arms in the air

Two metal bears whose noses point skyward

An Eskimo sculpture of a walrus with two gigantic tusks

An Eskimo bird

Two stuffed cloth parrots with big beaks

A large, brass statue of a penguin

A 10-foot-long collage that represents an African watering hole with zebras, horned buffalo, and elephants

A painted elephant with large tusks and a long trunk

A drawing of Koko the gorilla

Three small turtles, all with their necks poking out

A photo of Dizzy Gillespie, whose trumpet bell points upward at a 45-degree angle

A poster of several musicians playing a trombone, a saxophone, and other rather abstract "horns"

Another poster portraying two birdlike creatures

The Appel lithograph that lends its name to the subtitle of this chapter—*I Am an Animal*

On a visit to our apartment, Melanie Wallendorf was also struck by this proliferation of phallic symbols and related animal imagery. I recall that she took numerous photographs. Meanwhile, my own photos of the artistic objects just mentioned appear in the third part of my ACR trilogy (Holbrook, 1988b).

Historical Corroboration

One member of the Consumer-Behavior Odyssey inquired about the struggle against household pests in our New York City apartment. In this connection, most New Yorkers have battled against cockroaches. I am pleased to say that, with the aid of a miraculous white substance known as "Chinese chalk" and rumored to contain boric acid, we have kept our roach infestations more or less under control. In our previous apartment, however, the fight against cockroaches escalated to nearly cosmic proportions. A short story that I wrote in 1976 gave ample indication of my feelings concerning this plague. In retrospect, it now offers historical corroboration for the nearly traumatic role that the threat of invasion by intruding creatures has played in my psychic development. For example:

> December 7, 1975. I awakened from a vivid nightmare in which a large rat was devoured by an angry cockroach. Unable to sleep, I wandered into the kitchen in search of milk and cookies to settle my stomach. The fluorescent light revealed three fat roaches peacefully munching graham cracker crumbs on the formica counter. They reacted to my intrusion by disappearing into a tiny crevice behind the kitchen sink. . . . I glanced into the cabinet just in time to see a 2-inch roach disappear behind a stack of Royal Worcester dinner plates. (Holbrook, 1988a)

Archival Corroboration: Wolf Man, Too?

Readers familiar with Freud may note the corroborative similarity of the case described herein with that discussed in "History of an Infantile Neurosis" and referred to colloquially as *The Wolf Man* (Freud, 1918/1963). Both examples rely on an association of wolf imagery with the father figure, although the original Wolf Man's repressed homosexuality—as it emerges in his memories, dream, and phobia—appears to be quite different from the psychodynamics described in connection with my own experiences.

My picture of the Wolf Man is enriched by the recent reanalysis found in Nicholas Abraham and Marie Torok's book *The Wolf Man's Magic Word* (1986). These authors question Freud's interpretation and use an analysis based on what they call a "cryptonym" (literally, a "hidden name") to infer that the Wolf Man's dream-phobia resulted from an early seduction scene between brother and sister, a resulting introjection of the sister as a love object, a witnessing of the sister involved in an incestuous relationship with the father, and a subsequent association of the sister with the wolf (specifically, six wolves in the dream, in which the Russian *shiestorka*, or "a group of six," closely resembles *siestorka*, or "little sister"). The authors tie all of this to the patient's later neuroses concerning his nose and describe their unraveling of the cryptonym (*tieret*) as follows:

> Then we ventured a final hypothesis, and this turned out to be our lifesaver. . . . Why restrict our attention to the nightmares and phobias when the hypochondriac fears concerning the nose speak explicitly about scratch, scar, and cancer? Obviously, behind this was lurking the association, undoubtedly left nonverbalized, of a *lupus*, namely a *lupus seborrheus*. . . . How to link it to the seduction by the sister? Would she have touched him in a way that the child could have called "polish" . . . ? . . . We then turned to the word *tieret* and read: (1) to rub; (2) to grind, to crunch; (3) to wound; (4) to polish. . . . With all the necessary substitutions, the solution is simple: It concerns the association of the wolf with sexual pleasure obtained by rubbing. . . . By the same token, a whole area of the Wolf Man's enigmatic material was opened to our understanding. Lingering for the moment on the nose symptom, it became precise and concrete. The symptom had been produced, it was clear now, through the association of two words. . . . The hypochondriac *lupus*, coupled with the cryptonym "scar," did nothing more than show/hide the desire of a pleasurable rubbing applied to the "wolf" in order to make it stand up. "Sis, come and rub my penis," . . . It became obvious that this hidden sentence would be found everywhere in the Wolf Man's material. . . . What is at stake here is . . . a *metonymy* of words. The contiguity that presides over this procedure . . . arises from the lexical contiguity of the various meanings of the same words, this is, from the *allosemes*. . . . Having understood the real originality of this procedure, which lies in replacing a word by the synonym of its alloseme, we felt the need of applying to it a distinctive name, *cryptonymy*. (Abraham & Torok, 1986, pp. 17-19)

The validity of Abraham and Torok's interpretation via the cryptonym receives striking support from two further pieces of biographical material. First, the Wolf Man returns to the scene of his sister's suicide with the unconscious goal of climbing to the head of a river called the *Tierek*. Second, he falls in love with a woman named Theresa (cf. the Russian *Tiretsia* or "to rub oneself") whose diminutive is *Terka* (pronounced "Tierka"). Abraham and Torok end their initial account by commenting on this astounding "coincidence"

(p. 26)—the point, of course, being that in the use of symbolic meanings by the unconscious there are no coincidences.

Prior to writing the earlier sections of this essay, I had read neither Freud's case history of the Wolf Man nor Abraham and Torok's reinterpretation. However, I have since benefited from these interpretive analyses and from the lengthy autobiography written by the Wolf Man himself and edited by Muriel Gardiner (1971). Here, the Wolf Man reveals not only a forthright willingness to make his case public but also a remarkable sense of humor, as manifested by his ability, despite all of his problems, to take himself lightly. For example, in writing to the book's editor about her daughter's love of animals, the Wolf Man offers the following playful comment, one that seems poignantly appropriate to this book in general and to this essay in particular: "Nothing can be of greater value to a young person than a love of nature and understanding of natural science, particularly animals. Animals played a large part in my childhood also. In my case they were wolves" (p. 316).

Defense

Some readers might be made uncomfortable by my candid approach to a psychoanalytic interpretation of my collected artistic objects. For example, a former editor of the *Journal of Consumer Research* told me that he thought my writings on personal matters would one day prove embarrassing. Yet, embarrassing or not, I would suggest that the interpretation of some consumption phenomena requires this kind of in-depth introspective analysis. Here, I refer to the distinction—fundamental to Freudian thinking—between manifest and latent content (Freud, 1900/1965). Freud showed that dreams, slips of the tongue, neurotic symptoms, works of art, and many other everyday phenomena present manifest content at the overt level that disguises latent or covert meanings repressed as too threatening to be confronted openly.

In this view, every human life is a text and each text is a palimpsest containing multiple messages superimposed on one another with many layers of meaning hidden below the surface (Ricoeur, 1981). This basic conception of symbolic activity as grounded in repression and disguise has encouraged a wide range of interpretive projects in the theory of hermeneutics (Habermas, 1968; Rogers, 1987), semiotics (Eco & Sebeok, 1983; Umiker-Sebeok, 1987), and psychoanalytic artistic criticism (Bersani, 1986; Holland, 1973).

In this essay, I have drawn heavily on the interpretive approach introduced by Freud (1900/1965, 1908/1959, 1908/1963, 1914/1963, 1917/1977,

1918/1963). Here, I follow not only psychoanalysts but also philosophers (Kuhns, 1983), historians (Ginzburg, 1983), literary critics (Holland, 1973), and semioticians (Silverman, 1983) in regarding the Freudian view as a rich source of insights on the latent meaning of manifest artistic content:

> What characterizes psycho-analysis as a science is not the material which it handles but the technique with which it works. It can be applied to the history of civilization, to the science of religion and to mythology, no less than to the theory of the neuroses, without doing violence to its essential nature. What it aims at and achieves is nothing other than the uncovering of what is unconscious in mental life. (Freud, 1917/1977, p. 389)

Critiques

However, one must acknowledge basic questions concerning the scientific status of the psychoanalytic approach. For example, from the viewpoint of the hypothetico-deductive method, a scathing neopositivistic critique appears in the treatise by Grünbaum (1984). Along similar lines, Calder and Tybout (1987) have used neopositivistic criteria to argue that psychoanalysis is inherently unscientific:

> It may be that much work purporting to be scientific is in fact interpretive. . . . This has, for instance, long been a criticism of psychoanalytic work. . . . Freudian ideas are embraced by analysts without serious attempt at empirical refutation and are then used to interpret behavior. Such work is bogus from the standpoint of scientific knowledge. (p. 10)

This pronouncement betrays a disinterest in types of investigation that lead toward *idiographic*, or case-specific, as opposed to *nomothetic*, or universal, knowledge (Windelband, 1924, cited by Makkreel, 1975, p. 42). It also reflects a fear that unchecked introspection might encourage an anarchy of self-indulgence: "In an extreme form it could lead to *anarchy*. If construed as the 'anything goes' and 'why not call it science' of a Feyerabend, there is little to stop researchers from indulging in *anything that suits their fancy* in the name of scientific knowledge" (Calder & Tybout, 1987, p. 139, italics added).

This argument points to the difference between neopositivistic and post-positivistic views of science and interpretation, as in the debate between Hirsch (1967) and Gadamer (1975). Furthermore, the scientific status of psychoanalysis hinges on whether one regards it as a *natural science* (subject to testing via the standards of neopositivism) or as a *human science* (subject to different criteria of validity).

Natural and Human Sciences

If one views psychoanalysis as a natural science, Fisher and Greenberg (1985) have provided an exhaustive review of the empirical evidence bearing on "the scientific credibility of Freud's theories" and, with respect to the phenomena of present concern, have affirmed "the basic soundness of Freud's thinking about the . . . Oedipal and castration factors in male personality development" (p. 414):

> The literature has . . . affirmed certain aspects of the Oedipal concept, which is probably the most important segment in Freud's developmental explanatory scheme. There is fairly convincing proof that men do have . . . a history of sexually tinged rivalry with father for mother as a love object. The male does, as Freud proposed, experience castration anxiety. . . . Defensive reactions in the sexual realm . . . conform to Freud's Oedipal model. (Fisher & Greenberg, 1985, p. 400)

Conversely, if psychoanalysis is a human science, Habermas (1968) and Ricoeur (1981) have supported the Freudian approach as a process of hermeneutic self-reflection: "Psychoanalytic hermeneutics, unlike the cultural sciences, aims not at the understanding of symbolic structures in general. Rather, *the art of understanding* to which it leads is *self-reflection*" (Habermas, 1968, p. 228). In this view, self-reflection ultimately becomes the basis for a criterion of validity:

> A critical social science . . . take[s] into account that information about lawlike connections sets off a process of reflection in the consciousness of those whom the laws are about. . . . The methodological framework that determines the meaning of the validity of critical propositions of this category is established by the concept of *self-reflection*. (Habermas, 1968, p. 310)

This hermeneutic or semiological viewpoint accepts the potential personal validity of subjective self-knowledge gained via systematic introspection. It therefore embraces the proposition—central to the humanities at least since the time of Giambattista Vico (1744/1976)—that *humans can best understand the truths that humans themselves create* (Holbrook et al., 1989).

Thus, work in hermeneutics by Gadamer, Ricoeur, and Habermas has justified self-reflective psychoanalytic insights via the self-corrective process of a *hermeneutic circle,* in which one's preconceptions are adjusted against the evidence of a text so as to converge toward a valid interpretation. As Ricoeur (1981) has insisted, the text of interest may be any type of meaningful action (e.g., behavioral, narrative, imaginary). In short, any consumption activity— any aspect of one's own lived experience—can constitute a text suitable for self-reflective interpretation via subjective personal introspection (Hirschman & Holbrook, 1992; Holbrook & O'Shaughnessy, 1988).

Reliability and Validity

Beyond doubt, the introspective approach raises new challenges concerning issues of *reliability* and *validity* in the justification of conclusions based on subjective impressions, personal insights, and inward-looking self-reflections. I have already suggested some grounds for believing that justification in the form of *intersubjective consensus* is possible in the application of introspective methods. The criteria for establishing intersubjective agreement, however, thus far remain vague, at best, and require further specification. My own instincts, as illustrated by this chapter "I Am an Animal," suggest that the most promising direction for justification lies in the pursuit of corroborative supporting evidence (e.g., clinical, contextual, historical, archival).

In terms of reliability, such corroboration involves checks on *internal consistency.* For example, one seeks convergent details within the text of one's own private impressionistic experience. Memories in which the wolf phobia depended on being nipped in the seat by a yapping Chihuahua might not tell a convincingly coherent story. Recollections of being attacked by a gigantic collie are another matter.

Furthermore, corroborative validity entails the ability to *predict or anticipate* unexamined portions of the unfolding introspective account. For example, a trustworthy interpretation should anticipate a hitherto neglected fragment of evidence drawn from some as yet unexamined aspect of one's own life history or the observations of an outside analyst concerning relevant aspects of one's own overt behavior. Clearly, the reader's faith in the interpretation proposed earlier would suffer if I were to discover an article written by my own analyst in which she described my wolf phobia as a form of psychosis that involved hearing voices and seeing hallucinations.

Here, as always, the crux of the matter hinges on ensuring that the sources of such corroborative support for reliability and validity remain as intersubjectively persuasive as possible. The task of ensuring such consensus in the communal conversation presents formidable challenges to practitioners of the introspective approach and requires the further development of appropriate procedures and imaginative solutions (Holbrook & O'Shaughnessy, 1988).

The Value of Idiographic Knowledge

I believe that idiographic insights into consumption experiences (those based on just one or a few cases) are valuable as long as they provide examples of processes that might occur among different consumers in different contexts. Clearly, no one cares about bizarre events with little chance of recurrence. But, more and more, consumer researchers do care about uniquely personal consumption experiences that might shed some light on the nature of the human condition.

The illustrative psychoanalytic interpretation of an art collection presented here provides one such instance of complex human consumption. True, few consumers will be bit by large collies the day before their fathers come home from war and carry their mothers off to the north woods. Doubtless, still fewer will listen to *Peter and the Wolf* on days when their castration anxieties reach peak levels. Undeniably, most consumers will escape the terrors of the nocturnal phobia that appears to have colored my own artistic preferences so deeply. Inevitably, these others may not greet Karel Appel's *I Am an Animal* with the same gladness of heart that it inspires chez Morris the Cat.

But, for many, the *process* of consumption will contain *similar elements*. Art objects and various other possessions will convey hidden meanings that remain latent until carefully uncovered with the assistance of psychoanalytic interpretive techniques. No amount of mechanical content analysis of the objects' manifest message will reveal the emotionally charged connections and the unconscious meanings that lie buried below the surface. Only the most patient and honest probing of repressed thoughts and feelings can achieve an in-depth understanding of consumer behavior. In this, one's latent, repressed, unconscious wishes are like birds. One's manifest, surface, conscious consumption is like a pie. And when that pie is opened, the birds begin to sing.

❏ Conclusion

Those seeking applications of subjective personal introspection, with or without the clinical insights provided by psychoanalysis, need look no farther than the experiences of their own daily lives. We eat, drink, work, and converse with our families, friends, and colleagues on the basis of truths (not *the* Truth, but shared convictions about how the world operates) revealed to us, in part, by subjective personal introspection. Via such consensus-building conversations, the subjective may become intersubjective, though it will never become "objective" (in the sense of a correspondence theory of truth) or "impersonal" (in the sense of not involving people). To make a start, we need only consult Montaigne's "Book of the Self"—that is, the discourse on human nature that the French master has taught us as researchers to study—written in the text of our daily lives as ordinary consumers.

Ultimately, my conviction concerning the potential meaningfulness of subjective personal introspection rests less on a consideration of the various postmodern arguments reviewed earlier than on a conscious surrender to certain essentially romantic impulses discussed at the beginning of this chapter. Some thinkers—perhaps I should call them "feelers"—find themselves temperamentally drawn to accounts of lived experience. Such researchers—perhaps I should call them "explorers"—may wish to portray the human condition in terms of imaginative revelations, inner visions, and (yes) ecstatic passions that open themselves to access only via the paths of subjective personal introspection. Thus, the impetus of romanticism (versus, say, the posture of classicism) and the insights of introspection (in contrast, perhaps, to quantitative measures drawn from more mechanical methods) merge to support a project rooted in experiential consumption (where human experiences, as opposed to purchase decisions, lie at the heart of consumer behavior).

Those ready to embrace these aspects of humanity will find much of what I have said natural or even obvious. Those devoted to a more resolutely classical approach to the purportedly objective study of buying behavior will find my story mystical or even incomprehensible and will wonder—perhaps with some hostility—why I spend so much time and space talking about myself. "Who cares," they will ask, "about the adventures of Morris the Epicurean?" Or, to borrow a favorite phrase from the philosophy of Bill Wells (1993), "So what?"

I might reassure such critics by conceding that I do not wish to make exaggerated claims for the benefits to be gained from a romantically introspective approach to research on experiential consumption. Like any world-view, romanticism has its lacunae. Like any research style, introspection suffers from potential weaknesses. Like any focus, the consumption experience overlooks some important phenomena. Notice, however, that these concessions cut both ways. First, I would admit, subjective personal introspection faces certain limitations. But second, I would insist, so do other approaches.

This truism surfaced recently in considering the alternative approach represented by the well-publicized Consumer-Behavior Odyssey to which I have already referred. In general, the Odysseans did everything possible to follow the methodological dictates prescribed by the advocates of naturalistic inquiry (Hirschman, 1986a; Lincoln & Guba, 1985). These prescriptions call for (a) careful member checks and research audits and (b) taking pains to keep one's objective observations (as contained in one's field notes) separate from one's subjective impressions (as confessed in one's journal entries). We might wonder, however, whether these aspects of rigor, much touted in theory, have been achieved in practice.

First, there is the much-heralded matter of the *member check*, in which the researchers recontact their informants, present their conclusions, note divergences of the informants' views from their own interpretations, and refine their analyses accordingly. In my own experience as an informant for the Consumer-Behavior Odyssey, I can report a rather different outcome. Specifically, when confronted by the Odysseans' view of Morris-as-Great-White-Hunter, I disagreed vehemently. Indeed, so strongly did I disagree that I wrote not one but two lengthy manuscripts and made a carefully prepared audiovisual presentation complete with audiotapes and photographic slides devoted to (a) explaining to the world in general and to the Odysseans in particular exactly why I thought that the Great-Hunter interpretation was just plain wrong and (b) offering a considerable amount of corroborative evidence on behalf of that conclusion. Nevertheless, rather than revise or even qualify their analysis, the Odysseans made a videotape that prominently featured their Great-Hunter motif—complete with photographs of our house and its contents—and then toured the country, showing this film to literally hundreds of my past, present, and future colleagues. So much for the purported trustworthiness of the member check.

Second and much more fundamentally, we as researchers might strongly question the *feasibility* of ever removing subjectivity from one's observations (Geertz, 1973). Although Dan Sperber (1985) distinguishes between interpretive ethnography and theoretical anthropology in the apparent hope of keeping the two separate, the entire weight of Western philosophy argues against any such possibility (Bruner, 1986). Indeed, Richard Schweder (1986) has commented that ethnographies inevitably call forth a level of personal involvement something like that experienced in storytelling, and even Sperber (1985) has grudgingly admitted that "though they make . . . use of . . . experience, ethnographers achieve relevance in the manner of novelists" (p. 34): "These works . . . give us an insight into some fragments of human experience, and this, by itself, makes it worth the journey" (p. 34). Thus, for example, Norman Denzin (1989) follows C. Wright Mills (1959) in suggesting that "interpretive research begins and ends with the biography and the self of the researcher" (Denzin, 1989, p. 12):

> Interpretive interactionists find that their own worlds of experience are the proper subject matter of inquiry. . . . Interpretive interactionism asserts that meaningful interpretations of human experience can only come from those persons who have thoroughly immersed themselves in the phenomenon they wish to interpret and understand. (pp. 25-26)
>
> Such work will . . . involve researchers drawing upon their own biographical experiences as they formulate their interpretive work. (pp. 33-34)

On a similar theme, Renato Rosaldo (1987) argues for a "corrective to literal-mindedness" via the greater use of personal narratives and case histories:

> Personal narratives and case histories . . ., using the past tense and talking about particulars as they do, can depict the experience . . . in ways more difficult to achieve through normalizing discourse. . . . An increased disciplinary tolerance for diverse legitimate rhetorical forms could allow for reading and writing any particular text against other possible versions. Allowing forms of writing that have been marginalized or banned altogether to gain legitimacy could enable the discipline to approximate people's lives from a number of angles of vision. (p. 106)

Ultimately, Clifford Geertz (1988) tends to view ethnographies as aspiring toward the status of inspired poems or insightful novels in that "the writing of ethnography involves telling stories, making pictures, concocting symbolisms, and deploying tropes" (p. 140):

> To say it is art . . . is also to say the burden of authorship cannot be evaded. . . . Ethnography . . . is a work of the imagination. . . . The responsibility for

ethnography, or the credit, can be placed at no other door than that of the
romancers who have dreamt it up. (pp. 139-140)

Faced with the virtual impossibility of removing oneself from one's data,
one might plausibly respond by seeking an approach that openly acknowledges the self-reflective nature of the materials at hand. Toward this end,
rather than subscribe to the self-deluding pretense of maintaining separate
sets of "objective" field notes and "subjective" journal entries, I kept one
introspective log of my experiences on the odyssey (Holbrook, 1987b,
1991b). In this, I departed from the naturalistic methods prescribed by the
Odysseans. As noted by Holt (1991), however, "the trustworthiness criterion
and associated techniques proposed by . . . Wallendorf and Belk contradict
the nature of the interpretive task" (p. 59): "Specific techniques cannot act
as guarantors of privileged status in what is necessarily an interpretive
process" (p. 61). In the case of the material described in this chapter under
the heading "I Am an Animal," I believe that my introspective orientation
produced a better interpretation—one that is more personally useful, more
imaginatively meaningful, and more intersubjectively valid—than that available within the conventional limits of naturalistic inquiry (as represented by
the accounts provided by the Odysseans themselves). In short, I reject the
Morris-as-Great-White-Hunter conclusion in favor of one that regards
Morris as fearful of wolves but friendly to other members of the animal
kingdom. As mentioned earlier when discussing corroborative evidence,
those with real in-depth knowledge of me or my collection of artistic objects
have tended to agree.

All of this means we should avoid dismissing romantic approaches
(grounded in intuition or imagination) from the annals of consumer research
without examining the potential usefulness, meaningfulness, and validity of
subjective personal introspection (inward-looking, deep-probing self-
reflection) in studying a variety of different consumption experiences (some
merely hedonic, others profoundly ecstatic in nature). As I have tried to
show, facets of consumer aesthetics, deep meanings of possessions, and other
human responses to everyday consumer products may lend themselves to
investigation via the kind of subjective personal introspection that pursues
an essentially romantic orientation to explore the experiential aspects of
consumption. If so, somewhere in the scheme of things, Morris the self-
confessed animal may find his home as Morris the Epicurean Cat.

❏ Epilogue

Years after the issues discussed in this chapter first came to light, Melanie Wallendorf and Merrie Brucks combined forces to write a critique of subjective personal introspection, which appeared in the *Journal of Consumer Research* under the title "Introspection in Consumer Research: Implementation and Implications" (Wallendorf & Brucks, 1993). This article rehearses the methodological tenets from naturalistic inquiry that served as the basis for the Consumer-Behavior Odyssey, criticizes any research that departs from the prescribed techniques, and focuses most of its negative comments on an introspective essay by Stephen Gould (1991) entitled "The Self-Manipulation of My Pervasive, Perceived Vital Energy Through Product Use" and published in the same journal.

Given the relentlessness of this attack on the essay by Gould, perhaps I should feel grateful that my own earlier work in developing subjective personal introspection is largely ignored by Wallendorf and Brucks. However, I do note that these authors skewer their chosen example without mentioning that other introspective work—for example, that discussed in this chapter—has avoided many of the difficulties that they emphasize so insistently.

One might assume that this neglect of clear counterexamples to their criticisms stems from a lack of familiarity with, say, my ACR trilogy. But such an inference would be incorrect. Wallendorf spoke immediately after me at the ACR session where I presented "I'm Hip" (1986), edited the ACR volume that contained "The 25-Cent Tour" (1987), participated in the ACR sessions that included "From the Log" (1987) and "Meta-Meta-Meta-Analysis" (1988b), and made so many contributions to "I Am an Animal" (1988a) that I explicitly acknowledged her "helpful comments on an earlier draft." Hence, Wallendorf and Brucks had every reason to know that the charges they leveled at Gould did not apply with equal force to other examples of subjective personal introspection.

The critique by Wallendorf and Brucks appears to demand some reply from an author whose work they have inexplicably slighted. I want my reply to be gentle and friendly, rather than angry or querulous in tone. Toward this end, I have written the following poem entitled "On Reading Wallendorf and Brucks."

On Reading Wallendorf and Brucks

Since the critique of introspection
By Doctors Brucks and Wallendorf,
My formerly sincere affection
For that method has fallen off.

How could I choose to keep on working —
Applying an approach subjective —
When they brand this approach as shirking,
Decrying it as self-reflective?

These critics offer an attack —
Most thorough, careful, and well-schooled —
On one piece written three years back
By just one author: Stephen Gould.

They also cast a tacit cold look —
Although they do not stress this fact —
On some work done by Morris Holbrook,
Dismissed more by neglect than tact.

To summarize their Six Big Claims:
They say that introspection's hazy,
Egocentric in its aims,
And narcissistic if not lazy.

Claim One: *People forget things;* so
We cannot trust our own reflections
Even if these do seem to show
Deep meanings in our recollections.

Claim Two: Mistakes arise when we
Read texts to draw our inferences
Without attempts persistently
To heed *specific instances.*

Claim Three: We can avoid some errors —
On which both B. and W. frown,
Like lawyers who face similar terrors —
If we simply *write things down.*

Claim Four: We're fools if we contend
Self-understanding can be ample;
Thus, our critics recommend,
We *shun such an elitist sample.*

Claim Five: We should rely instead
On something that they call "*di-stance*" —
Which, like the two eyes in your head
Or like the two legs of my pants,

Stands astride interpretation
As ethnographers have approved —
One foot in "emic" participation,
The other "etically" removed.

Claim Six: Recall, the proverbial swallow
Does not make a summer. Hence,
A *thick description* must not wallow
In one's own experience.

(Though Clifford Geertz cites Gilbert Ryle
On how description can be "thick,"
The critics, in their trenchant style,
Perform a slick but crafty trick —

Defining *thick* as "macroscopic"
Or "cultural," to their satisfaction;
No matter that on this same topic
Ryle meant "*meaning* of an *action*.")

I cannot sue these folks for libel
Because they scarcely cite my name.
Not since they wrote the Holy Bible
Have authors seemed so free from blame.

So—chastened by this brave critique —
I shall no longer have the gumption
To hope that others want or seek
Analysis of *my* consumption.

Instead, I now expect to hide
From nasty jibes or dirty looks
Or threats of introspecticide
Inspired by Wallendorf and Brucks.

And yet. . . . And yet I must point out
That as I give up my old ways,
Something is lost without a doubt,
Deleted from my erstwhile gaze.

That thing, which seems to try to reach us,
Which I've pursued with wild ambition,
But which the critics find so specious?
In essence, the Human Condition.

Just as Montaigne in his essays
Delved deep where experience was rife,
Both to inform and to amaze
Us with details from his own life,

So must we struggle—like the one
Called *Marius* (Walt Pater's name) —
On this short day of "frost and sun,"
To burn with a "hard and gemlike flame."

In brief—within five words to cram
The central core of what is "real" —
Descartes?: "I think; therefore, I am";
My view?: "I am; therefore, I feel."

❏ Note

1. All excerpts from *The Complete Essays of Montaigne*, translated by Donald M. Frame, were reprinted with the permission of the publishers, Stanford University Press. © 1958 by the Board of Trustees of the Leland Stanford Junior University.

THE ROLE OF LYRICISM
IN CONSUMER RESEARCH

Skylark, Have You
Anything to Say to Me?

The lyric poet . . . through the medium of the emotions . . . has enabled us
to glimpse spiritual depths which until now were closed and inaccessible
to himself as well as to us. . . . Every great lyricist gives us knowledge of a
new feeling for the world. He shows us life and reality in a form in which
we feel we have never known it before. . . . All this "is" and "endures"; it
discloses to us a *knowledge* which cannot be grasped in abstract concepts,
which stands before us, nevertheless, as the revelation of something new,
something never before known or familiar.
—*Ernst Cassirer (1961), The Logic of the Humanities, p. 85*

❏ Introduction

Beyond Science

As the 1980s drew to an end, some consumer researchers delved more
deeply into interpretive approaches that gave birth to such projects as the
Consumer-Behavior Odyssey or the essays in subjective personal introspection described in the previous chapter. This postpositivistic push toward a
new conception of "scientific research" in studies of consumer behavior received formal recognition in such major works as Jean Umiker-Sebeok's

255

volume on the role of semiotics in marketing (1987), John O'Shaughnessy's hermeneutic approach (1987), Beth Hirschman's compilation on interpretive consumer research (1989), Rich Lutz's ACR address on the value of pluralism (1989), John Sherry's chapter on the postmodern turn in consumer research (1991), and the collaboration by Hirschman and Holbrook (1992) on the implications of regarding consumer behavior as a text that invites interpretation.

Together, these contributions represented a departure from the old neopositivistic canons and a broader acceptance—circa 1990—of approaches to consumer research that were called postpositivistic (Belk, 1991), interpretive (Hirschman, 1989), postmodern (Sherry, 1991), or pluralistic (Hirschman & Holbrook, 1992). In this emerging view, scientific research now included not only the old neopositivistic studies but also nonpositivistic approaches of many kinds—potentially including the sort of introspective essay described in Chapter 7—as summarized by Statement 7 in Figure 1.3 from Chapter 1: Scientific Research Is Studies.

But the constant need to defend one's work against the criticisms of those fighting to preserve the neopositivistic view—in other words, the status quo—eventually began to take its toll on at least one consumer researcher. After using all of my strength to argue for the scientific value of the interpretive approaches discussed in the previous chapter, I gradually asked myself an even more basic and potentially more disturbing question—namely, "What's so good about science?"

Here, if one ponders the examples set by such Nobel laureates as Linus Pauling (in his shaky claims on behalf of vitamin C) or David Baltimore (in his defense of Thereza Imanishi-Kari, who faked her data in their joint research), one cannot justify the prevailing tendency to use the term *scientific* as more or less synonymous with *good*. As a society, we have tended to treat anyone claiming to be a scientist as worthy of respect—no matter what that person's values or how outrageous that person's demands on credibility. We have, in short, made the logical error of confusing "science" with "goodness" and of assuming that making our studies more "scientific" automatically means making them "better."

But pursuing knowledge in this way does not necessarily move us closer to certain important truths about consumer behavior. Rather, *some truths may lie buried at a level of human experience too deep for science to penetrate.* As implied by the tradition of human studies descended from Giambattista Vico (1744/1976) and demarcated from the natural sciences by Wilhelm

Dilthey's distinction between *Naturwissenschaften* and *Geisteswissenschaften* (Makkreel, 1975), there exists a world of understanding beyond the sphere of traditional scientific knowledge in a realm of discourse called "the humanities." Being an old English major, I retain a large degree of respect for the humanities as a source of knowledge. In particular, for the humanities, the goal shifts from being more scientific to being more scholarly. The relevant phrase—Statement 8 in Figure 1.3 from Chapter 1—becomes: Research Is Studies.

As noted previously, every chapter in this book has a hero, someone who played a pivotal role in shaping developments that proved decisive in the history of my experiences as a consumer researcher. The heroes thus far have been influential teachers (John Howard), great thinkers (Phil Kotler, Sid Levy), intimate colleagues (Beth Hirschman, John O'Shaughnessy), famous friends in the field (Jim Bettman, Bob Ferber, Jack Jacoby)—in short, a list of "household names" in consumer research. In this chapter on my dawning appreciation for the value of scholarship, however, I believe that a key role was played by someone whose work may not be quite so familiar to most consumer researchers but who nonetheless has made a major contribution to the evolution in my view of the discipline. Specifically, I refer to Herbert J. Rotfeld, formerly a teacher at Penn State and now a professor at Auburn University in Alabama.

Herbert Rotfeld

I have never traveled to Penn State or visited Auburn University or, to the best of my recollection, met Herbert Rotfeld at any conference or professional meeting. The closest connection that I can trace between myself and Herb Rotfeld is the Auburn decal adorning the rear window of the pickup truck driven by my Aunt Betty from Montgomery. Nevertheless, I have been aware of his writings for a number of years, especially those from *Marketing News* and *Marketing Educator* (newsletters of the American Marketing Association). I wish to acknowledge my debt to one such piece in particular because—doubtless unbeknownst to Professor Rotfeld—it has exerted a major effect on me and, indeed, on my life as a consumer researcher.

I refer to an article by Rotfeld (1985) published in *Marketing News* and entitled "Marketing Educators Must Become More 'Scholarly.' " This short piece appeared at a moment when I was searching for ways to justify some of the departures from traditional thought described in this book. The problem, of course, was that such justifications did not exist ready-made and ripe for borrowing; rather, they needed to be developed in an agonizing process of self-discovery. Hence, I clutched at every straw or scrap of insight that I could find. And Herbert Rotfeld's push in the direction of scholarship provided one such invaluable clue to the puzzle.

By the end of the 1980s, even while defending the scientific status of interpretive studies, I had grown weary of pious pronouncements by the "scientists" in the field and leaned ever more strongly in the direction of the humanities. Indeed, I began to believe that entertainment and the arts provide routes to truth in consumer research every bit as valuable as the access afforded by traditional "science." This embrace of the humanities appeared in my collaboration with two other heroes in this story—namely, Steve Bell and Mark Grayson, both gifted students at Columbia. The resulting chapter, called "The Role of the Humanities in Consumer Research," was included in Hirschman's *Interpretive Consumer Research* (Holbrook et al., 1989). As implied by its title, this chapter represented a strong move in the direction of surrendering our unthinking obeisance to science in favor of incorporating insights gleaned from the arts and pop culture. Despite our vigorous attempts to justify this move philosophically, we lacked a suitable name to describe our humanistic leanings, one that could provide favorable connotations comparable to the cachet possessed by the hallowed term *scientific*. The piece by Herbert Rotfeld, which I discovered about the time we were writing "The Role of the Humanities," helped me realize that the word we needed—one commonly held in the highest esteem for the past few hundred years—was *scholarship*.

Scholarship

To me, the term *scholarship* implies a broad pursuit of knowledge far more sweeping and inclusive than that implied by the word *science*. Whereas I see *scientific* as suggesting a focus on rigor and a commitment to approved methods, I see *scholarly* as conveying a broad concern for wisdom and a devotion to insights gathered from various fields of inquiry. From this perspective, the scientist builds better instruments to use in the laboratory or designs improved techniques to employ in survey research; by contrast, the scholar finds undiscovered significance in obscure texts or spots meaningful connections between diverse literatures. Furthermore, science pursues the objective of *progress* (advancing the knowledge possessed by humankind or improving the world in some way), whereas scholarship directs much of its energy toward *self-development* (achieving a deeper fund of understanding based on work by other scholars). To some degree, where science is shared, scholarship is selfish. Where scientists generally contribute to the public fund of knowledge, scholars often invest in private human capital.

Distinctions

In *Merriam-Webster's Collegiate Dictionary* (1993), the two words of central concern here—namely, *science* and *scholarship*—appear on the same page. This dictionary defines *scholar* as "one who . . . studies" or "a learned person"; *scholarship* as "learning" or "knowledge"; and *scholarly* as "learned" or "academic" (p. 1045). By comparison, although *science* refers generally to "the state of knowing," it also refers more specifically to "a department of systematized knowledge as an object of study" or "natural science" (p. 1045); *scientist* refers to "a scientific investigator" (p. 1046); *scientific* refers to "exhibiting the methods or principles of science" (p. 1045); and *scientific method* refers to "procedures for the systematic pursuit of knowledge involving . . . the collection of data through observation and experiment, and the formulation and testing of hypotheses" (p. 1045). It seems clear, then, that the term *scholarship* is broader, *science* more restricted. The former includes the latter, but also a lot more. Indeed, the word *scientism*, which signifies "an exaggerated trust in the efficacy of the methods of natural science applied to all areas of investigation" (p. 1046), actually carries negative connotations associated with narrowness.

Given these distinctions, the point seems clear: If forced to choose between defining oneself as a scholar or a scientist, it is better to be a scholar. Or, to paraphrase Herbert Rotfeld, *consumer researchers should be more scholarly.*

Presidential Address

Having discovered this gospel of scholarship, I naturally wanted to share the good news—indeed, with something of the evangelical spirit that this religious metaphor implies. In October 1989, at the ACR conference in New Orleans, I got my big chance. Specifically, 2 years earlier, I had been elected president of the Association for Consumer Research. In this capacity, one serves for a period of 3 years, first as president-elect, then as president, then as past president. During this time, one has only a single real duty to perform—namely, to give a speech during lunch at the annual ACR conference held in the October of one's presidential year (sort of a "swan song" as one fades into the role of past president). This arrangement of responsibilities gives one 2 full years to worry over what to say in one's presidential address. Thus, the structure of the situation was perfectly calculated to give me heavy anxiety attacks, especially because, by the time I got my turn, almost every conceivably worthwhile thing had been said by my many distinguished predecessors.

In search of a suitably provocative topic, I decided to say a few words on behalf of scholarship in general and on behalf of greater sensitivity to one's own feelings when studying consumption experiences or consumer emotions in particular. Thus, my theme stressed the emotional aspects of consumption as its major focus, but it also considered a question not previously explored in our discourse on consumer research—namely, the *form* or the *rhetorical manner* in which studies of consumers are *expressed*. Introducing these issues concerning *self-expression* in consumer research, my speech raised the possibility of a less formal, more deeply engaged, lyrical approach to consumer research. And, in this, my presidential address challenged some of the most cherished beliefs held by my colleagues in the field.

In the remainder of this chapter, I present a revised version of the presidential address that I gave to the ACR conference in New Orleans—the birthplace of jazz (Holbrook, 1990c). Specifically, in the essay that follows, I advocate the goal of scholarship as worthy of pursuit beyond mere considerations of science and suggest the value of scholarly work in which consumer researchers express their own feelings.

Thus, in this essay I examine the role of lyricism in scholarly research on the consumption experience and on consumer emotions. I associate lyricism with a more personal expression of feelings and suggest that, as the content of consumer research deals increasingly with experiential or emotional phenomena, its style should adapt accordingly. It may depart from some traditional canons of science narrowly conceived but may be consistent with a broader conception of scholarship. In sum, in this essay I express the hope that consumer researchers may transcend some limitations of their conventionally impoverished language by drawing on the force of lyricism when writing on consumption experiences and consumer emotions.

❏ Emotions and Lyricism in Consumer Research

Feelings

Today—like yesterday and all the preceding days of my life—is a very emotional day for me. It is also a very emotional day, Dear Reader, for you. And indeed, it is a very emotional day for all consumers everywhere because emotion, I would argue, lies at the heart of the consumption experience as an inextricable part of the basic human condition.

As discussed in Chapters 4 and 5, this faith concerning the importance of emotional experiences in the lives of consumers has sustained me for a number of years and has, I am happy to say, begun to win acceptance from others doing excellent work in this area. In short, collectively, consumer researchers have now accepted emotion as an important topic for study. The remaining questions concern how to proceed when conducting research on the emotional aspects of the consumption experience.

In this connection, I argue that rather than perpetuate the customary pseudoscientific style of writing, consumer researchers should show more feeling in their discourse on emotion. They should, I believe, replace the typically cold, impersonal, dispassionate modes of communicating with brighter, warmer, richer, and more metaphoric uses of language. In other words, when speaking about emotional consumption experiences, consumer researchers should adopt a style more expressive or lyrical than what has prevailed.

This conviction accounts for the title of this chapter—namely, "The Role of Lyricism in Consumer Research." But the reader may still wonder how to explain the subtitle—"Skylark, Have You Anything to Say to Me?" I borrowed it from the first line of "Skylark," a wonderful old ballad written by Hoagy Carmichael and Johnny Mercer in 1941, repopularized by such singers as Bette Midler (1973) and Linda Ronstadt (1984), and characterized by Alec Wilder (1972) in *American Popular Song* as "remarkable" and "distinguished" (p. 383). "Skylark" has long been a favorite tune of jazz musicians, those most emotive of artists. Indeed, I can best account for my subtitle by recounting a brief story about a jazz singer whom I once heard on a trip to the South.

Marlene VerPlanck

A few years ago, my wife Sally, my son Chris, and I visited Charlotte, North Carolina, where friends took us to a concert to hear a marvelous singer named Marlene VerPlanck, whom I had admired greatly for many years via her recordings on the Audiophile label and who has a voice as pure as mountain snow.

As Marlene sang her first song, an up-tempo tune accompanied by the Loonis McGlohon Trio, I was in seventh heaven and only barely noticed a large, white-haired lady who came and sat on the seat directly in front of me. Then, after a brief announcement, the musicians began their version of "Skylark" (VerPlanck, 1979/1988). Following some slow, pensive chords from Loonis on the piano, Marlene returned to the microphone, closed her eyes, tilted back her head, and sang: "Skylark . . ., have you anything to say to me?" As she shaped this phrase, her words hit the air like little bells ringing sweet and clear above the crowd. The concert hall fell as quiet as a church. And in this reverent silence, the large, white-haired lady in front of me let out a clearly audible gasp of appreciation: "aaahhh."

After the intermission, Marlene introduced a few old friends from Charlotte scattered among the audience. She mentioned some local celebrities. Then she called on a more famous resident of Charlotte, the great operatic soprano Eileen Farrell. The spectators broke into a thunderous ovation, and the large, white-haired lady in front of me stood up and took a bow.

Eileen Farrell

Clearly, in that spontaneous gasp of appreciation, I had witnessed the immediate but deep emotional reaction of one great artist to another. My observation of Eileen Farrell admiring Marlene VerPlanck represents a facet of the consumption experience that usually occurs more privately. It represents a profound aesthetic response far deeper than anything that might be characterized as simple hedonic pleasure.

One does not gasp "aaahhh" in a concert unless one feels a profound aesthetic response verging on ecstasy. How can we as researchers account for this kind of transcendental consumption experience? In this case, I believe, the magic that so moved Eileen Farrell hinged on the utter perfection in Marlene VerPlanck's rendering of an achingly beautiful tune and its poignantly tender lyrics. It resulted from a brief but quintessential manifestation of what we might call *the power of lyricism*.

Lyricism

For years, as a student of English literature, I wondered what people meant when they talked about "lyricism." What makes a lyrical poem "lyrical"? Why are the words of a song called its "lyrics"? What is the connection with the little ancient harp known as a "lyre"?

In Greek mythology, Hermes (the messenger of the gods, who gave his name to hermeneutics) is credited with inventing the lyre, a small stringed instrument whose name is the root for the word *lyrical*. The great musician Orpheus used his lyre to soothe wild beasts, to move rocks, to make trees dance, and to stop the river of time. Robert Graves (1981) calls Orpheus "the most famous poet and musician who ever lived" (p. 44). In *The New Yorker*, Andrew Porter (1988) describes him as the "embodiment of music's power over the emotions" (p. 106): "Orpheus, who demonstrated that song can override the stern rules of the physical world—moving mountains, bringing the dead to life—remains the musicians' great hero" (p. 111).[1] In appreciation for these gifts, Apollo placed the lyre of Orpheus in heaven among the constellations of stars, where Lyra still resides—eternal, transcendent, beautiful.

According to Frye, Baker, and Perkins (1985), "Lyrical poetry began in ancient Greece in connection with music, as poetry sung, for the most part, to the accompaniment of a lyre" (p. 268). M. H. Abrams (1988) suggests:

> The term is now used for any fairly short, nonnarrative poem presenting a speaker who expresses a state of mind or a process of thought and feeling. . . . The lyric is uttered in the first person. . . . A lyric poem may be simply a brief expression of a mood or a state of feeling. (pp. 97-98)

In short, lyricism involves the expression of one's personal feelings.

W. R. Johnson (1982) emphasizes the first-person aspects of the classical lyric, as found in the patterns of pronouns in the "I-You poem" (p. 3) before its evolution toward more meditative forms. In other words, lyric poets speak about themselves in the first person. Thus, Johnson argues that "when the lyric poet casts his poem in the first-person singular . . ., the integrity of lyric form and lyric impulse remains intact" (p. 149). In terms of content, this first-person discourse dwells on the emotions of the speaker, whose feelings seek expression.

In the romantic tradition, the lyrical poem expresses "the spontaneous overflow of feeling" (Abrams, 1953, p. 97): "Poetry is the expression or over-flow of feeling, or emerges from a process of imagination in which feelings play the crucial part" (p. 101). Paraphrasing Pascal (1623-1662): We know truth less by reason than by the heart (Scruton, 1981, p. 45). Thus, Ernst Cassirer (1961) describes the lyric as follows: "There are, after all, only a few great and fundamental themes to which lyric poetry may apply itself. . . . Lyric poetry never leaves the sphere of human feelings. . . . Always lyric po-etry resolves itself into the 'natural forms of humanity' " (pp. 209-210).

As emphasized by Andrew Welsh (1978), these "natural forms" reflect the magic, incantatory, enchanting charm by which lyrical discourse acquires its power to move: "A special language of webs of sound and irregular rhythms different from the language used to communicate ordinary meanings . . . is a language of power, and that power comes primarily . . . from other meanings hidden deep in the sounds and rhythms" (p. 153).

In sum, although a variety of meanings have attached to the term, the adjective *lyrical* (with all of its suggestions of emotive power) literally means "suitable for singing." Although it would be redundant to apply the term to a song, one says that some *other* type of discourse or text is lyrical when one means that it is *like* a song. Like some primordial urge that gives birth to singing, *songlike, lyricism expresses emotion*. In "Skylark," the primary emotion expressed concerns a deep yearning for romantic love:

> Skylark, have you anything to say to me?
> Won't you tell me where my love can be?
> Is there a meadow in the mist,
> Where someone's waiting to be kissed?[2]

❏ *Two Roles for Emotions in Consumer Research*

I believe that such emotions deserve to play a part in consumer research in at least two senses. Accordingly, I say a few words about each role of emotions in consumer research and then elaborate at greater length on the second.

Role 1: Content or Substance

As already mentioned in Chapter 5, the first role of emotions in consumer research involves the way in which *consumption activities prompt emotional responses*. Clearly, as consumers, we feel joy, sadness, anger, fear, disgust, curiosity, love, and hate. In short, we shape our appreciative responses to consumption activities around our feelings as consumers. In this sense, how we *act* as consumers in making purchase decisions pales in importance when compared with how we *react* in the resulting emotions that move and stir our lived experiences. Valid consumer research must reflect this fact. It must reflect the role of emotion in its *content* or *substance*.

Role 2: Form or Style

As a second major role for emotions, I perceive a need for more lyricism in consumer research—the need to create a literature that sounds less matter-of-fact and more expressive, less humdrum and more songlike. Consumer research should better reflect the importance of feelings in its written *form* or *style*. This second point on the matching of substance and style argues for a mode of communicating in which the manner reflects the matter. In other words, as discussed in the following sections, I favor the production of texts that appear less "scientistic" (in the narrowly conceived view of science) and more "expressive" (from the broader perspective of humanism).

❑ Sound and Sense in Consumer Research

Languages of Thought and Feeling

As shown in Table 8.1, many thinkers have distinguished between scientific and poetic forms of discourse. According to this distinction, which I later find reason to question, the former conveys facts, whereas the latter expresses feelings.

Among the authors listed, literary critic I. A. Richards (1926/1935/1970) contrasted science (logical, factual) with poetry (emotional, feelingful). Similarly, M. H. Abrams (1979) drew a distinction between scientific and humanistic demonstrations:

───── **TABLE 8.1** ──
Traditional Contrasts Between Scientific and Poetic Discourse:
Reference Versus Emotion, Facts Versus Feelings

Author	Scientific Discourse	Poetic Discourse
I. A. Richards	Science—logical, factual	Poetry—emotional, feelingful
M. H. Abrams	Scientific demonstration	Humanistic demonstration
Roman Jakobson	Epic/narrative—referential, prosaic, third-person	Lyricism—emotive, songlike, first-person
Charles Morris	Scientific discourse— designative, informative	Poetic discourse—appraisive, valuative
Roland Barthes	Denotation	Connotation
Pierre Guiraud	Referential mode—logical, denotative, objective, scientific	Emotive mode—aesthetic, connotative, subjective, artistic
Jerome Bruner	Paradigmatic, scientific	Narrative, poetic
Peter Berger	Scientific	Subjective
C. P. Snow	Sciences	Humanities

A humanistic demonstration, unlike a scientific demonstration, is rarely such as to enforce the consent of all qualified observers. For it to carry the reader through its exposition to its conclusions requires some grounds for imaginative consent, some comparative ordering of values, some readiness of emotional response to the matters shown forth, which the reader must share with the author even before he begins to read; and these common grounds are no doubt in part temperamental, hence variable from reader to reader. (p. 194)

Linguists such as Roman Jakobson (1976) have separated lyricism (emotive, songlike, first-person) from epic or narrative (referring to a concrete object, prosaic, third-person). Semioticians have followed the lead of Charles Morris (1946) in emphasizing the difference between scientific discourse (designative, informative) and poetic discourse (appraisive, valuative): "The language of empirical science is adapted to expressing the truth and not the importance of its statements. Lyric poetry . . . uses terms . . . for . . . values and evaluations" (p. 58). In semiology, Roland Barthes (1964/1967) contrasted denotation and connotation, whereas Pierre Guiraud (1975) has distinguished the referential mode (logical, denotative, objective, scientific) from the emotive mode (aesthetic, connotative, subjective, artistic):

> The two principal modes of semiological expression are the referential (objective, cognitive) function and the emotive (subjective, expressive) function. They stand in antithetical opposition to one another to such an extent that the notion of a "double function" of language can be extended to all modes of signification. In fact, *understanding* and *feeling*, mind and soul, constitute two poles of our experience and correspond to modes of perception which are not only opposed but are inversely proportional. (p. 9)

Among social scientists, a psychologist like Jerome Bruner (1986) contrasts the paradigmatic with the narrative (p. 12) and scientific writing with the language of poetry (p. 22). Even the humanistically inclined sociologist Peter Berger (1963) suggests that one should not mix the scientific with the subjective, but rather should separate them as meticulously as meat and milk in a kosher kitchen (p. 124). And the self-proclaimed generalist C. P. Snow (1959/1964) once inflamed his colleagues by pointing to a rift between "the two cultures," by which he meant the sciences and the humanities.

I suggest, then, that a basic dichotomy or division—reference versus emotion, facts versus feelings, science versus poetry, logic versus lyric—has won wide acceptance and informs the literary efforts of most serious writers, whether scientists or humanists. Furthermore, in their eagerness to achieve the status of scientists, most consumer researchers have pursued the former and banished the latter from their language by striving to engage in a depersonalized, desiccated, and dispassionate sort of rhetoric under the guise of scientific rigor.

The Price of Dispassion

Yet, consumer research pays a heavy price for this retreat into a cold and colorless form of discourse. Often, any gains in factual accuracy and purported freedom from value-based biases are more than offset by an atmosphere of eviscerated indifference that prompts many readers to ask, in effect, "Who cares?"

Warm, passionate, value-laden feelings are not attributes that traditional consumer researchers appear to welcome; rather, they tend to opt for the scientific side of the contrasts shown in Table 8.1. Writing aimed in this direction overuses the *passive voice* ("was studied," "has been involved"), the verb *to be* (is, are, was, were), and a limited vocabulary of *stock terms* (e.g., interesting, important). Authors remove themselves from the scene and speak in disembodied voices, cleansing messy experience by bleaching it bland. Like the misbegotten production processes that have created crystal cola and clear beer, the preferred style of academic writing in consumer research puts feelings through the charcoal filter of scientism and removes most traces of humanity from our discourse on the consumption experience.

Sound and Sense

Consumer researchers might claim some legitimacy for cultivating dispassion or even indifference when they study such phenomena as brand choice or purchase decisions. But surely, when they come to phenomena related to consumers' emotions, they run the risk that their scientistic rhetoric may actually falsify the phenomena they claim to illuminate. In *The Philosophy of Rhetoric*, Richards (1936) acknowledges the "mysterious power" of using language that exemplifies what one describes (p. 121). His comment parallels Alexander Pope's more famous statement of the same thought in *An Essay on Criticism* (1711/1962):

> True ease in writing comes from art, not chance,
> As those move easiest who have learned to dance.
> 'Tis not enough no harshness gives offense,
> The sound must seem an echo to the sense. (ll. 362-365)

King Lear

That false attempts at scientific rigor via exaggerated precision or misplaced detachment in the realm of the emotions can do more harm than good appears clearly in Act 1 of Shakespeare's *King Lear* (1608/1970). The king immediately establishes his affinity with academic consumer researchers by announcing that he has "a constant wish to publish" (I.i.43). However, what he wants to "publish"—that is, to "proclaim"—is a clarification of his daughters' dowries. And toward that end, he asks the three girls to state their feelings toward him precisely in quantitative terms: "Which of you shall we say doth love us most/That we our largest bounty may extend" (I.i.51-52).

The only true response comes from Cordelia, who recognizes that she cannot weigh and objectify her emotions in this manner and therefore vows to say, "Nothing" (I.i.87-89): "Love, and be silent. . . . My love's/More ponderous than my tongue" (I.i.62, I.i.77-78). Lear's cruel and foreboding response—"Nothing will come of nothing" (I.i.90)—fails to recognize the folly of reducing the emotions to the scientistic mode of discourse and thereby lays a foundation for the tragedy that follows.

Inspired by *Lear*, consumer researchers concerned with emotion might wonder whether we, in our quest for a dispassionate language of facts and figures, might also have rushed straight into the arms of tragic miscomprehension.

❏ *Apologia*

Knowledge as the Social Construction of
Consensus via Conversations in a Community

As noted earlier, in a postmodern conception of science—perhaps one close to the post-Cartesian view (or nonview) articulated by Richard Rorty in *Philosophy and the Mirror of Nature* (1979)—knowledge is socially *constructed* and depends on a *consensus* born from *conversation* among people interacting in dialogues and discussions so that the *community* serves as the primary source of intersubjective validation:

> Justification is not a matter of a special relation between ideas (or words) and objects, but of conversation, of social practice. . . . The crucial premise of this argument is that we understand knowledge when we understand the social justification of belief, and thus have no need to view it as accuracy of representation. (pp. 170-171)

Via such conversations, we feel emotions. Those emotions must affect our work, whether we admit it or not. Denying this threatens our own humanity: "Scientism . . . is frightening because it cuts off the possibility of something new under the sun, of human life as poetic rather than merely contemplative" (Rorty, 1979, pp. 388-389). Those who write research reports devoid of emotion try to smuggle their feelings past the reader undetected. By

contrast, those reports might more honestly reflect the emotional underpinnings of the research.

This need for research to express its own emotional foundations becomes
especially apparent when the study focuses on emotion itself. In other words,
if we want to write about love, joy, ecstasy, or profound aesthetic rapture—
or alternatively about hate, sadness, boredom, or smoldering anger—we may
need to adopt a mode of discourse that lets the audience *feel* what we wish
to convey. If we want to claim that emotions matter, we may need to *show*
that they matter in the way we talk about them. In short, it does not suffice
just to follow the recommendations of Chapter 5 and to write *about emotion;*
rather, we must also aspire to scholarship that moves beyond mere science
by manifesting the personal involvement of an author who writes lyrically
with feeling.

The Distracting Context of Discovery

Few philosophers of science would readily agree with my argument thus
far. Norwood Russell Hanson (1958), Arthur Koestler (1964), Jacob
Bronowski (1965), or Augustine Brannigan (1981) have much to say about
the scientist's intuitive, playful, and creative but always socially embedded
subjective personal introspections; yet these and other thinkers tend to see
the researcher's own emotions as a mode of discovery, rather than as a mode
of justification (Deshpande, 1983). In this spirit, they implicitly consign
emotions to the front end of a hypothetico-deductive process (where theory
gets formulated), rather than to the back end (where results get reported).
Hence, they restrict emotions to the sphere of hypothesis generation but do
little to put feelings back into the discourse of research, where I believe they
belong.

To this distracting quasi-neopositivistic perspective, I have two responses.

Response 1

First, if consumer researchers wish to avoid watching their discipline
drained of its emotional fervor, perhaps they ought to reexamine their position. Here, I believe that academicians owe an allegiance to their profession
above and beyond what they owe to science narrowly conceived. As discussed earlier, the sine qua non for the academic profession is *scholarship* and
not science. Perhaps, then, what consumer researchers need most in study-

ing emotions is not so much science as liberal arts or other forms of scholarly work that somehow manage to preserve the researcher's feelings and to express them in ways open to the inspection of others.

Response 2

Second, maybe the conventional views of science are themselves wrong. Perhaps one cannot adequately explain the world in a discourse drained of its affective content. Perhaps we lose too much when we try to reduce our feelings to facts, our emotions to cognitions, our passions to thoughts.

Some of the more conventional perspectives on consumer research—for example, those using rational choice models of purchase decisions—may demand a logical, dispassionate approach. Such an approach can state axioms, deduce propositions, and test those hypotheses empirically. This precision proves comforting to the scientist and scholar alike.

But as consumer researchers focus on the role of emotion in the consumption experience, they should embrace a more impressionistic, metaphorical—yes, a more lyrical—approach to their topic. Furthermore, a mode of discourse that deals more with emotional content will communicate more effectively if it reflects the nature of its subject matter—that is, if it abandons the prosaic (scientistic) in favor of the expressive (poetic).

(Incidentally, as one immediate benefit from this awakening of lyricism, consumer researchers might overcome their semiofficial aversion to first-person pronouns. Increasingly, the pronouns *we* and even *I* might replace *you, it, they, he, she,* and [mercifully] *s/he*. Any trend that extinguishes the use of *s/he* cannot be all bad.)

In arguing for a more lyrical writing style in consumer research on emotions, I cite two potential sources of support: the first from scholarship in literary criticism, the second from the philosophy of science itself.

Support From Literary Criticism

First, as discussed by Abrams (1953) in *The Mirror and the Lamp,* classical literary critics believed strongly in "the basic neo-classic unifying principle of decorum" (p. 290) and argued for "the traditional consideration of style from the point of view of its appropriateness to the subject matter" (p. 234). This concept of *decorum* or appropriateness would suggest that research on consumer emotions ought to be couched in suitably engaged language whether or not those feelings are shared by the authors themselves. If shared, the issue is one of finding self-expression. If not shared, the issue is one of describing consumer emotions by conveying some sense of what those emotions feel like.

As noted earlier, this principle received its most famous articulation in Alexander Pope's aphorism: "The sound must seem an echo to the sense." In *The Rhetoric of Fiction*, Wayne Booth (1961/1983) invokes a comparable "process whereby substance and form, subject and treatment, matter and manner become fused" (p. 104). Frye et al. (1985) call this "the rhetorical device known as imitative harmony" (p. 269). Andrew Welsh (1978) also makes much of Pope's prescription: "Pope points to something that happens in the language of poetry, that sophisticated poets take the care to make happen and that readers of poetry have learned to admire" (p. 243).

Contemporary critics sometimes refer to Pope's dictum as the "imitative fallacy" (Alexander, 1992, p. 358) or "the fallacy of imitative form," which Christopher Lehmann-Haupt (1986) explains as "the error of, say, writing chaotic prose in order to convey a mood of chaos" (p. C21). Nevertheless, regarding this so-called fallacy, Lehmann-Haupt admits that experts he consulted reacted to his inquiries as if he were "trying to sell them hand cranks for starting cars" (p. C21). Indeed, adopting a less "cranky" posture, others have celebrated the wisdom of matching style to substance, form to content. This celebration appears stylistically wise and substantively correct (Hofstadter, 1979). In short, good writing requires some conformability between substance (matter) and the style (manner) in which it is communicated so as to achieve a unity of purpose and structure—a complementarity of content and form (Beardsley, 1979).

Support From the Philosophy of Science

Some newer trends in the philosophy of science provide a second argument for a more lyrical style of communication in consumer research on emotions. Recent philosophical movements draw on semiotics, hermeneutics, and rhetoric to question the clean dichotomies between facts (scientific discourse) and feelings (poetic discourse) listed in Table 8.1. For example, Umberto Eco's *Theory of Semiotics* (1976) tears apart Richards's positivistic theory of meaning and argues for an inextricable chain of denotation and connotation in which one cannot, in principle, remove the latter. It follows that *honest* science must *acknowledge* its own emotional and motivational bases: "Frequently to be really 'scientific' means not pretending to be more 'scientific' than the situation allows. . . . *Ceteris paribus* [all else being equal], I think that it is more 'scientific' not to conceal my own motivations, so as to spare my readers any 'scientific' delusions" (p. 29).

Eco's point recalls the perspective of Friedrich Nietzsche, who inveighed against even the possibility of value-free, dispassionate discourse and who purposely loaded his own style with exaggerations to serve as a constant reminder of its basis in personal interpretation: "Nietzsche uses . . . many styles . . . to suggest that there is no single, neutral language. . . . His constant stylistic presence shows . . . that the very distinction between the content of a view and the manner in which that view is presented is to be seriously questioned" (Nehamas, 1985, p. 37). According to Allan Megill (1985), Nietzsche called his *Birth of Tragedy* "music" and felt that it should be *sung* (p. 90).

Similarly, in *Personal Knowledge*, Michael Polanyi (1958) evinces a comparable distrust of objectivism and embraces the emotional—indeed, the impassioned—sources of both discovery and justification (thereby helping dissolve this problematic neopositivistic dichotomy). Polanyi (1958) rejects "the ideal of scientific detachment" and replaces it with "an alternative ideal of knowledge" based on "the *personal participation* of the knower in all acts of understanding" (p. vii): "Into every act of knowing there enters a tacit and passionate contribution of the person knowing what is being known, and . . . this coefficient is no mere imperfection, but a necessary component of all knowledge" (p. 312). In his view, despite the prevailing conception of science as based on "the disjunction of subjectivity and objectivity," each phase of scientific study requires "forms of persuasion which can induce a conversion" (p. 151) and, therefore, does entail "*persuasive* passion" (p. 159) in response to "a beauty that exhilarates and a profundity that entrances" (p. 15). For Polanyi, there is no such thing as divorcing the justification of knowledge from the passion of aesthetic appreciation:

> The affirmation of a great scientific theory is in part an expression of delight. The theory has an inarticulate component acclaiming its beauty. . . . A scientific theory which calls attention to its own beauty . . . is akin to a work of art . . . among the great systems of utterances which try to evoke and impose correct modes of feeling. (p. 133)

Thus, Polanyi adopts a view of scientific knowledge that readily accepts its own personal and emotional components: "Personal knowledge in science . . . commits us . . . to a vision of reality. . . . Like love, to which it is akin, this commitment is a 'shirt of flame,' blazing with passion and . . . consumed by devotion to a universal demand" (p. 64). In his view, science converges with art; thought with feeling; knowledge with passion; and truth—as Keats told us long ago in his "Ode on a Grecian Urn"—with beauty. Indeed, when at last he turns his attention to the human sciences (including biology), Polanyi (1958) proposes an even higher standard that sounds very much like a transported version of literary decorum:

> Facts about living things are more highly personal than the facts of the inanimate world. Moreover, as we ascend to higher manifestations of life, we have to exercise ever more personal faculties—involving a more far-reaching participation of the knower—in order to understand life. . . . As we proceed to survey the ascending stages of life, our subject matter will tend to include more and more of the very faculties on which we rely for understanding it. (p. 347)

More recently, in *Consequences of Pragmatism*, Rorty (1982) also inveighs against filtering the subjective components from one's thoughts (p. 194) and adopts a view in which social science approaches art: "What we hope for from social scientists is that they will act as interpreters for those with whom we are not sure how to talk. This is the same thing we hope for from our poets and dramatists and novelists" (p. 202).

Rorty's point gains impetus when coupled with the relativism of Paul Feyerabend's *Against Method* (1975). In "Is Science Marketing?" Peter and Olson (1983) capture the essence of Feyerabend's (1975) argument that when theories become *incommensurable* (not directly comparable in the same terms), the only possible justification of theoretical preferences becomes "judgments of taste" (p. 285); hence, "anything goes" (p. 296), including emotional propaganda (p. 154). In short, scientific justification rests not on proof, but on *persuasion*. Logically enough, this entails the use of *rhetoric*. Thus, in *Science in a Free Society*, Feyerabend (1982) calls on the rhetorical use of emotions to supplement reason in scientific argumentation: "I also favour imagination and emotion but I don't want them to *replace* reason, I want them to *limit it*, and to *supplement it*" (p. 189).

Rhetoric

As developed in a long tradition traced back to the Greeks by Perelman and Olbrechts-Tyteca (1958/1969), rhetoric is "the art of persuading" (p. 5) and "uses language to persuade and convince" (p. 8). Here, these authors depart from the concept of reasoning introduced by Descartes and dwell instead on argumentation: "The goal of all argumentation . . . is to create or increase the adherence of minds to the theses presented for their assent" (p. 45). In seeking this "adherence of minds," Perelman and Olbrechts-Tyteca place a strongly customer-oriented emphasis on "the essential role played by the audience" (p. 7) and repeatedly call attention to this basic principle in what consumer researchers might conceive as the "marketing of ideas": "The central principle, in this connection, is always adaptation to the audience" (p. 461). This orientation prepares the way for their almost scornful dismissal of scientistic detachment:

> The authors of scientific reports and similar papers often think that if they merely report certain experiments, mention certain facts, or enunciate a certain number of truths, this is enough of itself to automatically arouse the interest of their hearers or readers. This attitude rests on the illusion, widespread in certain rationalistic and scientific circles, that facts speak for themselves and make such an indelible imprint on any human mind that the latter is forced to give its adherence regardless of its inclination. (p. 17)

However widespread this illusion, Perelman and Olbrechts-Tyteca repeatedly argue that one cannot separate factual from evaluative meaning (p. 140) so that "the distinction between the emotive aspect and the descriptive aspect of a concept is questionable" (p. 447). Hence, artificial distinctions of the type listed earlier in Table 8.1 tend to blur:

> Nothing could be more arbitrary than the distinction made in textbooks between factual, neutral, descriptive speech, and sentimental, emotive speech. These distinctions have the sole advantage of drawing the student's attention to the fact that value judgments are very obviously introduced into argumentation, but they are harmful in that they imply that there are ways of expressing oneself that are per se descriptive, that there are speeches in which only facts, with their unquestionable objectivity, find place. (p. 150)

Thus, whatever one's aspirations, one can never remove values from scientific discourse; rather, "values enter, at some stage or other, into every argument" (p. 75). Even scientific arguments will include such emotional elements as "illustrations . . . chosen for their affective impact" (p. 360) and "feelings of the speaker" that "serve as an indication of sincerity" (p. 456) and as "means of obtaining the adherence of the audience through variations in the way of expressing thought" (p. 163).

Richard McKeon (1954, 1987) pursues a similar point of view, suggesting that "As an art of communication rhetoric has been designed to make use of all means of persuasion" (1987, p. 109). McKeon argues that "science . . . and . . . rhetoric . . . are not distinct in the context or in the techniques from which they arise, and . . . to separate them is to be guilty of unwarranted dichotomies and abstractions" (1954, p. 13). In his more recent essays, McKeon regards rhetoric as a path to "rejoining reason and sense, cognition and emotion" (1987, p. 13).

This "new rhetoric" has exerted considerable influence in a variety of disciplines. For example, in literary criticism, Wayne Booth (1961/1983) sees rhetoric as "the art of communicating with readers" or "the effort to help the reader grasp the work" and again gives a strong customer-oriented emphasis to the role of the audience. It follows that one cannot choose *whether*, but only *how*, to use rhetoric: "The author cannot choose to avoid rhetoric; he can choose only the kind of rhetoric he will employ" (p. 149). To put the same point somewhat differently, the author cannot manage to disappear; rather, "the author's judgment is always present, always evident to anyone who knows how to look for it" (p. 20). Neutrality is unattainable; the affective evaluations of an implied author always emerge.

In *Modern Dogma and the Rhetoric of Assent*, Booth (1974) has developed the relevance of what he calls "emotional proof" (p. 158)—that is, the use of feelings as evidence, as when "love constitutes a good reason" (p. 162). Such rhetorical devices, as well as other uses of figurative language (e.g., the animal metaphors, musical images, and other tropes found in this book), may play a role in helping to persuade readers (Abrams, 1988, pp. 64-68).

Philosophy of Science

Gradually, comparable viewpoints have flooded the philosophy of science. For example, in *The Return to Cosmology*, Stephen Toulmin (1982) gravitates toward a postmodern view of "the need to reinsert humanity into nature" (p. 210). He describes the view of science as objective versus subjective (p. 241) but brands the hope for objectivity "an Idol" (p. 248), proclaims the death of "the scientist as spectator" (p. 252), and adopts a postmodern perspective based on the metaphor of being "at home in the world of nature" (p. 272)—a metaphor that he illustrates with a quote from

T. S. Eliot's "Little Gidding" (1942/1962), in which "the rose" stands for contemplation and "the fire" represents passion, and "all shall be well . . . When
. . . the fire and the rose are one" (p. 145).[3]

In *The View From Nowhere*, Thomas Nagel (1986) voices a similar concern
for the absurdity of the Cartesian subject/object dichotomy (p. 220), acknowledges the limits of objectivity (p. 87), and seeks a possible harmony or
resolution in a respect for the particularism of aesthetic experience:

> The attitude of nonegocentric respect for the particular . . . is conspicuous as
> an element in aesthetic response, but it can be directed to all kinds of things,
> including aspects of one's own life. One can simply look hard at a ketchup
> bottle, and the question of significance from different standpoints will disap-
> pear. . . . The object engages us immediately and totally in a way that makes
> distinctions among points of view irrelevant. (pp. 222-223)

This possible mode of apprehending reality constitutes the essence of what
Morris Berman (playing on Max Weber) calls *The Reenchantment of the World*
(1981). Berman laments the divorce between scientists and poets, regrets the
consequent repudiation of emotion, and, in a telling play on words, characterizes the voice of dispassion as adopting the motto "Kill anything that
moves" (p. 120). Berman envisions a dissolution of the subject-object dichotomy via a "participating consciousness" that merges subject and object in a
holistic worldview: "Unless . . . participating consciousness can be restored
in a way that is . . . credible . . ., then what it means to be a human being
will forever be lost" (p. 132). For Berman, in such a participating consciousness, science is grounded in "the human experience of nature" (p. 187) where
"the important thing is that affect and analysis not be differentiated"
(p. 186).

Other Disciplines

Other commentators from diverse disciplines have focused on similar visions. For example, in *Literature and Science*, the novelist Aldous Huxley
(1963) described the merger of the subjective and objective that results in
samadhi and *satori* (p. 76). An occasional social scientist has pursued a comparable line of thought, as when the sociologist Richard Harvey Brown argued persuasively in favor of *A Poetic for Sociology* (1977). Among anthropologists, in *Works and Lives: The Anthropologist as Author*, Clifford Geertz

(1988) has acknowledged the role of rhetoric: "The relation between . . . the art of understanding . . . and . . . the art of presentation . . . is so intimate in anthropology as to render them at base inseparable" (p. 46). For Geertz, "ethnography . . . is a work of the imagination" (p. 140) wherein "the writing . . . involves telling stories, making pictures, concocting symbolism, and deploying tropes" (p. 140), all intended to produce conviction in the reader:

> The ability of anthropologists to get us to take what they say seriously has . . . to do with . . . their capacity to convince us that what they say is a result of their having . . . truly "been there." And that, persuading us that this offstage miracle has occurred, is where the writing comes in. (pp. 4-5)

Influenced by Geertz, Renato Rosaldo (1987) suggests that the traditional distancing rhetoric of ethnography fails when applied to deep emotional experiences: "Reports cast in the normalizing ethnographic idiom trivialize the events they describe by reducing the force of intense emotions to spectacle" (p. 99). To counter this tendency toward losing the phenomenon, Rosaldo proposes "a more personal, particularizing, experiential rhetoric" (p. 101).

Perhaps no social scientist has gone farther than the economist Donald McCloskey (1985) in analyzing the scientific use of persuasive techniques. Calling on the work of Feyerabend, Booth, Polanyi, Toulmin, and Rorty (among others previously discussed), McCloskey sees effective rhetoric as enhancing the persuasiveness of the scientific "conversation" as it moves toward intersubjectivity (p. 27). In the spirit of McCloskey, Wassily Leontief (1986), a Nobel laureate, reviewed some work by Kenneth Boulding in the following terms:

> The indisputable success of Mr. Boulding's writing is probably to a considerable extent due to his truly magisterial style—one is tempted to say, his rhetoric. . . . If the purpose of communication is to persuade, then oratorical discourse, which exploits to the full the emotional suggestiveness and occasional ambiguity of common language, should prove to be quite effective. (p. 7)[4]

Toward a Third Culture

Perhaps more than any other thinker, Charles Davy (1978) captures the essence of the proposed alliance between science and lyrical poetics in

Towards a Third Culture. Davy mourns our loss of an integrative "participating consciousness" and describes our present "onlooker consciousness" as a condition in which "thinking and feeling tend to fall apart" (p. 64). He speaks disparagingly of our resulting loss of meaning: "When Imagination fails, the measurable becomes the measure of all things" (p. 71). To counteract this tendency, he proposes a richer "third culture" combining science, religion, and art: "The third culture . . . will retain the particular virtues of the scientific outlook—disciplined thinking, respect for facts, testing by experiment—but it will use them differently. . . . It will be . . . also a religious and an artistic culture" (p. 93). In the third culture, with more humanizing influences (p. 104) and renewed imagination (p. 115), "the poet and the artist are . . . clairvoyant in . . . perceiving more in the world than most of us do" (p. 116). In short, Davy (1978) reviews the progress from a participating to an onlooking consciousness as moving from an earlier poetic language to a current scientific discourse that has grown cold, lifeless, and empty. He envisions the birth of the third culture by comparing the creative imagination of humans with renewal in a new season of growth:

> Summer comes first: the time when nature is abundant and men in their activities and feelings go out into nature. . . . Evolution proceeded to autumn; the skies of consciousness darkened and men turned their thoughts to earth. We are now in winter . . . but the imagination of man has power to quicken the dry earth and bring in a new season. (pp. 172-173)

Shelley's Skylark

The "new season" to which Davy tacitly refers recalls words written by another prophet of imaginative experience, the poet Percy Bysshe Shelley, whose "Ode to the West Wind" (1820/1962) asks what Abrams (1988) considers "the most famous rhetorical question in English" (p. 161): "If Winter comes, can Spring be far behind?" Shelley's ode implores the inspiriting wind to "Make me thy lyre" (l. 57). In this, it reminds us of our concern for lyricism, of Johnny Mercer's lyrics to "Skylark," and therefore of Shelley's own "To a Skylark" (1820/1962). Shelley hails the skylark as a "blithe Spirit" who "Pourest thy full heart/In profuse strains of unpremeditated art." With significance, the second stanza of Mercer's lyrics manages to combine Shelley's Skylark and West Wind imagery:

> O, Skylark, have you seen a valley green with Spring,
> Where my heart can go a-journeying,
> Over the shadows and the rain
> To a blossom-covered lane?
>   —Carmichael & Mercer, 1941[2]

Concerned as it is with the fertility of a green valley and the fecundity of a blossom-covered lane, this second stanza seems to celebrate a feminine point of view—one that calls on both an imaginative vision and a concern for matters of the heart. "Skylark" thereby raises some implicit but nonetheless important questions concerning the role of feminism in consumer research.

❏ The Relevance of Feminism

The Liberation of Morris the Cat

When I gave my presidential address to the Association for Consumer Research in 1989, I had recently been reading some enlightening writers who have applied the perspective of feminism to the philosophy of science. My remarks on that occasion represented the first instance when anyone in our discipline had publicly defended a more feminist approach to consumer research (Holbrook, 1990c). Doubtless, my own abilities in this direction suffer from limitations imposed by the psychological sex role into which society has enculturated me. Thus, in 1993, I welcomed the broader-based treatments of feminism in consumer research presented by Julia Bristor and Eileen Fischer (1993), by Beth Hirschman (1993), and by Barbara Stern (1993).

Bristor and Fischer (1993) distinguish among three feminist perspectives of relevance to consumer research.

1. *Liberal feminism* denies the relevance of differences between the sexes and works toward achieving equal opportunities for women.
2. *Women's voice/experience feminism* assumes that the experiences of women differ from those of men so that women speak in different voices that deserve empowerment.
3. *Poststructuralist feminism* sees the opposition of male masculinity and female femininity as pervasive in a dominant discourse that hegemonically shapes consciousness via influences that deserve to be challenged.

At the risk of considerable oversimplification, I suggest that the work of Hirschman (1993) grows primarily from the "liberal" tradition, that the approach of Stern (1993) reflects the "poststructuralist" viewpoint, and that my own comments emphasize the role of women's experience in giving them a different voice. Thus, my own reflections bear primarily on a small subset of the problems that interest feminists—namely, the connections among feminism, female experience, women's voices, and the philosophy of science.

In *The Flight to Objectivity*, Susan Bordo (1987) argues that conventional scientific epistemology—that is, the neopositivistic theory of knowledge—rests on a dualism of Self versus Other descended from a Cartesian mistrust of subjectivity that is fundamentally masculine in its psychological origins and that reflects the "wrenching tear" experienced in the male child's emotional separation from his mother (p. 57). The resulting separation anxiety precipitates an anxious reaction against emotion and a flight to objectivity (p. 76). This "flight" produces a masculinized psyche in which feelings become irrelevant: "Thus, the specter of infantile subjectivism is overcome by the possibility of a cool, impersonal, distanced cognitive relation to the world" (p. 99). Bordo protests this masculine notion that reason should be "free from contamination by emotion, instinct, will, sentiment, and value" (p. 116).

On a related theme, Evelyn Fox Keller (1985) emphasizes that the feminine viewpoint (subjective, emotional, personal, nurturing), as opposed to the masculine viewpoint (objective, rational, impersonal, power oriented), retains a sense of the union between mother and child, thereby permitting a resolution of the Cartesian dichotomy in the form of a subject-object merger. In Keller's memorable words, science "is a form of love" (p. 117) based on an empathy and intimacy in which "self and other, mind and nature survive not in mutual alienation . . . but in structural integrity" (p. 165).

Along similar lines, Wendy Hollway (1989) describes the historical masculinization of science in which "men . . . avoided the affective by producing it as a particularly feminine characteristic" so that "the affective was expunged simultaneously from scientific, rational and male thought" (p. 110). Hollway inveighs against what she calls "sexist regimes of truth" (p. 45) and proposes to replace these by a method focusing on the subjectivity of meanings in the framework of interpersonal discourse (p. 67)—that is, on a linguistic construction of subjective reality (p. 82) with emphasis given to "the part played by gender difference" (p. 86). Her feminist position focuses on

"women's experience" (p. 106) and on its implications for "gendered subjectivity" (p. 108). In this light, Hollway expands Keller's emphasis on separation anxiety and reaches a similar conclusion that "being a woman provides
advantageous conditions for identification with the person or people participating in the research" (p. 127).

Thus, Bordo, Keller, and Hollway encourage a feminine perspective in
science with a special language comparable to that described in Carol
Gilligan's *In a Different Voice*. Gilligan (1982) characterizes feminine dis-
course by its caring, interpersonal connections and supportive feelings
wherein "women not only define themselves in a context of human relationship but also judge themselves in terms of their ability to care" (p. 17). In
Women's Ways of Knowing, Mary Field Belenky and her colleagues (Belenky,
Clinchy, Goldberger, & Tarule, 1986) emphasize the key importance of
Gilligan's metaphor for epistemological progress via "gaining a voice" (p. 16).
For them, this feminine voice involves "connected," as opposed to "separate," knowing (p. 101). Connected knowing entails a trust in personal experience and a capacity for empathy (pp. 112-113). It aspires toward "a more
authentic voice" (p. 209) and attains a "passionate" understanding by
"knowers who enter into a union with that which is to be known" (p. 141).

According to Jean Baker Miller in *Toward a New Psychology of Women*
(1976), this authentic feminine voice exerts a humanizing influence by "expressing the emotional and personal qualities that are inherent in all experience" (p. 25). Miller sees women as socialized into this role—that is,
"trained to be involved with emotions and with the feelings occurring in the
course of all activity" (p. 39). She adds that "men can also go on to enlarge
their emotional experience" (p. 46). Indeed, male scientists who suppress
this feminine side of knowledge falsify the reality that confronts at least
half the population—namely, the reality described by such works as Jessie
Bernard's *The Female World* (1981) and Anne Wilson Schaef's *Women's Reality* (1985).

A Female Backlash

Predictably, my ACR presidential address horrified many men in the audience by telling them that, when addressing such topics as consumer emotions, they should learn to speak in a more feminine voice. The more macho
members of ACR were appalled at the thought that they should talk more
like women by openly expressing their feelings. In retrospect, their reaction

appears inevitable. Many male ACR members have carefully cultivated an essentially masculine, emphatically neopositivistic style of discourse from which they have successfully removed all empathetic feelings or emotional expression. These men take pride in their patriarchal patois and would not change it for the world.

But I had not adequately anticipated that, apparently, many female members of ACR feel exactly the same way. Such women have suffered so intensely from the pressures against being feminine in a discipline geared toward masculine values—the aversion to women's perspectives in a discourse dominated by an old-boy network of scientific speech—that they have struggled for years to become manlike in their use of words and masculine in their scientistic language.

Such ACR women may regard themselves as "feminists" in the sense (referred to earlier as "liberal feminism") that they believe women can become "just like men." But after heroic efforts to become more masculine in their thought and speech, they do not subscribe to the "women's voice" feminism that says women are and should be different because they reflect a different *psychology* (Miller); because they perceive a different *reality* (Bernard; Schaef); because they experience *alternative ways of knowing* (Belenky); and because they speak in a different *voice* (Gilligan). Nor do they subscribe to the more feminine view of *science* (Keller) that *rejects* the masculine *objectivist epistemology* (Bordo) and that *embraces* a more feminine *openness to intersubjectivity* (Hollway). Having worked so hard to win the acceptance of their male colleagues, these female consumer researchers do not want to hear that they have made a big mistake. They especially do not want to hear this from Morris the Liberated Cat (who, presumably, cannot fully appreciate the issues at stake because he is, after all, a man).

Reaffirmation

Given this tension between the "liberation" of Morris the Cat and the "female backlash" just described, I wish to reaffirm my original position with respect to feminism in consumer research. Like the distinguished feminists reviewed here, I do believe in the existence of a feminine side to science—one that listens more attentively to the emotional aspects of human experience, one that seeks a nurturing union of the author (as the subject) with the consumer (as the object of study), one that speaks in a different, more lyrical voice. Furthermore, I recommend that consumer researchers prize these characteristics in their research, cultivate them where they already exist, and develop them where social pressures have conspired to stamp them out. I therefore believe that all consumer researchers should open their work to a greater infusion of these more feminine impulses and should, in this sense, learn to speak "girl talk."

In short—when the occasion calls for it, as when addressing the emotional aspects of consumption experiences—both the women and the men who conduct consumer research must think, feel, and write in a manner more feminine. But unfortunately, I must also warn that consumer researchers who take this approach will inevitably encounter difficulties associated with the pioneering lyrical spirit, as clearly foretold in the third stanza of Carmichael and Mercer's "Skylark":

> And, in your lonely flight,
> Haven't you heard the music in the night —
> Wonderful music —
> Faint as the will-o'-the-wisp,
> Crazy as a loon,
> Sad as a gypsy serenading the moon?[2]

❑ *Home, Again*

Danger Signs

Consumer researchers who follow my advice, embark on a "lonely flight," and yield to the lyrical spirit of "music in the night" when writing their next paper on consumer emotions will probably find cause to appreciate Johnny Mercer's powers of prophesy. The first reviewer will say that the logic is "faint as a will-o'-the-wisp"; the second will say that the method is "crazy as a loon"; the third will say that the results and conclusions are "sad as a gypsy serenading the moon"; and the editors will reject the manuscript (saying that they have read it carefully and agree with the reviewers' many helpful comments).

This will happen because, as members of a discipline clothed in the sanctimonious remnants of the neopositivistic patrimony, consumer researchers have learned to deny their feminine side and to signal that they do not care very much about each other's feelings. Thus, consumer researchers dutifully suppress their emotions and squelch any trace of self-revelation. If an occasional author dares to violate this norm, the work is declared "self-indulgent," "solipsistic," or "expressive" (used as a pejorative term in such epithets as "paroxysms of self-expression"). In this, consumer researchers imply that they do not care very much about each other or, ultimately, even about themselves.

Houses and Homes

If we as researchers were to view the discipline of consumer research metaphorically as a dwelling place, it would appear that consumer researchers have constructed a house in which there is no room for the researcher's emotions. This style of architecture violates an important principle that I learned one summer when I undertook some home improvements.

In June 1989, as my friends who saw my scratched and splintered fingers can attest, I invested a good deal of time building bookcases in our apartment to accommodate my rapidly growing collection of paperbacks and compact discs, all of which I loved too dearly to part with but had no place to keep. Later, I spent a happy month of July at the University of British Columbia in Vancouver as the guest of Rick Pollay and Carole Christopher. The moment I walked into their house, I was struck by its carefully planned use of space. Rick is an eminent collector of antique relics from advertising (his "advertiques") and has meticulously designed every square inch of his study to store his collection of advertising treasures. I felt strongly that Rick's example validated my own adventures in the construction of bookshelves. And after sensing this validation, I finally realized that it hinged on a very simple principle—namely, that without a place to keep things that we cherish, things that stir our emotions, things that add meaning to our lives, a house would be deeply flawed.

Yet, consumer researchers have chosen to dwell (but perhaps not fully to live) in such a deeply flawed house—a house with no place to put the things that matter most to many people—namely, a house with no room for their own feelings. Such a house may be, in the words of Graham Nash, "a very, very, very fine house" (Crosby, Stills, Nash, & Young, 1970). But such a house is not a home.

Better Homes and Gardens

Remembering the skylark's warm, green valley and the need to build bookshelves to hold our most deeply meaningful treasures, consumer researchers need better homes and gardens. This need corresponds directly to the metaphors in the last stanza of Johnny Mercer's great lyrics:

> Skylark, I don't know if you can find these things,
> But my heart is riding on your wings;
> So, if you see them anywhere,
> Won't you lead me there;
> O, Skylark, won't you lead me there.[2]

In this almost prayerful conclusion, the lyricist asks for a place where the heart can reside. Analogously, I ask for an annex to the grounds and for some new rooms with new views from new windows in the mansion where those who labor in the field of consumer research have erected their edifice. I ask for an open embrace by consumer researchers of the attempt to express deeply felt emotions. I ask consumer researchers to abandon their mercilessly scientistic stance—the paternalistic neopositivism, the he-man hypothetico-deductivism—and to start caring profoundly about one another's deepest passions and truest selves. I ask for greater acceptance of lyricism in consumer research because I believe that the lyrical resonance with which consumer researchers convey their feelings to one another will greatly facilitate their ability to understand and communicate the nature of the emotional phenomena that pervade the consumption experience.

❑ Epilogue

Three Illustrations

I might illustrate what I regard as the restorative power of lyricism with three analogies drawn from music and, therefore, closely linked to singing. Here, as in Chapter 2 on theory development as a jazz solo, the parallels between the scholarly activities of an academic and the creative endeavors of an artist again become unmistakable. Once more, I believe, lyricism may achieve a transcendence from the mundane to the extraordinary, from the ridiculous to the sublime.

Art Pepper

Consider, for example, the work of the great jazz saxophonist Art Pepper. By the account found in his own autobiography—entitled, with heavy irony, *Straight Life* (Pepper & Pepper, 1979)—Pepper was for many years a complete scoundrel, an obsessive profligate, an unrepentant bum, and a hardened criminal. He took drugs with reckless abandon, robbed filling stations, and spent most of his adulthood in prison. Nor was Pepper one of those gentle junky jazz musicians—like, say, Charlie Parker, who never hurt anyone but himself. Rather, Pepper was a callous convict, a self-proclaimed sociopath whose only concern for law, order, or decency boiled down to the fear of being caught and whose career as a felon culminated in a sentence to serve time at San Quentin.

So addicted was Art Pepper to his life of drugs and crime that, in the documentary film *Notes From a Jazz Survivor* (McGlynn, 1982), he offered a detailed comparison between criminal activities and playing jazz. Thus, he describes the musicians in his band—Bob, the bassist; Milcho, the pianist—as different kinds of guys whom he might take along when committing a robbery. Clever though the comparison might seem, it conveys a distressing picture of Art Pepper as a deeply disturbed man. And when he connects all of this hate with beauty, it makes one's blood run cold:

> There's a lot of parallels in being a criminal and being a jazz musician. Bob—he's careful; he's always there, you know; so he keeps us from going insane, you know. He's like the guy that's cool that would carry the gun in a robbery if you only had one gun, because he would be the one least likely to use it. But, with me, I would use it the *second* that anything went wrong, you know, and *love* using it. So would Milcho. If the two of us went on a robbery and we had guns, it would be a violent robbery, I mean . . . I mean, *really* violent, you know, because we're both *filled* with *hate*, you know. . . . Hate and beauty are so close.

Yet, Pepper had one saving grace—namely, his total honesty of self-expression—found, for example, in his unfathomable ability to tell the sordid story of his own depravity in the form of that amazingly candid autobiography. This honesty also infused his playing and revealed itself in a surprisingly lyrical temperament.

Art Pepper's alto style incorporated an almost excruciating lyricism, a penchant for the immediate outpouring of feelings and for the unconstrained expression of emotions. As he describes one of his most celebrated recordings—entitled *Art Pepper Meets the Rhythm Section* (Pepper, 1957)—for example, he emerged from a drug-induced torpor, picked up a broken-down horn that he had not touched in months, and somehow blew chorus after chorus of inspired jazz melodies, torn not from a printed score but from the tormented depths of his own tortured soul. In short, Art Pepper's lyrical gifts transformed this otherwise unsavory character into a poet of emotional expression and a prophet of beauty.

Paul Desmond

Paul Desmond, another magnificent alto saxophonist, was perhaps the most lyrical soloist that jazz has ever known. He spun lilting melodic patterns out of airy nothingness in a constantly inventive stream of musical sequences composed of repeated thematic ideas and their developing variations. Desmond's lyricism appeared to elevate his vision beyond the commonplace world.

On one mournful day only a few weeks before his untimely death, Paul Desmond summoned all of his waning strength, endured his pain, and blew one of his most beautiful solos on the title tune from an album with Chet Baker called *You Can't Go Home Again* (Baker, 1977), just before collapsing from overexertion. Betraying no hint of his physical anguish, Desmond's playing is all tenderness. Thus does the magic of lyricism lift one's spirits to heights otherwise unattainable and elevate one's powers of communication.

Pepper and Desmond Play "Skylark"

Interestingly, both Art Pepper and Paul Desmond recorded "Skylark," the leitmotif for this chapter. Pepper played it on an early album in which he accompanied Hoagy Carmichael performing some of his own tunes (Carmichael, 1956); Desmond offered his rendition on one of the last recordings he made (1974).

Pepper may have been uncomfortable with the unsympathetic character of Carmichael's labored singing style. For whatever reasons, his performance sounds even darker and more brooding than usual, filled with rhythmic displacements and bent tones that suggest pain and doubt.

By contrast, Desmond's version of this piece conjures up impressions of sweetness and light. He alters some of its chords and melody lines in ways characteristically Desmondian and toys effortlessly with melodic sequences in his typically playful dialectic of implication, surprise, and resolution.

Although Pepper's and Desmond's treatments of "Skylark" differ markedly in tone, both share an intense lyricism. Pepper seems to cry through his horn. Desmond seems to smile.

Dinah Washington

Dinah Washington began as a gospel singer and carried the fervor of that style into her later work as a jazz and pop vocalist. Her energetic and feelingful recordings of such songs as "What a Diff'rence a Day Made" (n.d.) completely mask what was for her an agonizing disability. Specifically, Dinah Washington stuttered, stuttered so badly that she could scarcely conduct a coherent conversation. Hence, her ability to communicate via conventional means was severely curtailed. But, as often happens in the case of stuttering, her problem disappeared when she raised her voice in song. Dinah Washington sang like an angel. And her lyrical gift conquered her verbal nemesis.

Art, Paul, Dinah, and Consumer Research

Consumer researchers who embark on the study of consumption experiences in general and emotions in particular venture forth into new and intellectually perilous areas of inquiry. Like jazz musicians coping with the melodic and harmonic structure in a difficult piece of music, they face threatening risks and potential dangers. But, also like jazz musicians, consumer researchers enjoy the opportunity to express themselves through the power of their lyrical gifts.

We have a choice. We can cultivate a bland form of scientistic discourse that conveys little more than does a hopeless stutter. We can let our voices stammer and falter, gasping for words and heaving huge sighs of helpless inarticulateness. Or we can learn from Art Pepper, Paul Desmond, and Dinah Washington. We can lift every voice and sing. We can let our feelings show. We can express our emotions, welcoming them in ourselves and in others as integral components of the consumption phenomena that we wish to understand. If we can follow the latter path, we may open a way to the contribution to be gained from the role of lyricism in research on consumer emotions in the consumption experience.

Skylark Immortal

In this book in general and in this chapter in particular, I have borrowed heavily—for illustrations, anecdotes, stories, and metaphors—from the animal kingdom and from the world of music. When I am not preoccupied with animal imagery, music is often my major leitmotif. And, of course, when I refer to "Skylark," I refer to both the animal and the song. Hence, in its combination of animal imagery with the role of song in the expression of our deepest feelings, the skylark embodies the central theme of this chapter on the power of lyricism in consumer research. Although Hoagy Carmichael and Johnny Mercer doubtless did not spend much time thinking about the study of consumption, this potential role of lyricism concerned them implicitly when they asked, "Skylark, have you anything to say to me?" Before them, the skylark had attracted the poet Shelley in his tribute to the "blithe spirit" that pours forth its "full heart" in song. In a poem called "Shelley's Skylark," Thomas Hardy (1887/1955) reminded us that we should cherish Shelley's metaphor as an emblem of the immortal spirit that raises its lyrical voice to the heights of ecstasy:

> Somewhere afield here something lies
> In Earth's oblivious eyeless trust
> That moved a poet to prophecies —
> A pinch of unseen, unguarded dust:
>
> The dust of the lark that Shelley heard,
> And made immortal through times to be —
> Though it only lived like another bird,
> And knew not its immortality. . . .
>
> Go find it, faeries, go and find
> That tiny pinch of priceless dust,
> And bring a casket silver-lined,
> And framed of gold that gems encrust;
>
> And we will lay it safe therein,
> And consecrate it to endless time;
> For it inspired a bard to win
> Ecstatic heights in thought and rime.

❑ *Notes*

1. Reprinted by permission; © 1988 Andrew Porter. Originally in *The New Yorker*.

2. *Skylark*, by Johnny Mercer and Hoagy Carmichael. Copyright © 1941 (Renewed) WB Music Corp (ASCAP) and Hoagy Carmichael Pub. All rights reserved. Used by permission of Warner Bros. Publications Inc., Miami, FL 33014.

3. Excerpt from "Little Gidding" in *Four Quartets,* copyright 1943 by T. S. Eliot and renewed 1971 by Esme Valerie Eliot, reprinted by permission of Harcourt Brace & Company and Faber and Faber Ltd.

4. Leotief (1986), p. 7. Copyright © 1986 by The New York Times Company. Reprinted by permission.

DOGMATISM AND CATASTROPHE IN THE DEVELOPMENT OF MARKETING THOUGHT

> We desperately need some sort of spiritual center that can help us feel good about the kind of research we do. Toward that end, we must find, elevate, and proclaim whatever is noble, worthwhile, and profound in the development of marketing thought.
>
> —*AMA Task Force (1988), "Developing, Disseminating, and Utilizing Marketing Knowledge," p. 17*

❑ Introduction

For Fun

By the time I reached the stage of aspiring to scholarship above and beyond mere science in consumer research, I had pretty much concluded that any serious academic activity aimed at raising interesting questions about the nature of consumption qualifies as meaningful and worthwhile. From this perspective, the consumer researcher alone is the sole arbiter of what constitutes valuable work on his or her own agenda. Here, the standards for value may depend on a burning desire to understand some phenomenon for

292

the purpose of figuring out how to make money from it or on nothing more than a whim motivated by idle curiosity. Furthermore, I had come to believe that work focused on my own subjective personal introspections and expressed in a lyrical style might contribute to the understanding of consumer behavior as part of the human condition. This book may be taken as an extended example of what happens if these beliefs are put into practice.

Some readers, especially those with a practical bent, may find it difficult to imagine where consumer researchers' minds might wander if they willingly submitted to their own idle curiosity. One illustration occurred when my wife Sally and I accompanied Robert Schindler to a neighborhood Mexican restaurant called Caramba. The events on that occasion say something about where consumer research comes from.

One summer evening in 1987, Robert Schindler spent a night on our couch en route to visiting some relatives in New Jersey. It happens that, like Sally and me, Robert loves spicy food. So we took him to Caramba, a then-new but now-defunct place just up the street at 96th and Broadway, known less for its culinary refinement than for its mind-boggling, machine-made frozen margaritas. After a couple of these refreshing drinks—which were churned out by a large contraption something like a Dairy Queen dispenser, which tasted like what God must have had in mind when he invented the lime tree, and which contained so much alcohol that they could be served only in New York City (where one need not worry about having to drive home)—Robert, Sally, and I began to reminisce and to recall music we liked from the good old days. After a while, we noticed that we all carried especially warm feelings for certain musical artists (the Beatles, the Stones, and Simon and Garfunkel in the case of Robert) as opposed to others (Elvis Presley, Chuck Berry, and Little Richard in the case of Sally). The question that entertained us, of course, was *why*.

By the end of this margarita-enriched evening, we had evolved the hypothesis that our differences in tastes might depend on the discrepancies in our ages and that this phenomenon, in turn, might suggest the importance of a critical period in our lives during which we had latched on to the music that was popular—something like the way baby birds imprint on objects (usually their mothers) that they encounter during a certain critical period (as demonstrated by the great ethologist Konrad Lorenz, often shown in pictures walking across a field and followed by a long line of young geese). This speculation gave birth to some research in which Robert and I played popular music from the last 50 years for people varying widely in age.

Specifically, Holbrook and Schindler (1989) drew on 28 hit records from the years 1932 (the Mills Brothers singing "Smoke Rings") to 1986 (Peter Gabriel performing "Sledgehammer"). We played 30-second excerpts from these musical selections in random orders for 108 respondents who varied in age from 16 to 86 years old and who rated each piece on a 10-point scale from 1 (*I dislike it a lot*) to 10 (*I like it a lot*). These liking scores were standardized within respondents (across stimuli) and were then averaged across respondents for each song-specific age (the date of the recording minus the date of the respondent's birth). These song-specific ages ranged from –39 to 85, meaning that the youngest respondent was minus 39 years old when "Smoke Rings" hit the popularity charts, whereas the oldest respondent was 85 years in age when "Sledgehammer" became a hit. With song-specific age (SSA) as our key independent variable and mean liking as our key dependent variable, we regressed mean liking on SSA and SSA-squared across the 124 SSA levels from –39 to 85. That regression produced a strong fit ($R = 0.84$) with a highly significant negative contribution due to SSA-squared ($t(121) = -16.52$, $p < 0.0001$). As shown in Figure 9.1, this result indicated an inverted U-shaped relationship. Simple calculus showed that a preference peak occurred at a song-specific age of about 23.5 years old.

In short, this study demonstrated a strong age-related preference peak for music popular when the respondent was in late adolescence or early adulthood (in his or her early 20s). Needless to say, a study like this raises as many questions as it answers, one of the most conspicuous concerning the issue of whether the phenomenon of a critical period found for popular music (the peak preferences associated with late adolescence or early adulthood) would occur for other products as well (say, movies, movie stars, clothing styles, other fashion-related items, automobiles, furniture, or food). Pursuing such questions, Robert and I launched a series of studies that have coalesced around the theme of *nostalgia* and that have generally supported (a) the role of the *critical period* in establishing age-related preferences for time-dated objects of consumption, (b) the role of *nostalgia proneness* as an individual characteristic associated with preference differences among consumers, and (c) the role of a *nostalgic shift* due to the *interaction* of (a) and (b) such that the age-related preference peak tends to occur at an earlier age for consumers higher in nostalgia proneness. We have shown these and comparable effects for such products as Oscar-winning motion pictures (Holbrook, 1993c, 1994d; Holbrook & Schindler, 1994b), photographs of movie stars (Holbrook & Schindler, 1994a), and advertisements in fashion magazines

Musical preference

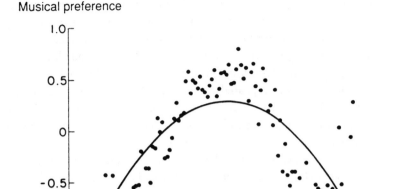

Song-specific age

Figure 9.1. Relationship Between Song-Specific Age and Musical Preference

SOURCE: From "Some Exploratory Findings on the Development of Musical Tastes," by M. B. Holbrook and R. M. Schindler (1989), Journal of Consumer Research, 16, p. 122. Published by University of Chicago Press. Copyright © Journal of Consumer Research, Inc., 1989. Reprinted with permission.

(Schindler & Holbrook, 1993). Other work, still in progress as I write this, has begun to investigate the roles of (a) an age-related preference peak, (b) nostalgia proneness, and (c) the nostalgic shift in tastes for such products as automobiles and food. Whether this work on nostalgia will ultimately make an important contribution remains to be judged in about the year 2050 and need not trouble us here. Rather, my central point concerns the issue of why Robert and I pursued this particular stream of consumer research.

The simple answer is: For fun. We followed our idle curiosity. We honored our scholarly inclinations. We submitted to our scientific intuitions. Emphatically, we did not consider whether the results would prove relevant to marketing managers. We did not anticipate lucrative consulting contracts. We did not hope to provide tools useful to top executives in the entertainment industry.

This freedom to pursue one's own intellectual instincts is a characteristic of the academic life that I value above all others. In consumer research, as emphasized in Chapter 6, nothing can substitute for academic freedom. This is one reason why I enjoy sitting with Robert and Sally while guzzling frozen margaritas in Mexican restaurants. Caramba has vanished by now, but other Mexican restaurants have appeared on the Upper West Side to take its place. And we have also begun to frequent Italian places that serve formidable deep-dish pizzas. The last time Robert and I dined at such an establishment in Chicago, we mused about how some people manage to love certain foods that we happen to hate—say, root beer, licorice, cotton candy, chocolate-covered marshmallow cookies, and clove-flavored chewing gum. We have not yet begun our root beer study, but I look forward to exploring this issue.

Meanwhile, the point of central importance at the moment is that, in a world of truly free inquiry, consumer research does not "equal" any particular type or group of studies. Indeed, except in the loosest sense, "research" does not necessarily entail conducting "studies" at all. One can do one's research in the library or in one's own imagination. Hence, in Statement 9 of Figure 1.3 from Chapter 1, *Studies* and *Is* are crossed out, leaving only *Research*. Consumer research just *is*. It can—and should—be anything we want it to be. From intellectual liberty comes scholarly progress.

From Marketing Research to Research in Marketing

If this principle applies to the study of consumption, one might also ask what relevance it carries for the broader investigation of marketing. This question served as the impetus for the next phase in my development.

Prior to 1990, I believed that *consumer research* should pursue topics of interest *for their own sake*, whereas *marketing research* should aspire to *managerial relevance*. In essence, this is the position for which I argue at length in Chapter 6 and that constituted one of the great debates in the field during the mid-1980s. But by 1990, influenced by such thinkers as Sid Levy (1976) and Beth Hirschman (1986b), I had come to adopt a much broader view of research *in* marketing and to realize that many of the arguments raised about the role of managerial relevance in consumer research applied with equal force to *research in marketing*.

And who, the reader might ask, was the hero of this particular revelatory moment? Here, I have no trouble in identifying one or two intellectual antagonists (say, Fred Webster or Connie Pechmann, whose contributions concern us in what follows). But the identification of a chief protagonist poses more problems. Instead of one or two key figures, those deserving credit (or blame) for shaking up my conception of research in marketing include a whole group of people known officially as the AMA Task Force. My participation on this task force during the late 1980s did much to shape my views on the importance of academic freedom—not only for consumer research (as argued earlier) but also, more generally, for research in marketing (as argued here). Once again, I found myself in a highly public debate with some very important people. In this chapter, I tell the story of that debate and its impact on my views concerning the development of marketing thought (Holbrook, 1989a).

❏ A Debate on the Development of Marketing Thought

The AMA Task Force

For a few years, during the late 1980s, I participated in a kind of cross between a think tank, a discussion group, and a consciousness-raising seminar, sponsored by the American Marketing Association (AMA). Officially named the Task Force on the Development, Dissemination, and Utilization of Marketing Thought, it came to be known to its members as the AMA Task Force. Under the chairmanship of Kent Monroe, the AMA Task Force combined the efforts of 11 members who (with 3 exceptions) came directly from academia and who (perhaps inevitably) brought their perspectives as teachers, scholars, and scientists to bear on issues concerning the development, dissemination, and utilization of marketing knowledge.

We met a few times a year for 3 years in such cities as Atlanta, St. Petersburg, Chicago, and New York. We thought and talked, studied and argued, wrote and revised for countless hours. We covered as much as we could of the current prospects for knowledge development in marketing. (So much time did this consume that we never got as far as worrying about the dissemination or use of marketing knowledge.) For me, the main appeal of these activities arose from my chance to share in the intellectual excitement generated by this distinguished set of colleagues. We seldom reached unanimity, but we had fun arguing. Or, at least, I did.

As a by-product of that dialogue, we produced a lengthy document that ultimately appeared (greatly condensed) in the October 1988 *Journal of*

Marketing (AMA Task Force, 1988). I shall not try to provide any sort of comprehensive encapsulation of the recommendations in the full task force report. At the broadest level, we touched on the different constituencies of marketing knowledge, on the structural impediments to its development and dissemination, on the role of doctoral programs in marketing, on problems in the career cycles of marketing academicians, and on possible improvements in the vehicles through which we communicate with one another. But perhaps the key lesson emerging from all of these deliberations concerns the miracle that occurred in our ability to achieve any sort of consensus at all.

Those who participated on the AMA Task Force tended to approach virtually any problem from as many different orientations as the number of different people involved. Paul Bloom would politicize the issue; Bart Weitz would look for its hard-headed managerial implications. Al Wildt would build a quantitative model of the relevant marketing phenomenon; Beth Hirschman would rhapsodize over its hidden beauties. Jerry Zaltman would interpret the key theoretical underpinnings; Alice Tybout would deduce hypotheses and submit these to rigorous attempts at falsification. Diane Schmalensee would draw up a detailed list of subproblems; Bill Wilkie would search for the big picture. Chairman Monroe would seek an orderly approach to defining the task with which the committee was charged, setting priorities and assigning responsibilities; Morris the Cat would pursue every conceivable tangent.

Yet, despite these enriching differences in viewpoint, most members of the AMA Task Force did share one basic perspective that permitted them to work together in a fruitful conversation. That perspective reflected a tacit premise that the development of marketing knowledge reflects the efforts of marketing academicians who have devoted their lives to this discipline, that it therefore involves the universities and their business schools, and that this circumscribed world of discourse addresses the issues about which the mostly academic members of the task force were best qualified to comment insightfully. In other words, given its composition, the AMA Task Force tended to approach its job from the implicit perspective of the academic researcher and scholar.

The Debate

The report of the task force appeared in conjunction with constructive comments by Gil Churchill, Robert Garda, and Shelby Hunt, together with a critique by Fred Webster (at the time, executive director of the Marketing Science Institute). Located in Cambridge, Massachusetts, about halfway between Harvard and MIT, the Marketing Science Institute (MSI) is an organization that funnels funds from corporations into research by academicians. Needless to say, its principals have maintained an earnest devotion to the enterprise of encouraging marketing research that furthers the interests of business managers. Apparently, Fred Webster shared this prevailing MSI perspective.

In essence, Webster (1988) found the work of the task force "disappointing" (p. 48) because of its apparent disregard for "issues of concern to marketing managers, issues of marketing practice that could reasonably be expected to provide direction for rigorous marketing inquiry" (p. 49). In Webster's view,

> The Task Force, dominated as it is by marketing educators rather than practitioners, elected to address some rather parochial and self-serving issues. . . . If one were to ask marketing managers and students to define a set of issues relating to knowledge in the field of marketing, chances are good that none of the Task Force's concerns would be high on their lists. (p. 48)

These words conveyed the view that the task force contributed nothing of importance to present and future marketing managers.

Then, Webster (1988) explicitly turned to a paragraph that I have used as an epigraph to this chapter and that I happen to have written myself. I felt proud of its inclusion in the final task force report. And I believed that we had accomplished something meaningful by calling attention to the value of a "spiritual center" and to the importance of "whatever is noble, worthwhile, and profound in the development of marketing thought." Webster, however, surprised me greatly by concluding that "such a plaint implies personal judgments . . . and moral imperatives that seem strangely out of place in an assessment of the state of marketing knowledge" (p. 49).

In a manner reminiscent of the controversy reported in Chapter 6, Fred Webster's revival of related issues in the broader context of the AMA Task Force suggested the need for a new debate. It happened that one of our task force members, Paul Bloom, played a major role in organizing the 1989 Summer Educator's Conference of the American Marketing Association in Chicago. For this occasion, he honored the work of the AMA Task Force by planning a special plenary session devoted to considering the work of the task force in general and the criticisms raised by Fred Webster in particular.

Plenary means, literally, that "everybody comes." And lots of people did come—lured, in part, by the hotness of the topic and, in part, by the list of speakers that Paul Bloom put together. Besides Chairman Monroe (soon-to-become-editor for the *Journal of Consumer Research*), Paul recruited three superstars from the galaxy of those committed to the task of building knowledge regarded as high in managerial relevance. Steve Greyser from Harvard upheld the values espoused by the MSI (for whose interests he has long served as an ardent champion). From California, Lyman Porter represented the views reported in his influential book with Lawrence McKibbin, *Management Education and Development* (1988). And Dean Don Jacobs from Northwestern's Kellogg School of Management embodied the position of a business school administrator. One could not have assembled a group more influentially committed to the advancement of knowledge intended to guide the practice of marketing managers.

And arguing on behalf of the opposed point of view—debating the gospel of managerial relevance before a crowd of righteous believers, preaching apostasy to a room full of devout disciples—the panel of speakers included one lonely and pathetic figure . . . Morris the Cat.

In retrospect, I cannot imagine what mixture of New York narcissism and Cholbrookian chutzpah moved me to accept this particular invitation to make a speech. I do recall, however, that as the day for the debate approached, I regarded my speaking assignment with growing apprehension. I dimly realized that I would face united opposition and that even my most sincere convictions would not necessarily save me from public humiliation. Nevertheless, rushing onto terrain where rational angels would surely have feared to tread, I somehow found the nerve to deliver the message that follows (Holbrook, 1989a).

❑ Dogs and Cats

True Brutality

Overall, I believe that many in the field share Fred Webster's concerns and that these criticisms reflect some measure of factual accuracy regarding the main focus of the task force. The point on which some might disagree with Fred relates not so much to his descriptive premises as to his prescriptive conclusions. Those conclusions invoke an emphasis on the importance of managerial relevance that some scholarly researchers simply do not accept as a standard by which they should live their lives. I hasten to add, however, that when I wrote a reply to Fred's critique, one of our mutual friends (who is sympathetic to Fred's position) told me that my rhetoric was "brutal."

According to a different Webster—namely, the imaginary one behind *Merriam-Webster's Collegiate Dictionary* (1993)—the word *brutal* means "befitting a brute" (p. 147), where a *brute* is a *beast* or an *animal*. Here, I believe that our friend has suggested an apt metaphor in whose terms we might characterize and clarify this whole debate. In that spirit, I propose to cast the contrast between the academic and managerial perspectives into a comparison between some familiar members of the animal kingdom.

Canine Versus Feline

Referring to the two perspectives that I wish to contrast as managerial and academic research, let us compare their differences to those between a dog and a cat. I suggest that researchers who pursue *managerial relevance*, as opposed to those who care mostly about *academic scholarship*, reveal temperaments, orientations, or predispositions relatively more *canine*, as opposed to *feline*.

To familiarize myself with the contrasting characteristics of these two species, I have read Vicki Hearne's insightful collection of philosophical essays on animal training, entitled *Adam's Task*. In this work, Hearne (1987) conveys her deep sense of a fundamental difference that drives to the heart of this debate.

For Vicki Hearne, training a dog consists in the essence of what we mean when we ask it to "go fetch." We teach the dog to run and get a stick or a bird and to present it or drop it at our feet—preferably without first chewing it to pieces. The goal here, for both the trainer and the dog, is *obedience*, where "absolute obedience . . . confers nobility, character and dignity on the dog" (p. 43). Everybody knows that dogs can be trained in this fashion, that they are basically anxious to please, and that they therefore respond to positive praise or negative correction by learning to obey our commands.

In this, dogs resemble researchers who seek to pursue managerial relevance. Such researchers voluntarily take their direction(s)—sort their priorities or respond to instructions—in a way that honors the interests of
business practitioners. Figuratively or sometimes even literally, such researchers follow orders. They thereby please managers a great deal because
managers are accustomed to giving directions and like it a lot when their
commands are obeyed. In a sense, then, the managerially oriented researcher
resembles a golden retriever or a pointer—that is, someone who retrieves the
desired information or who points to useful knowledge—basking in the
warm praise and creature comforts to be obtained by pleasing one's master.
This idea appeared vividly in a *New Yorker* cartoon by P. Steiner (1990) of
two dogs walking down the sidewalk and one saying to the other: "It's always
'Sit,' 'Stay,' 'Heel'—never 'Think,' 'Innovate,' 'Be yourself' " (p. 30).[1]

By contrast, we all hold very different expectations of a cat. According to
Hearne (1987), "most house cats would rather die than obey a direct order"
(p. 56). Cats are famous for their independence. Paul Fussell (1983) quotes
Jean-Jacques Rousseau as deploring the "despotic instinct" of ailurophobes:
"They do not like cats because the cat is free . . . will never consent to become a slave . . . will do nothing to your order, as the other animals do"
(p. 96). To this, Hearne (1987) adds a corroborative story on animal experiments in comparative psychology:

> I used to hear older experimenters advising younger ones about working with
> cats. It seems that under certain circumstances, if you give a cat or cats a
> problem to solve or a task to perform in order to find food, they work it out
> pretty quickly, and the graph of their comparative intelligence shows a sharply
> rising line. But, as I heard, "the trouble is that as soon as they figure out that
> the researcher or technician *wants* them to push the lever, they stop doing it;
> some of them will *starve* to death rather than do it." (pp. 224-225)

In short, a cat refuses to respond obediently, in a linear way, to our expectations. For this reason, a cat always pursues a circuitous route: "It is profoundly important to him that he avoid the stupidities of straight lines"
(p. 227). Most important, cats reject the "emotional bribery" (p. 240) implicit in a system of training by means of reward and punishment: "Hence
the grammars of approval and disapproval . . . are refused utterly by cats"
(p. 238). This means, of course, that you cannot teach a cat to "go fetch."
When you return home in the evening, you will find your cat curled immov-

ably in front of the fireplace. Your cat will not budge to go and fetch your pipe and slippers or to retrieve your newspaper. Your cat could not care less about whether you have the information you want.

Herein, your cat resembles the academic researcher, who will also refuse to gather the information that you seek. Rather, like the cat, academic researchers pursue the circuitous path to knowledge, more or less indifferent to the approval or disapproval of their masters (the marketing managers) and ready to starve—or at least to dwell in dignified academic penury— before succumbing to the pressures implicit in the dictates of managerial relevance.

DOGmatism and CATastrophe

Given the contrast that I have just drawn, it should surprise no one that those pursuing managerial relevance and those devoted to academic scholarship tend to look askance on one another's "pet" projects. From the feline perspective of the academic scholar, the demands of managerial relevance appear DOGmatic. From the canine perspective of the researcher oriented toward managerial relevance, the irresponsibility of those who follow their own circuitous path appears CATastrophic. Hence, a deep ambivalence emerges from the difference between practitioner-oriented dogs and academically inclined cats.

Even while stressing the value of obedience training, Vicki Hearne (1987) recognizes the relative merits of stubborn independence: "What we have made mistakes about is the nature of certain virtues, especially the willingness to please" (p. 232). In other words, Hearne deeply distrusts the fragility of any bond based on the need for constant approval. Such a distrust dictates a considerable respect for cats. Clearly, we might expect anyone named Morris to carry this sentiment past the point of respect to the level of admiration. And I do.

Support

All of this reflects my disagreement with those who attack academic scholarship on the grounds of its deficiencies in managerial relevance. But with such notable authorities as Steve Greyser (Myers et al., 1980), Fred Webster (1988), and Lyman Porter (Porter & McKibbin, 1988) boosting the cause of managerial relevance, I entertain few illusions about my power to defend my position through the use of mere animal metaphors. I therefore briefly return for support to an unquestioned authority on the issues we address—namely, the late commissioner of baseball.

A. Bartlett Giamatti

Before he took over as head of the National League and later as the full-fledged commissioner of this country's national pastime, A. Bartlett Giamatti served as the president of Yale University and, prior to that, as a professor of English, Italian, and comparative literature. From the perspective of these academic positions, Giamatti wrote some essays later collected in *A Free and Ordered Space: The Real World of the University*. Here, Giamatti (1988) insists on the ideals of a liberal education based on "a spirit that studies a subject simply for and in itself, without concern for the practical consequences of such study" (p. 109), as formulated in the explicitly anti-utilitarian views of John Henry Cardinal Newman's *The Idea of a University*:

> That alone is liberal knowledge . . . which stands on its own pretensions, which is independent of sequel, expects no complement, refuses to be *informed* (as it is called) by any end. . . . The most ordinary pursuits have this specific character, if they are self-sufficient and complete; the highest lose it, when they minister to something beyond them. (Newman, quoted by Giamatti, 1988, p. 167)

Following Newman, Giamatti passionately advocated the liberal ideal of knowledge pursued for its own sake as an end in itself. His essays resound with a devotion to independent thinking and to the kind of free but disciplined inquiry alluded to in his title. In a congeries of consonant concord, Giamatti consistently chooses words beginning with the letter *c*, such as "civility" (p. 12), "conversation" (p. 24), "collegiality" (p. 39), "community" (p. 39), "cooperation" (p. 80), "conviction" (p. 81), "congregation" (p. 87), "complex consensus" (p. 99), "connecting" (p. 99), "common interest" (p. 99), "competition, compromise, and consensus" (p. 113), "citizens" (p. 196), "collaborative" (p. 197), "care" (p. 197), "communicate" (p. 216), "connectedness" (p. 216), "cherish" (p. 219), "cohesive" (p. 231), "capacious" (p. 231), and "creation of knowledge for its own sake" (p. 119). In short, whenever Giamatti seeks the mot juste, he turns—perhaps without conscious intention—to c-words. We might contrast these with m-words, found ubiquitously in the business lexicon, such as *money, materialism, mechanical, mercenary, merchandise, machinery, mandate, mastery, manager,* and *market*—in short, those words that form the basic rhetoric of Managers concerned with Marketing in the Métier of Making Money.

Giamatti (1988) unflinchingly recognized that his commitment to "the freely inquiring mind, supportive of the right of other minds freely to inquire" (p. 46) drove a wedge between the objectives of education and those of business:

> A college or university is an institution where financial incentives to excellence are absent, where the product line is not a unit or an object but rather a value-laden and life-long process; where the goal of the enterprise is not growth or market share but intellectual excellence. (p. 37)

As one would expect from his advocacy of liberal education, Giamatti showed a deep concern for the central issues raised by "private-sector sponsorship of research," the tension between views of "knowledge as property versus knowledge as a free good," and questions about "how to manage the company's need to treat knowledge as property and the university's need to provide free access to, and open discussion of, the results of research" (p. 182). On these and related issues, Giamatti (1988) remained unshakable in his dedication, on behalf of the university, to basic research as the pursuit of knowledge for its own sake: "Basic research—that is, investigation that seeks new knowledge and understanding rather than solutions to immediate problems—is the essential nature of research on the part of all scholars" (p. 247). This celebration of basic research elevates the essentially feline virtue of independence to a high place (p. 258). Such a vantage point ensures vigilance concerning the need to keep the competing canine virtue of obedience in check:

> The norms of University research remain and must remain those of free access to information, independent assessment of evidence, the capacity freely to publish results subject to review by peers. To those who fear that the private sector will impose requirements on the University that would violate the academic integrity and processes that lie at the heart of our place, I say I understand the concern and will not ever dismiss it. No money offered from

any quarter that would require inappropriate promises or behavior will be accepted. (pp. 257-258)

Priorities

As I cannot emphasize strongly enough, the commitment to free inquiry goes beyond the assurance that important research findings will be openly published and in addition embraces the principle that the direction of research efforts—that is, the problems attacked, the questions studied, the issues investigated—must remain a matter for free, open, and self-determined choice. Thus, Giamatti (1988) reiterated this point almost obsessively:

> The University exists . . . to foster . . . the free exchange of ideas. . . . Individual members of the faculty pledge themselves to the open, unimpeded, and objective pursuit of ideas. . . . It is essential to protect academic freedom. . . . The university will not accept . . . infringement upon . . . the faculty's free inquiry. . . . The constant challenge for the university is . . . to cherish learning, and its pursuit, for its own sake. (pp. 261-269, passim)

Giamatti was by no means the only university president to care deeply about issues concerning the potentially distorting influence of corporate sponsorship on university research. Indeed, a conference at the University of Pennsylvania (Langfitt, Hackney, Fishman, & Glowasky, 1983) addressed what one academic leader called "the threatened diversion . . . from teaching and basic research into more applied investigation" (U. Penn's Hackney, 1983, p. xiii). Various other university spokespersons pointed to "the need for caution" (NYU's Fusfeld, 1983, p. 14), the danger of "seducing . . . faculty into . . . narrower . . . research" (U. of Washington's Omenn, 1983, p. 21), "the possible erosion of basic academic values" (Rensselaer's Low, 1983, p. 68), and threats to the tradition wherein "our universities encourage researchers . . . to pursue their scholarly goals in whatever directions seem . . . most promising to them" (Johns Hopkins's Muller, 1983, p. 147).

Meanwhile, as already noted in Chapter 6, the Pajaro Dunes Conference, also attended by the presidents of several major universities, pondered the ties of business to academia and stressed that this type of relationship raises the possibility of distorting academic objectives ("University/Industry Ties," 1982). About the same time, Harvard's Derek Bok (1982) voiced his concern "that programs to exploit technological development will confuse the university's central commitment to the pursuit of knowledge" (p. 142). Later, on the occasion of Harvard's 350th anniversary celebration, Bok charged that "some professors were becoming increasingly caught up in the contemporary pursuit of affluence, undermining the mission of the university" (Butterfield, 1986, p. 14).[2]

Here, the major concern stems from the possibility that those who pay for university research may gain the power to direct and potentially to distort its focus. Boffey (1984) reports this fear that "the growing collaboration between the universities and industry . . . may eventually destroy the very values of unfettered scientific inquiry that make academic research unique" (pp. C1, C9): "Nicholas Wade . . . warned that the directions of academic research might be dictated by commercial interests, that the credibility of the universities might be damaged and that the public might be deprived of independent scientific advice if academics become subservient to industrial sponsors" (p. C9).[3] In other words, those in the know fear that he who pays the piper calls the tune (Foote, 1984, p. A31) or that "the talent follows the money" with consequences that might "distort and skew scientific research" (Jennings, quoted by Berger, 1988, p. A14).[4] Such anxieties recall Clark Kerr's (1982) limerick about the "Young Lady From Kent" who was lavishly wined and dined: "She knew what it meant—but she went" (p. 69). Apparently, in academic research as elsewhere, there is no such thing as a free lunch.

By the early 1990s, the concerns raised by university administrators swelled to a crescendo that found its way onto the front page of the *New York Times* under the title "Business and Scholarship: A New Ethical Quandary"—"Critics are asking whether growing financial incentives for scientists will dictate research priorities, impede the sharing of information, promote fraudulent work and increase conflicts of interest" (Leary, 1989, p. A1).[5] In short, the bottom line concerns the setting of intellectual priorities and whether they are for sale.

An Illustration of Priority Warping

Readers might be thinking to themselves that the worries just expressed represent merely hypothetical possibilities troublesome only to the sorts of neurotic people who would choose to live their lives in the ivory tower of academia. Hence, before continuing, it might be helpful to mention a rather vivid illustration of the problems that can arise when commercial interests distort the direction of science or when the profit motive infects the purity of scholarship. I refer to the controversies that surrounded the research conducted by Stanley Pons and Martin Fleischmann on low-temperature nuclear fusion at the University of Utah. This fiasco shows what can happen when the canons of commercialization, the materialistic goals of monetary gain, and the pursuit of patent protection conspire to guide the course of scientific endeavor.

When Pons and Fleischmann first announced their purported breakthrough on March 23, 1989, the frenzy of excitement over the potential profits from a theoretically unlimited supply of cheap energy quickly reached proportions that the *New York Times,* in another front-page story, labeled "Fusion Furor" (Wilford, 1989, p. A1). But from the beginning, the scientific dedication to free and open inquiry broke down. While the University of Utah "applied for patents on the cold-fusion technique," its celebrity researchers provided "few details of how the experiment was conducted and checked out" (Wilford, 1989, p. B6). This withholding of information frustrated attempts to replicate the Utah results, led to loud complaints from other scientists, and encouraged skepticism because the work had been "shrouded in secrecy, supposedly due to patents" (Wilford, 1989, p. B6).[6] Ultimately, this skepticism blossomed into suspicion and discredit when Pons and Fleischmann "declined to collaborate with other laboratories on experiments that would help dispel doubts about their work" because "Utah lawyers became uneasy with . . . possible conflicts over intellectual property rights" (Broad, 1989a, p. C8).[7] Finally, a Utah spokesman admitted that "the scientists want to tell everything, but the patent attorneys tell us to say absolutely nothing" (Broad, 1989b, p. A20).[8] Meanwhile, the popular press summarized this perversion of science as an object lesson in corporate finance:

> The discovery . . . could be worth a fortune. Keeping some of the secrets to themselves could serve to protect their financial interests. . . . The awesome potential of the alleged discovery explains why so many people are badgering Pons and Fleischmann for information, and why they are giving it out so cautiously. (Lemonick, 1989, p. 74)[9]

Crease and Samios (1989) sized up the situation as follows: "With their findings almost universally discredited, Pons and Fleischmann continue to cling to their assertion that they have found something new. . . . Pons and Fleischmann apparently fell victim to the experimental scientist's worst nightmare . . . self-deception" (p. 35).[10] In the last analysis, Broad (1990) suggests, the Pons-Fleischmann phenomenon has reflected "zealotry" inspired by interest in "the commercialization of the discovery" and by "profit seeking rather than scientific peer review" (p. C12).[11]

(Notice, by the way, the proliferation of f-words in the language used to describe this situation—"fusion furor," "frenzied race to be the first to confirm . . . the findings," "few details," "fortune," "filed five patent applications," "findings . . . discredited," "factor at work," "fell victim," "Fleischmann," and the oft-repeated "financial interests." This stream of f-words reminds us alliteratively of a troubling concern lurking in the background: "fraud.")

❑ The Glaring Exception

All of this sounds like Bart Giamatti's worst nightmare. Yet, the Utah upheaval and resulting disrepute of Professors Pons and Fleischmann mirror the conditions under which many researchers in marketing live on a daily basis. The difference, of course, is that, in the case of business research, nobody notices. In business research, we simply accept the smothering veil of secrecy that accompanies the tempting apple of commercial gain. In business research, the taking for granted of greed as the foundation for value goes almost unquestioned.

Shared Assumptions

The assumption that research in marketing should address questions dictated by the profit motive of business managers pervades the ethos of professional schools, Business Departments, and Marketing Divisions in this nation's universities. Almost nobody questions the bedrock belief that research in marketing should aspire to increasing profits and improving the bottom line—that marketing academics are properly the minions of managers. I find this shared assumption rampant in the aforementioned works by Myers et al. (1980), by Porter and McKibbin (1988), and by Webster (1988).

For example, Webster (1988) stresses that marketing research requires both scientific rigor and managerial relevance: "The rigor and relevance dichotomy is not only false but counterproductive and misleading. Good research in marketing, by definition, has both. Relevance requires concern for and interaction with marketing managers and the problems they face" (pp. 50-51). This argument echoes the ardent managerialism advocated by Myers et al.'s (1980) Commission on the Effectiveness of Research and Development for Marketing Management (CERDMM): "Early on, the Commission adopted the position that the objective of research should be to improve marketing management practice" (p. 11). From this perspective: "The Commission's view was that if marketing knowledge over the long run is to be considered 'effective,' it should contribute something to improved decision making or other aspects of marketing management practice in the industrial sector" (pp. 143-145). CERDMM's viewpoint encourages an active role for business managers in determining the direction of research in marketing:

> To facilitate or accelerate the development of useful managerial research, we need to identify and define topics considered significant in the business community, have a mechanism for helping to develop and shape the research ideas to be employed in addressing those topics, and develop a base of funding to support the time and efforts of the researchers involved. (p. 10)

Indeed, in this view, "even basic research in marketing should make some contribution to 'solving a specific business problem' or 'improving the effectiveness of marketing management' " (p. 154). Thus, Myers et al. (1980) gravitate toward the conclusion expressed by Howard Westing (1977) in his article for the *Marketing News* entitled "Marketing Educators Must Switch to Helping Real World Meet Real Problems": "The fact of the matter is that we are not an academic discipline. . . . Our goal should be to try to make business more proficient and efficient. . . . We are all professional disciplines, rather than academic disciplines" (quoted by Myers et al., 1980, p. 245). For support, the authors cite businesspeople who complained to CERDMM that "very many academic marketing researchers . . . have no real knowledge of marketing problems" (p. 242), that "the academics are simply ignorant of the problems of practical implementation" (p. 242), and that "the knowledge generators would be well served to develop more client-effective channels of communication with the marketing managers" (p. 243).

The same themes reappear in Porter and McKibbin's (1988) study for the American Assembly of Collegiate Schools of Business (AACSB), rather aggressively entitled *Management Education and Development: Drift or Thrust Into the 21st Century?* Reflecting its AACSB parentage, this study emphasizes criticisms that "business school faculties lack sufficient breadth of understanding of real-world business problems" (p. 132): "Research being turned out by business schools is largely trivial and irrelevant. It does not, say the critics, address . . . the most important problems and issues faced by business. . . . Critics claim that . . . business school research is . . . not relevant to the 'real' problems of business" (pp. 168-170). Despite some second thoughts later raised by Porter (1989), Porter and McKibbin (1988) never seriously question their central insistence on "the issue of how to increase the impact of business school research on the practicing profession" (p. 180).

The monograph *Drift or Thrust* certainly seems to have caught the temper of the times, circa 1990. Thus, a related article in *Business Week* by John Byrne (1990) carried the following somewhat wordy but nonetheless pointed title: "Is Research in the Ivory Tower 'Fuzzy, Irrelevant, Pretentious'? B-schools stress scholarly papers, but a lot of what emerges has no value for the manager" (p. 62). In this article, Byrne (1990) describes the amazement expressed by Richard R. West (then the dean of the Business School at New York University) over "what he considers the overemphasis placed on scholarly research at most business schools" (p. 62). After this appallingly anti-intellectual comment, Byrne goes on to quote Scott S. Cowen (Management School dean at Case Western Reserve), as follows: "As much as 80% of management research may be irrelevant. . . . I wonder if the majority of it is of any significant value to executives in terms of influencing their daily actions, behaviors, or business practices" (p. 62).

The arguments and conclusions just summarized clearly favor a role for management interests in guiding the direction of business research. This premise serves as "the predominant research mission" of the MSI (Myers et al., 1980, p. 158) and appears to motivate such glaring gestures as the unsolicited letter to our AMA Task Force from the president of a strategy-research organization who complained as follows:

> The task force is overloaded with academics—the very people who I feel have done a terrible job in obtaining and conveying useful knowledge to those in the business and marketing community who need their help. . . . If the task force is to help overcome the obvious problems in marketing knowledge accumulation, . . . it would conduct in-depth interviews with the management

users themselves to learn how to orient basic and applied research to their requirements.

This letter routinely expresses a prevailing doctrine on the birthright of managers to direct the course of business-related research. Few would be so foolhardy as to attack this pervasive ideology. Few, therefore, will spontaneously embrace my comparison between managerial and academic researchers—paralleling the difference between dogs and cats—or my insistence on the need to find a place for the latter in the marketing menagerie.

Task Force Redux

The purpose of a university and the people in it is to create knowledge. This creation of knowledge depends fundamentally on free inquiry cherished for its own sake as an end in itself. As argued by Bronowski (1965): "In science, there is no substitute for independence" (pp. 61-62). In the context of marketing, Sid Levy (1976) would agree: "A marketing science should be demarcated that does not do *marketing research* but that does *research into marketing*. It should be a pursuit of knowledge, as distinguished from its application, candidly and proudly so" (p. 580).

It follows that any force that impedes the freedom of inquiry must be resisted as inherently inconsistent with the core objectives of academic scholarship. In the case of research devoted to the pursuit of managerial relevance, researchers face the danger that outside interests—extrinsic, as opposed to intrinsic, value—may determine or distort the directions of their investigations. This danger mounts rapidly when external business interests pay for the research in question, whether through expense reimbursements, honorariums, grant funding, or consulting fees.

The resulting intrusion of outside interests into the research process constitutes a potential threat to the independence of free inquiry that should stir concerns among all those affiliated with the academic process, including those who live and work in schools of business. We have seen that members of the university in other fields and disciplines do show such concerns. Yet, no one shows any real concern for this problem when it arises in the case of business schools.

Thus, business schools generally and Marketing Departments in particular take for granted a situation that has raised considerable alarm when it has affected other disciplines. Business professors cheerfully welcome—indeed, avidly seek—corporate funding, consulting relationships, and self-imposed mandates of managerial relevance without ever noticing, let alone questioning, the inevitably associated damage to free inquiry.

In my view, the main accomplishment of the AMA Task Force was that it partially succeeded in resisting this dominant ethos of managerial relevance. As a group, the task force kept in mind the difference between managerial and academic research, couching its major recommendations in terms designed to further academic research in marketing without special attention to advancing managerial marketing research. It thereby departed from the perspective adopted by other comparable groups. For me, this difference in viewpoint, so deplored by Webster (1988), represents the crowning achievement of the task force in that it questions some pervasive but insidious premises that richly deserve to be repudiated.

In making this claim, I may go farther than some members of the AMA Task Force would find comfortable. Indeed, I realize that my own views on this subject are fairly extreme and that I may be reading messages into the task force report that it does not, in fact, contain. If so, let me reassure the reader that I do not wish to become Morris the Martyr. Rather, I only want to put in a kind word or two for the perspective of Morris the Cat.

❑ The Celebration of Cats

Cats Are Curious

The fellows of the AMA's 1987 Doctoral Consortium conveyed a relevant message when they thoughtfully gave me a copy of the book by Roger Caras (1986) entitled *A Celebration of Cats*. Caras (1986) repeatedly disputes the stereotypical image of cats as aloof and insists instead that "What cats are is individualistic" (p. 15). Indeed, the cat shows a profound interest or even a life-threatening curiosity in human affairs, but little servility or deference to its master, which Caras considers an explanation for why Alexander the Great, Napoleon, and Hitler all hated cats (p. 17). The dog, by contrast, seeks to please by its obedience. Robert Stearns (1976) draws this comparison as follows: "There is the ridiculous idea that dogs are superior to cats because cats cannot be trained. A cat will not jump into a lake and bring back a stick; would you?" (p. 287).

Managers Manage

It seems natural that business managers should prefer the canine to the feline personality. After all, managers manage. They are accustomed to giving directions. When confronted by research, it is not surprising that they want to control it too.

My own essentially feline view is that academic researchers—whatever the cost in terms of esteem or wealth—must resist such attempts at domination, all the more because the managerial credo generally appears in terms that, on the surface, sound so plausible. Indeed, the advocates of managerial relevance in marketing research couch their message to academicians in language that seems quite conciliatory. "Be reasonable," they say; "Be of assistance to others." "Be useful," they suggest; "Give us information helpful in doing our jobs better." "Be accommodating," they urge; "Compromise and respect the needs, pressures, and dictates of the real world." But, in essence, this message that sounds so constructive masks a threatening implication: "Be untrue to what you care about most and what you think matters. Distort your own voice. Renounce the integrity of your own vision. And do all this with an ingratiating deference—a bow of the head, a wag of the tail—and gratitude to us for letting you be relevant."

Cruelty to Cats

This attitude on the part of those who preach managerial relevance has caused much hardship among the academicians who devote themselves to the more basic and less applied side of science and scholarship. But, surely, history has taught us by now that we should never mistreat our cats (Caras, 1986; Fireman, 1976).

The Egyptians worshipped cats as divine, and the Greeks also regarded them as godlike creatures. But cats lost ground with the Romans, who cynically carried them into battle against the Egyptians, knowing that the latter would rather sacrifice a city than risk harming a cat. And with the spread of Christianity during the Middle Ages, cats fell under suspicion as symbols of

Satan. By papal decree, cruel persecution was turned against cats: "During the Middle Ages, . . . hundreds of thousands of cats were destroyed in ceremonies presided over by priests, and hundreds more were crucified and flayed" (Bay, 1976, p. 11). Thus, false assumptions about the evil nature of cats led to their being "crucified or thrown howling into ovens" (Voight, 1976, p. 17): "Convinced that destruction, usually by fire or some other hideous means, was the only way to be free of these devils, superstitious people in medieval times continued an unparalleled and wanton killing of cats, generally in a sacrificial manner" (Jackson, 1976, p. 33).

As documented in Robert Darnton's *Great Cat Massacre* (1984), such horrific practices continued well into the 18th century. But, by then, they had already produced their most horrendous consequences when, in the 14th century, the purgation of cats permitted a tremendous increase in the European rat population. This infestation of rodents precipitated the black plague and thereby led directly to the deaths of three out of every four people in Europe (Voight, 1976, p. 18). No wonder the Irish adopted their signal proverb: "Beware of people who dislike cats" (Caras, 1986, p. 134).

The moral, of course, is that people should cherish cats. Analogously, we as researchers should treasure the academic individualists who stubbornly insist on doing research that managers find useless. Indeed, we should round up all of the researchers who bravely refuse to care about managerial relevance and—far from treating them like outcasts or disciples of the devil— should thank them for it.

Conclusion

Those who teach consumer behavior or marketing must recognize and preserve the honorable difference between the academic and managerial sides of research. If nothing else, the AMA Task Force report serves to call attention to this divergence in viewpoints. If nothing else, it reminds us that marketing academics pursue certain promising if circuitous paths that deserve the respect of their more managerially inclined colleagues. And, if nothing else, it thereby justifies the conclusion that researchers in marketing desperately need some sort of spiritual center to help them feel good about the kind of research they do and that, toward this end, they must *find, elevate, and proclaim whatever is noble, worthwhile, and profound in the development of marketing thought.*

❑ Epilogue

A Critique by Cornelia Pechmann

My original thoughts on "Dogmatism and Catastrophe in the Development of Marketing Thought" (Holbrook, 1989a) elicited a rejoinder from my friend Cornelia (Connie) Pechmann (1990), who disagreed with certain aspects of my case against the quest for managerial relevance. The theme of my chapter on the skylark demands that I respond to Connie's critique in a lyrical way. Hence, I confine myself to quoting the gist of her argument and to presenting a short poem that reflects my feelings (Holbrook, 1990a).

To summarize Connie's claims in her own words:

> Morris Holbrook . . . asserted that mandating consumer behaviorists' research to be managerially relevant . . . precludes us from conducting research that is intrinsically motivated. . . . According to Holbrook, researchers who pursue managerial relevance are . . . funded by corporations. . . . However, managerially relevant research frequently is not funded by corporations. . . . Grants frequently are allocated on the basis of the research's perceived relevance, but this is not to say that managers necessarily dictate the questions to be addressed. . . . Holbrook's condemnation of managerially relevant research is based primarily on the inherent dangers of relying on private-sector funding rather than on conducting managerially relevant research. . . . Managerially relevant research . . . does not limit academic freedom. Even researchers who pursue managerial relevance are free to choose what questions they ask as long as the answers might potentially be of interest to their constituencies. . . . I find managerially relevant research to be highly intrinsically rewarding. . . . My objective is to increase the effectiveness of marketers. . . . Therefore, I would like to make a simple suggestion to Morris Holbrook and other likeminded individuals. . . . To truly gain our respect, you must be respectful of our right to do research that we are intrinsically motivated to do—namely, research that will be of value to managers, students, consumers, and/or regulators. (Pechmann, 1990, passim)

Here, Connie makes some good points—especially (a) her distinction between the target of relevance and the source of funding and (b) her correct insistence that academic freedom entails the right to choose topics of interest to managers. But, as I have indicated in this chapter, I do disagree with other aspects of her analysis. To keep the resulting exchange as light in tone as possible, I have taken to versification in what—if my verse did not so strongly offend the standards of managerial relevance—might otherwise qualify as *dog*gerel.

If the events described in my poem were performed as a theatrical production, the marketing manager would play the role of Dog; Morris would play the role of Cat; and Connie Pechmann (as befits the French-German translation of "Peche-Man" as "Fish-Person") would play the role of Fish.

DOG(matism), CAT(astrophe), and FISH(iness)

A cat and a dog once got into a fight;
They argued all night about which one was right.
The cat said that felines should be independent;
The dog said that all pets should become more relevant.

The dog growled at the cat; the cat hissed at the dog;
The two animals had an intense dialogue;
But impassioned debate did not help them agree
About what—in essence—it means to be free.

The cat thought that freedom's what pleases a *cat.*
The dog—at considerably greater length
　　and in a tone of high seriousness
　　with many pious references
　　to societal benefits —
　　put forward a definition of freedom
　　as something which involves
　　a readjustment of priorities
　　toward more practical objectives
　　by getting feedback on exactly what it is
　　that your master wants
　　and then doing precisely *that.*
Clearly, as noted by every spectator,
These creatures had need of a smart arbitrator.

So along came a fish with her finny tail wagging
And said, "I do hope I don't seem to be bragging,
But I find, on freedom, my time is best spent
If I remain sublimely indifferent.

In fact, this repression of my every wish
Has earned me my epithet, 'cold as a fish.'
Like me, you should learn to forget you're a pet
And to swim in the sea but not even get wet."

❑ *Notes*

1. Peter Steiner in *The New Yorker*, June 25, 1990. © 1990 The New Yorker Magazine, Inc.

2. Butterfield (1986), p. 14. Copyright © 1986 by The New York Times Company. Reprinted by permission.

3. Boffey (1984), pp. C1, C9. Copyright © 1984 by The New York Times Company. Reprinted by permission.

4. Berger (1988), p. A14. Copyright © 1988 by The New York Times Company. Reprinted by permission.

5. Leary (1989), p. A1. Copyright © by The New York Times Company. Reprinted with permission.

6. Wilford (1989), pp. A1, B6. Copyright © 1989 by The New York Times Company. Reprinted with permission.

7. Broad (1989a), p. C8. Copyright © 1989 by The New York Times Company. Reprinted with permission.

8. Broad (1989b), p. A20. Copyright © 1989 by The New York Times Company. Reprinted with permission.

9. Lemonick (1989), p. 74. Copyright © 1989 Time Inc. Reprinted by permission.

10. Crease and Samios (1989), p. 35. Copyright © 1989 by The New York Times Company. Reprinted with permission.

11. Broad (1990), p. C12. Copyright © 1989 by The New York Times Company. Reprinted with permission.

I'M HIP

An Autobiographical Account of
Some Musical Consumption Experiences

Music's my life,
And ev'ry day I live it,
And it's a good life too.
                    —Billy Preston, "Music's My Life,"
                              Music Is My Life, (1972)[1]

❏ **Introduction**

New Possibilities

Previous chapters have led us through a process of chipping and tearing at the original view of consumer research with which we began a quarter-century ago until almost every vestige of the conventional wisdom has been stripped away. The reader will recall that we started, in the early 1960s, with the pervasive doctrine that "Scientific Marketing Research Is Neopositivistic Managerially Relevant Studies of Decisions to Buy Goods and Services" (Statement 1 in Figure 1.3 from Chapter 1). One by one, in chapter after chapter, aspects of this traditional view have been discarded until, by now, little remains of the traditional credo with which we began—indeed, little more than the single word *Research* (Statement 9 in Figure 1.3 from

Chapter 1). Thus—in the mid-1990s, as we rapidly approach the next mil-lenium—we confront the challenge of doing consumer research with a new freedom in concepts, methods, and aims that is as promising in its opportu-nities as it is terrifying in its uncertainties.

In a sense, during the past three decades, consumer researchers have shredded the map that used to chart their course and that offered safe guid-ance in approaching the discipline. Some will regard the uncharted territory that now lies ahead as a vast wasteland of potential dangers—something like a huge desert in which one seeks a safe oasis of security. Others will see the new vistas of empty space that have unfolded as a sort of clean slate, a tabula rasa, on which they can fill in the blanks with new approaches to the study of consumption.

I tend to subscribe to the latter view. The history of consumer research, as recounted in this book from a subjective personal introspective point of view, has produced a kind of mental housecleaning in which the broom of pluralism has swept the cobwebs of old superstitions from the attic of our collective mind. That mind now lies open to a great variety of possibilities. One such possibility (among many alternatives) serves as the theme for this chapter and is summarized by Statement 10 in Figure 1.3 from Chapter 1: Humanistic Consumer Research in Marketing Includes Interpretive Intrin-sically Motivated Studies of Experience in the Consumption of Artwork and Entertainment.

Specifically, if we recall the series of stages in which this book has pro-gressed, we see that one possible course (among others) for a consumer re-searcher moving from the 1960s through the 1990s toward the year 2000 has involved the following:

- ❑ Replacing a focus on *marketing* with one directed toward *consumers* (Chap-ter 2)
- ❑ Shifting from a concern for *goods and services* to an interest in *artwork and entertainment* (Chapter 3)
- ❑ Abandoning the preoccupation with *buying* in favor of work on *consumption experiences* (Chapter 4)
- ❑ Worrying less about *decisions* to choose brands than about *emotional experi-ences* in product acquisition, usage, and disposition (Chapter 5)
- ❑ Striving less to achieve extrinsically motivated objectives of *managerial relevance* than to pursue an *intrinsically motivated* quest for knowledge valued as an end in itself (Chapter 6)

❑ Regarding the old *neopositivistic* philosophy of science as the antiquated precursor to a broadened range of alternative approaches that include *interpretive* or postpositivistic methods (Chapter 7)

❑ Seeing these interpretive approaches as replacing mere *science* or old-fashioned scientism with real scholarship in the best sense of a *humanistic* devotion to learning (Chapter 8)

❑ Demanding that distortions in priorities associated with the "canine" view of *marketing research* surrender to the felicities found in a more "feline" freedom for *research in marketing* (Chapter 9)

The upshot of all of these proposals for modifications and changes in our view of consumer research is to recommend one potential approach (among the various pluralistic possibilities) structured along the lines just described:

Humanistic Consumer Research in Marketing Includes Interpretive Intrinsically Motivated Studies of Experience in the Consumption of Artworks and Entertainment.

This proposed approach retains our expanded focus on *consumers* (Chapter 2); *artwork and entertainment* (Chapter 3); *consumption* (Chapter 4); emotional *experiences* (Chapter 5); *intrinsically motivated* curiosity (Chapter 6); subjective personal introspection as a viable *interpretive* source of insights (Chapter 7); a resulting *humanistic* bent toward lyricism in the expression of one's own feelings (Chapter 8); and a concomitant "catastrophic" insistence that one's own research *in* marketing is what one wants it to be (Chapter 9).

Illustration: Sonata Allegro

We now need, it seems to me, an illustration of what the sort of approach just described abstractly might actually look like if one really dared to do it in the real world of consumer research. As I suggest in Chapter 1, such concrete examples of the research style currently under consideration have remained few and far between. Isolated attempts have appeared in the work of Beth Hirschman (1991) and Steve Gould (1991). But the only sustained effort, to my knowledge, occurred in my so-called ACR trilogy summarized in Chapter 7 and its aftermath in subsequent autobiographical essays. Here, as promised earlier, I devote much of Chapter 10 to an illustration taken from that original trio of examples. Specifically, I present my subjective personal introspections under the title "Exposition: I'm Hip."

Exposition

The reader will notice that this autobiographical "exposition" talks about my own consumption experiences from a rather personal point of view. In this essay, I describe my subjective feelings connected with the role of music in my life. I introspect deeply on the meaning of these musical consumption experiences and try to communicate lyrically something of the emotional resonance involved. Of course, I treat the theme of hipness in the tongue-in-cheek manner that it deserves and do not hesitate to make fun of its author, who is nothing if not comical. I reproduce "I'm Hip" here in a version quite close to its original form (Holbrook, 1986e), with just a few minor revisions added to improve accuracy, clarity, or gracefulness wherever possible.

Sonata Form

More recently, I have returned to this theme concerning the role of music in my life. In particular, I have written three additional autobiographical pieces that describe important moments in my musical consumption experiences and that I include here to complete a sort of *sonata allegro*. As usual, the sonata form follows the structure described by *The Harvard Brief Dictionary of Music*, progressing from the "Exposition" through a "Development" to a "Recapitulation" followed by a "Coda":

> In the *exposition* the main . . . ideas are "exposed." . . . The *development* serves to "develop" the thematic material introduced in the exposition. . . . Dynamic growth, tension, and dramatic conflict [are] characteristic of the development section. . . . Another important trait of the development section is the extended use of modulation, leading into various keys, often far removed from the main key. The *recapitulation* is essentially a restatement of the exposition (though it can be shortened or extended) with a modification of the key scheme. . . . The *coda* varies greatly in length and importance. . . . The coda often assumes considerable proportions and great importance. (Apel & Daniel, 1960, pp. 276-277)

Development

Analogously, the present "Development" modulates from a major to a minor key and describes a "Lesson in Humility." Full of tension and conflict, it recounts my "growth pains" in learning that a career as a jazz musician did

not seem to lie within my grasp. Somber in tone, it conveys a feeling of sadness or even despair far removed from the mood of the exposition.

Recapitulation

The "Recapitulation" returns to a happier theme and restates the positive
mood of the exposition. I wrote it as a tribute to my hero Dizzy Gillespie on
the occasion of his 75th birthday (Holbrook, 1992). Unfortunately, with
Dizzy's death at the age of 75, it has also become a memorial; but, nonetheless, it reiterates the positive force of jazz in my life, with extensions concerning the joy that I once felt when two jazz geniuses—Diz and his great pianist,
Junior Mance—treated me with kindness and respect. As a further extension, to the best of my autoethnographic ability, it presents my sense of how
a common love for music can erase differences between generations, between ethnic groups, and between socioeconomic backgrounds. With luck,
it captures the essence of my consumption experience when, for a brief moment, two heroes acted as friends. In their honor, it is entitled "Just Dizzy,
Junior, and Me on the Way to Our Gig."

Coda

The "Coda" describes some insights that struck me with great force when
I revisited an old film called *The Benny Goodman Story* (Rosenberg & Davies,
1955). Considered afresh, after 40 years of forgetfulness, this movie clearly
contains a relevant subtext that appears to have exerted a strong unconscious influence on my personality and characteristic perspectives. On the
basis of this moment of epiphany, further clarified by the insights of my friend
Ellen Day (Holbrook & Day, 1994), I suggest some connections between
Benny as a jazz musician and myself as a teacher of consumer research.

❏ Exposition: *I'm Hip*

> I'm hip; I'm no square;
> I'm alert, I'm awake, I'm aware. . . .
> Like dig: I'm in step;
> When it was hip to be hep, I was hep. . . .
> —Dave Frishberg (1981), "I'm Hip" [2]

For most of my life, I have tried very hard to be hip. Growing up, I was never the smartest student at school, the best football player on the team, the most popular guy in the class, the most successful in winning student elections, or the biggest hit with the girls at the small female prep school down the street. But I had one consolation. Even if I wasn't better than my classmates at anything important, I was hipper than at least 99% of the other students at the Milwaukee Country Day School. I knew that just as surely as I know that vanilla tastes better than tutti-frutti.

Very early, I learned that the rules for being hip are actually quite simple. They follow a straightforward four-step procedure:

1. Find out what most people like.
2. Treat that with complete indifference (or, when pressed, with scornful contempt).
3. Ferret out some obscure treasure admired by, at most, a few cognoscenti (or, if necessary, by some other group of weirdos).
4. Elevate that piece of obscurity to a lofty status of extravagant admiration and treat anyone who cannot appreciate it with pity (sometimes mixed with disdain).

In Milwaukee, Wisconsin—where people like Liberace were born and raised; where Lawrence Welk ruled in Saturday evening prime time; where weekday afternoon radio consisted mostly of polka bands and Hawaiian guitars; where the best-known products had names like Miller and Pabst; and where the Braves with Hank Aaron and Warren Spahn were unanimously regarded as the town's greatest cultural achievement—being hip was easy. The four steps come naturally to someone inhabiting a city whose cachet depended on the reputation of its leading brand of beer—namely, "Schlitz, the Beer That Made Milwaukee Famous."

At home, things were different. Some of the earliest sounds that I can remember hearing were the tinkling notes of my father's piano as he played Teddy Wilson and Fats Waller arrangements of songs like "China Boy" and "Just a Girl That Men Forget," transcriptions he had painstakingly read and scrupulously committed to memory when he was probably still himself scarcely more than a young boy. On many evenings, I fell asleep with that sweet music ringing gently in my ears. Thus, I learned to love jazz at a very early age. I suppose you could say that, for a little kid, I was pretty hip.

I also remember my grandmother effortlessly sight-reading Chopin, with her long, delicate fingers skimming across the keys of her ebony Steinway. And I recall Teenie, our beautiful housekeeper, pouring out her soul in melodious spirituals as she glided through her chores. Everywhere, I was surrounded by graceful music. Soon, I wanted to make some music of my own.

My dad, Sandy, taught me some simple, one-finger tunes on the piano but realized very quickly that, for the sake of my development and his nerves, I needed more professional instruction. So, at the age of 6, I started lessons with Helen, a friend of my parents who came from the old school of piano teaching. Helen awarded a gold star if you practiced faithfully and learned your lesson for that week or a red star if you did not. She lived by the rule that three red stars meant termination. Thanks to gentle but constant prodding from my mother, May, I never received one of those dreaded red stigmata, but even then I was hip enough to know that red stars belonged in Moscow, not Milwaukee. Later, much later, I learned the difference between extrinsic and intrinsic motivation and realized that musical activities properly belong in the latter category where even positive external rewards can exert disincentive effects. Meanwhile, Helen taught me to play a few classical compositions, dragging me through such bleak exercises as Mozart's Piano Sonata in C-Major (that supremely annoying piece of juvenalia otherwise known as "In an Eighteenth Century Drawing Room"). After 4 years, I could stumble through about three pages of its first movement, but the main lesson I learned from Helen was an abiding sense of what the experience curve means when it says that you need to double the number of trials in order to attain a 20% improvement in performance. This doubling and redoubling of effort grew increasingly tedious. Somewhere between the 10- and 20-thousandth repetition, my spirit broke. Increasingly, in my frustration, I would lean forward and bite our piano. This noble Steinway still bears ancient teeth marks along its front edge. Realizing that this modus operandi was noticeably less than hip—with support from Sandy and May (who had doubtless grown tired of reminding me to practice)—I asked for a new instructor, someone a little closer to jazz.

By this route, I came to study with Tommy, Milwaukee's leading jazz musician and, purely and simply, the greatest teacher that I have ever known. Since then, I have attended various schools, studied under innumerable professors, and watched many academic colleagues, but I have never encountered Tommy's equal in communicating his vast knowledge and love of his subject matter. Tommy lived and breathed jazz. His students lived and breathed jazz with him.

Tommy started me on boogie-woogie versions of "St. Louis Blues" and "Basin Street," moved me into jazzier swing and show tunes like "Moonglow" and "A Foggy Day," and gradually began showing me chords, harmonic progressions, and the techniques of improvisation. His empathy, patience, and enthusiasm deeply conveyed his passion for music. They instilled in me a lasting faith in his credo: "If it *sounds* right, it *is* right." Tommy was the quintessence of hipness, the prototype, the ideal. He approached the Platonic Form for Hip. Tommy *sounded* right. Tommy *was* right.

So, under Tommy's guidance, I marched to the tune of a different drummer, one with a rhythmically advanced sense of time. While everybody else in Milwaukee was listening to Rosemary Clooney's "Come On-A My House," Doris Day's "Che Sera Sera," and Patti Page's "How Much Is That Doggy in the Window," I cultivated a devoted attachment to Sandy's collection of Benny Goodman records—precariously breakable 78s and scratchy old 33s that even he had largely forgotten about.

I found exactly two other contemporaries, Johnny and Steve, who shared my worshipful fondness for singers like Bing Crosby, Ella Fitzgerald, and Louis Armstrong and for musicians like Lionel Hampton, Gene Krupa, and the King of Swing himself. Johnny and I memorized the Bing-and-Gary duets by singing them with each other for hours over the telephone. Steve and I played and replayed Goodman's 1938 Carnegie Hall concert in amazed admiration for the intricacies of the wonderful trumpet solos by Harry James and Ziggy Elman. When the film *The Benny Goodman Story* appeared, Steve and I were in ecstasy. I tried to learn to play the trumpet, but this task proved impossible for a young man with a horn, an entire mouthful of braces, and an orthodontist whose weekly machinations vividly presaged Sir Laurence Olivier's sadistic performance in *The Marathon Man*. For a while, I even persuaded some of my friends to call me Ziggy. They cooperated but probably did not understand that it was my way of retaliating against society's devotion to Eddie Fisher and "Oh, My Papa." (I still have my shiny Holton trumpet hanging in our bookcase—unused but not forgotten.)

The arrival of Elvis Presley gave me something new and much more formidable to detest. At this critical moment, Johnny left town to attend Deerfield Academy in Massachusetts. Steve, my confrere in vintage-1938 tastes, deserted me, bought a black leather jacket, grew ducktails, and practiced wildly gyrating dances on the tiptoes of his white sweat socks. Things got lonely. I was the only one in my eighth-grade class who thought—no, knew!—that Elvis was terrible. Cherishing my adolescent musical iconoclasm like a rare diamond, I searched for a way to remain hip.

Two things saved me. The first involved my discovery of the cool school of West Coast jazz. Gerry Mulligan, Chet Baker, Paul Desmond, Stan Getz, and their cohorts brought me into an ethereal world of restrained, cerebral, progressive music that none of the other eighth graders knew, cared about, or could understand—even if they had been willing to listen to it, which they were not. I was in orbit. I had found something wonderful that no one else liked. In fact, I had found something supremely beautiful that everyone else hated. I had reached the outer sphere of hipness where few ever tread.

My second salvation came from forming a band or what, in those days, we called a "combo." This combo consisted of Howie on guitar, Kenny on bass, Stu on drums, and me on piano or (later) vibes. We learned tunes like "How High the Moon," "Pick Yourself Up," and "Jumpin' With Symphony Sid." In other words, we shunned anything remotely popular. Sometimes, we played for parties or dances, but mostly the combo just practiced by ourselves on Sunday afternoons that were long and arduous for us—no doubt even longer and still more arduous for our bewildered parents—as we fumbled and argued our way through incorrect chord changes and botched melody lines.

The other guys in the combo came from public school. I only saw them on weekends. The rest of the time, surrounded by preppy little eighth graders who showed an ironic fondness for Elvis and other greased-up, hip-swinging hillbillies, I pursued my own splendid musical isolation. My classmates thought that "hip(s)" was a (plural) noun. I knew that, for me, it was a (singular) adjective. Sometimes, I felt a little outcast in my wayward tastes. But, if you let that sort of thing bother you, then you're not really very hip.

Finally, in the first year of high school, Peter arrived. Pete came from across town, where he had pursued a roughly parallel development of musical sensibilities. The major difference was that Pete had listened to a wider array of the new jazz than I had heard. Peter exposed me to Miles Davis, Sonny Rollins, and Thelonious Monk. I had to scramble to compete. I dug back into the recent past and came up with Charlie Parker, Dizzy Gillespie, and Horace Silver. Pete reciprocated with Art Pepper, Lee Konitz, and Jimmy Giuffre. I countered with Clifford Brown, Milt Jackson, and Hampton Hawes. These were times of enormous growth in our evolving musical tastes—times in which, almost every day, we discovered some new form of stupendous greatness—for example, Clifford Brown's solo on "Gertrude's

Bounce" or Milt Jackson's re-creation of "Over the Rainbow" or the amazing "lost" chord that Hampton Hawes plays midway through his choruses on "Green Leaves of Summer." All profoundly inspirational to Peter and me. Even someone who is very hip needs a kindred spirit. Peter and I spurred each other on.

Once a week or whenever we could pry some allowance money from one of our parents, Pete and I traveled downtown to Radio Doctor's—our mecca—Milwaukee's best record dealer and the finest jazz outlet I would see until I reached New York and found places like Sam Goody's and King Karol or, later, J&R and Tower Records. These weekly pilgrimages to Radio Doctor's invariably produced fabulous discoveries. After hours of sampling every new release in sight and driving the store's otherwise amiable owner ("Doctor" Stu) nearly crazy, we would triumphantly make our purchase, climb back on the bus, and head for the turntable at my house. (Those recordings usually cost $4.98. Thirty years later—before the widespread adoption of compact discs—the same items, in reissues faithful to the originals, typically carried prices of $4.99. I can think of no other consumer product with as low a long-run rate of inflation.) I began to regard record stores as my homes away from home. Years later, on the traumatic afternoon when John F. Kennedy was shot, I went straight to the nearest music shop and stood there for 3 hours, with my ears buried in headphones, listening to all of the new jazz releases. Once again, the owner thought that I was very strange, but it made me feel better, like a visit home.

More recently, as I read the musical biography of Gerry Mulligan by Jerome Klinkowitz (1991), the following acknowledgment leapt off the page with the force of a startling revelation:

> My most personal affectionate gratitude is shared by everyone who buys jazz records—gratitude for the clerks and owners who keep shops stocked, who are often archivists themselves, who think of digging out an odd album that includes one's favorite, and—in the case of selling records to a kid just barely into his teens with collecting ambitions far deeper than his pockets—who give a break on the price. To . . . Ron and Gordy at the old Radio Doctor's Shop downstairs on Wells Street in the lost Milwaukee of my childhood, I'm thankful for making such listening possible. (p. xii)

Klinkowitz (1991) goes on to begin his "Introduction" with the following description of a Gerry Mulligan concert:

Milwaukee, 13 January 1959, during the inevitable week of winter's sub-
basement, when the temperature is in the teens below zero and the wind
whistles off the Lake. A concert in jazz by the Gerry Mulligan Quartet at
Downer College. . . . And the concert is in a snug, quaintly medieval hall—
beamed ceiling, half-timbered walls, leaded windows, the works—providing a
spot of warmth and light in this alien, forbidding world. . . . The north side
was new, jazz was new, and the whole atmosphere was something different. . . .
Never underestimate the effect of a jazz concert on a fifteen-year-old in the
1950s. (p. 1)

I was also 15 years old in 1959. And I well know that this account of the
magical concert by Gerry Mulligan at Downer College rings true because,
like Jerome Klinkowitz, *Peter and I were there.*

Of course, Peter and I alienated all of our classmates; after all, as I've said,
that is part of the point of being hip. While everyone else in our high school
was enjoying Harry Belafonte and the Kingston Trio, I entertained myself by
writing editorials for the student newspaper (*The Ledger*), pointing out the
inanity of lyrics such as "Banua, Banua,/Banua, Oh-Oh;/Banua, Banua,/
Baby I don't know."

During our last year at Country Day, Peter and I brought some 45 rpm jazz
records to school and played them incessantly on the little phonograph in
the senior room, to the exasperated distraction of our fellow students. One
day, while we were gone, Dave (captain of the football, hockey, and baseball
teams) used our collection of cherished 45s as Frisbees and sailed them, one
by one, out the senior room window into the cool spring daylight. These
gems, including one or two rare items like Oscar Peterson's unavailable recording of "The Golden Striker," were never recovered or replaced. Dave's
Crime Against Art will forever serve as my touchstone for the Apotheosis of
Anti-Hip.

At graduation, partly because Pete wrote the descriptions, my school yearbook confirmed that I had achieved the status of "the class's leading non-
conformist." But clouds had begun to form on the horizons of my hipness.
First, in an episode that I discuss further in the "Development" section of
this chapter, I had spent part of the previous summer at the Lenox School of
Jazz, where some of my greatest idols (including John Lewis and Milt Jackson
from the Modern Jazz Quartet) had made it very clear to me that they did
not exactly consider me ready for the Jazz Big Time. Needless to say, they
were right. Most of those distinguished leaders in the field could not even

find enough work to keep their own bands together. And they were musical geniuses! Certainly, that bitter economic reality did not augur well for me. I realized that eventually I would need some other profession.

Second, Ornette Coleman had burst onto the jazz scene, with his little white plastic alto sax, playing music that was too far advanced even for our studiously abstruse tastes. Listening to Ornette's honks and squeaks, Peter and I began to wonder whether we would be hip to the jazz wave of the future.

Third, my self-proclaimed hipness had earned me acceptance at Harvard College. I have already confessed that I was not the most intelligent, popular, or athletic student at Country Day. But these were not the criteria of major importance to Harvard's admissions office. Harvard was looking for people who were hip. I was hip, so they took me. The only trouble was that they also admitted about 1,246 other freshmen, every one of whom was at least as hip as I was . . . or, mostly, much hipper. This staggering competition doubtless accounts for the miserably stressful pressure that I encountered in college. In the land of the blind, the man with one eye is king. In Milwaukee, the person who dug Charlie Parker was about as hip as you can get. I had spent my first 18 years achieving a blissful degree of utter hipness in my own narrow little world. But, all at once, I found myself in the midst of hipsters in every domain—music, art, literature, films—claiming interests so esoteric that they tapped levels of nonconformity whose existence I had scarcely suspected. Suddenly, surrounded by the Harvard intelligentsia, I felt positively square by comparison.

Surviving this threat to my unconventionality with my hipness intact proved difficult, but I did it. My deus ex machina was the Beatles. Everybody—the Yale men, the Princeton boys, and even the Harvard students—everybody loved the Beatles. It was impossible to dislike their insouciant blend of good spirits and hard-driving rock. Impossible, that is, for everyone but me. With total dedication and fierce perseverance, I managed to accomplish this unexampled feat. I practiced by playing myself Bill Evans and Jim Hall records through earphones while all others in the house were blasting "I Want to Hold Your Hand" or "I Saw Her Standing There" at peak volumes on their portable stereos. I had triumphed. At last, everyone at Harvard enjoyed something immensely popular that I could detest with self-righteous scorn.

This ploy sustained me through my difficult college years and brought me into the late 1960s to face the new traumas of Columbia University's MBA program, the rigors of life in New York City, the Vietnam War, and a draft board who simply did not understand that I was much too hip (not to mention cowardly) to serve in the U.S. Army. Through this pain, I was sustained by Sally, my wonderful new bride, who served not only as a great comfort and shelter against world chaos but also as a constantly reassuring model of pristine squareness. She disliked jazz and loved the Beatles. I loathed the Beatles and adored Paul Desmond. We preserved this delicately balanced symbiosis throughout the terrifying years of the Johnson administration. From a safe distance, I sympathized with those involved in the Columbia sit-ins and riots. I admired the guts of the student protestors, even the ones who disrupted my academic training. They worked for peace. But except for attending a few protest marches, political rallies, and demonstrations in Central Park, I remained aloof. After all, Mark Rudd, Tom Hayden, Abbie Hoffman, Jerry Ruben, and the other student protestors were merely hippies and yippies. By contrast, I myself was hip.

Then something terrible happened. Jazz died—or at least it went into deep hibernation for a while. Peter, who had come to New York to earn his MA in English at Columbia and had then returned to Milwaukee to marry my next-door neighbor, Susie, and to teach at Country Day, now moved with Susie to Dublin to begin his never-to-be-finished doctoral dissertation on Wilkie Collins. Meanwhile, all of our favorite jazz musicians entered semi-retirement (Paul Desmond, Gerry Mulligan); went to jail (Art Pepper, Hampton Hawes); moved to Europe (Art Farmer, Dexter Gordon); or did all three (Chet Baker). I was left with nothing to listen to, nobody to listen to it with, and a baby on the way.

The sudden total eclipse of jazz in my life, the consciousness raised by impending fatherhood, the agony of the Vietnam era, and deep doubts about whether it was hip to pursue an MBA career produced two momentous consequences: first, a decision to enter Columbia's PhD program in marketing and, second, an embarrassing regression in my musical tastes. I clung to what little security I could find, sought safety in numbers, and began listening to the Stones, the Who, Traffic, Cream, Simon and Garfunkel, Jefferson Airplane, and, yes, even the Beatles. Just before the Beatles broke up, I fell in love with *Abbey Road* and started working my way backward through their oeuvre, buying all of their recordings in retrograde order and finishing with *Meet the Beatles*, the album that features "I Want to Hold Your Hand." When the rumor started that Paul was dead, I was as concerned as their most loyal fan. Soon, the group itself had perished and I had to look elsewhere for musical sustenance. Thus does hipness founder when it crashes against the rocky shores of the Principle of Irony.

Christopher, weighing almost 9 pounds and replete with adorable charm from the moment he was born, arrived to fill the breach. His delivery was 3 weeks late, but we finally induced labor by taking him in utero to a Procol Harum concert at the Fillmore East and letting the ear-shattering, nerve-grinding, belly-thumping sounds of "Salty Dog" and "Whiter Shade of Pale" disturb his peaceful slumber in the womb. Suddenly, my world was filled with new life in the form of Christopher and countless rock groups and artists that were springing up like wildflowers: the Band, Joe Cocker, Blind Faith, James Taylor, Blood-Sweat-and-Tears, Van Morrison, Jackson Browne, and so on. Bob, an old classmate from Country Day, moved to New York, entered a partnership with Albert Grossman, and began managing such rock stars as Dylan, the Band, Janis Joplin, Seatrain, Blood-Sweat-and-Tears, and Procol Harum. Thanks to Bob's generosity, Sally and I were flooded with reviewer's copies of LPs and free concert tickets. Whenever we could find and afford baby-sitters, we went down to the Fillmore. We heard everybody. Maybe it wasn't very hip, but it sure was fun.

I even learned to play a sort of watered-down version of rock on the piano. My fumbling efforts in this direction led to constant feuds with our downstairs neighbors, Valerie and Barbara, who were themselves struggling young musicians and who did not appreciate my musical assault on their folky sensibilities. On the very afternoon that my new baby grand arrived (inherited from my grandfather), Valerie paid me a nasty visit within 10 minutes after I started practicing. We endured many such unpleasant scenes, letters to the landlord from both sides, poundings on their ceiling (our floor), and (once) the arrival of the police (whom I called in a brilliant stroke of one-upmanship). But, despite this harassment, I finally learned to play songs like "Ruby Tuesday," "Both Sides Now," and "Bridge Over Troubled Water" in a kind of compromise jazz-rock style.

For a while, I took this reawakened interest in performing into All Angels, the Episcopal church near where we lived. Paul and I showed up there at about the same time, filled with an urge to play some jazz-tinged rock or rock-tinged jazz and convinced that religious services provided an appropriate milieu for that activity. The easiest thing to find was piano players; so I learned to play the Fender bass and let Zooey handle the piano chores. Mac, a marketing professor at Columbia, played electronic keyboards in the band. I wrote countless jazz-rock arrangements of old Episcopal hymns like "Holy,

Holy, Holy," "Praise to the Lord," and "Children of the Heavenly King." Moreover, I adopted the philosophy—which I still hold, more than ever— that any music is suitable for church as long as it is played with the right religious feeling (a subtle variation on Tommy's old doctrine that if it *sounds* right, it *is* right). This credo worked well for tunes like "Let It Be" and "Put Your Hand in the Hand"; but it broke down when, on one inspired Sunday morning, I played "Ben" (Michael Jackson's theme music for the movie about a large rat) during Holy Communion. This song deals with the themes of friendship and loyalty, and it sounded right to me at the time. After all, unlike Willard, Ben was a *good* rat. However, besides establishing my credentials as one of the early Michael Jackson fans, this experience (and many others like it) prompted increasing attempts by the clergy to control my selection of musical material. Angered, however unreasonably, I rationalized that I was too hip for organized religion.

I turned instead to psychotherapy. In 5 years of Freudian analysis (four times a week on the couch), Lila listened in about equal proportions to stories about (a) my musical adventures, (b) my trials in the PhD program and tribulations in beginning my first teaching job at Columbia, and (c) the rest of my many problems and interests. Needless to say, thanks to the first of these content areas, Lila has become the hippest psychoanalyst in New York. She has witnessed endless attempts to unravel the mystery of the tingle that starts at the base of my spine and charges upward into goosebumps on the back of my neck. For example, I spent months on the couch trying to figure out why Ray Charles moves me so deeply, deciding that it has something to do with Teenie and those spirituals I heard as a child, but concluding that these revelations only begin to scratch the surface. Similar, still-unresolved questions surround my responses to Paul Desmond, Art Pepper, Bill Evans, and Hampton Hawes. The closest I ever came to understanding my rapturous reactions to Milt Jackson was the analogy that, for me, he does on the vibraphone what Earl Monroe did on the basketball court. As they used to say, Earl the Pearl was a magician—so loose and free, yet deadly accurate. Finally, after such speculations had run rampant for 2 or 3 years, Lila pointed out to me that, if I ever wanted to finish psychoanalysis, I had better move on to other matters. (She might have said, "Fish or cut bait." But, as I recall, "Shit or get off the pot" was the way she put it.)

Although Lila (like a true Freudian) seldom spoke, a few of her rare but incredibly perceptive comments changed my life forever. One day, after listening to about 40 minutes of diatribe on my agonies concerning a particularly difficult and unrewarding piece of marketing research, she innocently asked why I did not do more work like the project for a jazz radio station (WRVR) that I was enjoying so much. I decided that she was right and extrapolated her comment to cover most of my research activities. As my guiding principle, I adopted the goal of getting the names of my favorite singers and musicians into the major journals. Thus did Roberta Flack and Ray Charles soon find their ways, respectively, into the *Journal of Consumer Research* (Holbrook, 1977) and the *Journal of Applied Psychology* (Holbrook & Williams, 1978). Encouraged by this initial success, I have continued to seek homes for my musical heroes in the various publications related to the field of consumer research. I have experienced the thrill of putting Paul Desmond into the *Journal of Marketing Research*, James Taylor into *Marketing Science*, Bill Evans into the *Journal of Marketing*, Chet Baker into the *Journal of Retailing*, Art Pepper into *Advances in Consumer Research*, Jim Hall into the *Journal of Consumer Psychology*, Lee Konitz into *Empirical Studies of the Arts*, John Lewis into *Marketing Letters*, Sarah Vaughan into the *Psychology of Music*, and Dave Frishberg into the *ACR Newsletter.*

Thanks to Lila, jazz reentered my life in a big way. Along with other aspects of my youth, I began reexamining my jazz roots and learned that they were stronger than my branches into church music and rock 'n' roll. Moreover, many of my long-lost jazz heroes had awakened from their slumbers and were returning to the recording studios. Albums by Paul Desmond, Bill Evans, Hampton Hawes, Gerry Mulligan, Chet Baker, Art Farmer, Art Pepper, Zoot Sims, and others—sometimes with the masters playing rock tunes, as in Desmond's *Bridge Over Troubled Water* or Baker's *Blood, Chet, and Tears* (n.d.)—flooded onto the market. I began writing guest reviews for a short-lived jazz publication called *Different Drummer.* These reviews paid a mere $4.00 apiece, not even enough to cover the purchase price of the recording, but somehow their appearance in print always cheered me up as a token of my reemerging jazz consciousness. A typical example was my review of Oscar Peterson's *Great Connection* (1971):

> Most of Oscar Peterson's more successful albums recently have been collaborations with other gifted and forceful soloists such as Herb Ellis (MPS), Milt Jackson (MPS), or Joe Pass (Pablo). Somehow, when Oscar sinks comfortably into the cozy familiarity of the conventional piano-bass-drums trio, he seems to lose the urge to experiment with new ideas. . . . The present disc documents

this less interesting facet of Peterson's pianistic personality. We are offered routine run-throughs of old chestnuts like "Younger Than Springtime," "Soft Winds," "Just Squeeze Me," and "On the Trail." . . . Aside from bassist Pedersen's heroic comping and finger-bruising solos, the most captivating moments on the disc occur in Peterson's intriguingly lugubrious reading of "Smile." Elsewhere, Oscar simply reaffirms his supreme technical command over the keyboard. And that's not exactly faint praise. (Holbrook, 1974, p. 22)

Meanwhile, my old friend Peter had abandoned Wilkie Collins, moved to London, written a best-selling horror story, and earned so much money that the British tax system compelled his return to the United States. He arrived in New York full of ideas about new people worth hearing (Scott Hamilton, Warren Vaché) and old people worth rehearing (Billie Holiday, Lester Young). As always, his instincts proved infallible. I spent days pawing through secondhand record bins in search of old Holiday and Young recordings I had been too ignorant to buy when I was a child and they had been easy to find. Tantalized and encouraged by these events, I entered a new period of hipness from which I hope never to recover, as hipness ripens into eccentricity.

But another force had also emerged on my musical scene: Christopher. Somehow, amidst all of these other happenings, Chris had reached early adulthood, had learned to play Mozart and Bach like an angel, had stubbornly repudiated jazz, and had built a passionate devotion to rock. Moreover, he had developed the strong conviction that he is a lot hipper than his old man. Could I passively withstand this new questioning of my hipness? Of course not.

So, I tried to catch up by listening to Christopher's favorite recordings of U2, the Smiths, the Minutemen, Talking Heads, the Replacements, Sonic Youth, the Butthole Surfers, the Violent Femmes, and Killing Joke. What generally greeted my ears when I played the albums Chris lent me was somewhere between a wailing screech and a screeching wail. Synthesizers appeared to have banished real musical instruments, and vocal noises seemed to have replaced language. I hated this music instinctively. Listening to it was nearly torture. But I forced myself to do it. I must keep up with the times. After all, I'm hip, and I need a constantly replenished supply of popular music that I can hate.

Occasionally, however, Chris found something about which we could enjoy a meeting of the minds. The videotape of "We Are the World" (reputed at the time to be the largest selling single recording in history) served as a spectacular case in point. Chris could justifiably proclaim the virtues of heartfelt performances by Michael Jackson and Bruce Springsteen. We could both agree on the merits of Stevie Wonder's impassioned outpouring and Cyndi Lauper's 2 seconds of pure brilliance. And I could have the satisfaction of insisting that the whole production should be interpreted not only in light of its worthwhile social cause but also as a crowning tribute by Quincy Jones to the work and spirit of Ray Charles. Obviously, it seems to me, the entire piece builds ineluctably toward his style and reaches its culmination in his melismatic embellishments of the refrain.

Chris has graduated from college now—a nice little place called Carleton, in Minnesota, about a half-hour south of Minneapolis—and has moved out of our apartment to start his own life a few blocks uptown. So I no longer hear so much grating racket emanating until late into the night from the crack underneath his bedroom door. I miss him and his raucous din very much. But I'm still hip enough to know noise when I hear it.

Meanwhile, I have suffered the trauma of watching my vast collection of hip jazz recordings become technologically obsolete. After fighting the trend for as long as I could, I have started replacing them—the ones I can find—with compact discs. At last count, I had about 2,500 jazz CDs. But these merely scratch the surface of the wonderful sounds on LP that will probably be lost forever.

Before concluding this autobiographical exposition, I think I should recount what has happened to the characters in my little introspective saga. My grandmother has passed away; her magnificent ebony Steinway now sits unused and gathers dust. Teenie has moved back home to Tuskeegee, Alabama. Until his death in July 1992, I still sometimes heard Sandy play the old Wilson and Waller arrangements that May and I continue to cherish via our home recordings.

Helen has mercifully stopped teaching by the star system. Meanwhile, the nonpareil Tommy has retired and moved to the Wisconsin Dells, where he doubtless remains prototypically hip. When Beth and I did our first book, *Symbolic Consumer Behavior* (Hirschman & Holbrook, 1981), we dedicated it with great affection to one of her professors (Robert Burns) and to Tommy Sheridan (my hero), "whose support and stimulation best conveyed the process of learning and the meaning of esthetic experience" (p. iv). At the time, I wrote Tommy a letter of retrospective appreciation. I learned later that my letter had meant enough to Tommy for him to frame it. And I was filled with happiness.

After college and the Peace Corps, Johnny returned to Milwaukee and lived for a while in my grandfather's old house before seeking new homes in Brooklyn, Los Angeles, and Portland; we have stayed in touch, but he doesn't listen much to Bing Crosby anymore. Steve teaches aviation at the University of Illinois; we had a wonderful visit recently, but I doubt that he remembers Ziggy's solo on "And the Angels Sing." Kenny the bassist went into medicine, I believe. Stu the drummer wound up in Los Angeles, changed his name to David, and began working in marketing, advertising, and public relations. Howie the guitarist came to New York, changed his name to Hod, worked as a musician, and even made some recordings with his own groups, but died tragically in an automobile accident after moving out to the West Coast. By a strange turn of coincidence, Hod's younger brother, Michael, has become a highly respected sociologist and has even served on the policy board for the *Journal of Consumer Research.* Small world, I guess.

Peter's novels, always filled with the names of jazz musicians, have achieved fabulous success. In *Shadowland,* he provided the ultimate description of life at Country Day circa 1960 and included a flattering but largely fictional account of my own struggling efforts as a jazz pianist:

> Morris, standing on the side of the room with the other members of his trio, looked crippled with stage fright. . . . The three of them filed up the stairs to the stage. Brown picked up his bass, Morris said, "One . . . one . . . one . . . one," and they began playing "Somebody Loves Me." It sounded like sunlight and gold and fast mountain springs, and I switched off everything else and just listened to the music. . . . During Morris' last number I heard . . . him insert a quote from "Hail, Hail, the Gang's All Here" into his solo. . . . He was having, under trying circumstances, the best time he could, which is one definition of heroism. (Straub, 1980, pp. 115-116)

Peter and Susie have moved back to New York permanently and, to my joy, have once again become our near neighbors. They now number many great jazz musicians among their friends and lend these artists their unstinting support. Peter has written some terrific liner notes for musicians on the Concord Jazz label such as Scott Hamilton, Rosemary Clooney, and—yes—Gerry Mulligan.

Dave reappeared as my classmate in Columbia's MBA program and has since moved to Connecticut, where he now works as an executive head-

hunter. He recently found a first-class top-management position for one of
our mutual friends from Country Day.

Ornette, who still specializes in honks and squeaks, showed up in my office one day wanting to know how to reach a wider audience. I told him I
didn't think someone as hip as he is could do that. The Modern Jazz Quartet—perhaps after being as mean to each other as they had been to me—
broke up for a while but later regrouped and played as miraculously as ever
before their drummer, Connie Kay, passed away.

Harvard still stands on the banks of the Charles, and a recent directory
of my classmates confirms their continued hipness: Almost all of them are
college professors.

Sally, still very precious to me after more than a quarter century of marriage, continues to dislike most jazz; we have finally reached a compromise
in our mutual fondness for Bach and black gospel music played at peak volume on the car stereo.

Bob left rock management and began investing in other types of commercial properties; he also manages Peter. Valerie and Barbara still live in the
same building and probably still infuriate their new neighbors in our old
apartment. Paul and Zooey remain active in church music; both have
learned to fit themselves into the liturgy better than I ever could; Mac has
moved through the stage of serving as a dean and has returned to his role as
one of our school's finest teachers. Lila still practices psychoanalysis in New
York; I remain grateful to her insights and for the suggestion that resulted in
my populating some of the journals with the names of my favorite singers and
musicians.

Chris continues as a source of joy in our lives; I marvel at his ability to
absorb Bach and Mozart—and, more recently, some of the jazz greats—while
simultaneously admiring Sonic Youth. For several years, Chris and I made
Christmas tapes containing samples of our playing and distributed these to
our long-suffering friends. Typically, Chris would play a few selections from
his classical repertoire. I would rattle through a few dimly remembered jazz
pieces and would end with a reworking of some old Episcopal hymn that I
used to play in church.

The words to one of these hymns remind me of the place for music in my
life, with feelings akin to those expressed by Billy Preston in the epigraph to
this chapter. These words from the hymnal refer, literally, to the eternality
and everlasting nature of God Himself. But, for me, they also convey something of the power in music to last forever. Like other artistic forms, music in

general and jazz in particular are ultimate consumer durables. They endure from year to year and from generation to generation. They attain a spiritual and nearly godlike permanence:

> Abide with me: Fast falls the eventide;
> The darkness deepens; Lord, with me abide:
> When other helpers fail and comforts flee,
> O thou who changest not, abide with me
>
>   —Monk, 1861, "Abide With Me"

❑ *Development: A Lesson in Humility*

> A . . . lack of rapport was noted by *Down Beat* in connection
>   with an attempt by Paul Desmond to buy a Dacron blanket.
> "I'm sorry sir," said the salesgirl. "We seem to be all out of
>   Dacron blankets. But wouldn't you like to look at this one?"
> "No. I don't think so. I want Dacron."
> "But, sir, this one is down. It's real down."
> "I'm hip," said Desmond. "But I still want Dacron."
>
>   —Leonard Feather and Jack Tracy (1963),
>   *Laughter From the Hip*, pp. 152-153

In the summer of 1960, as a budding young jazz pianist, I persuaded my parents to send me to study at the Lenox School of Jazz for 2 weeks at the end of August, just before the start of my senior year in high school. At that time, the Lenox School was a well-known summer music camp stationed at Music Inn near Tanglewood in Pittsfield, Massachusetts. The school had gained considerable fame for bringing together musicians of great stature—such as Dizzy Gillespie, Jimmy Giuffre, J. J. Johnson, Jim Hall, Oscar Peterson, Herb Pomeroy, George Russell, Gunther Schuller, and the members of the Modern Jazz Quartet—to instruct fledgling jazz players (the most illustrious of whom had been Ornette Coleman of later Free-Jazz fame). John Lewis (pianist of the Modern Jazz Quartet) played the role of the school's director, with the other members of the quartet also serving as faculty.

It so happened that, at the time, no one in music mattered more to me than did the Modern Jazz Quartet in general and its vibraharpist, Milt Jackson, in particular. I knew every note of their records by heart and, as noted earlier, had joined together with three other kids from Milwaukee to form a group called the Baywood Jazz Quartet that emulated these idols from the Modern Jazz Quartet as closely as humanly possible. The word *Baywood* came from combining parts of the names of the suburbs where the four of us lived. I lived in Shore*wood*; the other three lived in Whitefish *Bay*.

In this group, I played piano and vibes. Kenny Schoeninger played acoustic bass, with Stu Langer on drums and Howard Schudson on guitar. Every Saturday or Sunday (depending on the schedules of Howie's basketball and tennis teams), we four would practice for hours on end, trying to perfect our Lewis- and Jackson-inspired licks and striving to keep our tempos from speeding up or dragging while still making all of the right chord changes. Sometimes the Baywood group would play for high school dances or for fraternity parties. Stu and Howie were Jewish, so the quartet also performed at quite a few bar mitzvahs. Always, we took our music very seriously—so seriously that we argued incessantly about who was playing too loud, who sped up during the last chorus of "Perdido," and whose latest arrangement deserved the most rehearsal time.

By dint of heroic preparations, letters from supporters, tuition money from our parents, and lots of chutzpah, three of us—Kenny, Stu, and I—managed to get ourselves accepted for admission to the summer program at the Lenox School of Jazz. Howie stayed behind to work on earning money for college. Ironically, much later, Howie was the only member of the Baywood Jazz Quartet ever to work as a professional musician. After moving to New York and changing his name to Hod David, he had a folk-rock band briefly during the 1960s; embarked on a career as a songwriter during the 1970s; and, in about 1975, moved to Los Angeles, where he died tragically when his car collided with a fire truck. But, if Hod was the one with the most talent and the greatest long-range dedication, the other three were the ones with the biggest short-term enthusiasm and the deepest devotion to the Modern Jazz Quartet.

So we three Baywoods packed into Stu's 1955 Buick with a trailer on the back filled by Stu's drums, Kenny's bass, and a small attaché case full of my own arrangements and compositions plus a tuning wrench. We headed east on Route 80, flying along the highway while we scat-sang chorus after chorus of such favorite jazz anthems as "Ornithology" and "Line for Lyons." Kenny sang a bass part—"Dum-di-dum dum dum, dum dum-di-dum dum"—while Morris scatted an improvised melody and Stu beat time on the leatherette dashboard with a ballpoint pen. Stu insisted that the big Buick handled best at high velocities. So he kept the speedometer at about 90 miles per hour most of the way. This plus God's blessings carried us in record time to Wheatleigh Hall at Music Inn in the beautiful Berkshires, where the mountain air was crisp and fresh, where the musicians were stupendous, and where the atmosphere had all the conviviality of a 24-hour-a-day cutting contest.

I shall never forget the first time I met my idol Milt Jackson, also known as "Bags." The morning schedule for the first day of classes designated 10:00 a.m. in Tent B as the time and place for me to meet with the great master of the vibraharp. As I approached the tent, practically trembling with excitement, I could hear the clear bell-like tones of Milt's vibes wafting toward me in the breeze. Bags had started to play Benny Golson's intricate piece called "I Remember Clifford," a tune that the nonpareil vibraharpist had recently recorded on one of my most cherished phonograph albums.

Clear, unaccompanied melody came at me in an inviting rush. Oh, it was beautiful. Crystalline scales flowed up and down the bars of the vibes as Jackson worked his magic upon them. A clever turn of phrase prepared the way for a long arpeggio up to a high note that hung there in the crisp morning air like a perfect flower at the end of a long stem. An even higher note glistened brightly before Jackson manipulated his variable vibrato-producing resonators and caused it to shimmer and then to fall away in a hushed tremolo.

As I approached, I heard my idol say to no one in particular, "Great tune. I think it's another 'Round Midnight.'"

From there, however, the lesson ran downhill fast. Jackson began by suggesting that we play a duet for a while on a still-untitled "Blues in F" that he had just finished writing. Speechless with excitement, I comped while Bags soloed. After running circles around me for a couple of minutes (sort of like what one might expect if Michael Jordan decided to play a little one-on-one with, say, Danny DeVito), the vibraharpist stopped abruptly and asked me what tunes I liked to play. Feeling humiliated and not knowing the best answer to this question—though, apparently, "Blues in F" had been ruled out—I picked up my well-worn book of lead sheets and pushed it at the vibist. Jackson began leafing through it with a deeply quizzical expression on his face and then started to laugh.

"What's so funny?" I asked.

"Lullaby of Birdland," replied the older man.

To this day, I still do not understand what Milt Jackson found so hilarious about "Lullaby of Birdland."

> **Q:** Could it have been that "Lullaby" was written by a white British pianist (George Shearing)?
>
> **A:** Hardly, because Shearing had worked with any number of great African American artists, including Nat Cole, Denzil Best, Al McKibbon, and Wes Montgomery.
>
> **Q:** Could it have been that Jackson had instantly found flaws in my arrangement of this piece?
>
> **A:** Not likely, because it soon turned out that Bags could barely read, much less write, music himself.
>
> **Q:** Could it have been that Jackson had somehow taken an instant dislike to me and just wanted to make an inept young fledgling feel small and inferior?
>
> **A:** Maybe, because I soon found Jackson's contempt mirrored in the sentiments of the other faculty members at the Lenox School of Jazz.

At any rate, on the following day, my idol Bags departed to attend his sick mother in Detroit. Although I have sat in the audience at many MJQ concerts since then, I have never again met Milt Jackson face-to-face. He remains an *idol*, but now I have sense enough to know that this word means "a false god."

Meanwhile, we members of the Baywood Jazz Quartet who had made the trip from Milwaukee quickly discovered that our musical skills did not measure up to those possessed by the other summer campers. We Baywoods were the youngest students at Lenox that year. I was the only person at the camp who had still not graduated from high school (with the exception of some much older musicians on the faculty who had probably never even attended high school). And, unfortunately, I was no child prodigy. My musical skills were simply not as developed as those who had completed college-level courses in music schools like Berkelee or who had worked professionally for a few years. So, I found myself on the bottom of every musical pile, low man on the totem pole in every hierarchy of talent and training. Remarkably, the Lenox faculty in general and such members of the Modern Jazz Quartet as Milt Jackson or John Lewis in particular seemed to enjoy reminding me of my deficiencies whenever possible.

Finally, one evening, John Lewis summoned all of the student pianists to a hastily convened meeting held on the stage at Music Inn (the same spot where Duke Ellington had performed a few nights earlier). Seven of us appeared, ranging in age from 16 (me) to about 40 or 50 (a well-seasoned and extremely pleasant black man from Detroit who had played professionally for at least a quarter of a century). John Lewis and Gunther Schuller sat at a card table on one end of the stage, taking notes while each pianist played three pieces—one solo, one with a rhythm section of bass and drums, and one with the rhythm plus a tenor saxophonist (J. R. Monterose). To my horror, the bassist and drummer were none other than Percy Heath and Connie Kay from the Modern Jazz Quartet.

The prospect of playing together with these giants of jazz before two of the most learned men in the field made me so nervous that my hands literally grew numb as I took my place on the piano bench. The trio swung into a blues, "Blue Monk," with me playing the familiar melody that I had performed thousands of times. Everything went pretty well until the time came for me to solo. Then I found that my fingers, frozen stiff with stage fright, just did not work properly. My already limited technique had deserted me completely. I vainly stabbed at the keys with stiff digits, hoping that maybe I at least sounded like a bad imitation of Thelonious (who did, in fact, tend to play that way), though I had never before tried to copy his style. While I struggled on in agony, Gunther Schuller rose and walked around me in a circle, staring at my hands and thereby prompting even stronger feelings of panic with even worse pianistic results.

At the end of this terrible ordeal—after I had stumbled my way through an error-enriched solo version of "Someone to Watch Over Me" and a botched attempt to accompany J. R. Monterose on "All the Things You Are" (with the saxophonist expressing some disappointment that we could not perform the tune in his favorite key of G-flat, a key in which I could barely play the major scale, let alone negotiate the chord changes to such a complex piece)—I took my turn sitting at the card table with the two Master Teachers. They told me, not kindly, that I did not appear suited for a career in jazz.

"You have to know your material *perfectly* when you get up to play in public," said Lewis. "But it sounded like you got lost on the bridge to that . . . solo piece" (as if the performance had failed so badly that he could not even recognize the familiar Gershwin melody).

"And your phrasing on that blues was very strange," added Schuller. "Especially the way you seemed to lag behind the chord changes, still playing one chord after the next one had already started."

In their way, both men emphasized that I clearly did not belong in the world of music, that I showed no evident talent, that I had no hope of a successful career in jazz, and that my future—if, indeed, I had one anywhere—obviously lay in some other field of endeavor. I believed them. Devoutly.

I returned to Milwaukee from the Lenox School of Jazz with a rather damaged ego and a greatly altered sense of my musical abilities. I never again assumed that I had any real aptitude as a musician. I never again dreamed that I might one day make my living as a jazz pianist. And I never again had much faith in my competence to judge my own work. Someone, it seemed, always had a better sense of my worth than I did. Someone, it has seemed, always tends to find me wanting. And someone, it seems, is always more than happy to tell me about it.

In a way, I suppose, the faculty members at the Lenox School of Jazz did me a big favor. They may have saved me from a fate comparable to that suffered by Sissy Spacek in a film produced for Public Television in which she plays the role of Verna, an eager but immensely untalented singing dancer who tours the U.S. Army bases in Europe during World War II. Verna falls madly in love with a young officer played by William Hurt, who proposes marriage. But Sissy turns Bill down because she feels driven to pursue her "gift" as an entertainer. The more seasoned performers (Sally Kellerman and Howard da Silva) confront Sissy with the facts that she has no talent, that she will fail miserably in her intended career, and that she should return immediately to Bill and beg him for forgiveness. But, stubbornly, Sissy perseveres in her hopelessly inept efforts to sing and dance (a role, by the way, in which she is truly wonderful). Finally, she enjoys a brief moment of glory when her clumsy performance cheers up some wounded soldiers in a dismal basement hideout while German bombs explode overhead. But, the next day, Sissy's Jeep hits a land mine. And, when the dust has settled, Verna lies in the road—dead as a doornail.

As I said, maybe I should feel more appreciation for how John Lewis, Gunther Schuller, and Milt Jackson treated me. After all, by scaring me off, they saved me from throwing away my life in unrequited efforts to become a jazz musician. They protected me from trying to be like them. I suppose I really should experience some sense of gratitude. But I do not.

❑ Recapitulation: *Just Dizzy, Junior,*
and Me on the Way to Our Gig

When he celebrated his 75th birthday on October 21, 1992, John Birks "Dizzy"
Gillespie ranked, unarguably, as the World's Greatest Living Jazz Musician and,
arguably, as one of the most important artistic geniuses that America has ever pro-
duced. Moreover, Dizzy's generosity and encouragement touched the lives of count-
less younger musicians and fellow musical travelers. In the account presented here,
some details have been disguised to protect the privacy of the peripheral characters
involved. But most of the story that follows is true—especially the parts about
Junior, Dizzy, and how graciously they treated a young kid who worshipped them.

"*You're* not from Milwaukee," said Dizzy to my mother.

"No, ah'm from Mun-gum-ri," she shot back at him in her best hoked-up
version of a mock-Alabama drawl, while I nervously stood next to her—
staring in wonder at the world-famous trumpet player and musical genius,
John Birks ("Dizzy") Gillespie.

Dizzy's acute ears (honed on years of practice while growing up in
Cheraw, South Carolina) had detected the vestigial traces of my mother's
Southern accent, just as (honed on the sounds of jazz in the big band era of
the 1930s) they had detected the possibilities for developments in tonal freedom, harmonic complexity, and rhythmic abandon that had flowered under
his inspired influence into be-bop. Now, years later, Dizzy had transcended
his role as a pioneer in the bop revolution and had emerged as a reigning
master of the jazz tradition.

The year was 1960. I was only a junior in high school—just 16 years of
age, barely old enough to drive a car—but already an aspiring jazz pianist in
love with the music that flowed from the contributions of Charlie Parker,
Bud Powell, Thelonious Monk, Miles Davis, and, of course, Dizzy himself.
As we shook hands, I felt almost speechless with reverence.

"What d'you do?" he asked kindly.

"Fine, thanks," I said. "And you?"

"Not how," he replied. "*What* do you do?"

"Oh, go to school," I confessed. But then I brightened, "And play a little
piano."

"A pianist!" Dizzy beamed, as if I had just revealed myself to be his long-
lost cousin. "Here, meet my piano man, Junior."

But, to me, Junior Mance needed no introduction. I had been listening to his recordings for months, ever since Verve had released his first trio album with Ray Brown on bass. I had struggled to memorize Junior's licks and had tried in vain to copy that soulful keyboard feeling of his. His music radiated warm, happy, gospel-flavored earthiness. A completely distinctive sound. (Twenty years later, after moving to New York, I stepped off an elevator at the United Nations Plaza Hotel, heard two notes of piano coming from a bar down the hall, and announced to my wife Sally, "That's Junior Mance." Those two bell-like tones did it for me, like one of Pavlov's dogs. And it *was* Junior Mance!)

Earlier that week, I had dragged my parents down to Gallagher's—the local nightclub where Dizzy's band was playing and where I could gain admission only if accompanied by an adult—to sit for hours while I swooned over the beauty of the music. Junior had played swinging chorus after swinging chorus, building to shouting climaxes of rumbling churchlike chords that rose in the air like great balloons of ecstatic sound. His version of "Willow, Weep for Me" swelled mightily. The piano almost seemed to levitate.

Indeed, this band from 1959/1960 was one of the best Dizzy ever put together. Junior played piano with a rhythm section composed of the sturdy Lex Humphries on drums and the magnificent Sam Jones on bass. Les Spann excelled on both flute and guitar, playing the latter in an octave-based style that closely paralleled the approach popularized by Wes Montgomery a few years later. But the real magic came from Dizzy's horn.

As a trumpeter, Dizzy Gillespie ranked as one of the great virtuosos of all time. Music poured from the bell of his strangely upturned instrument in a torrent of unbridled inventiveness. Simple phrases played with razor-sharp rhythmic precision gave way to cascades of jagged-edged 16th notes that would spiral upward through the top harmonic intervals of the underlying chord structure—flatted 9ths, augmented 11ths, diminished 13ths—always ending on some completely unexpected turn of phrase, some total surprise. Dizzy astounded jazz listeners with his ceaseless creativity. His innovations—the incorporations of Latin rhythms, the intricate compositions, the futuristic big band arrangements, the incomparable scat singing, the matchless sense of humor—influenced many. But few ever managed to imitate his trumpet style because it is just too hard to play like that. (The only one who has come close is Jon Faddis, but at what sacrifice to his own originality one can only guess.)

The night we had heard him at Gallagher's, Dizzy had played two stirring sets. He opened with a moving version of his classic "Con Alma" (Spanish for "With Soul"). He sailed happily through a delightfully funny rendition of "Umbrella Man" ("Doodle-lama-lama doodle-lama-lama doodle-lama-yay; any umbrellas, any umbrellas, to fix today?"). He played his heart out on a Latin-tinged swinger called "Lorraine" (for his wife). He triumphed in a send-up of rock 'n' roll based on "School Days" (complete with boringly re-petitive background patterns and a sing-song melody that contrasted vio-lently with his brilliant trumpet solo). He roared mightily on his great composition "Night in Tunisia" (with a stop-time segue from the tune to the improvised chorus that set my hair on end). He clowned his way through a devilishly clever "Sunny Side of the Street" ("Grabbin' up your hats, coats, boots, and everything; leave your worries on the doorstep 'cause we're goin' bye-bye . . ."). And he swung his tail off on an up-tempo "Salt Peanuts" (fea-turing his patented trumpet pyrotechnics).

That was Dizzy. Endless variety. Total genius.

My excitement had peaked the next day when my family had received an invitation from our friend Val LeBar to come for dinner with Dizzy as the fea-tured guest of honor. We drove the 10 miles out to Val's house at about 5 p.m. My parents and I took separate cars because, later, I would have to go down-town to play for a party with my own combo—the Baywood Jazz Quartet.

It gets dark very early in Milwaukee during the winter months. So, even though the hour was young, the sky had already turned pitch black by the time we found Val's house. Bracing against the frigid January air, we crunched through the snow, down her long driveway, and into her cozy and spacious living room.

Looking radiant, Val had made her elaborate introductions all around. Musicians met corporate lawyers, physicians, and newspaper editors. Guys from the band greeted housewives and teenagers. Dizzy flirted with my mom.

Soon, we all went to the buffet for a feast of beef stroganoff. Val stood by, looking proud and smoothing the side of her sleek black cocktail dress. A member of Milwaukee's aristocracy, she also ranked as one of its bona fide intellectuals. Val was hardly what you would call matronly. But, despite her svelte and chic appearance, she was a good jazz mother. She had raised her daughter, Jill, to be a jazz musician. And now she was trying to help me.

Quite gifted, Jill played the piano better than I did. She once astonished me by executing a flawless blues in G-flat—for me, the most difficult of all keys. But, tonight, Jill was away at college—Sarah Lawrence, as I recall—so I had Dizzy and Junior all to myself.

Dizzy sat on the piano bench, spooning meat and noodles into his big cheeks with obvious delight and smirking like a happy baby.

My mother and I sat on the floor, balancing our plates precariously on our knees, at the Master's feet.

"This is real nice," said Diz. "Great to have a good home-cooked meal. That right, Junior?"

"Sure is," said Junior appreciatively. "It surely is."

During dinner, we chatted about the music business. I asked a lot of stupid questions like, "Where do you get your trumpet rebuilt?" "Who writes the arrangements for your quintet?" and "Where does the band go after Milwaukee?" Really dumb questions—every one of which Dizzy and Junior answered as politely as if they had been formulated by Socrates.

Eventually, I mentioned that I would have to leave soon to go to my engagement with the Baywoods. Dizzy perked up. It turned out that he and Junior had come in a taxicab and needed a ride downtown. Given that the bar where our combo would play was only about half a block from Gallagher's, I was thrilled to oblige.

When we left Val's house, we discovered that a light snow had begun to fall. The three of us trudged through the new dusting of powder to my mother's blue-and-white Oldsmobile. We wiped a thin layer of snowflakes from the front and back windshields, got the Olds started, and edged her out onto Lake Drive, headed south.

Within moments, I heard loud snoring from the back seat. Dizzy had sprawled out and fallen fast asleep.

Junior and I talked as we drove toward downtown Milwaukee. We passed my high school, and I told him about my unhappy experiences on the Country Day football team.

"Wouldn't catch *me* playin' football," Junior said wisely. "Bad for the hands."

"I know," I agreed. "But here everyone *has* to play. We only have 25 kids in our class. The varsity needs somebody to scrimmage with. That's what they use *me* for. I try to make fists and to keep my fingers curled under so they won't get stepped on."

We continued down Lake Drive. The scene was beautiful. Icy crystals hung from the trees and sparkled in their branches under the tall streetlamps. Banks of snow along the curb looked like gigantic down pillows. And, in the back seat, Dizzy snored a little louder.

Suddenly, the car hit a patch of ice and skidded sideways slightly. I slammed on the brakes and slid some more to the left, frantically turning the wheels into the skid the way we had been taught to do in driver's education class. Luckily for us, no car was coming from the other direction because the Oldsmobile ended up on the wrong side of the yellow line.

"Whoa, there," said Junior.

"Yeah," I said, trying to seem calm. "Bad spot on the road."

But I had seen a terrible vision. For a split second, I had imagined our car careening across the roadway and into a telephone pole on the other side. My mind's eye had pictured the dread headline in the *Milwaukee Sentinel* the next morning: "World's Greatest Jazz Musician Killed in Auto Accident; Local Youth Also Dead."

I edged back into my lane and slowed to a crawl. I stopped conversing with Junior and stared at the street in front of me, painfully conscious of every vibration of the steering wheel, fixated on each nuance of the engine noises, deeply aware of even the slightest loss of traction.

We edged past the park where the tennis courts used to be flooded for ice skating. Under the lights, against the dark sky, brightly colored parka-wrapped bodies whirled on the rink as the snow came down all around. I relaxed a little but maintained my slow and careful pace.

Then I heard another strange sound from the back seat—a sort of beelike buzzing, high in pitch, rising and falling over the span of about two octaves. I risked a glance in the rearview mirror and saw Dizzy's famous cheeks bulging out around a small shiny object that he held against his lips. Dizzy had begun to practice scales on his mouthpiece. He was getting ready for work.

We cruised down the outer drive—past Bradford Beach, where we could see inky Lake Michigan starting to freeze up along the shore; past the Yacht Club, whose windows blazed brightly in the rooms where all of the sailors had gone to escape from the impenetrable cold on the water; and past the duck pond, on which the winter's surface of ice lay knee-deep in gleaming snow. The buzzing sounds from the back seat now seemed strangely cheerful, almost soothing amidst all of these stark contrasts between white snow and black night. Suddenly, I felt an immense sense of peace. If only for a brief time, we were together—compatriot spirits—just Junior, Dizzy, and me on the way to our gig.

❑ *Coda: Benny*

> You smile, and the angels sing;
> And though it's just a gentle murmur at the start,
> We kiss, and the angels sing
> And leave their music ringing in my heart.
>
> —Johnny Mercer and Ziggy Elman (1939),
> "And the Angels Sing"[3]

About 40 years ago, Steve Allen—affable host of *The Tonight Show*, passable screen actor, and creator of numerous admirable comic inventions—played the title role in a movie called *The Benny Goodman Story*. Donna Reed played Benny's major romantic interest, Alice. And, remarkably, many of the great musicians of the Goodman era played themselves. Thus, major speaking parts featured such luminaries as Teddy Wilson (the great jazz pianist who sparkled in Goodman's small groups and made immortal recordings with people like Billie Holiday and Lester Young), Gene Krupa (the visually wondrous drummer who chewed gum so hard and hit every cymbal stroke with such conviction that he appeared to imbue each movement with his whole heart), and Lionel Hampton (the multitalented vibraharpist who teamed with Wilson and Krupa in the quartet under Goodman's leadership to form the first racially integrated musical group to reach national prominence). Lesser on-screen roles included Kid Ory (great New Orleans trombonist), Buck Clayton (master trumpeter from the old Count Basie Band), Stan Getz (tenor sax giant of a later era), Harry James (famous trumpet player and band leader), and Martha Tilton (re-creating her historic collaboration with Ziggy Elman on "And the Angels Sing" from the 1938 Carnegie Hall concert).

Overall, the movie ranks as Grade-B cinema with Grade-A music. The B rating results from a sappy (historically inaccurate) love story that clutters up the music. But beneath the saccharine sentiments of the main plot in which Alice woos Benny, one does catch the hint of a subtext with great potential interest to consumer researchers who teach courses in marketing. Specifically, one gets a glance at the old debate between the product and customer orientations as these apply to the problem of giving the public what it wants.

In one crucial scene from the *The Benny Goodman Story*, Benny meets John Hammond and his sister Alice, Gene Krupa, and Teddy Wilson in a bar where Teddy is playing the piano. Here, Benny wins Alice's respect by revealing that he wants to form his own band to play the kind of music that *he* wants to play. In this, stubbornly, he knows what he wants; he believes that the music he cares about—improvised "hot" jazz—does have an audience; he believes that this audience can be reached through dance music; and he intends to pursue these convictions. The dialogue makes these points with great economy.

TEDDY: Hi, Benny. Keeping busy?

BENNY: Oh, a few record dates, Ted.

GENE: Can't live off that.

JOHN: You should have stuck with Pollack. He died here in New York, but he's doing all right on the road.

BENNY: Yeah, playing those same old stock arrangements.

GENE: I heard Kel Murray's after you, Benny—offered you real dough.

BENNY: I turned him down, Gene.

JOHN: Turned him down? Why?

BENNY: Same reason I left Ben Pollack. I want a band that plays "hot" music, that really "takes off."

GENE: And where would it play? There's no place outside of Harlem for a band like that.

TEDDY: Yeah—like Fletcher Henderson always says—"hot" bands are "cold turkey" in this town.

BENNY: I don't know about that. It's never been tried.

GENE: Never been tried? What about Pollack and the others?

BENNY: Not the way I mean. I have a few ideas; I don't know if they're crazy.

JOHN: What kind of ideas, Benny?

BENNY: Uh, they're *musical* ideas; I can't put them into words. But when we get together in a joint like this and jam, the people come in and they sit down and they listen. The reason they sit and listen is because that's the way we play. . . .

TEDDY: Well, what are you aiming at? Gonna get up a band of your own?

BENNY: It looks like I'd have to.

GENE: Be *practical*, Benny. You wouldn't make a nickel. What can you hope for—a few recordings, a college prom, maybe? . . . *Nobody wants* this kind of music.

BENNY: *I do.*

TEDDY: I know how you feel, but it's hopeless, Benny. It's a wild dream. *Don't be that way.*

> **BENNY:** I can't help the way I am. [Rising] I'll see you later. [To Alice] It's nice to have met you.
>
> **JOHN:** He's one of the greatest clarinetists in the business. And the *stubbornest*.
>
> **ALICE:** John, every hot musician isn't another Paganini.
>
> **JOHN:** As it happens, Benny *is*.
>
> **ALICE:** Oh, come now.
>
> **JOHN:** Some day, I'll prove it to you.
>
> **ALICE:** Well, I must say, Benny does have his own strange kind of *integrity*. I admire him for *that*.[4]

Later, Alice finds Benny desperately trying to earn some money (so that he can support his widowed mother) by playing in a dance band led by that selfsame Kel Murray, who features the sort of Mickey Mouse music—those bland and boring "stock arrangements"—that Alice knows Benny hates. She comments to her date: "Why that's Benny Goodman. . . . I can't believe it—Benny with a band like this." Then she chides Benny directly; and he responds defensively.

> **ALICE:** I'm disappointed in you.
>
> **BENNY:** Disappointed? Why?
>
> **ALICE:** This is the kind of music you *don't* like, isn't it?
>
> **BENNY:** It sure is.
>
> **ALICE:** Well, I expected you to stick to your *convictions*.
>
> **BENNY:** My *convictions* haven't changed.[4]

Minutes later, Benny walks off the bandstand and quits this thankless job. Alice experiences a moment of guilt: "I feel terrible. . . . He had a job; *now* all he has are his *convictions*. I'm afraid I'm to blame."

Immediately, Benny begins to put together a band of his own. Things do start out promisingly as the Goodman Band wins some support on the "Let's Dance" radio show broadcast from New York. Indeed, in one beautifully dramatic moment, we see Kel Murray finish his set and play the program's theme song in his annoyingly schmaltzy, music-box style. The stage revolves, with the Goodman Band on the other side of the backdrop. And just as Kel Murray concludes his insipid rendition, Benny's men begin their rousing version of "Let's Dance."

But, when the sponsor cancels this radio show, the Goodman Band reluctantly hits the road. Subsequent scenes show the band failing commercially in one venue after another. For example, at a place called Elitch's Gardens in Denver, the club owner, an obnoxious fellow named Clark, accosts Goodman for purveying an insufficiently low-brow brand of entertainment.

CLARK: What do you call that song? Has it got a name?

BENNY: Yeah, "Down South Camp Meeting."

CLARK: Don't you guys play any tangos?

BENNY: No we don't, Mr. Clark.

CLARK: How about some comedy numbers? Don't you have funny hats?

BENNY: No, we do not.

CLARK: There's a guy down at the Casino. He's got gold derbies, trick hats, musical saws—real good stuff. And *he's* grabbing all the *business.*

BENNY: I'm sorry, Mr. Clark. You're not looking for a band; you're looking for a three-ring circus.[4]

Thus, the Goodman Band fails in town after town until finally it reaches California, where at the Palomar Ballroom, Benny defiantly insists on playing *their* music to honor the arrival of Alice, who has journeyed all the way from New York to hear the band play what threatens to be its swan song. Just after Alice walks in, Benny calls for the first tune of the evening:

BENNY: Well, this is our last night, fellas. We got together so we could play *our* kind of music, and so far nobody has let us. Well, we're going to play it tonight, *whether they like it or not.* We're gonna do all our big numbers, right on down the line. We'll start with "One O'Clock Jump."[4]

As the band launches into this swing classic, couples float onto the dance floor. Stan Getz solos beautifully on tenor sax. More dancers emerge. Benny plays a powerful chorus. Some more people rise from their tables and start to dance. Buck Clayton's strong trumpet pulls a few more onto the floor. By the time the band has reached the famous shouting riffs traded between trombones, saxophones, and trumpets in the concluding ensemble, the crowd has grown so dense that the people can no longer dance. They can only stand still, watch attentively, and listen appreciatively. After the music ends, the audience erupts in wild applause, cheering ecstatically. Alice radiates admiration for Benny. Goodman has triumphed. He has launched what we all know in retrospect will become a career as one of the great icons of American popular culture—the King of Swing.

Never missing a chance to drive this point home, the movie repeats similar patterns of success two more times. First, back in New York, Benny still worries that the local folks will not appreciate his music (what with "hot" bands getting a "cold" reception in New York and all). As he faces his opening at the Paramount movie theater—scheduled for the inauspicious hour of 10 a.m.—he feels considerable trepidation. But when the Paramount's feature film ends and the Goodman Band ascends on the platform stage, again playing its urgent version of "Let's Dance," a sold-out crowd goes crazy with excitement. In one of those great Hollywood clichés, the next tune (a raging "Bugle Call Rag") moves the young fans to leap from their seats in a frenzy and to dance wildly in the aisles.

But, second, the real point is that, beyond dancing, people have started to listen. So, to make Benny's triumph complete, the band plays its famous concert at Carnegie Hall. Again, Benny feels apprehensive about public acceptance but determined not to compromise his standards. Indeed, these ambivalent feelings give him one more chance to display his stubborn commitment to integrity. Just before the concert, we see Benny, his manager Willard Alexander, his brother Harry, and his musical guru Fletcher Henderson agonizing in a solemn powwow.

WILLARD:	No tickets left, Benny. They've been sold out for 3 days. We even have 'em sitting on the stage.
BENNY:	Sold out . . .?
HARRY:	Every seat in the house taken. And not by kids either. Not at *these* prices.
BENNY:	A tall house, full of long-hairs. People who have never heard our kind of music before.
HARRY:	You're taking an awful chance. You know that, don't you, Benny?
BENNY:	Yep. We should have had more time. We need more than one rehearsal. . . . We never should have gotten into this. . . .
WILLARD:	Now listen, Benny. If you're that worried, we can call it off. We still have time.
BENNY:	Naw, we'll go through with it.
HARRY:	Your whole reputation is at stake, Benny. Don't take a chance like this. *Don't be that way.*

FLETCHER: Say, Benny, about the programs. We've got to get it to the printers. We've got to finish laying it out. For instance, what are you gonna open with?

BENNY: Well, let's see. Maybe that new tune we just did. The Edgar Sampson thing. That might be all right.

FLETCHER: What are you going to call it?

BENNY: Oh . . . how about "Don't Be That Way"? That's what I've heard all my life. Every time I've wanted to try something new, someone always said, "Don't be that way." Well, this concert's something new. So maybe that would be a good idea for the opening tune.[4]

On the evening of the concert, everyone feels huge anxiety. But, as Goodman's great musicians play their masterful swing, stuffed shirts begin to pat their feet, long-hairs begin to bob their heads in time to the music, and the cultural elitists of New York begin to listen attentively. Harry James, Ziggy Elman, Teddy Wilson, Lionel Hampton, Gene Krupa all play their hearts out. Alice—who has had a falling out with Benny because of his tendency toward aloofness—shows up and smiles lovingly as Benny woos her with his clarinet. Finally, Benny has achieved their dream and has gained legitimacy by playing to a receptive crowd of musical aristocrats at Carnegie Hall.

The moral is clear: Do what you believe in; follow your deepest convictions; be stubborn; maintain your integrity; and someday you will reach an audience of appreciative listeners, make lots of money, and marry Donna Reed.

I saw this movie for the first time the week it came out, in 1955, when I was barely 12 years old and thought that Benny Goodman had hung the stars. At the time, I related primarily to the music, had zero interest in the love story, and could not have cared less about the marketing phenomena associated with the subtext on the consumer aesthetics of the big-band business. I just enjoyed Benny, Gene, Teddy, Lionel, and—especially—Harry and Ziggy.

More recently, in June 1993, I watched the film again on cable TV. This time, the music still sounded great. Donna Reed looked vastly improved. But what struck me most forcefully was the poignant analogy between the business-related subtext and my own experiences as a teacher of consumer behavior. Indeed, I now realize with a stunning sense of epiphany that, without awareness, my initial exposure to *The Benny Goodman Story* those many years ago changed my life by influencing me unconsciously to behave as I have subsequently behaved, in and out of the classroom.

Grade-B movie or not, *The Benny Goodman Story* makes a cinematically powerful case for stubborn integrity in following one's convictions, whether in music or in teaching.

When applied to the *music business*, these ideals imply an abhorrence of stock arrangements and a fierce devotion to playing one's own impassioned improvisations. In short, corny or not, this movie captures the essence of jazz: *Improvisatory freedom* toward the end of *self-expression*.

When applied to *teaching*, the same ideals imply an abhorrence of standardized courses and a fierce devotion to conveying one's own sincerest intellectual commitments. In short, dangerous or not, this analogy captures the essence of scholarship: *Academic freedom* toward the end of *self-understanding*.

Thus, long buried in my unconscious childhood memories, the subtext of *The Benny Goodman Story* carries such strong meanings for me that, when I accidentally saw this film again after all these years, it evoked an overwhelmingly strong resonance of self-recognition.

Not everybody in our discipline shares the beliefs of Morris the Cat concerning the nature of consumer research. To recapitulate briefly, Morris believes in the feline virtues of independence, espouses a deep commitment to academic freedom, favors scholarship conducted for its own sake as an end in itself, and remains steadfastly indifferent to the canine merits of obedience to marketers as the reward-controlling masters who set priorities for studies that aim at managerial relevance. So, like Benny in the movie, Morris holds some strong convictions. The question of interest at the moment, so insistently enunciated by the Goodman film, concerns the issue of what happens when those convictions collide with the traditional norms for teaching marketing courses in an MBA program.

Here, the metaphorical force of the analogy with *The Benny Goodman Story* appears inescapable. Just as most dance audiences in the 1930s wanted dull, repetitive, bland stock arrangements performed by schlock merchants like Guy Lombardo (or the fictitious Kel Murray) to fulfill all of their expectations and to lull them into a deep, quasi-somnambulant sense of security, so too do many MBAs expect a marketing course to focus on strategic implications for managerially relevant applications. The verdict for anyone who believes that business education should be a little bit different is simple: "*Don't be that way.*"

But, like Benny, Morris must contend with his convictions. For example, one of these convictions concerns the need for a course about consumers and only consumers. This need follows from a clear chain of logic. Specifically, as noted earlier, if a *business* consists of *managers* in a relationship with *customers*, then both managers and customers deserve attention in a business school curriculum. Yet, 90% of all business courses focus entirely on the managerial side (e.g., finance, accounting, management, operations research, money and banking). Of the remaining 10%, mostly marketing courses, 9 of 10 deal primarily with the interaction between managers and customers from the perspective of the former participants (e.g., marketing strategy, marketing research, advertising management, product policy, personal selling, pricing). Thus, no more than 1% of the courses in a business curriculum devote their full attention to the customer in general or to the consumer in particular. Obviously, from the perspective of the university (where intellectual integrity is supposed to matter) and in contrast with that of the executive-training program or the trade school (where immediate usefulness and quick fixes are the order of the day), this situation creates a grotesque imbalance of emphasis that begs for correction.

Continuing the analogy, in the eyes of Morris the Cat, most business school courses resemble the standardized stock arrangements of traditional dance bands from the 1930s. Like Kel Murray in *The Benny Goodman Story*, they give the audience what it expects—namely, an emphasis on managers. They thereby neglect the "hot" topics in consumer research. Yet, Morris holds the conviction that, in an academic university, these topics in consumer research deserve representation and therefore merit an offering by at least one instructor in at least one class—namely, by Morris in his course on consumer behavior.

Just as Benny Goodman in the film pursued his convictions with what John Hammond called his "stubbornest" dedication and what Alice admired as "his own strange kind of integrity," Morris has departed from the MBA norms and has challenged the conventions of the managerial mentality by introducing a course in consumer behavior designed to focus on consumer research without obsessive emphasis on practical applications. Just as some people liked Benny's music but others did not, some students appear to appreciate the change of pace in this class on consumer research, whereas others seem to resist the violation of their expectations. And just as Benny hoped that some enthusiastic fans would ultimately discover that his music was good for listening, Morris hopes that a sufficient number of MBAs—say, about 40 per term (roughly 10% of the market)—will ultimately decide that he has something valuable to say and will find his lectures worth hearing.

Clearly, for both Benny Goodman and Morris the Cat, the marketing strategy in question contains sizeable elements of *product orientation*—that is, a tendency toward following one's own convictions in hopes of finding an adequate audience. Thus, when Gene Krupa warns that "Nobody wants this kind of music," Benny replies, "I do." Similarly, when conventional wisdom warns that "Nobody wants a course on consumers," a few of us reply, "We do." The question therefore arises whether one can justify departing from the approved marketing conventions of *customer orientation*—that is, an eagerness to give customers what they want—in the areas of art and teaching. In both cases, I believe, the answer is yes.

First, as Beth Hirschman noted in the pages of the *Journal of Marketing* (1983) and as Holbrook and Zirlin described in their piece for *Advances in Nonprofit Marketing* (1985), one often finds that a strong tendency toward product orientation guides the work of artists. Artistic integrity demands that artists produce offerings that *they* think are good; that they remain true to their own creative visions; that they pursue originality, inventiveness, and innovativeness; and that they please themselves in hopes that what they offer will please not so much the mob as posterity. And if we have any sense, as an audience for the arts, we would not want it any other way. When art goes commercial, it dies. It dries up and withers away, sometimes to be reincarnated as schlock or kitsch.

Second and similarly, teachers must shoulder an obligation to offer what *they* think matters; to profess what they believe to be the truth according to their own scholarly lights; to honor the value of divergent thinking, their own and that of their students; to follow their own insights in hopes that these may exert enough influence to change the way people think. This is what universities—including their MBA courses, as opposed to executive-training programs or trade schools—are all about. And if we have any sense, as participants in the educational process, we would not want it any other way. When education sells out, it, too, becomes cheap and vulgar.

But how far can we push this righteously stubborn product orientation before it verges on egocentric obstinacy? How much can we honor conviction before it becomes arrogance? How often can we force exasperated people to say "Don't Be That Way" before our deviant posture signifies not integrity but insularity, not self-understanding but solipsism?

Here, in part, one answer lies in the well-worn strategy of *selective market segmentation.* This strategy of *selectivity* and *concentration* (sometimes referred to as "niche" marketing) suggests that because different people have different tastes, no one offering can appeal to all customers with equal force. It therefore makes sense to find a market segment whose needs and wants are not well-satisfied by available offerings and to design a marketing mix to attract this target segment as strongly as possible.

For example, in the film, Benny Goodman willingly abandons the waltz-worshipping, champagne-swilling "squares" (whose tastes are already well-satisfied by Kel Murray and the other faceless bands that play "stock arrangements") and caters instead to a small but vibrant set of "hep" listeners (who can appreciate the kinds of sounds made by Count Basie, Duke Ellington, Fletcher Henderson, Chick Webb, and Goodman himself). Although perhaps fewer than 10% of the population, this segment of "hep" listeners cares enough about "hot" music—with enough passion as it turns out—to make Goodman a hit.

On similar logic, any marketing teacher knows that he or she cannot appeal to everyone with a course that stresses the customer's side of the business and that eschews the ordinary obeisance to the interests of managers as embodied by the conventional standardized team-taught group-think syllabus. Clearly, those cookie-cutter courses serve the sizeable segments of student "squares" who simply seek some stories about business success. But does there perhaps exist a selective group of "hip" students who care about such "cool" topics as consumers and the nature of the consumption experience?

Such questions haunt me every time I enter the classroom. After I receive my course evaluations—often with some appreciative words from the hip folks but sometimes with a few unkind comments from the aforementioned squares—the latter sometimes disturb and even depress me for weeks. In this, it appears that marketing instructors bear a close resemblance to bandleaders. Both face the public knowing that they perform a creative task in which artistic or professional integrity will guarantee rejection by some or even most of their audience. Both know that the more complex, challenging, and countercultural they make their offering—the more it surprises, confounds, and violates expectations—the fewer audience members will appreciate it. Both must try to strike a delicate balance between commitments to their art and concessions to popular tastes. Both orchestrate performances intended as unique and challenging for people who might prefer something easier to digest. And, if the room does not fill up, both tend to blame themselves. Thus rages the age-old tension between crass commercialism and sincere convictions. How much truth must one demand from oneself? How

much audience acceptance is enough? These questions pose difficult dilem-
mas with which both artists and professors must wrestle.

Unfortunately, in the case of the real-life Benny Goodman (as opposed to
the fictitious character found in the film), this struggle appears to have fos-
tered or encouraged a rather offensive private personality. From the written
record, we learn that this undisputed clarinet virtuoso and musical perfec-
tionist beat his band into shape through the use of cruelty and nastiness.
Historical accounts suggest that Goodman would rather humiliate a musician publicly than gently point out his mistakes in private. By all reports,
Benny preferred to embarrass someone with sarcasm rather than to ask
nicely.

Appalling as such charges sound, they come through loud and clear in the
biographical writings. For example, in his book *Jazz Anecdotes*, the author
and bassist Bill Crow (1990), who often played with Goodman and who
knew all of the key musicians involved, describes the King of Swing in less
than flattering terms:

> Benny Goodman has probably generated more anecdotes than any other
> musician. He was a superior instrumentalist and an extremely successful
> bandleader. He was also absent-minded, inscrutable, ruthless, and often infu-
> riating. His eccentricities on and off the bandstand gave the musicians who
> worked for him abundant material for backstage stories. (p. 255)

In *From Birdland to Broadway*, Crow (1992) renders the following account of
his own experiences in the Goodman Band:

> I had been warned by many of Benny's ex-sidemen that he was a tough
> bandleader to work for. . . . Benny drove a hard bargain on my salary. . . . He
> was a little patronizing, and would get on different guys about inconsequential
> things. . . . We were all proud of the band, and we couldn't understand why
> Benny didn't feel that way too. . . . Instead, he seemed to be always on his guard
> against us, as if we had been shanghaied and had to be watched for signs of
> mutiny. He rarely expressed approval, undermined everyone's musical confi-
> dence, and rarely seemed to appreciate his best soloists. . . . Benny eventually
> made us all unhappy. (p. 195)

The noted jazz historian John Lincoln Collier (1989) summarizes Benny
Goodman's character flaws as follows:

> A series of pieces . . . by Bill Crow . . . constituted a fairly complete catalogue of all the criticisms which have been leveled at Goodman by musicians—his insensitivity, his tendency to shove himself into the spotlight, his public butt-scratching, his niggling over money and his general attitude that he was King and the musicians were lackeys expected to accept with a smile whatever abuse he heaped upon them. . . . It must be borne in mind that Goodman treated his musicians far worse than he treated most other people in his life. . . . But it cannot be denied that he treated musicians badly. (p. 355)

But I did not know all that when I went to watch the reunion concert by the Benny Goodman Quartet—given at Carnegie Hall in the early 1970s on the same stage where, almost 40 years earlier, Goodman had achieved the triumph that put him on the cultural map for all time. All four members of the classic quartet showed up—Teddy Wilson, Lionel Hampton, Gene Krupa, and Benny himself—standing about where they had stood in 1938 and again in the movie 15 years later. Each had turned gray, gone white, or lost most of his hair. All had reached senior citizen status. None played at anywhere near his career peak. But Gene Krupa gave the performance of a lifetime. And I shall never forget it.

For years, Gene had suffered from leukemia and on this particular evening, heavily medicated, barely had the strength to climb onto his drum stool. But as the music hit its groove, Gene began to swing with that old conviction—once again rising to the occasion and once again tapping out every rhythmic subtlety with those wonderful facial expressions that told the audience he meant every cymbal stroke with his whole heart and soul. Soon, Gene's energy had returned and, in those transcendent moments, had lifted the spirits of every person seated in that great concert hall.

Gene maintained his magic spark all evening, drumming with a miraculous command summoned from some deep well of courage known only to great artists. After the last tune—"Sing, Sing, Sing," featuring a drum solo—the other musicians helped Gene to his feet to acknowledge the thunderous ovation. Rumors said that Gene collapsed backstage, too exhausted to play an encore or even to take a well-deserved curtain call. He died only a few weeks later.

Would Gene Krupa have pushed himself to those limits for a music in which he did not believe with a relentless passion that lasted all of his life? I don't think so. Would the world have been a poorer place if he had not? I believe it would have. For artists and for teachers, the lesson seems pretty clear: Play what you feel; say what you mean.

Not all professors face the challenge to perform with the sort of heroic dedication displayed by Gene Krupa. Yet, in their own humble way, perhaps teachers also have some reason to hope that their audiences might respect the efforts and sacrifices that they do make. Particularly when we risk unpopularity in order to convey something in which we believe, we might hope that at least a few students might appreciate our attempts to confound their expectations by telling them the truth. And from this hope, we may derive the energy to be different, to struggle against mediocrity, to seek self-understanding.

In this small way, sadder but wiser, we resemble the partly fictitious hero of *The Benny Goodman Story*. Like Benny in the movie—confronting small audiences with fierce convictions—we face some tough choices between telling our students what we know they want to hear and sharing what we honestly believe. Perhaps *The Benny Goodman Story* seems so touching because the film suggests a happy ending for people who confront these vexing questions with integrity. In this motion picture, the hero clings to his convictions until, through sheer stubbornness, he achieves popular approval at the Palomar Ballroom, mass acceptance at the Paramount Theater, and critical acclaim at Carnegie Hall. Thus does this film suggest to a weary teacher that somehow telling the truth might one day inspire a room full of students to take notice. Thus does it suggest a perfect world in which brilliant clarinet playing wins the heart of a fair lady, in which Donna Reed remains forever young, in which artistry conquers ethnic differences, and in which endless practice of efforts toward self-improvement really does get you to Carnegie Hall. Thus—as Benny, Gene, Teddy, Lionel, Harry, and Ziggy play majestically in a joyous image of harmonious fulfillment—does it offer the beautiful vision of a transcendent moment in which, moved by honest integrity, an audience of music lovers—or students—might sit very still. And listen.[5]

❑ Notes

1. © 1971 Irving Music Inc. All rights reserved. International © secured. Used by permission.

2. "I'm Hip" words by David Frishberg, music by Robert Dorough. Copyright © 1981 Swiftwater Music and Aral Music. Used by permission. All rights reserved.

3. *And the Angels Sing*, by Ziggy Elman and Johnny Mercer. Copyright © 1939 WB Music Corp. (Renewed). All rights reserved. Used by permission of Warner Bros. Publications Inc., Miami, FL 33014.

4. Copyright © by Universal City Studios, Inc. Courtesy of MCA Publishing Rights, a Division of MCA, Inc.

5. Thanks to Ellen Day for permission to draw on our collaborative research.

EPILOGUE
The Turtle

The flowers appear on the earth; the time of the singing of birds is come, and the voice of the turtle is heard in our land.
—The Song of Solomon, 2:12

❏ *In Memoriam: Bart Giamatti*

Surely, the previous chapters—especially Chapters 6 and 9—will have suggested how deeply I was saddened by the death of A. Bartlett Giamatti, whose passing occurred after I had written the bulk of my original reflections on dogs and cats, bears and baseball, prior to their subsequent revision and integration into this book. In particular, my comparison of academic and managerial research has drawn heavily on the wisdom articulated by Giamatti during his service as president of Yale University. His presidential communications bristled with ideas relevant to the work of consumer researchers as scholars.

When Bart Giamatti died at the tragically young age of 51, well-known by virtue of his role as the commissioner of baseball, eulogies and encomiums filled the pages of the *New York Times* for several days. In one of the nicest remembrances, Robert Semple (1989) touched on the values central to Giamatti's concerns:

363

Giamatti's eloquent and even romantic devotion to traditional values explains him. It explains his passion, as student and teacher, for English literature and the classical poets; his commitment, as a college president, to learning for its own sake; his reverence, as baseball commissioner, for old ball parks, orderly crowds, green grass, blue skies and games in the afternoon. (Semple, 1989, p. A18)[1]

In another tribute, Edward Fiske (1989) drew on Giamatti's essentially romantic conviction that "two of his great loves, baseball and literature, were spiritual cousins":

The national pastime, he said, is "an oft-told tale. . . . Indeed, its basic motif—leaving home and struggling to return—is as ancient as Homer. All literary romance . . . derives from the 'Odyssey' and is about rejoining." (Fiske, 1989, p. B10)

Incredibly, in his intellectual pursuits, Giamatti confronted the same character-testing trials and tribulations that afflict the rest of us less epic scholars: "Shortly after assuming the Yale presidency he was asked to contribute an article on the liberal arts to the *New York Times* that turned out to be uncharacteristically diffuse and . . . was rejected" (Fiske, 1989, p. B10). Imagine! Even A. Bartlett Giamatti, president of Yale, suffered the indignity of having an invited paper rejected by something less than a first-tier academic journal. At times like these, only his moral courage could have sustained him: "Bart Giamatti brought passion to whatever he felt called to do. He cared about Yale and baseball and scholarship and the English language, and pursued all of these with gusto, dignity, eloquence and wit" (Fiske, 1989, p. B10).[2]

Comparing the ballpark to the gridiron—as George Carlin did so engagingly in the passage quoted earlier (Chapter 6)—one somehow doubts that Bart Giamatti had much love for football. If this hunch is correct, I find this imputed feeling easy to share. In that spirit, with admiration and appreciation, I declare Bart Giamatti the hero of this epilogue and dedicate the following brief essay to his memory. Consistent with my earlier reflections on the skylark, the epigraph to this chapter refers to the plaintive cooing of the turtledove. However, the following essay recalls the more earthy, the more lowly, the more four-legged sort of turtle with whom I also have good reason to identify.

❏ The Turtle

At that painful moment in my early existence when my future vocations, career choices, love life, and other biographical details still remained most elusively in doubt—that time known officially as adolescence and characterized unofficially by a chronic and unquenchable edginess—the one fact I knew for certain concerned my own hopeless inadequacies as a football player. I acquired this one incontrovertible piece of information about my God-given talents and aspirations (or rather my stupendous lack thereof) by virtue of my participation, as a junior and senior in high school, on the Milwaukee Country Day School varsity football team. It was there, in that dread arena of terrible humiliation, that I laid claim to a nickname that haunted me for most of my 11th- and 12th-grade years: The Turtle.

For 2 years, my classmates called me "The Turtle"—all day, every day. They greeted me with this epithet first thing in the morning. They whispered it at me in the middle of junior-level chemistry, senior-level physics, and college-level calculus. They invoked it to taunt me in the lunchroom. And, after school, they embarrassed me at the drive-in frozen custard stand by announcing it in front of the assembled girls from Downer, our sister institution. But most of all, they used it relentlessly and accurately in the place where I had earned it, on the football field.

Those who know me as a relatively scrawny 148-pound ectomorph may react with surprise to the intimation that I once disported myself on the gridiron at a Midwestern high school. I can relieve their incredulity, however, by confessing that, as an ectomorph with the food-craving passion of an endomorph, I weighed 185 pounds at the start of my senior year, a bulk that placed me high enough in my school's chunkiness hierarchy to ensure—nay, to demand—my reluctant presence on the team.

I refer, of course, to the second-string team. Clearly, my rotundity and general lack of coordination rendered any chance of my playing on the real team unthinkable. But, with a typical class size of only about 25 boys, the coach needed all of the big bodies he could muster, flabby or not. Specifically, he needed our otherwise inadequate second-string torsos so that the first string could practice its plays against some resistance, however feeble. According to the official rationale, this would help people like me lose weight and build character (the two being viewed, incidentally, as roughly synonymous). But I was only fat, not completely stupid. So, I could plainly see that the real reason for my presence on the field entailed my ability to serve as a sort of human blocking dummy. In short, my mission was to scrimmage.

This destiny at a school whose dual mottoes I still recall—"*alis volat propriis*" ("he flies by his own wings") and "don't wait to become a great man, be a great boy"—confronted me with some rather daunting problems of a practical nature resulting from my typical assignment to the defensive line at the position of center, through which our stellar fullback (who comprised 195 pounds of solid muscle and who enjoyed grinding chubby people under his spikes for fun) ran most of his drills. As a fledgling but hopeful pianist, I took umbrage at the frequency with which I got my fingers trampled under the merciless fullback's sharply pointed hard rubber cleats. Inevitably, if only for survival, I invented a sort of self-protective strategy.

My defensive posture featured a special technique that I developed slowly as a way of getting under the action so that the violence of the colliding helmets and clashing shoulder pads could pass above me, leaving me relatively unscathed below. I called this evasive approach my "turtle stance." Basically, it involved crouching down on all fours, with my big belly as close to the ground as humanly possible, and then springing forward on the artless pretense of trying to burrow beneath the offensive center.

Needless to say, all opponents—even those most devoted to the game of football—were smart enough to figure out that they could easily foil my tortoiselike tactics by simply falling on top of me. This they learned quite rapidly, thereby gaining the satisfaction of sprawling on me and teasing me with my reptilian eponym while I cowered below, hunching over my curled-up fists and deriving some rueful encouragement from the morbid consolation that the charging fullback was stepping on *them*.

Obviously, these habits of self-protective conduct failed utterly to endear me to my coach, and I thereby definitively avoided the remotest possibility of playing in any real game. Finally, on one crisp Saturday afternoon that I shall never forget, the bitter Milwaukee wind sent goose bumps down my exposed neck and into the top of my green-and-gold jersey. I sat huddled on the sidelines and hopefully waited for the game to end so that I could retire from the October chill to the relative safety of the locker room and the warm security of the shower. But our team somehow surged so far ahead of its rivals on the playing field that the masterminds on our bench began to seek variety and, casting about for something truly novel to try, conceived the misbegotten idea of inserting me into the action.

Once I had gained my position on the line of scrimmage, feeling indeed like a terrified turtle on an endless expanse of cold and cheerless grass, it took the offensive center exactly two plays to discern the correct maneuver needed to foil my defensive strategy. Subsequently, he landed repeatedly with bone-crushing vehemence on my exposed backside.

But in the fleeting window of opportunity that transpired before the sturdy lineman learned regularly to squash me beneath his sweaty elbows and knees, I once successfully burrowed under his shins and emerged on the other side, in Beulah Land, incredulously wondering what to do next. There, during that unprecedented visit to the offensive backfield (so green, so lush, so tranquil beyond the pale of the thrashing bodies behind me), I suddenly encountered a gracefully fleeing fullback who, like a galloping gazelle, tried to glide past me on a smooth swing around the right end. Wildly, wantonly, witlessly, I flung myself at him and wrapped my arms around his legs in a lunging embrace.

To my total astonishment and utter delight, he collapsed on the spot amidst a gratifying crash and clatter of plastic pads and other protective paraphernalia. I thus enjoyed a brief but boundless moment of ecstatic insight, an evanescent epiphany of the second down with 3 yards to go. I discovered that even the fleetest fullback will fall if you fly through the air and grab him by his knees.

More recently, as presaged in the preceding chapters, it has often occurred to me that some aspects of consumer research resemble the purposelessly violent clash of a football game. By analogy, the reviewers compose the first-string team. They follow the instructions of their coaches, the editors. The hapless writers serve as the scrubs against whom the real team needs to scrimmage. The prospective author gets dashed to the ground by Reviewer A, bashed in the head by Reviewer B, and smashed in the groin by Reviewer C. The righteous editors solemnly proclaim that these punishments befit the writer's laziness and incompetence. Then they run the same play again. And again. And again. Over and over and over.

Extending this analogy a bit, I have begun to wonder whether one might not benefit from adopting some kind of novel intellectual posture. Something, perhaps, reminiscent of the turtle stance. Something seen as so lowly that it merely creeps and crawls on the ground beneath the austere majesty and awesome grandeur of science. Something, say, like literary criticism or hermeneutic interpretation or semiotic analysis or the humanities in general or aesthetics in particular. Something—O, Unthinkable—like the lyrical expression of emotional experience or the subjective personal introspective essay. Something, in short, like the position arrived at in compiling the 10 preceding chapters of this book and summarized by the postmodern pluralistic posture represented by Statement 11 in Figure 1.3 from Chapter 1: Scientific and Humanistic Marketing and Consumer Research Includes Neopositivistic and Interpretive Managerially Relevant and Intrinsically Motivated Studies of Decisions to Buy Goods and Services and of Experiences in the Consumption of Artwork and Entertainment.

With such a stance, one might play the research game from a defensive posture so radical that the linemen, the fullbacks, and even the coaches have not encountered it yet. Of course, as soon as they caught on, one would regularly end up with one's face in the mud and somebody else sitting on top. But, until they did. . . .

Until they did catch on, one might escape punishment for just a short time. Just once, like The Turtle on a memorable Saturday in October long ago, one might burrow underneath the fray and break through to the light on the other side. One might recapture, however evanescently, that brief but boundless moment of ecstatic insight in which fleeing truth crashes in around us, arrested in midflight by the urgent grasp of our wildest lunging embrace.

❑ Notes

1. Semple (1989), p. A18. Copyright © 1989 by The New York Times Company. Reprinted by permission.
2. Fiske (1989), p. B10. Copyright © 1989 by The New York Times Company. Reprinted by permission.

REFERENCES

Abbott, L. (1955). *Quality and competition.* New York: Columbia University Press.

Abraham, N., & Torok, M. (1986). *The wolf man's magic word: A cryptonymy* (N. Rand, Trans.). Minneapolis: University of Minnesota Press.

Abrams, M. H. (1953). *The mirror and the lamp: Romantic theory and the critical tradition.* New York: Oxford University Press.

Abrams, M. H. (1963). English romanticism: The spirit of the age. In N. Frye (Ed.), *Romanticism reconsidered* (pp. 26-72). New York: Columbia University Press.

Abrams, M. H. (1971). *Natural supernaturalism.* New York: Norton.

Abrams, M. H. (1979). Rationality and imagination in cultural history. In W. C. Booth (Ed.), *Critical understanding: The powers and limits of pluralism* (pp. 176-194). Chicago: University of Chicago Press.

Abrams, M. H. (1988). *A glossary of literary terms* (5th ed.). New York: Holt, Rinehart & Winston.

Ajzen, I., & Fishbein, M. (1980). *Understanding attitudes and predicting social behavior.* Englewood Cliffs, NJ: Prentice Hall.

Alderson, W. (1957). *Marketing behavior and executive action.* Homewood, IL: Irwin.

Alexander, J. (1992). General theory in the postpositivist mode: The "epistemological dilemma" and the search for present reason. In S. Seidman & D. G. Wagner (Eds.), *Postmodernism and social theory: The debate over general theory* (pp. 322-368). Cambridge, MA: Blackwell.

Alston, W. P. (1967). Pleasure. In P. Edwards (Ed.), *The encyclopedia of philosophy* (Vol. 6, pp. 341-347). New York: Macmillan.

AMA Task Force. (1988). Developing, disseminating, and utilizing marketing knowledge. *Journal of Marketing, 52* (October), 1-25.

369

Anderson, P. F. (1983). Marketing, scientific progress, and scientific method. *Journal of Marketing, 47*(Fall), 18-31.

Anderson, P. F. (1986). On method in consumer research: A critical relativist perspective. *Journal of Consumer Research, 13*(September), 155-173.

Anscombe, G. E. M. (1957). *Intention*. Ithaca, NY: Cornell University Press.

Apel, W., & Daniel, R. T. (1960). *The Harvard brief dictionary of music*. Cambridge, MA: Harvard University Press.

Armstrong, E. A. (1963). *A study of bird song*. London: Oxford University Press.

Arnheim, R. (1966). *Art and visual perception*. Berkeley: University of California Press.

Auerbach, E. (1953). *Mimesis: The representation of reality in Western literature* (W. R. Trask, Trans.). Princeton, NJ: Princeton University Press.

Auerbach, E. (1969). Philology and *Weltliteratur. Centennial Review, 13*(Winter), 1-17.

Bagozzi, R. P. (1986). *Principles of marketing management*. Chicago: Science Research Associates.

Baker, C. (n.d.). *Blood, Chet, and tears* [Record album]. Verve (V6-8798).

Baker, C., with Desmond, P. (1977). You can't go home again (By D. Sebesky). On *You can't go home again* [Recording]. A&M (CD0805).

Barthes, R. (1967). *Elements of semiology* (A. Lavers & C. Smith, Trans.). New York: Hill & Wang. (Original work published 1964)

Barthes, R. (1983). *The fashion system* (M. Ward & R. Howard, Trans.). New York: Hill & Wang. (Original work published 1967)

Bartlett, J. (1992). *Familiar quotations* (16th ed.) (J. Kaplan, Ed.). Boston: Little, Brown.

Barzun, J. (1975). *Classic, romantic, and modern*. Chicago: University of Chicago Press. (Original work published 1943)

Baudrillard, J. (1981). *For a critique of the political economy of the sign* (C. Levin, Trans.). St. Louis: Telos.

Bay, T. (1976). The social history of the cat. In J. Fireman (Ed.), *Cat catalog: The ultimate cat book* (pp. 10-16). New York: Workman.

Bazerman, C. (1987). Codifying the social scientific style: The APA publication manual as a behaviorist rhetoric. In J. S. Nelson, A. Megill, & D. N. McCloskey (Eds.), *The rhetoric of the human sciences* (pp. 125-144). Madison: University of Wisconsin Press.

Beardsley, M. (1979). Verbal style and illocutionary action. In B. Lang (Ed.), *The concept of style* (pp. 149-168). Philadelphia: University of Pennsylvania Press.

Beardsley, M. C. (1981). *Aesthetics: Problems in the philosophy of criticism* (2nd ed.). Indianapolis: Hackett.

Becker, G. S. (1976). *The economic approach to human behavior*. Chicago: University of Chicago Press.

Becker, H. S. (1978). Arts and crafts. *American Journal of Sociology, 83*(4), 862-889.

Becker, H. S. (1982). *Art worlds*. Berkeley: University of California Press.

Beers, H. A. (1968). *A history of English romanticism in the eighteenth century.* New York: Dover. (Original work published 1899)

Belenky, M. F., Clinchy, B. M., Goldberger, N. R., & Tarule, J. M. (1986). *Women's ways of knowing: The development of self, voice, and mind.* New York: Basic Books.

Belk, R. W. (1986). What should ACR want to be when it grows up? In R. J. Lutz (Ed.), *Advances in consumer research* (Vol. 13, pp. 423-424). Provo, UT: Association for Consumer Research.

Belk, R. W. (Ed.). (1991). *Highways and buyways: Naturalistic research from the consumer behavior odyssey.* Provo, UT: Association for Consumer Research.

Belk, R. W., Bahn, K. D., & Mayer, R. N. (1982). Developmental recognition of consumption systems. *Journal of Consumer Research, 9* (June), 4-17.

Belk, R. W., & Pollay, R. W. (1985). Images of ourselves: The good life in twentieth century advertising. *Journal of Consumer Research, 11* (March), 887-897.

Belk, R. W., Wallendorf, M., Sherry, J. F., Jr., & Holbrook, M. B. (1991). Collecting in a consumer culture. In R. W. Belk (Ed.), *Highways and buyways: Naturalistic research from the consumer behavior odyssey* (pp. 178-215). Provo, UT: Association for Consumer Research.

Belk, R. W., Wallendorf, M., Sherry, J., Holbrook, M. B., & Roberts, S. (1988). Collectors and collecting. In M. J. Houston (Ed.), *Advances in consumer research* (Vol. 15, pp. 548-553). Provo, UT: Association for Consumer Research.

Bellante, D., & Foster, A. C. (1984). Working wives and expenditure on services. *Journal of Consumer Research, 11* (September), 700-707.

Ben-David, J. (1972). *Trends in American higher education.* Chicago: University of Chicago Press.

Berger, J. (1988, September 16). Academic research for financial gain. *New York Times,* p. A14.

Berger, P. L. (1963). *Invitation to sociology: A humanistic perspective.* New York: Anchor.

Berger, P. L., & Luckmann, T. (1966). *The social construction of reality: A treatise in the sociology of knowledge.* New York: Anchor.

Berkvist, R. (1980, September 22). Innaurato's characters even surprise himself. *New York Times,* p. C16.

Berlyne, D. E. (1960). *Conflict, arousal, and curiosity.* New York: McGraw-Hill.

Berlyne, D. E. (1969). Laughter, humor, and play. In G. Lindzey & E. Anderson (Eds.), *The handbook of social psychology* (Vol. 3, pp. 795-852). Reading, MA: Addison-Wesley.

Berlyne, D. E. (1971). *Aesthetics and psychobiology.* New York: Appleton-Century-Crofts.

Berlyne, D. E. (Ed.). (1974). *Studies in the new experimental aesthetics.* New York: John Wiley.

Berman, M. (1981). *The reenchantment of the world.* Ithaca, NY: Cornell University Press.

Bernard, J. (1981). *The female world.* New York: Free Press.

Bernstein, R. J. (1971). *Praxis and action: Contemporary philosophies of human activity.* Philadelphia: University of Pennsylvania Press.

Bernstein, R. J. (1983). *Beyond objectivism and relativism: Science, hermeneutics, and praxis.* Philadelphia: University of Pennsylvania Press.

Bersani, L. (1986). *The Freudian body: Psychoanalysis and art.* New York: Columbia University Press.

Bettman, J. R. (1970). Information processing models of consumer behavior. *Journal of Marketing Research, 7,* 370-376.

Bettman, J. R. (1979). *An information processing theory of consumer behavior.* Reading, MA: Addison-Wesley.

Bettman, J. R., Johnson, E. J., & Payne, J. W. (1991). Consumer decision making. In T. S. Robertson & H. H. Kassarjian (Eds.), *Handbook of consumer behavior* (pp. 50-84). Englewood Cliffs, NJ: Prentice Hall.

Bloch, P. H. (1982). Involvement beyond the purchase process: Conceptual issues and empirical investigation. In A. Mitchell (Ed.), *Advances in consumer research* (Vol. 9, pp. 413-417). Ann Arbor, MI: Association for Consumer Research.

Bloch, P. H., & Bruce, G. D. (1984). Product involvement as leisure behavior. In T. C. Kinnear (Ed.), *Advances in consumer research* (Vol. 11, pp. 197-202). Provo, UT: Association for Consumer Research.

Boffey, P. M. (1984, July 17). Industry takes dominant science role. *New York Times,* pp. C1, C9.

Bok, D. (1982). *Beyond the ivory tower.* Cambridge, MA: Harvard University Press.

Booth, W. C. (1974). *Modern dogma and the rhetoric of assent.* Chicago: University of Chicago Press.

Booth, W. C. (1983). *The rhetoric of fiction* (2nd ed.). Chicago: University of Chicago Press. (Original work published 1961)

Bordo, S. (1987). *The flight to objectivity: Essays on Cartesianism and culture.* Albany: State University of New York Press.

Bosanquet, B. (1915). *Three lectures on aesthetics.* London: Macmillan.

Boyd, H. W., Jr., & Levy, S. J. (1963). New dimensions in consumer analysis. *Harvard Business Review, 41* (November/December), 129-140.

Brannigan, A. (1981). *The social basis of scientific discoveries.* Cambridge, UK: Cambridge University Press.

Brinberg, D., & Wood, R. (1983). A resource exchange theory analysis of consumer behavior. *Journal of Consumer Research, 10* (December), 330-338.

Brinton, C. (1967). Romanticism. In P. Edwards (Ed.), *The encyclopedia of philosophy* (pp. 206-209). New York: Macmillan.

Bristor, J. M., & Fischer, E. (1993). Feminist thought: Implications for consumer research. *Journal of Consumer Research, 19* (March), 519-536.

Broad, W. J. (1989a, May 30). At conference on cold fusion, the verdict is negative. *New York Times,* pp. C1, C8.

Broad, W. J. (1989b, June 14). Effort to verify fusion experiment collapses. *New York Times,* p. A20.

Broad, W. J. (1990, October 30). Cold fusion still escapes usual checks of science. *New York Times*, pp. C1, C12.

Broad, W. J., & Wade, N. (1982). *Betrayers of the truth.* New York: Simon & Schuster.

Brody, J. E. (1985, October 16). Strategies for coping with a pet's death, which can be as painful as that of a friend. *New York Times*, p. C8.

Bronowski, J. (1965). *Science and human values.* New York: Harper & Row.

Brooks, H. (1978). The problem of research priorities. In G. Holton & R. S. Morison (Eds.), *Limits of scientific inquiry* (pp. 171-190). New York: Norton.

Brown, R. H. (1977). *A poetic for sociology: Toward a logic of discovery for the social sciences.* Cambridge, UK: Cambridge University Press.

Bruner, J. (1986). *Actual minds, possible worlds.* Cambridge, MA: Harvard University Press.

Burke, K. (1969). *A rhetoric of motives.* Berkeley: University of California Press.

Butterfield, F. (1986, September 7). Harvard president deplores the pursuing of affluence. *New York Times*, p. 14.

Byrne, J. A. (1990, October 29). Is research in the ivory tower "fuzzy, irrelevant, pretentious"? *Business Week*, pp. 62-64.

Cacioppo, J. T., Losch, M. E., Tassinary, L. G., & Petty, R. E. (1986). Properties of affect and affect-laden information processing. In R. A. Peterson, W. D. Hoyer, & W. R. Wilson (Eds.), *The role of affect in consumer behavior: Emerging theories and applications* (pp. 87-118). Lexington, MA: D. C. Heath.

Calder, B. J., & Tybout, A. M. (1987). What consumer research is. *Journal of Consumer Research*, *14*(June), 136-140.

Campbell, C. (1987). *The romantic ethic and the spirit of modern consumerism.* Oxford, UK: Basil Blackwell.

Campbell, J. (with Moyers, B.). (1988). *The power of myth* (B. S. Flowers, Ed.). Garden City, NY: Doubleday.

Campbell, K. (1984). *Body and mind* (2nd ed.). Notre Dame, IN: University of Notre Dame Press.

Caras, R. (1986). *A celebration of cats.* New York: Simon & Schuster.

Carlin, G. (1975). Baseball and football. In *An evening with Wally Londo* [Record album]. Los Angeles: Little David Records (LD 1008).

Carlston, D. E. (1987). Turning psychology on itself: The rhetoric of psychology and the psychology of rhetoric. In J. S. Nelson, A. Megill, & D. N. McCloskey (Eds.), *The rhetoric of the human sciences* (pp. 145-162). Madison: University of Wisconsin Press.

Carmichael, H. (with Pepper, A.). (1956). Skylark (By H. Carmichael & J. Mercer). On *Hoagy sings Carmichael* [Record album]. Capitol-Pacific Jazz (CDP 7 46862 2).

Carmichael, H., & Mercer, J. (1941). Skylark [Song]. Los Angeles: Warner Chappel Music.

Carroll, J. D. (1972). Individual differences and multidimensional scaling. In R. N. Shepard, A. K. Romney, & S. B. Nerlove (Eds.), *Multidimensional scaling:*

Theory and applications in the behavioral sciences (Vol. 1, pp. 105-155). New York: Seminar.

Cassirer, E. (1961). *The logic of the humanities* (C. S. Howe, Trans.). New Haven, CT: Yale University Press.

Catford, L., & Ray, M. (1991). *The path of the everyday hero: Drawing on the power of myth to meet life's most important challenges.* Los Angeles: Jeremy P. Tarcher.

Chamberlin, E. H. (1956). *The theory of monopolistic competition.* Cambridge, MA: Harvard University Press.

Clark, N. B. (1984, June 18). When naming a cartoon character, the creators were bearish on Yogi. *Sports Illustrated,* p. 6.

Cohen, J. B., & Areni, C. S. (1991). Affect and consumer behavior. In T. S. Robertson & H. H. Kassarjian (Eds.), *Handbook of consumer behavior* (pp. 188-240). Englewood Cliffs, NJ: Prentice Hall.

Cohen, J. M. (1933). Introduction. In *The confessions of Jean-Jacques Rousseau* (J. M. Cohen, Trans.) (pp. 7-14). Harmondsworth, UK: Penguin.

Coleridge, S. T. (1948). Dejection: An ode. In E. Bernbaum (Ed.), *Anthology of romanticism* (pp. 177-179). New York: Ronald Press. (Original work published 1802)

Collier, J. L. (1989). *Benny Goodman and the swing era.* New York: Oxford University Press.

Connors, M. (1986, December 1). A research odyssey. *Adweek,* pp. 4-6.

Cooper-Martin, E., & Holbrook, M. (1993). Ethical consumption experiences and ethical space. In L. McAlister & M. L. Rothschild (Eds.), *Advances in consumer research* (Vol 20, pp. 113-118). Provo, UT: Association for Consumer Research.

Corporate/university ties growing stronger. (1983, January 3). *Chemical and Engineering News,* pp. 32-33.

Crease, R. P., & Samios, N. P. (1989, September 24). Cold fusion confusion. *New York Times Magazine,* pp. 34-38.

Crosby, D., Stills, S., Nash, G., & Young, N. (1970). Our house. (By G. Nash). On *Deja vu* [Record album]. Atlantic (SD 7200).

Crow, B. (1990). *Jazz anecdotes.* New York: Oxford University Press.

Crow, B. (1992). *From Birdland to Broadway: Scenes from a jazz life.* New York: Oxford University Press.

Csikszentmihalyi, M. (1975). *Beyond boredom and anxiety.* San Francisco: Jossey-Bass.

Csikszentmihalyi, M., & Rochberg-Halton, E. (1981). *The meaning of things: Domestic symbols and the self.* Cambridge, UK: Cambridge University Press.

Darnton, R. (1984). *The great cat massacre: And other episodes in French cultural history.* New York: Vintage.

Davy, C. (1978). *Towards a third culture.* Edinburgh, Scotland: Floris.

De Lacy, P. H. (1967). Epicurus. In *The encyclopedia of philosophy* (Vol. 3, pp. 3-5). New York: Macmillan.

Denzin, N. K. (1984). *On understanding emotion.* San Francisco: Jossey-Bass.

Denzin, N. K. (1989). *Interpretive interactionism.* Newbury Park, CA: Sage.

DePree, M. (1989). *Leadership is an art.* New York: Dell.

DePree, M. (1992). *Leadership jazz.* New York: Currency.

Descartes, R. (1986). *Meditations on first philosophy* (B. Williams, Trans.). Cambridge, UK: Cambridge University Press. (Original work published 1641)

Deshpande, R. (1983). "Paradigms lost": On theory and method in research in marketing. *Journal of Marketing, 47*(Fall), 101-110.

Desmond, P. (1974). Skylark (By H. Carmichael & J. Mercer). On *Skylark* [Record album]. CBS-CTI (ZK 44170).

Dichter, E. (1947). Psychology in marketing research. *Harvard Business Review, 25*(Summer), 432-443.

Dichter, E. (1949). A psychological view of advertising effectiveness. *Journal of Marketing, 14*(July), 61-66.

Dichter, E. (1960). *The strategy of desire.* Garden City, NY: Doubleday.

Diderot, D. (Ed.). (1964). Regrets on parting with my old dressing gown. In *Rameau's nephew and other works by Denis Diderot* (J. Barzun & R. H. Bowen, Trans.) (pp. 309-317). New York: Bobbs-Merrill. (Original work published c. 1760)

Donovan, R., & Rossiter, J. (1982). Store atmosphere: An environmental psychology approach. *Journal of Retailing, 58*(Spring), 34-57.

Dornbusch, R. R., & Fischer, S. (1984). *Macro-economics* (3rd ed.). New York: McGraw-Hill.

Douglas, M. (with Isherwood, B). (1979). *The world of goods.* New York: Norton.

Drucker, P. (1954). *The practice of management.* New York: Harper.

Ducasse, C. J. (1979). Art and the language of the emotions. In M. Rader (Ed.), *A modern book of esthetics* (pp. 67-70). New York: Holt, Rinehart & Winston.

Eco, U. (1976). *A theory of semiotics.* Bloomington: Indiana University Press.

Eco, U., & Sebeok, T. A. (Eds.). (1983). *The sign of three: Dupin, Holmes, Peirce.* Bloomington: Indiana University Press.

Eliot, T. S. (1962). Four quartets (1935-1942). In *The complete poems and plays* (pp. 117-145). New York: Harcourt, Brace & World. (Original work published 1942)

Engel, J. F., Kollat, D. T., & Blackwell, R. D. (1968). *Consumer behavior.* New York: Holt, Rinehart & Winston.

Farley, J. U., & Ring, L. W. (1970). An empirical test of the Howard Sheth model of buyer behavior. *Journal of Marketing Research, 7*(November), 427-438.

Feather, L., & Tracy, J. (1963). *Laughter from the hip: The lighter side of jazz.* New York: Da Capo.

Fennell, G. (1982, February). *Terms v. concepts: Market segmentation, brand positioning, and other aspects of the academic-practitioner gap.* Paper presented at the Winter Educators' Conference of the American Marketing Association, Chicago.

Fennell, G. (1985). Things of heaven and earth: Phenomenology, marketing, and consumer research. In E. C. Hirschman & M. B. Holbrook (Eds.), *Advances in consumer research* (Vol. 12, pp. 544-549). Provo, UT: Association for Consumer Research.

Feyerabend, P. (1975). *Against method: Outline of an anarchistic* theory of knowledge.* London: Verso.

Feyerabend, P. (1982). *Science in a free society.* London: Verso.

Fireman, J. (Ed.). (1976). *Cat catalog: The ultimate cat book.* New York: Workman.

Fishbein, M., & Ajzen, I. (1975). *Belief, attitude, intention and behavior.* Reading, MA: Addison-Wesley.

Fisher, S., & Greenberg, R. P. (1985). *The scientific credibility of Freud's theories and therapy.* New York: Columbia University Press.

Fiske, E. (1989, September 6). Lessons. *New York Times*, p. B10.

Fitzsimons, G. J., Block, L. G., & Holbrook, M. B. (1993). *Marketing, consumption, and the pursuit of beauty: Some lessons from popular culture.* Unpublished manuscript, Columbia University, Graduate School of Business.

Foote, E. T. (1984, November 13). College is big business: But will education survive? *New York Times*, p. A31.

Frame, D. M. (1958). Introduction. In *The complete essays of Montaigne* (D. M. Frame, Trans.) (pp. v-xiv). Stanford, CA: Stanford University Press.

Fraser, K. (1985). *The fashionable mind.* Boston: Nonpareil.

Freud, S. (1959). The relation of the poet to day-dreaming. In E. Jones (Ed.), *Collected papers* (Vol. 4, pp. 173-183). New York: Basic Books. (Original work published 1908)

Freud, S. (1963). The relation of the poet to day-dreaming. In P. Rieff (Ed.), *Character and culture* (pp. 34-43). New York: Collier. (Original work published 1908)

Freud, S. (1963). The Moses of Michelangelo. In P. Rieff (Ed.), *Character and culture* (pp. 88-106). New York: Collier. (Original work published 1914)

Freud, S. (1963). From the history of an infantile neurosis. In P. Rieff (Ed.), *Three case histories* (pp. 187-316). New York: Collier. (Original work published 1918)

Freud, S. (1965). *The interpretation of dreams* (J. Strachey, Trans.). New York: Avon. (Original work published 1900)

Freud, S. (1977). *Introductory lectures on psychoanalysis* (J. Strachey, Trans.). New York: Norton. (Original work published 1917)

Friedman, M. (1985). The changing language of a consumer society: Brand name usage in popular American novels in the postwar era. *Journal of Consumer Research, 11* (March), 927-938.

Friedman, M. (1991). *A "brand" new language: Commercial influences in literature and culture.* Westport, CT: Greenwood.

Frishberg, D. (1981). I'm hip (By D. Frishberg & R. Dorough). On *The Dave Frishberg songbook* [Record album]. Omnisound Jazz (N-1040).

Frishberg, D. (1987). Zoot walks in (By D. Frishberg, Z. Sims, & G. Mulligan). On *Can't take you nowhere* [Record album]. Fantasy (FCD-9651-2).

Frye, N. (1963). The drunken boat: The revolutionary element in romanticism. In N. Frye (Ed), *Romanticism reconsidered: Selected papers from the English Institute* (pp. 1-25). New York: Columbia University Press.

Frye, N. (1968). *A study of English romanticism.* Chicago: University of Chicago Press.

Frye, N., Baker, S., & Perkins, G. (1985). *The Harper handbook to literature.* New York: Harper & Row.

Fusfeld, H. I. (1983). Overview of university-industry research interaction. In T. W. Langfitt, S. Hackney, A. P. Fishman, & A. V. Glowasky (Eds.), *Partners in the research enterprise: University-corporate relations in science and technology* (pp. 10-19). Philadelphia: University of Pennsylvania Press.

Fussell, P. (1983). *Class.* New York: Summit.

Gadamer, H.-G. (1975). *Truth and method* (G. Barden & J. Cumming, Eds.). New York: Crossroad.

Gans, H. J. (1974). *Popular culture and high culture: An analysis and evaluation of taste.* New York: Basic Books.

Gardiner, M. (Ed.). (1971). *The wolf-man by the wolf-man.* New York: Basic Books.

Gardner, B. B., & Levy, S. J. (1955). The product and the brand. *Harvard Business Review, 33*(March-April), 33-39.

Geertz, C. (1973). *The interpretation of cultures.* New York: Basic Books.

Geertz, C. (1988). *Works and lives: The anthropologist as author.* Stanford, CA: Stanford University Press.

Geist, W. E. (1985, October 16). The selling of the comet, 1985. *New York Times,* p. B3.

Giamatti, A. B. (1983). Free market and free inquiry: The university, industry, and cooperative research. In T. W. Langfitt, S. Hackney, A. P. Fishman, & A. V. Glowasky (Eds.), *Partners in the research enterprise: University-corporate relations in science and technology* (pp. 3-9). Philadelphia: University of Pennsylvania Press.

Giamatti, A. B. (1988). *A free and ordered space: The real world of the university.* New York: Norton.

Gilligan, C. (1982). *In a different voice: Psychological theory and women's development.* Cambridge, MA: Harvard University Press.

Ginzburg, C. (1983). Morelli, Freud, and Sherlock Holmes: Clues and scientific method. In U. Eco & T. A. Sebeok (Eds.), *The sign of three* (pp. 81-118). Bloomington: Indiana University Press.

Giorgi, A. (1970). *Psychology as a human science: A phenomenologically based approach.* New York: Harper & Row.

Goffman, E. (1959). *The presentation of self in everyday life.* Garden City, NY: Doubleday.

Goldman, A. I. (1970). *A theory of human action.* Princeton, NJ: Princeton University Press.

Goleman, D., Kaufman, P., & Ray, M. (1992). *The creative spirit.* New York: Dutton.

Good, G. (1988). *The observing self: Rediscovering the essay.* London: Routledge.

Goodall, J. (1971). *In the shadow of man.* Boston: Houghton Mifflin.

Goodell, W. F. (1968). *Memorandum re conflict of interest.* New York: Columbia University.

Gore, A., Jr. (1983). Recombinated institutions: The changing university-corporate relationship. In T. W. Langfitt, S. Hackney, A. P. Fishman, & A. V. Glowasky

(Eds.), *Partners in the research enterprise: University-corporate relations in science and technology* (pp. 121-127). Philadelphia: University of Pennsylvania Press.

Gould, S. J. (1991). The self-manipulation of my pervasive, perceived vital energy through product use: An introspective-praxis perspective. *Journal of Consumer Research, 18*(September), 194-207.

Graves, R. (1981). *Greek myths.* Garden City, NY: Doubleday.

Gray, W. (1985). *Homer to Joyce.* New York: Macmillan.

Green, P. E., & Carmone, F. J. (1970). *Multidimensional scaling and related techniques in marketing research.* Boston: Allyn & Bacon.

Green, P. E., & Srinivasan, V. (1978). Conjoint analysis in consumer research: Issues and outlook. *Journal of Consumer Research, 5*(September), 103-123.

Grünbaum, A. (1984). *The foundations of psychoanalysis: A philosophical critique.* Berkeley: University of California Press.

Guignon, C. B. (1983). *Heidegger and the problem of knowledge.* Indianapolis, IN: Hackett.

Guiraud, P. (1975). *Semiology.* London: Routledge & Kegan Paul.

Habermas, J. (1968). *Knowledge and human interests* (J. J. Shapiro, Trans.). Boston: Beacon.

Hackett, G. (1985, January 21). Newsmakers. *Newsweek,* p. 48.

Hackney, S. (1983). Prologue. In T. W. Langfitt, S. Hackney, A. P. Fishman, & A. V. Glowasky (Eds.), *Partners in the research enterprise: University-corporate relations in science and technology* (pp. xi-xv). Philadelphia: University of Pennsylvania Press.

Hagstrom, W. O. (1965). *The scientific community.* Carbondale: Southern Illinois University Press.

Haitch, R. (1985, October 13). Burying pets. *New York Times,* p. B1.

Hampshire, S. (1982). *Thought and action.* Notre Dame, IN: University of Notre Dame Press.

Hanson, N. R. (1958). *Patterns of discovery.* Cambridge, UK: Cambridge University Press.

Hardy, T. (1955). Shelley's skylark. In G. B. Woods & J. H. Buckley (Eds.), *Poetry of the Victorian period* (pp. 926-927). Chicago: Scott, Foresman. (Original work published 1887)

Havlena, W. J., & Holbrook, M. B. (1986). The varieties of consumption experience: Comparing two typologies of emotion in consumer behavior. *Journal of Consumer Research, 13*(December), 394-404.

Hawes, D. K., Talarzyk, W. W., & Blackwell, R. D. (1975). Consumer satisfactions from leisure time pursuits. In M.-J. Schlinger (Ed.), *Advances in consumer research* (Vol. 2, pp. 817-836). Chicago: Association for Consumer Research.

Hearne, V. (1987). *Adam's task: Calling animals by name.* New York: Vintage.

Helgeson, J. G., Kluge, E. A., Mager, J., & Taylor, C. (1984). Trends in consumer behavior literature: A content analysis. *Journal of Consumer Research, 10*(March), 449-454.

Henderson, J. M., & Quandt, R. E. (1958). *Microeconomic theory: A mathematical approach*. New York: McGraw-Hill.

Hendricks, J., & Parker, C. (1959). Now's the time [Recorded by D. Lambert, J. Hendricks, & A. Ross]. On *The swingers* [Record album]. Hollywood, CA: World Pacific Records.

Hickrod, L. J. H., & Schmitt, R. L. (1982). A naturalistic study of interaction and frame: The pet as "family member." *Urban Life, 11*(April), 55-77.

Hicks, J. R. (1946). *Value and capital* (2nd ed.). Oxford, UK: Clarendon.

Highwater, J. (1981). *The primal mind*. New York: Harper & Row.

Hirsch, E. D., Jr. (1967). *Validity in interpretation*. New Haven, CT: Yale University Press.

Hirschman, E. C. (1980). Attributes of attributes and layers of meaning. In J. C. Olson (Ed.), *Advances in consumer research* (Vol. 7, pp. 7-11). Ann Arbor, MI: Association for Consumer Research.

Hirschman, E. C. (1983). Aesthetics, ideologies, and the limits of the marketing concept. *Journal of Marketing, 47*(Summer), 45-55.

Hirschman, E. C. (1985a). Primitive aspects of consumption in modern American society. *Journal of Consumer Research, 12*(September), 142-154.

Hirschman, E. C. (1985b). Scientific style and the conduct of consumer research. *Journal of Consumer Research, 12*(September), 225-239.

Hirschman, E. C. (1986a). Humanistic inquiry in marketing research: Philosophy, method, and criteria. *Journal of Marketing Research, 23*(August), 237-249.

Hirschman, E. C. (1986b). Marketing, intellectual creativity, and consumer research. In R. J. Lutz (Ed.), *Advances in consumer research* (Vol. 13, pp. 433-435). Provo, UT: Association for Consumer Research.

Hirschman, E. C. (1987). Movies as myths: An interpretation of motion picture mythology. In J. Umiker-Sebeok (Ed.), *Marketing and semiotics: New directions in the study of signs for sale* (pp. 335-373). Berlin: Mouton de Gruyter.

Hirschman, E. C. (Ed.). (1989). *Interpretive consumer research*. Provo, UT: Association for Consumer Research.

Hirschman, E. C. (1991). Presidential address: Secular mortality and the dark side of consumer behavior: Or how semiotics saved my life. In R. H. Holman & M. R. Solomon (Eds.), *Advances in consumer research* (Vol. 18, pp. 1-4). Provo, UT: Association for Consumer Research.

Hirschman, E. C. (1993). Ideology in consumer research, 1980 and 1990: A Marxist and feminist critique. *Journal of Consumer Research, 19*(March), 537-555.

Hirschman, E. C. (1994). Consumers and their animal companions. *Journal of Consumer Research, 20*(March), 616-632.

Hirschman, E. C., & Holbrook, M. B. (Eds.). (1981). *Symbolic consumer behavior*. Ann Arbor, MI: Association for Consumer Research.

Hirschman, E. C., & Holbrook, M. B. (1982). Hedonic consumption: Emerging concepts, methods, and propositions. *Journal of Marketing, 46*(Summer), 92-101.

Hirschman, E. C., & Holbrook, M. B. (1986). Expanding the ontology and methodology of research on the consumption experience. In D. Brinberg & R. J. Lutz (Eds.), *Perspectives on methodology in consumer research* (pp. 213-251). New York: Springer-Verlag.

Hirschman, E. C., & Holbrook, M. B. (1992). *Postmodern consumer research: The study of consumption as text.* Newbury Park, CA: Sage.

Hofstadter, A. (1979). On the interpretation of works of art. In B. Lang (Ed.), *The concept of style* (pp. 67-91). Philadelphia: University of Pennsylvania Press.

Hofstadter, R. (1955). *Academic freedom in the age of the college.* New York: Columbia University Press.

Holbrook, M. B. (1974). Oscar Peterson. *Different Drummer, 1*(December), p. 22.

Holbrook, M. B. (1975). *A study of communication in advertising.* Unpublished doctoral dissertation, Columbia University, Graduate School of Business.

Holbrook, M. B. (1977). Comparing multiattribute attitude models by optimal scaling. *Journal of Consumer Research, 4*(December), 165-171.

Holbrook, M. B. (1978). Beyond attitude structure: Toward the informational determinants of attitude. *Journal of Marketing Research, 15*(November), 545-556.

Holbrook, M. B. (1980). Some preliminary notes on research in consumer esthetics. In J. C. Olson (Ed.), *Advances in consumer research* (Vol. 7, pp. 104-108). Ann Arbor, MI: Association for Consumer Research.

Holbrook, M. B. (1981). Integrating compositional and decompositional analyses to represent the intervening role of perceptions in evaluative judgments. *Journal of Marketing Research, 18*(February), 13-28.

Holbrook, M. B. (1982). Mapping the market for esthetic products: The case of jazz records. *Journal of Retailing, 58*(Spring), 114-129.

Holbrook, M. B. (1984). Theory development is a jazz solo: Bird lives. In P. F. Anderson & M. J. Ryan (Eds.), *Proceedings of the 1984 AMA Winter Educators' Conference* (pp. 48-52). Chicago: American Marketing Association.

Holbrook, M. B. (1985a). The consumer researcher visits Radio City: Dancing in the dark. In E. C. Hirschman & M. B. Holbrook (Eds.), *Advances in consumer research* (Vol. 12, pp. 28-31). Provo, UT: Association for Consumer Research.

Holbrook, Morris B. (1985b). Why business is bad for consumer research: The three bears revisited. In E. C. Hirschman & M. B. Holbrook (Eds.), *Advances in consumer research* (Vol. 12, pp. 145-156). Provo, UT: Association for Consumer Research.

Holbrook, M. B. (1986a). Aims, concepts, and methods for the representation of individual differences in esthetic responses to design features. *Journal of Consumer Research, 13*(December), 337-347.

Holbrook, M. B. (1986b). *Consumer misbehavior: The nature of irregular, irrational, illegal, and immoral consumption.* Unpublished manuscript, Columbia University.

Holbrook, M. B. (1986c). Emotion in the consumption experience: Toward a new model of the human consumer. In R. A. Peterson, W. D. Hoyer, & W. R.

Wilson (Eds.), *The role of affect in consumer behavior: Emerging theories and applications* (pp. 17-52). Lexington, MA: D. C. Heath.

Holbrook, M. B. (1986d). *Greatness in consumption.* Unpublished manuscript, Columbia University, Graduate School of Business.

Holbrook, M. B. (1986e). I'm hip: An autobiographical account of some musical consumption experiences. In R. J. Lutz (Ed)., *Advances in consumer research* (Vol. 13, pp. 614-618). Provo, UT: Association for Consumer Research.

Holbrook, M. B. (1986f). Whither ACR? Some pastoral reflections on bears, Baltimore, baseball, and resurrecting consumer research. In R. J. Lutz (Ed.), *Advances in consumer research* (Vol. 13, pp. 436-441). Provo, UT: Association for Consumer Research.

Holbrook, M. B. (1987a). An audiovisual inventory of some fanatic consumer behavior: The 25-cent tour of a jazz collector's home. In M. Wallendorf & P. F. Anderson (Eds.), *Advances in consumer research* (Vol. 14, pp. 144-149). Provo, UT: Association for Consumer Research.

Holbrook, M. B. (1987b). From the log of a consumer researcher: Reflections on the odyssey. In M. Wallendorf & P. F. Anderson (Eds.), *Advances in consumer research* (Vol. 14, pp. 365-369). Provo, UT: Association for Consumer Research.

Holbrook, M. B. (1987c). Mirror, mirror, on the wall, what's unfair in the reflections on advertising? *Journal of Marketing, 51* (July), 95-103.

Holbrook, M. B. (1987d). O, consumer, how you've changed: Some radical reflections on the roots of consumption. In F. Fırat, N. Dholakia, & R. Bagozzi (Eds.), *Philosophical and radical thought in marketing* (pp. 156-177). Lexington, MA: D. C. Heath.

Holbrook, M. B. (1987e). Progress and problems in research on consumer esthetics. In D. V. Shaw, W. S. Hendon, & C. R. Waits (Eds.), *Artists and cultural consumers* (pp. 133-146). Akron, OH: Association for Cultural Economics.

Holbrook, M. B. (1987f). Some notes on the banausic interrelationships among marketing academics and practitioners. In R. W. Belk & G. Zaltman (Eds.), *Proceedings of the Winter Educators' Conference* (pp. 342-343). Chicago: American Marketing Association.

Holbrook, M. B. (1987g). The study of signs in consumer esthetics: An egocentric review. In J. Umiker-Sebeok (Ed.), *Marketing and semiotics: New directions in the study of signs for sale* (pp. 73-121). Berlin: Mouton de Gruyter.

Holbrook, M. B. (1987h). What is consumer research? *Journal of Consumer Research, 14* (June), 128-132.

Holbrook, M. B. (1988a). The psychoanalytic interpretation of consumer research: I am an animal. *Research in Consumer Behavior, 3,* 149-178.

Holbrook, M. B. (1988b). Steps toward a psychoanalytic interpretation of consumption: A meta-meta-meta-analysis of some issues raised by the consumer behavior odyssey. In M. J. Houston (Ed.), *Advances in consumer research* (Vol. 15, pp. 537-542). Provo, UT: Association for Consumer Research.

Holbrook, M. B. (1989a, September). Aftermath of the task force: Dogmatism and catastrophe in the development of marketing thought. *ACR Newsletter,* pp. 1-11.

Holbrook, M. B. (Ed.). (1989b). *John A. Howard: A life in learning* [Videotape interview]. Chicago: American Marketing Association.

Holbrook, M. B. (1989c, June). "These foolish things," "The dear departed past," and the songs of David Frishberg: A commentary and critique [President's column]. *ACR Newsletter*, pp. 1-8.

Holbrook, M. B. (1990a, September). Holbrook's reply to Pechmann: Prelude and poem. *ACR Newsletter*, p. 4.

Holbrook, M. B. (1990b, December). On hatching a program of consumer research: An elephant's faithful one hundred percent. *ACR Newsletter*, pp. 15-18.

Holbrook, M. B. (1990c). The role of lyricism in research on consumer emotions: Skylark, have you anything to say to me? In M. Goldberg, G. Gorn, & R. Pollay (Eds.), *Advances in consumer research* (Vol. 17, pp. 1-18). Provo, UT: Association for Consumer Research.

Holbrook, M. B. (1991a). Discussion group 4: The effectiveness of emotional ads and campaigns in a complex media environment. In C. Yoon (Ed.), *Tears, cheers, and fears: The role of emotions in advertising* (Conference Summary, Report No. 91-112, pp. 49-50). Cambridge, MA: Marketing Science Institute.

Holbrook, M. B. (1991b). From the log of a consumer researcher. In R. W. Belk (Ed.), *Highways and buyways: Naturalistic research from the consumer behavior odyssey* (pp. 14-33). Provo, UT: Association for Consumer Research.

Holbrook, M. B. (1991c). Romanticism and sentimentality in consumer behavior: A literary approach to the joys and sorrows of consumption. *Research in Consumer Behavior*, 5, 105-180.

Holbrook, M. B. (1992). Just Junior, Dizzy, and me on the way to our gig. *Marketing Signs*, 14-15, 1, 15-18.

Holbrook, M. B. (1993a). *Daytime television game shows and the celebration of merchandise: The Price Is Right*. Bowling Green, OH: Bowling Green State University Popular Press.

Holbrook, M. B. (1993b). The nature of customer value: An axiology of services in the consumption experience. In R. T. Rust & R. L. Oliver (Eds.), *Service quality: New directions in theory and practice* (pp. 21-71). Newbury Park, CA: Sage.

Holbrook, M. B. (1993c). Nostalgia and consumption preferences: Some emerging patterns of consumer tastes. *Journal of Consumer Research*, 20(September), 245-256.

Holbrook, M. B. (1993d). On the new nostalgia: "These foolish things" and echoes of the dear departed past. In R. B. Browne & R. J. Ambrosetti (Eds.), *Continuities in popular culture: The present in the past & the past in the present and future* (pp. 74-120). Bowling Green, OH: Bowling Green State University.

Holbrook, M. B. (1994a). Axiology, aesthetics, and apparel: Some reflections on the old school tie. In M. DeLong & A-M. Fiore (Eds.), *Aesthetics of textiles and clothing: Advancing multi-disciplinary perspectives*. (ITAA Special Publication #7; pp. 131-141). Monument, CO: International Textile and Apparel Association.

Holbrook, M. B. (1994b). Ethics in consumer research: An overview and prospectus. In C. T. Allen & D. R. John (Eds.), *Advances in consumer research* (Vol. 21, pp. 566-571). Provo, UT: Association for Consumer Research.

Holbrook, M. B. (1994c). Loving and hating New York: Some reflections on the Big Apple. *International Journal of Research in Marketing, 11* (September), 381-385.

Holbrook, M. B. (1994d). Nostalgia proneness and consumer tastes. In J. A. Howard, *Buyer behavior in marketing strategy* (2nd ed., pp. 348-364). Englewood Cliffs, NJ: Prentice Hall.

Holbrook, M. B. (1994e). Postmodernism and social theory. *Journal of Macromarketing, 13* (Fall), 69-75.

Holbrook, M. B., & Batra, R. (1987). Assessing the role of emotions as mediators of consumer responses to advertising. *Journal of Consumer Research, 14* (December), 404-420.

Holbrook, M. B., Bell, S., & Grayson, M. W. (1989). The role of the humanities in consumer research: Close encounters and coastal disturbances. In E. C. Hirschman (Ed.), *Interpretive consumer research* (pp. 29-47). Provo, UT: Association for Consumer Research.

Holbrook, M. B., & Bertges, S. A. (1981). Perceptual veridicality in esthetic communication: A model, general procedure, and illustration. *Communication Research, 8* (October), 387-424.

Holbrook, M. B., Chestnut, R. W., Oliva, T. A., & Greenleaf, E. A. (1984). Play as a consumption experience: The roles of emotions, performance, and personality in the enjoyment of games. *Journal of Consumer Research, 11* (September). 728-739.

Holbrook, M. B., & Corfman, K. P. (1985). Quality and value in the consumption experience: Phaedrus rides again. In J. Jacoby & J. C. Olson (Eds.), *Perceived quality: How consumers view stores and merchandise* (pp. 31-57). Lexington, MA: D. C. Heath.

Holbrook, M. B., & Day, E. (1994). Reflections on jazz and teaching: Benny, Woody, and we. *European Journal of Marketing, 28* (8/9), 133-144.

Holbrook, M. B., & Dixon, G. (1985). Mapping the market for fashion: Complementarity in consumer preferences. In M. B. Solomon (Ed.), *The psychology of fashion* (pp. 109-126). Lexington, MA: D. C. Heath.

Holbrook, M. B., & Gardner, M. P. (1993). An approach to investigating the emotional determinants of consumption durations: Why do people consume what they consume for as long as they consume it? *Journal of Consumer Psychology, 2* (2), 123-142.

Holbrook, M. B., & Grayson, M. W. (1986). The semiology of cinematic consumption: Symbolic consumer behavior in *Out of Africa. Journal of Consumer Research, 13* (December), 374-381.

Holbrook, M. B., & Hirschman, E. C. (1982). The experiential aspects of consumption: Consumer fantasies, feelings, and fun. *Journal of Consumer Research, 9* (September), 132-140.

Holbrook, M. B., & Hirschman, E. C. (1993). *The semiotics of consumption: Interpreting symbolic consumer behavior in popular culture and works of art.* Berlin: Mouton de Gruyter.

Holbrook, M. B., & Holloway, D. V. (1984). Marketing strategy and the structure of aggregate, segment-specific, and differential preferences. *Journal of Marketing, 48*(Winter), 62-67.

Holbrook, M. B., & Howard, J. A. (1977). Frequently purchased nondurable goods and services. In R. Ferber (Ed.), *Selected aspects of consumer behavior* (pp. 189-222). Washington, DC: National Science Foundation.

Holbrook, M. B., & Huber, J. (1979a). Separating perceptual dimensions from affective overtones: An application to consumer research. *Journal of Consumer Research, 5*(March), 272-283.

Holbrook, M. B., & Huber, J. (1979b). The spatial representation of responses toward jazz: Applications of consumer esthetics to mapping the market for music. *Journal of Jazz Studies, 5*(Spring/Summer), 3-22.

Holbrook, M. B., & Lehmann, D. R. (1981). Allocating discretionary time: Complementarity among activities. *Journal of Consumer Research, 7*(March), 395-406.

Holbrook, M. B., Lehmann, D. R., & O'Shaughnessy, J. (1986). Using versus choosing: The relationship of the consumption experience to reasons for purchasing. *European Journal of Marketing, 20*(8), 49-62.

Holbrook, M. B., & Olney, T. J. (in press). Romanticism and the wanderlust: An effect of personality on consumer preferences. *Psychology & Marketing.*

Holbrook, M. B., & O'Shaughnessy, J. (1984). The role of emotion in advertising. *Psychology & Marketing, 1*(2), 45-64.

Holbrook, M. B., & O'Shaughnessy, J. (1988). On the scientific status of consumer research and the need for an interpretive approach to studying consumption behavior. *Journal of Consumer Research, 15*(December), 398-402.

Holbrook, M. B., O'Shaughnessy, J., & Bell, S. (1990). Actions and reactions in the consumption experience: The complementary roles of reasons and emotions in consumer behavior. *Research in Consumer Behavior, 4*, 131-163.

Holbrook, M. B., & Ryan, M. J. (1982). Modeling decision-specific stress: Some methodological considerations. *Administrative Science Quarterly, 27*, 243-258.

Holbrook, M. B., & Schindler, R. M. (1989). Some exploratory findings on the development of musical tastes. *Journal of Consumer Research, 16*(June), 119-124.

Holbrook, M. B., & Schindler, R. M. (1991). Echoes of the dear departed past: Some work in progress on nostalgia. In R. H. Holman & M. R. Solomon (Eds.), *Advances in consumer research* (Vol. 18, pp. 330-333). Provo, UT: Association for Consumer Research.

Holbrook, M. B., & Schindler, R. M. (1994a). Age, sex, and attitude toward the past as predictors of consumers' aesthetic tastes for cultural products. *Journal of Marketing Research, 31*(August), 412-422.

Holbrook, M. B., & Schindler, R. M. (1994b). *Market segmentation based on age and attitude toward the past: Concepts, methods, and findings concerning nostalgic influences on customer tastes.* Unpublished manuscript, Columbia University, Graduate School of Business.

Holbrook, M. B., & Williams, R. S. (1978). A test of the correspondence between perceptual spaces based on pairwise similarity judgments collected with and without the inclusion of explicit ideal objects. *Journal of Applied Psychology, 63,* 373-376.

Holbrook, M. B., & Zirlin, R. B. (1985). Artistic creation, artworks, and aesthetic appreciation: Some philosophical contributions to nonprofit marketing. In R. W. Belk (Ed.), *Advances in nonprofit marketing* (Vol. 1, pp. 1-54). Greenwich, CT: JAI.

Holland, N. N. (1973). *Poems in persons: An introduction to the psychoanalysis of literature.* New York: Norton.

Hollway, W. (1989). *Subjectivity and method in psychology: Gender, meaning, and science.* Newbury Park, CA: Sage.

Holman, R. H. (1980). A transcription and analysis system for the study of women's clothing behavior. *Semiotica, 32*(12), 11-34.

Holman, R. H. (1981). Product use as communication: A fresh look at a venerable topic. In B. M. Enis & K. J. Roering (Eds.), *Review of marketing* (pp. 106-119). Chicago: American Marketing Association.

Holt, D. B. (1991). Rashomon visits consumer behavior: An interpretive critique of naturalistic inquiry. In R. H. Holman & M. R. Solomon (Eds.), *Advances in consumer research* (Vol. 18, pp. 57-62). Provo, UT: Association for Consumer Research.

Holton, G. (1978). From the endless frontier to the ideology of limits. In G. Holton & R. S. Morison (Eds), *Limits of scientific inquiry* (pp. 227-241). New York: Norton.

Holton, G., & Morison, R. S. (Eds.). (1978). *Limits of scientific inquiry.* New York: Norton.

Horn, J. C., & Meer, J. (1984, August). The pleasure of their company. *Psychology Today, 18,* pp. 52-58.

Hospers, J. (1967). Problems of aesthetics. In P. Edwards (Ed.), *The encyclopedia of philosophy* (Vol. 1, pp. 35-56). New York: Macmillan.

Howard, J. A. (1963a). *Marketing: Executive and buyer behavior.* New York: Columbia University Press.

Howard, J. A. (1963b). *Marketing management.* Homewood, IL: Irwin.

Howard, J. A. (1977). *Consumer behavior: Application of theory.* New York: McGraw-Hill.

Howard, J. A. (1983). Marketing theory of the firm. *Journal of Marketing, 47*(Fall), 90-100.

Howard, J. A. (1989). *Consumer behavior in marketing strategy.* Englewood Cliffs, NJ: Prentice Hall.

Howard, J. A. (1994). *Buyer behavior in marketing strategy* (2nd ed.). Englewood Cliffs, NJ: Prentice Hall.

Howard, J. A., & Sheth, J. N. (1969). *The theory of buyer behavior.* New York: John Wiley.

Huber, J. (1975). Predicting preferences on experimental bundles of attributes: A comparison of models. *Journal of Marketing Research, 12*(August), 290-297.

Hudson, L. A., & Ozanne, J. L. (1988). Alternative ways of seeking knowledge in consumer research. *Journal of Consumer Research, 14*(March), 508-521.

Huizinga, J. (1938). *Homo ludens.* New York: Harper & Row.

Hunt, S. D. (1983). *Marketing theory: The philosophy of marketing science.* Homewood, IL: Irwin.

Hunt, S. D. (1991). Positivism and paradigm dominance in consumer research: Toward critical pluralism and rapprochement. *Journal of Consumer Research, 18*(June), 32-44.

Hunter, J. (1983). Truth and effectiveness in revelatory stories. *ReVision, 6*(Fall), 3-15.

Hutt, P. B. (1978). Public criticism of health science policy. In G. Holton & R. S. Morison (Eds.), *Limits of scientific inquiry* (pp. 157-170). New York: Norton.

Huxley, A. (1963). *Literature and science.* New Haven: Leete's Island Books.

Hyde, L. (1983). *The gift: Imagination and the erotic life of property.* New York: Vintage.

Jackson, L. G. (1976). Lore and legends of the cat. In J. Fireman (Ed.), *Cat catalog: The ultimate cat book* (pp. 31-35). New York: Workman.

Jacoby, J. (1975). Consumer psychology as a social psychological sphere of action. *American Psychologist, 30*(October), 977-987.

Jacoby, J. (1978). Consumer research: A state of the art review. *Journal of Marketing, 42*(April), 87-96.

Jacoby, J. (1985a). Serving two masters: Perspectives on consulting. In E. C. Hirschman & M. B. Holbrook (Eds.), *Advances in consumer research* (Vol. 12, p. 144). Provo, UT: Association for Consumer Research.

Jacoby, J. (1985b). The vices and virtues of consulting: Responding to a fairy tale. In E. C. Hirschman & M. B. Holbrook (Eds.), *Advances in consumer research* (Vol. 12, pp. 157-163). Provo, UT: Association for Consumer Research.

Jakobson, R. (Ed.). (1976). The contours of *The Safe Conduct.* In L. Matejka & I. R. Titunik (Eds.), *Semiotics of art: Prague school contributions* (pp. 188-196). Cambridge: MIT Press.

Jaynes, J. (1976). *The origin of consciousness in the breakdown of the bicameral mind.* Boston: Houghton Mifflin.

Jefferson, E. (1968). Now's the time (By C. Parker & E. Jefferson). On *There I go again* (1980) [Record album]. Prestige (P-24095).

Jenkins, I. (1962). Romanticism. In D. D. Runes (Ed.), *Dictionary of philosophy* (pp. 272-273). Totowa, NJ: Littlefield, Adams.

Jeske, L. (1981, August). Jimmy Knepper. *Down Beat, 48,* pp. 14-17, 66-67.

Johnson, W. R. (1982). *The idea of lyric: Lyric modes in ancient and modern poetry.* Berkeley: University of California Press.

Jones, R. S. (1982). *Physics as metaphor.* New York: New American Library.

Jorgensen, D. L. (1989). *Participant observation: A methodology for human studies.* Newbury Park, CA: Sage.

Joyce, J. (1986). *Ulysses* (H. W. Gabler, Ed.). New York: Vintage. (Original work published 1922)

Kant, I. (1957). Critique of the aesthetical judgement. In T. M. Green (Ed.), *Kant selections* (pp. 375-445). New York: Scribner. (Original work published 1790)

Kassarjian, H. H. (1974). Projective methods. In R. Ferber (Ed.), *Handbook of marketing research* (pp. 3-85 through 3-100). New York: McGraw-Hill.

Kassarjian, H. H. (1983). Social values and the Sunday comics: A content analysis. In R. P. Bagozzi & A. M. Tybout (Eds.), *Advances in consumer research* (Vol. 10, pp. 434-438). Ann Arbor, MI: Association for Consumer Research.

Kaufmann, W. (1974). *Nietzsche: Philosopher, psychologist, antichrist* (4th ed.). Princeton, NJ: Princeton University Press.

Keats, J. (1948). Ode on melancholy. In E. Bernbaum (Ed.), *Anthology of romanticism* (pp. 820-821). New York: Ronald Press. (Original work published 1820)

Kehret-Ward, T., & Yalch, R. (1984). To take or not to take the only one: Effects of changing the meaning of a product attribute on choice behavior. *Journal of Consumer Research, 10*(March), 410-416.

Keller, E. F. (1985). *Reflections on gender and science.* New Haven, CT: Yale University Press.

Kennedy: Future academic research policy. (1982, July 19). *Chemical and Engineering News*, pp. 35-40.

Kermode, F. (1957). *Romantic image.* New York: Routledge & Kegan Paul.

Kerr, C. (1982). *The uses of the university.* Cambridge, MA: Harvard University Press.

Kidd, I. G. (1967). Cyrenaics. In P. Edwards (Ed.), *The encyclopedia of philosophy* (Vol. 2, pp. 286-287). New York: Macmillan.

Kiley, T. D. (1983). Licensing revenue for universities: Impediments and possibilities. In T. W. Langfitt, S. Hackney, A. P. Fishman, & A. V. Glowasky (Eds.), *Partners in the research enterprise: University-corporate relations in science and technology* (pp. 59-67). Philadelphia: University of Pennsylvania Press.

King, S., & Straub, P. (1984). *The talisman.* New York: Viking.

Klinkowitz, J. (1991). *Listen: Gerry Mulligan, an aural narrative in jazz.* New York: Schirmer.

Koestler, A. (1964). *The act of creation.* New York: Dell.

Köhler, W. (1925). *The mentality of apes.* New York: Harcourt, Brace.

Kordig, C. R. (1978). Discovery and justification. *Philosophy of Science, 45,* 110-117.

Kotler, P. J. (1972). A generic concept of marketing. *Journal of Marketing, 36*(April), 46-54.

Kotler, P. J. (1988). *Marketing management* (6th ed.). Englewood Cliffs, NJ: Prentice Hall.

Kotler, P. J., & Levy, S. J. (1969). Broadening the concept of marketing. *Journal of Marketing, 33*(January), 10-15.

Kruskal, J. B., & Wish, M. (1978). *Multidimensional scaling.* Beverly Hills, CA: Sage.

Kuhn, T. S. (1970a). Reflections on my critics. In I. Lakatos & A. Musgrave (Eds.), *Criticism and the growth of knowledge* (pp. 231-278). Cambridge, UK: Cambridge University Press.

Kuhn, T. S. (1970b). *The structure of scientific revolutions* (2nd ed.). Chicago: University of Chicago Press.

Kuhn, T. S. (1977). *The essential tension: Selected studies in scientific tradition and change.* Chicago: University of Chicago Press.

Kuhns, R. (1983). *Psychoanalytic theory of art: A philosophy of art on developmental principles.* New York: Columbia University Press.

Lakoff, G., & Johnson, M. (1980). *Metaphors we live by.* Chicago: University of Chicago Press.

Lambert, D., Hendricks, J., & Ross, A. (1959). Now's the time (By C. Parker & J. Hendricks). On *The swingers* [Record album]. World Pacific Records (WP-1264).

Lancaster, K. (1971). *Consumer demand: A new approach.* New York: Columbia University Press.

Lancaster, K. (1974). *Variety, equity, and efficiency.* New York: Columbia University Press.

Langfitt, T. W., Hackney, S., Fishman, A. P., & Glowasky, A. V. (Eds.). (1983). *Partners in the research enterprise: University-corporate relations in science and technology.* Philadelphia: University of Pennsylvania Press.

Leary, W. E. (1989, June 12). Business and scholarship: A new ethical quandary. *New York Times,* p. A1.

Lefferts, N. E. (1985, July 28). What's new in the pet business. *New York Times,* p. F15.

Lehmann-Haupt, C. (1986, June 9). The 4 deadly fallacies, pathetic and otherwise. *New York Times,* p. C21.

Lemonick, M. D. (1989, May 8). Fusion illusion? *Time,* pp. 72-77.

Leong, S. M. (1985). Metatheory and metamethodology in marketing: A Lakatosian reconstruction. *Journal of Marketing, 49*(Fall), 23-40.

Leontief, W. (1986, January 12) A + B = goodness. *New York Times Book Review,* p. 7.

Levey, M. (1985). Introduction. *Marius the epicurean,* by Walter Pater (pp. 7-26). Harmondsworth, UK: Penguin.

Levitt, T. (1960). Marketing myopia. *Harvard Business Review, 38*(July/August), 45-56.

Levitt, T. (1962). *Innovation in marketing.* New York: McGraw-Hill.

Levy, S. J. (1959). Symbols for sale. *Harvard Business Review, 37*(July-August), 117-124.

Levy, S. J. (1976). Marcology 101 or the domain of marketing. In K. L. Bernhardt (Ed.), *Marketing: 1776-1976 and beyond* (pp. 577-581). Chicago: American Marketing Association.

Levy, S. J. (1981). Interpreting consumer mythology: A structural approach to consumer behavior. *Journal of Marketing, 45* (Summer), 49-61.

Lewin, K. (1936). *Principles of topological psychology* (F. Heider & G. M. Heider, Trans.). New York: McGraw-Hill.

Lewin, K. (1951). *Field theory in social science: Selected theoretical papers* (D. Cartwright, Ed.). Chicago: University of Chicago Press.

Lincoln, Y. S., & Guba, E. G. (1985). *Naturalistic inquiry.* Beverly Hills, CA: Sage.

Lindblom, C. E., & Cohen, D. K. (1979). *Usable knowledge.* New Haven, CT: Yale University Press.

Lipsey, R. G., & Steiner, P. O. (1969). *Economics* (2nd ed.). New York: Harper & Row.

Lothrop, Lee & Shepard Books. (1982). *Goldilocks and the three bears.* New York: Walker.

Low, G. M. (1983). The organization of industrial relationships in universities. In T. W. Langfitt, S. Hackney, A. P. Fishman, & A. V. Glowasky (Eds.), *Partners in the research enterprise: University-corporate relations in science and technology* (pp. 68-80). Philadelphia: University of Pennsylvania Press.

Lurie, A. (1981). *The language of clothes.* New York: Vintage.

Lutz, R. J. (1985, Winter). Call for papers: 1985 ACR conference. *ACR Newsletter, 15,* pp. 5-7.

Lutz, R. J. (1989). Presidential address, 1988: Positivism, naturalism and pluralism in consumer research, paradigms in paradise. In T. K. Srull (Ed.), *Advances in consumer research* (Vol. 16, pp. 1-8). Provo, UT: Association for Consumer Research.

Makkreel, R. A. (1975). *Dilthey: Philosopher of the human studies.* Princeton, NJ: Princeton University Press.

Mandler, G. (1975). *Mind and emotion.* New York: John Wiley.

Marshall, A. (1920). *Principles of economics.* New York: Macmillan.

Martineau, P. (1957). *Motivation in advertising.* New York: McGraw-Hill.

McCloskey, D. N. (1985). *The rhetoric of economics.* Madison: University of Wisconsin Press.

McCracken, G. (1988). *Culture as consumption: New approaches to the symbolic character of consumer goods and activities.* Bloomington: Indiana University Press.

McGlynn, D. (Producer and Director). (1982). *Notes from a jazz survivor* [Documentary videotape]. Los Angeles: Winter Moon Productions.

McKeon, R. (1954). *Thought, action, and passion.* Chicago: University of Chicago Press.

McKeon, R. (1987). *Rhetoric: Essays in invention and discovery* (M. Backman, Ed.). Woodbridge, CT: Ox Bow.

McKusick, H. (1957). Now's the time (By C. Parker). On *Cross section—saxes* [Record album]. Decca (DL 79209).

McMurry, R. N. (1944). Psychology in selling. *Journal of Marketing, 9* (October), 114-118.

Meer, J. (1984, August). Pet theories. *Psychology Today, 18,* pp. 60-67.

Megill, A. (1985). *Prophets of extremity: Nietzsche, Heidegger, Foucault, Derrida.* Berkeley: University of California Press.

Mercer, J., & Elman, Z. (1939). And the angels sing [Song]. Los Angeles: Warner Chappel Music.

Merriam-Webster's collegiate dictionary (10th ed.). (1993). Springfield, MA: Merriam-Webster.

Metzger, W. P. (1955). *Academic freedom in the age of the university.* New York: Columbia University Press.

Meyer, L. B. (1956). *Emotion and meaning in music.* Chicago: University of Chicago Press.

Meyer, L. B. (1967). *Music, the arts, and ideas.* Chicago: University of Chicago Press.

Mick, D. G. (1986). Consumer research and semiotics: Exploring the morphology of signs, symbols, and significance. *Journal of Consumer Research, 13*(September), 196-213.

Midler, B. (1973). Skylark (By H. Carmichael & J. Mercer). On *Bette Midler* [Record album]. Atlantic (SD 7270 0598).

Miller, J. B. (1976). *Toward a new psychology of women.* Boston: Beacon.

Mills, C. W. (1959). *The sociological imagination.* New York: Oxford University Press.

Milton, J. (1957). Lycidas. In M. Y. Hughes (Ed.), *John Milton: Complete poems and major prose* (pp. 120-125). New York: Odyssey. (Original work published 1637)

Milton, J. (1957). Paradise lost. In M. Y. Hughes (Ed.), *John Milton: Complete poems and major prose* (pp. 206-469). New York: Odyssey. (Original work published 1674)

Milwaukee Country Day School. (1961). *The arrow.* Milwaukee: Author.

Miniard, P. W., & Cohen, J. B. (1983). Modeling personal and normative influences on behavior. *Journal of Consumer Research, 10*(September), 169-180.

Mitroff, I. I., & Kilmann, R. H. (1978). *Methodological approaches to social science.* San Francisco: Jossey-Bass.

Monk, W. H. (1940). Abide with me (Hymn No. 467, 1940 hymnal) [Hymn]. (Original work published 1861)

Montaigne, M. de. (1958). *The complete essays of Montaigne* (D. M. Frame, Trans.). Stanford, CA: Stanford University Press. (Original work published 1595)

Moore, W. L., & Holbrook, M. B. (1982). On the predictive validity of joint-space models in consumer evaluations of new concepts. *Journal of Consumer Research, 9*(September), 206-210.

Moorman, C. (1984, February). *The prepared mind.* Paper presented at the American Marketing Association Winter Educators' Conference, Ft. Lauderdale.

Morris, C. (1946). *Signs, language, and behavior.* New York: George Braziller.

Morris, R. T. (1941). *The theory of consumer's demand.* New Haven, CT: Yale University Press.

Muller, S. (1983). REACTORS . . . Steven Muller. In T. W. Langfitt, S. Hackney, A. P. Fishman, & A. V. Glowasky (Eds.), *Partners in the research enterprise: Uni-*

versity-corporate relations in science and technology (pp. 146-147). Philadelphia: University of Pennsylvania Press.

Muncy, J. A., & Fisk, R. P. (1987). Cognitive relativism and the practice of marketing science. *Journal of Marketing, 51* (January), 20-33.

Murray, T. (1980). *Developing the ability to relate scarcity and communication value: How children come to use products as linguistic units.* Unpublished doctoral dissertation, University of Washington.

Myers, J. G., Massy, W. F., & Greyser, S. A. (1980). *Marketing research and knowledge development: An assessment for marketing managers.* Englewood Cliffs, NJ: Prentice Hall.

Nagel, T. (1986). *The view from nowhere.* New York: Oxford University Press.

Nehamas, A. (1985). *Nietzsche: Life as literature.* Cambridge, MA: Harvard University Press.

Nelkin, D. (1978). Threats and promises: Negotiating the control of research. In G. Holton & R. S. Morison (Eds.), *Limits of scientific inquiry* (pp. 191-210). New York: Norton.

Nelson, J. S. (1987a). Seven rhetorics of inquiry: A provocation. In J. S. Nelson, A. Megill, & D. N. McCloskey (Eds.), *The rhetoric of the human sciences* (pp. 407-434). Madison: University of Wisconsin Press.

Nelson, J. S. (1987b). Stories of science and politics: Some rhetorics of political research. In J. S. Nelson, A. Megill, & D. N. McCloskey (Eds.), *The rhetoric of the human sciences* (pp. 198-220). Madison: University of Wisconsin Press.

Nelson, J. S., Megill, A., & McCloskey, D. N. (Eds.). (1987). *The rhetoric of the human sciences: Language and argument in scholarship and public affairs.* Madison: University of Wisconsin Press.

Neslin, S. A. (1981). Linking product features to perceptions: Self-stated versus statistically revealed importance weights. *Journal of Marketing Research, 18* (February), 80-86.

Newman, J. W. (1955). Looking around: Consumer motivation research. *Harvard Business Review, 33* (January/February), 135-144.

Newman, J. W. (Ed.). (1966). *On knowing the consumer.* New York: John Wiley.

Nickols, S. Y., & Fox, K. D. (1983). Buying time and saving time: Strategies for managing household production. *Journal of Consumer Research, 10* (September), 197-208.

Nicosia, F. M. (1966). *Consumer decision processes.* Englewood Cliffs, NJ: Prentice Hall.

Nozick, R. (1981). *Philosophical explanations.* Cambridge, MA: Harvard University Press.

O'Guinn, T. C., & Faber, R. J. (1989). Compulsive buying: A phenomenological exploration. *Journal of Consumer Research, 16* (September), 147-157.

O'Guinn, T. C., Wei-Na Lee, & Faber, R. J. (1986). Acculturation: The impact of divergent paths of buyer behavior. In R. J. Lutz (Ed.), *Advances in consumer research* (Vol. 13, pp. 579-583). Provo, UT: Association for Consumer Research.

Oliver, R. L. (1984). *Expressions of satisfaction up and down the phylogenetic continuum* (Special Topic Session). Washington, DC: Association for Consumer Research.

Oliver, R. L., & Bearden, W. O. (1985). Crossover effects in the theory of reasoned action: A moderating influence attempt. *Journal of Consumer Research, 12*(December), 324-340.

Olson, J. C. (1982). Presidential address—1981: Toward a science of consumer research. In A. Mitchell (Ed.), *Advances in consumer research* (Vol. 9, pp. v-x). Ann Arbor, MI: Association for Consumer Research.

Omenn, G. S. (1983). University-corporate relations in science and technology: An analysis of specific models. In T. W. Langfitt, S. Hackney, A. P. Fishman, & A. V. Glowasky (Eds.), *Partners in the research enterprise: University-corporate relations in science and technology* (pp. 23-32). Philadelphia: University of Pennsylvania Press.

O'Neill, E. (1957). *A touch of the poet.* New York: Vintage.

Osborne, H. (1970). *Aesthetics and art theory.* New York: E. P. Dutton.

O'Shaughnessy, J. (1987). *Why people buy.* New York: Oxford University Press.

O'Shaughnessy, J. (1992). *Explaining buyer behavior: Central concepts and philosophy of science issues.* New York: Oxford University Press.

O'Shaughnessy, J., & Holbrook, M. B. (1988). Understanding consumer behavior: The linguistic turn in marketing research. *Journal of the Market Research Society, 30*(2), 197-223.

Packard, V. (1957). *The hidden persuaders.* New York: Pocket Books.

Parker, C. (1988). Now's the time (By C. Parker). On *The complete Charlie Parker Savoy sessions* [Record album]. Savoy Jazz (ZDS 5500-1). (Original work recorded 1945)

Parker, C. (1988). Now's the time (By C. Parker). On *BIRD: The complete Charlie Parker on Verve* [Record album]. Verve (CD 837 152-2). (Original work recorded 1953)

Parsons, T. (1937). *The structure of social action.* New York: Free Press.

Pater, W. (1947). Conclusion to *The Renaissance.* In F. W. Roe (Ed.), *Victorian prose* (pp. 572-575). New York: Ronald Press. (Original work published 1873)

Pater, W. (1947). Romanticism. In F. W. Roe (Ed.), *Victorian prose* (pp. 583-590). New York: Ronald Press. (Original work published 1876)

Pater, W. (1985). *Marius the epicurean* (M. Levey, Ed.). Harmondsworth, UK: Penguin. (Original work published 1885)

Patterson, F. (1985). *Koko's kitten.* New York: Scholastic.

Patterson, F., & Linden, E. (1981). *The education of Koko.* New York: Holt, Rinehart & Winston.

Pechmann, C. (1990, June). Response to President's Column, September 1989. *ACR Newsletter,* pp. 5-7.

Pepper, A. (1957). Imagination (By J. Burke & J. Van Heusen). On *Art Pepper meets the rhythm section* [Record album]. Contemporary (JCD 688 7532 or VDJ 1556E or S7532).

Pepper, A., & Pepper, L. (1979). *Straight life: The story of Art Pepper.* New York: Schirmer.

Perelman, C., & Olbrechts-Tyteca, L. (1969). *The new rhetoric: A treatise on argumentation* (J. Wilkinson & P. Weaver, Trans.). Notre Dame, IN: University of Notre Dame Press. (Original work published 1958)

Pessemier, E. A. (1977). *Product management: Strategy and organization.* New York: John Wiley.

Peter, J. P., & Olson, J. C. (1983). Is science marketing? *Journal of Marketing, 47*(Fall), 111-125.

Peterson, O. (1971). *Great connection* [Record album]. MPS (CD 821 851-2).

Pine-Coffin, R. S. (1961). Introduction. In R. S. Pine-Coffin (Ed.), *Confessions* by St. Augustine (pp. 11-17). Harmondsworth, UK: Penguin.

Pirsig, R. M. (1974). *Zen and the art of motorcycle maintenance: An inquiry into values.* New York: Bantam.

Platt, J. (1970). *Perception and change.* Ann Arbor: University of Michigan Press.

Playboy Home Video. (1993). *Celebrity centerfold: Dian Parkinson* [Videotape]. Beverly Hills, CA: Playboy Entertainment Group.

Polanyi, M. (1958). *Personal knowledge: Towards a post-critical philosophy.* Chicago: University of Chicago Press.

Pollay, R. W. (1985). The subsiding sizzle: A descriptive history of print advertising, 1900-1980. *Journal of Marketing, 49*(Summer), 24-37.

Pollay, R. W. (1986). The distorted mirror: Reflections on the unintended consequences of advertising. *Journal of Marketing, 50*(April), 18-36.

Pope, A. (1962). An essay on criticism. In M. H. Abrams, et al. (Eds.), *The Norton anthology of English literature* (Vol. 1, pp. 1432-1444). New York: Norton. (Original work published 1711)

Popper, K. (1968). *The logic of scientific discovery.* New York: Harper Torchbooks. (Original work published 1959)

Popper, K. (1976). *Unended quest: An intellectual autobiography.* La Salle, IL: Open Court.

Porter, A. (1988, June 6). Musical events: Another Orpheus sings. *New Yorker,* pp. 106-111.

Porter, C. (1957). *Silk stockings* [Movie]. Culver City, CA: MGM/UA Home Video.

Porter, L. W. (1989, Spring). Business school faculty as constructive critics of business. *Selections,* pp. 27-31.

Porter, L. W., & McKibbin, L. E. (1988). *Management education and development: Drift or thrust into the 21st century?* New York: McGraw-Hill.

Preston, B. (1972). Music's my life. On *Music is my life* [Record album]. A&M Records (SP 3516).

Ratchford, B. T. (1975). The new economic theory of consumer behavior: An interpretative essay. *Journal of Consumer Research, 2*(September), 65-75.

Ratchford, B. T. (1979). Operationalizing economic models of demand for product characteristics. *Journal of Consumer Research, 6*(June), 76-87.

Ray, M., & Myers, R. (1986). *Creativity in business.* Garden City, NY: Doubleday.

Reichenbach, H. (1938). *Experience and prediction*. Chicago: University of Chicago Press.

Reingen, P. H., Foster, B. L., Brown, J. J., & Seidman, S. B. (1984). Brand congruence in interpersonal relations: A social network analysis. *Journal of Consumer Research, 11* (December), 771-783.

Reinhold, R. (1984, July 8). Rigors of the road. *New York Times Magazine*, p. 38.

Richards, I. A. (1936). *The philosophy of rhetoric*. New York: Oxford University Press.

Richards, I. A. (1970). *Poetries and sciences: A reissue of science and poetry (1926, 1935) with commentary*. New York: Norton. (Original work published 1927, 1935)

Ricoeur, P. (1976). *Interpretation theory: Discourse and the surplus of meaning*. Fort Worth: Texas Christian University Press.

Ricoeur, P. (1981). *Hermeneutics and the human sciences: Essays on language, action and interpretation* (J. B. Thompson, Ed. and Trans.). Cambridge, UK: Cambridge University Press.

Robinson, J. (1954). *The economics of imperfect competition*. New York: Macmillan.

Rogers, E. M. (1987). The critical school and consumer research. In M. Wallendorf & P. F. Anderson (Eds.), *Advances in consumer research* (Vol. 14, pp. 7-11). Provo, UT: Association for Consumer Research.

Ronstadt, L. (1984). Skylark (By H. Carmichael & J. Mercer). On *Lush life* [Record album]. Asylum (60387-1).

Rook, D. W. (1985). The ritual dimension of consumer behavior. *Journal of Consumer Research, 12* (December), 251-264.

Rook, D. W. (1987). The buying impulse. *Journal of Consumer Research, 14* (September), 189-199.

Rorty, R. (1979). *Philosophy and the mirror of nature*. Princeton, NJ: Princeton University Press.

Rorty, R. (1982). *Consequences of pragmatism*. Minneapolis: University of Minnesota Press.

Rorty, R. (1987). Science as solidarity. In J. S. Nelson, A. Megill, & D. N. McCloskey (Eds.), *The rhetoric of the human sciences* (pp. 38-52). Madison: University of Wisconsin Press.

Rosaldo, R. (1987). Where objectivity lies: The rhetoric of anthropology. In J. S. Nelson, A. Megill, & D. N. McCloskey (Eds.), *The rhetoric of the human sciences* (pp. 87-110). Madison: University of Wisconsin Press.

Rosen, C., & Zerner, H. (1984). *Romanticism and realism: The mythology of nineteenth-century art*. New York: Viking.

Rosenberg, A. (Producer), & Davies, V. (Director). (1955). *The Benny Goodman Story* [Film]. Universal City, CA: Universal City Studios.

Rosenzweig, R. M. (1983). The Pajaro Dunes Conference. In T. W. Langfitt, S. Hackney, A. P. Fishman, & A. V. Glowasky (Eds.), *Partners in the research enterprise: University-corporate relations in science and technology* (pp. 33-39). Philadelphia: University of Pennsylvania Press.

Rotfeld, H. (1985, July 19). Marketing educators must become more "scholarly." *Marketing News*, pp. 35-36.

Rousseau, J.-J. (Ed.). (1933). *The Confessions* (J. M. Cohen, Trans.). Harmondsworth, UK: Penguin. (Original work published 1782)

Ruesch, J., & Kees, W. (1956). *Nonverbal communication*. Berkeley: University of
California Press.

Russell, R. (1973). *Bird lives! The high life and hard times of Charlie (Yardbird) Parker.*
New York: Charterhouse.

Ryan, M. J., & Bonfield, E. H. (1975). The Fishbein extended model and consumer
behavior. *Journal of Consumer Research, 2*(September), 118-136.

Ryle, G. (1949). *The concept of mind.* New York: Barnes & Noble Books.

St. Augustine. (1961). *Confessions* (R. S. Pine-Coffin, Trans.). Harmondsworth, UK:
Penguin. (Original work published c. 400)

Samuelson, P. A. (1948). Consumption theory in terms of revealed preference. *Eco-
nomica, 15*(November), 243-253.

Sanders, C. R. (1990). Excusing tactics: Social responses to the public misbehavior
of companion animals. *Anthrozoos, 4,* 82-90.

Santayana, G. (1896). *The sense of beauty.* New York: Dover.

Schaef, A. W. (1985). *Women's reality: An emerging female system in a white male society.* New York: Harper & Row.

Schaper, E. (1967). Pater, Walter Horatio. In P. Edwards (Ed.), *The encyclopedia of
philosophy* (Vol. 6, pp. 56-57). New York: Macmillan.

Scheffler, I. (1982). *Science and subjectivity* (2nd ed.). Indianapolis, IN: Hackett.

Schiller, F. (1965). *On the aesthetic education of man* (R. Snell, Trans.). New York:
Frederick Ungar. (Original work published 1795)

Schindler, R. M., & Holbrook, M. B. (1993). Critical periods in the development of
men's and women's tastes in personal appearance. *Psychology & Marketing,
10*(November/December), 549-564.

Schneckloth, T. (1979, February 22). John Abercrombie: A direction of his own.
Down Beat, 46, pp. 16-17, 42, 46.

Schudson, M. (1984). *Advertising, the uneasy persuasion: Its dubious impact on American society.* New York: Basic Books.

Schwab, R. (1984). *The oriental Renaissance: Europe's rediscovery of India and the East,
1680-1880* (G. Patterson-Black & V. Reinking, Trans.). New York: Columbia
University Press.

Schweder, R. (1986, September 21). Storytelling among the anthropologists. *New
York Times Book Review,* pp. 1, 38-39.

Schweder, R. A. (1988, February 28). The how of the world. *New York Times Book
Review,* p. 13.

Scitovsky, T. (1976). *The joyless economy: An inquiry into human satisfaction and dis-
satisfaction.* New York: Oxford University Press.

Scruton, R. (1981). *From Descartes to Wittgenstein: A short history of modern philosophy.* New York: Harper & Row.

Sebeok, T. A. (1981). *The play of musement.* Bloomington: Indiana University Press.

Sebeok, T. A., & Umiker-Sebeok, J. (1981). Smart simians: The self-fulfilling prophecy and kindred methodological pitfalls. In T. A. Sebeok (Ed.), *The play of
musement* (pp. 134-209). Bloomington: Indiana University Press.

Semple, R. (1989, September 5). Bart Giamatti's journey: Searching for values amid human frailty. *New York Times*, p. A18.

Seuss, Dr. (a.k.a. Theodor Seuss Geisel). (1940). *Horton hatches the egg.* New York: Random House.

Shakespeare, W. (1970). *King Lear* (A. Harbage, Ed.). Harmondsworth, UK: Penguin. (Original work published 1608)

Shelley, P. B. (1962). Ode to the west wind. In M. H. Abrams, et al. (Eds.), *The Norton anthology of English literature* (Vol. 2, pp. 422-424). New York: Norton. (Original work published 1820)

Shelley, P. B. (1962). To a skylark. In M. H. Abrams, et al. (Eds.), *The Norton anthology of English literature* (Vol. 2, pp. 448-451). New York: Norton. (Original work published 1820)

Sherry, J. F., Jr. (1983). Gift giving in anthropological perspective. *Journal of Consumer Research, 10*(September), 157-168.

Sherry, J. F., Jr. (1991). Postmodern alternatives: The interpretive turn in consumer research. In T. S. Robertson & H. H. Kassarjian (Eds.), *Handbook of consumer behavior* (pp. 548-591). Englewood Cliffs, NJ: Prentice Hall.

Sheth, J. N. (1979). The surpluses and shortages in consumer behavior theory and research. *Journal of the Academy of Marketing Science, 7*(Fall), 414-427.

Sheth, J. N. (1982). Consumer behavior: Surpluses and shortages. In A. A. Mitchell (Ed.), *Advances in consumer research* (Vol. 9, pp. 13-19). Ann Arbor, MI: Association for Consumer Research.

Shils, E. (1983). *The academic ethic.* Chicago: University of Chicago Press.

Shimp, T. A., & Kavas, A. (1984). The theory of reasoned action applied to coupon usage. *Journal of Consumer Research, 11*(December), 795-809.

Shropshire, W., Jr. (1981). *The joys of research.* Washington, DC: Smithsonian Institution Press.

Shulman, J. (1980). Measuring consumer tastes in popular music. In J. C. Olson (Ed.), *Advances in consumer research* (Vol. 7, pp. 25-27). Ann Arbor, MI: Association for Consumer Research.

Silverman, K. (1983). *The subject of semiotics.* New York: Oxford University Press.

Simon, P. (1975). Still crazy after all these years. On *Still crazy after all these years* [Record album]. Columbia (PC 33540).

Sirgy, M. J. (1982). Self-concept in consumer behavior: A critical review. *Journal of Consumer Research, 9*(December), 287-300.

Snow, C. P. (1964). *The two cultures: And a second look.* Cambridge, UK: Cambridge University Press. (Original work published 1959)

Solomon, M. R. (1983). The role of products as social stimuli: A symbolic interactionism perspective. *Journal of Consumer Research, 10*(December), 319-329.

Solomon, M. R., & Anand, P. (1985). Ritual costumes and status transitions: The female suit as totemic emblem. In E. C. Hirschman & M. B. Holbrook (Eds.), *Advances in consumer research* (Vol. 12, pp. 315-318). Provo, UT: Association for Consumer Research.

Sperber, D. (1985). *On anthropological knowledge.* Cambridge, UK: Cambridge University Press.

Spiggle, S. (1985). 7-Up art, Pepsi art, and Sunkist art: The presentation of brand symbols in art. In E. C. Hirschman & M. B. Holbrook (Eds.), *Advances in consumer research* (Vol. 12, pp. 11-16). Provo, UT: Association for Consumer Research.

Stearns, R. (1976). Dogs are not purrfect. In J. Fireman (Ed.), *Cat catalog: The ultimate cat book* (p. 287). New York: Workman.

Steiner, P. (1990, June 25). [Cartoon]. *New Yorker*, p. 30.

Stephenson, W. (1967). *The play theory of mass communication.* Chicago: University of Chicago Press.

Stern, B. B. (1989). Literary criticism and consumer research: Overview and illustrative analysis. *Journal of Consumer Research, 16*(December), 322-334.

Stern, B. B. (1993). Feminist literary criticism and the deconstruction of ads: A postmodern view of advertising and consumer responses. *Journal of Consumer Research, 19*(March), 556-566.

Sternberg, J. von (1968). *The blue angel.* London: Lorrimer. (Original work published 1930)

Stevens, W. (Ed.). (1961). *The collected poems.* New York: Knopf.

Stewart, Z. (1979, January 1-February 15). Griffin. *Musician, 16,* pp. 46-49, 62.

Straub, P. (1980). *Shadowland.* New York: Coward, McCann & Geoghegan.

Sudnow, D. (1978). *Ways of the hand.* New York: Knopf.

Supersax. (1977). Now's the time. (By C. Parker). On *Chasin' the bird* [Record album]. Pausa (PR 7038).

Terrace, H. S. (1985). *In the beginning was the "name."* Unpublished manuscript, Columbia University.

Thayer, L. (1982). Human nature: Of communication, of structuralism, of semiotics. *Semiotica, 41,* 25-40.

Thomas, L. (1979). *The medusa and the snail: More notes of a biology watcher.* New York: Bantam.

Thompson, C. J., Locander, W. B., & Pollio, H. R. (1989). Putting consumer experience back into consumer research: The philosophy and method of existential-phenomenology. *Journal of Consumer Research, 16*(September), 133-146.

Tolman, E. C. (1959). Principles of purposive behavior. In S. Koch (Ed.), *Psychology: A study of a science* (Vol. 2, pp. 92-157). New York: McGraw-Hill.

Toulmin, S. (1982). *The return to cosmology: Postmodern science and the technology of nature.* Berkeley: University of California Press.

Tucker, W. T. (1967). *Foundations for a theory of consumer behavior.* New York: Holt, Rinehart & Winston.

Tucker, W. T. (1974). Future directions in marketing theory. *Journal of Marketing, 38*(April), 30-35.

Tybout, A. M., & Hauser, J. R. (1981). A marketing audit using a conceptual model of consumer behavior: Application and evaluation. *Journal of Marketing, 45*(Summer), 82-101.

Umiker-Sebeok, J. (Ed.). (1987). *Marketing and semiotics: New directions in the study of signs for sale.* Berlin: Mouton de Gruyter.

Unger, L. S., & Kernan, J. B. (1983). On the meaning of leisure: An investigation of some determinants of the subjective experience. *Journal of Consumer Research*, 9(March), 381-392.

University/industry ties pondered. (1982, April 5). *Chemical and Engineering News*, p. 4.

Veblen, T. (1967). *The theory of the leisure class*. New York: Penguin. (Original work published 1899)

Veblen, T. (1954). *The higher learning in America: A memorandum on the conduct of universities by business men*. Stanford, CA: Academic Reprints. (Original work published 1918)

VerPlanck, M. (1988). Skylark (By H. Carmichael & J. Mercer). On *Marlene Ver-Planck loves Johnny Mercer* [Record album]. Audiophile (APCD-138). (Original work recorded 1979)

Vessels, J. (1985). Koko's kitten. *National Geographic, 167*(January), 110-113.

Vico, G. (1976). *The new science* (T. G. Bergin & M. H. Fisch, Trans.). Ithaca, NY: Cornell University Press. (Original work published 1744)

Voight, J. (1976). The black death plague and the cat. In J. Fireman (Ed.), *Cat catalog: The ultimate cat book* (pp. 17-19). New York: Workman.

Von Oech, R. (1983). *A whack on the side of the head: How to unlock your mind for innovation*. New York: Warner.

Von Wright, G. H. (1983). *Practical reason*. Ithaca, NY: Cornell University Press.

Wallendorf, M. (1980). The formation of aesthetic criteria through social structures and social institutions. In J. C. Olson (Ed.), *Advances in consumer research* (Vol. 7, pp. 3-6). Ann Arbor, MI: Association for Consumer Research.

Wallendorf, M. (1985, October). *Inner direction as a social character for consumer research*. Paper presented at the Fall Conference of the Association for Consumer Research, Las Vegas.

Wallendorf, M., & Arnould, E. (1991). "We gather together": Consumption rituals of Thanksgiving Day. *Journal of Consumer Research, 18*(June), 13-31.

Wallendorf, M., & Belk, R. W. (1987). Deep meaning in possessions. [Videotape]. Cambridge, MA: Marketing Science Institute.

Wallendorf, M., & Brucks, M. (1993). Introspection in consumer research: Implementation and implications. *Journal of Consumer Research, 20*(December), 339-359.

Wallendorf, M., & Reilly, M. D. (1983). Ethnic migration, assimilation, and consumption. *Journal of Consumer Research, 10*(December), 292-302.

Washington, D. (n.d.). What a diff'rence a day made. On *What a diff'rence a day makes!* [Record album]. Mercury (SR 60158).

Wayda, S. (1991, December). Dian Parkinson, come on down! *Playboy, 38*, pp. 94-101.

Weber, M. (1946). Science as a vocation. In H. H. Gerth & C. W. Mills (Eds.), *From Max Weber: Essays in sociology* (pp. 129-156). New York: Oxford University Press. (Original work published 1919)

Webster, F. E., Jr. (1988). Comment. *Journal of Marketing, 52*(October), 48-51.

Wellek, R. (1981). *A history of modern criticism 1750-1950: 2. The romantic age.* New York: Cambridge University Press. (Original work published 1955)

Wells, W. D. (1993). Discovery-oriented consumer research. *Journal of Consumer Research, 19*(March), 489-504.

Welsh, A. (1978). *Roots of lyric: Primitive poetry and modern poetics.* Princeton, NJ: Princeton University Press.

Westing, H. (1977, July 29). Marketing educators must switch to helping real world meet real problems. *Marketing News.*

Whorf, B. L. (1956). *Language, thought, and reality: Selected writings of Benjamin Lee Whorf.* New York: John Wiley.

Whyte, L. L. (1961). A scientific view of the "creative energy" of man. In M. Philipson (Ed.), *Aesthetics today* (pp. 349-374). New York: World.

Wilde, O. (1962). *The picture of Dorian Gray.* New York: New American Library. (Original work published 1891)

Wilder, A. (1972). *American popular song: The great innovators, 1900-1950.* New York: Oxford University Press.

Wilford, J. N. (1989, April 24). Fusion furor: Science's human face. *New York Times,* pp. A1, B6.

Wilkie, W. L., & Pessemier, E. A. (1973). Issues in marketing's use of multi-attribute attitude models. *Journal of Marketing Research, 10*(November), 428-441.

Wind, Y. J. (1982). *Product policy: Concepts, methods, and strategy.* Reading, MA: Addison-Wesley.

Windelband, W. (1924). Geschichte und Naturwissenschaft. *Praeludien* (Vol. 2). Tuebingen, Germany: J. C. B. Mohr.

Winn, R. B. (1962). Epicurean school. In D. D. Runes (Ed.), *Dictionary of philosophy* (p. 93). Totowa, NJ: Littlefield, Adams.

Woods, W. A. (1981). *Consumer behavior.* New York: North Holland.

Wordsworth, W. (1948). The tables turned. In E. Bernbaum (Ed.), *Anthology of romanticism* (pp. 189-190). New York: Ronald Press. (Original work published 1798)

Wordsworth, W. (1948). The recluse (Introduction to "The excursion"). In E. Bernbaum (Ed.), *Anthology of romanticism* (pp. 277-278). New York: Ronald Press. (Original work published 1814)

Wright, P. (1975). Consumer choice strategies: Simplifying vs. optimizing. *Journal of Marketing Research, 12*(February), 60-67.

Yalch, R. F. (1985, Spring). From the editor. *ACR Newsletter, 15,* p. 2.

Yalow, R. S. (1981). Biomedical investigation. In W. Shropshire (Ed.), *The joys of research* (pp. 101-115). Washington, DC: Smithsonian Institution Press.

Yeats, W. B. (1956). Adam's curse. In *The collected poems of W. B. Yeats* (pp. 78-79). New York: Macmillan. (Original work published 1904)

Yeats, W. B. (1956). Among school children. In *The collected poems of W. B. Yeats* (pp. 212-214). New York: Macmillan. (Original work published 1928)

INDEX

ABOUT THE AUTHOR

Morris B. Holbrook (Ph.D., Columbia University) is the W. T. Dillard Professor of Marketing in the Graduate School of Business at Columbia University. He graduated from Harvard College with a BA in English and received his MBA and PhD in marketing from Columbia. Since 1975, he has taught courses at the Columbia Business School in such areas as marketing strategy, sales management, research methods, consumer behavior, and commercial communication in the culture of consumption. His research has appeared in many journals and has covered a wide variety of topics in marketing and consumer behavior, with a special focus on issues related to communication in general and to aesthetics, semiotics, hermeneutics, advertising, the media, art, and entertainment in particular. Recent books include *Daytime Television Game Shows and the Celebration of Merchandise: The Price is Right*; *The Semiotics of Consumption: Interpreting Symbolic Consumer Behavior in Popular Culture and Works of Art* (with Elizabeth C. Hirschman); and *Postmodern Consumer Research: The Study of Consumption as Text* (with Elizabeth C. Hirschman). The author's hobbies include playing the piano, attending jazz and classical concerts, watching movies, going to the theater, collecting musical recordings, and being kind to cats.

419